# RABELAIS'S CARNIVAL

The New Historicism: Studies in Cultural Poetics
Stephen Greenblatt, General Editor

1. *Holy Feast and Holy Fast: The Religious Significance of Food to Medieval Women,* by Caroline Walker Bynum

2. *The Gold Standard and the Logic of Naturalism: American Literature at the Turn of the Century,* by Walter Benn Michaels

3. *Nationalism and Minor Literature: James Clarence Mangan and the Emergence of Irish Cultural Nationalism,* by David Lloyd

4. *Shakespearean Negotiations: The Circulation of Social Energy in Renaissance England,* by Stephen Greenblatt

5. *The Mirror of Herodotus: The Representation of the Other in the Writing of History,* by François Hartog, translated by Janet Lloyd

6. *Puzzling Shakespeare: Local Reading and Its Discontents,* by Leah S. Marcus

7. *The Rites of Knighthood: The Literature and Politics of Elizabethan Chivalry,* by Richard C. McCoy

8. *Literary Practice and Social Change in Britain, 1380–1530,* edited by Lee Patterson

9. *Trials of Authorship: Anterior Forms and Poetic Reconstruction from Wyatt to Shakespeare,* by Jonathan Crewe

10. *Rabelais's Carnival: Text, Context, Metatext,* by Samuel Kinser

11. *Behind the Scenes: Yeats, Horniman, and the Struggle for the Abbey Theatre,* by Adrian Frazier

12. *Literature, Politics, and Culture in Postwar Britain,* by Alan Sinfield

13. *Habits of Thought in the English Renaissance: Religion, Politics, and the Dominant Culture,* by Debora Kuller Shuger

# RABELAIS'S CARNIVAL

## TEXT, CONTEXT, METATEXT

SAMUEL KINSER

University of California Press
*Berkeley • Los Angeles • Oxford*

University of California Press
Berkeley and Los Angeles, California

University of California Press, Ltd.
Oxford, England

**Library of Congress Cataloging-in-Publication Data**

Kinser, Sam.
  Rabelais's carnival : text, context, metatext / Samuel Kinser.
    p.   cm.—(The New historicism ; 10)
  Bibliography: p.
  Includes index.
  ISBN 0-520-06522-0 (alk. paper)
  1. Rabelais, François, ca. 1490–1553?—Criticism and
interpretation. 2. Carnival in literature.  I. Title.  II. Series.
PQ1694.K56  1990
843'.3—dc20                                    89-33814
                                                  CIP

Printed in the United States of America
1  2  3  4  5  6  7  8  9

# Contents

*List of Figures*                                          vii

*Foreword*                                                 ix

*Introduction*                                              I

PART ONE   TEXT/CONTEXT                                     7

  1. Paratexts and Printing                      17

  2. Modes of Representation                      46

PART TWO   MAKING IT STRANGE                               61

  3. Who Is Quaresmeprenant?                      69

  4. What Makes Sausage-People Fight?             93

  5. Perversity and Patriarchy                   III

PART THREE   NORMALIZATION                                125

  6. Post-Renaissance Metatexts                 131

  7. Semiotics and Criticism                    162

PART FOUR   TEXT, SUBTEXT, COUNTERTEXT                    181

  8. Communalism                                187

  9. Mockery                                     214

  10. Bakhtin's Discovery                        248

*Afterword*                                                261

*Appendix 1: Context*                                             265

*Appendix 2: The Carnival-Lent Tradition and*
*Quaresmeprenant*                                                 270

*Appendix 3: Cannibals, Pantagruel, and the Spirit of*
*the Queen of Navarre*                                            272

*Appendix 4: Friar John's Breviary, and Others*                  275

*Bibliography*                                                    281

*Index*                                                           289

# Figures

1. Anonymous, Title page to Rabelais, *Gargantua* (1547).    27

2. Frans Hoghenberg, Engraving, *Fat Carnival with all his Guests Comes Here to Quarrel with Thin Lent* (1558).    49

3. Anonymous, Section D of the Engraved Illustrations to Olaus Magnus, *Carta Marina* (1539).    65

4. Section A of the Illustrations to Olaus Magnus, *Carta Marina:* Piglike Sea Monster near Faroe Islands (1539).    104

5. Anonymous, Title page to Rabelais, *Gargantua* (ca. 1544).    153

6. The Mixed, Alternating Stresses of Textual Meaning.    164

# Foreword

François Rabelais (1483?–1553) is the Renaissance incarnate.

—So?

He represents the panoply of learning, the excitement of sixteenth-century men, Columbus's heirs and Petrarch's, at the prospect of a suddenly expanding world.

—And then?

He expressed the spirit of the people, their exuberant refusal to be captured by the reassurances, in heaven as on earth, offered by church and state authority.

—All this is true . . . and irrelevant. All this is metatext, and metatext is all, or almost all, interpretation. In its first freshness it widens one's eyes, offering an unaccustomed vision of a text. But soon the vision is replaced by an image, and then (if the metatext is as effective as it is interesting) by a statue, indeed an icon, of the author. A "classic" text, like Rabelais's, like Petrarch's, like Shakespeare's, accumulates images and icons around itself. If it did not, it would not be read. Metatext accommodates the text to new circumstances, insuring its relevance now, guaranteeing its irrelevance in the future, until another metatext can be imagined.

In the academies Rabelais's icon remains that imagined by the Romantic poet Victor Hugo, the one described in the first paragraphs: Rabelais, the embodiment of Europe's rebirth, Rabelais the humanist, Rabelais the royalist, Rabelais the spirit of Humanity. Remember the sixteenth century, remember the springtime of the French state, the state of Francis I and Henry II, remember those days of ardent moral reform, the early days of Lutheran and Calvinist enthusiasm before the sclerosis of creeds set in.

This Rabelais has become irrelevant because its meaning has been reduced to plaster. Its hard edges and precise lineaments have been worn away by repetitious handling. It has come to fit the contours of the Curriculum. No one *reads* Rabelais in these conditions. To be made to learn about the text in this way insures that it will not be read. Meta-text has obscured the text, overshadowing it with images.

Outside the academies a reaction has taken form. In the 1960s and 1970s a new metatext was proposed: Rabelais the embodiment of verbal richness, Rabelais the word player, Rabelais's text as a mixture of texts, his text as nothing but intertexts, as a scrambling of words, as a Carnival of verbality.

All this is true and not yet irrelevant. Is there a way to forestall its reduction to a plaster mold? That is the theme of this book.

The new metatext asserts among other things that Rabelais's writing is "carnivalesque." This idea of the work will be tested here as the means to more general critical ends. Mikhail Bakhtin's *Rabelais and His World* (1965) is at the origin of this idea. Unlike most other versions of the new metatext, which have applied to Rabelais New-Critical, formalist, and structuralist ideas of self-generating textuality, Bakhtin employs historical and ideological as well as structural and semiotic methods of analysis. He does this by alluding to something inherent in the text, its structure, and its semiotics: the "carnivalesque spirit."

The meaning of Carnival and the meaning of Rabelais's novels are said to be intertwined: Bakhtin, of course, is referring to the meaning of the pre-Lenten festivity as experienced in the sixteenth century. Yet he does not offer descriptions of particular late medieval or Renaissance Carnivals. Bakhtin's carnivalesque spirit hovers over many sixteenth-century activities—marketplace slang, student farces, charivaris, and other public amusements and festivities—rather than inhabiting the pre-Lenten occasion exclusively. Bakhtin does not even analyze in any detail the only place in Rabelais's work where that author discusses Carnival in more than a few phrases, chapters 29 to 42 of his *Fourth Book*.[1]

1. Mikhail Bakhtin, *Rabelais and His World* (Moscow, 1965; trans., Cambridge, Mass., 1968) discusses "carnivalesque spirit" throughout his book; for a first definition, see 8–12. In this book I have used capitals and small letters to distinguish the broad and narrow meanings of this kind of festivity current in present-day Euro-American usage. Carnival with a capital "C" refers to the particular occasion, the period preceding Ash Wednesday in Roman Catholic

The idea that Rabelais's novels exhibit a carnivalesque spirit asserts something about how as well as why Rabelais's text has passed from reader to reader, accumulating metatexts and acquiring the status of a classic. If a carnivalesque text upsets and inverts expectations, one needs to know how Rabelais acquired a carnivalesque vocabulary and how he adapted it to bookmaking. Rabelais's strategies as an author were molded by the character of book production and consumption in his time, which was quite special. When his first publications appeared in 1532, the printed book was only sixty years old in France and less than one hundred years old in the Western world. Its parts and form, its privileges and also its limits, its relation to political, economic, and ideologically controlling factors, were still inchoate. Rabelais's allegedly carnivalesque text is related to the new horizon opened by that print revolution which with the computer has in our time taken a new turn.

So, after all, this analysis of Rabelais's Carnivalism is not just a means to more general critical ends. Its four parts have a certain independence, and they may seem to turn away from each other as the reader follows on. Bookmaking, and making Carnival; studying Rabelais's statements about Carnival, particularly in the *Fourth Book*, and studying critics' interpretations of those statements, particularly Bakhtin's; relating text to context, and both of these to metatext: these subjects cohere, but

---

custom; the period may extend any time from one or two days to six or eight weeks, depending on local tradition. Carnival with a small "c" refers to a more general category of festivities characterized by glittering spectacle and fantasy; in English and American milieus such spectacle has been commercialized and refers to a place where sideshows and thrilling rides are proposed to the public, regardless of the time of year. The broad and narrow meanings coexist in Europe outside England and have persisted in many Protestant, as well as Catholic, locales. The narrow meaning has been largely lost in Anglo-American areas, except around New Orleans. Bakhtin's term "carnivalesque spirit" is an abstraction from the narrow meaning; it does not refer to carnival as spectacle and fantasy, and yet it is not intended to evoke the pre-Lenten occasion alone. "Carnivalesque spirit" is political: it derides serious, "official" thought and behavior; it brings the high low. I have followed the translators of Bakhtin's work in using "carnivalesque" and "carnivalesque spirit" in this study with small letters to indicate its broad meaning, while cautioning readers here not to confuse Bakhtin's broad meaning with that generally current in Anglo-American usage.

they cohere by facing each other, by confronting no less than comple-
menting each other, like the double-sided two facing pages by means
of which they pass to you.[2]

2. Portions of this book were presented in a lecture at French House, Columbia University, in November 1980. I wish to thank French House and the
members of the Columbia Department of French for their hospitality on that
occasion. I am deeply indebted to Barbara Bowen, Sean Shesgreen, and Tzve-
tan Todorov for mental stimulation of every kind in relation to this project. As
will be apparent to readers of chapter 1, I am also very sensitive to and grateful
for the contributions of the many persons and institutions with whom and with
which I have worked in elaborating the "paratexts" of this book, in particular
the governing committees and staff of the Department of History and Cheryl
Fuller of the Liberal Arts and Sciences Word Processing Center at Northern
Illinois University. Financial aid for this book's publication from the College
of Liberal Arts and Sciences, Northern Illinois University, is also gratefully
acknowledged.

# Introduction

Rabelais wrote four books and part of a fifth, published posthumously, about an imaginary family of giants: Grandgosier and Gargamelle, their child, Gargantua, and Gargantua's son, Pantagruel. Gargantua and his parents were not the author's invention. They existed in an anonymous chapbook called *The Great and Inestimable Chronicles of the Grand and Enormous Giant Gargantua,* published in 1532 shortly before Rabelais invented the first of his books. Rabelais's first invention told the story of Gargantua's son Pantagruel and his boon companions (*Pantagruel,* 1532), perhaps because Rabelais's first thought was to build upon the stories about Gargantua that had just been published; he praises extravagantly the prosaically written *Great Chronicles* and their giant hero in the prologue to *Pantagruel.*

Praise of Gargantua was good advertisement for Rabelais's stories not only because of the recently published chapbook but also because Gargantua, unlike Pantagruel, was apparently a familiar name to Frenchmen who never read books. Stories about the giant and place-names associated with his deeds have left their mark on the French countryside at hundreds of points; they are specially concentrated in northwest Normandy and Upper Brittany, just to the north and west of the Loire Valley where Rabelais sets his stories. Oblique references in written sources allow Gargantua to be traced as an element of oral mythology from the twelfth century; it is plausible to suppose that his name and figure were slowly taking form in oral tradition for hundreds of years before that.[1]

1. On the complex issues of Rabelais's relation to oral tales and written chapbooks about Gargantua see Rabelais, *Oeuvres,* ed. Abel Lefranc, et al., Volume I (Paris, 1913), introduction; *The Tale of Gargantua and King Arthur,* ed. Huntington Brown (Cambridge, Mass., 1932), introduction; *Le Vroy Gargantua,* ed. Marcel Françon (Paris, 1949), 121–33; and esp. Henri Dontenville, *Histoire et géographie mythiques de la France* (Paris, 1973). See also chs. 1 and 2 of my forthcoming *Birth of Gargantua, Festive Culture in Late Medieval and Early Modern*

This vast oral tradition was an opportunity and a constraint. Some effort would be needed to translate oral style into written terms. But at the same time the aura of folkloric fantasy surrounding Gargantua afforded the author a fictive looseness, an area where inventive play with his subject could be expected and could resonate with stories already told. If commercial success is any evidence, Rabelais seems to have combined these elements very effectively. Like the chapbooks, which retailed the life of Gargantua in six new variants and an unknown number of printings in 1533 and 1534, the story of Gargantua's son, *Pantagruel,* was reprinted at least seven times in the same two years.[2]

There was another reason for this success. *Pantagruel* was written to appeal to both broad popular audiences and intellectual elites, for it combined tall tales with elaborate erudition. Before he became a storyteller, Rabelais had established himself through letters, personal contacts, and public lectures as a learned student of Greek and Roman medicine and law. He had in 1530 graduated from the faculty of medicine at Montpellier and had practiced at Narbonne. In 1532, the very year in which he published *Pantagruel,* he also edited the Latin letters of a Ferrara physician, edited and translated several medical works by Hippocrates and Galen, and also edited a will by one Ioannes Cuspidius, supposedly an ancient Roman, with notes about the Roman law governing contracts of sale (Rabelais's source has since proved to be an Italian fifteenth-century forgery). The most serious reflection of these interests in *Pantagruel* is a chapter in which the hero receives a letter from his father Gargantua prescribing the course of studies that Pantagruel should follow and lauding the recent revival of ancient learning. A few chapters later, however, Pantagruel is shown judging a dispute

---

*Times,* reviewing the question in detail together with this and other relevant secondary literature.

Pantagruel too existed before Rabelais's fictions but independently from Gargantua. He was a small devil who raised the thirst of good drinkers, particularly in Lent. See, e.g., vv. 92–96 of "La dure et cruelle Bataille et paix du glorieux sainct Pensart à l'encontre de Caresme, composée par le Prince de la Bazoche d'Issouldun," a law student's farce played at Tours in 1485, published in 1490 at Paris, and edited by Jean-Claude Aubailly in his *Deux Jeux de Carnaval* (Geneva, 1977). Unlike Gargantua, Pantagruel has not been plausibly located up to now in unlettered milieus.

2. *A New Rabelais Bibliography: Editions of Rabelais before 1626,* ed. Stephen Rawles and Michael Screech (Geneva, 1987), 65–91; henceforth cited as *NRB.*

between Lord Kissmyarse and Lord Suckfizzle, an episode followed by another in which Pantagruel's friend Panurge confounds an English scholar's philosophico-theological arguments by coughing, humming, clenching his teeth, sticking out his tongue, playing with his codpiece, and gesticulating with obscene verve.[3] The book's broadly popular traits are sometimes transfigured into serious occasions of reflection, and then again the latter are dissolved with laughter-provoking absurdities.

These kinds of narrative reversals were amplified and given more sophisticated form in *Gargantua* (1535),[4] the *Third Book* (1546), and finally the *Fourth Book* (1552), which is our particular interest here. Why did Rabelais turn aside from his learned studies and editions to write these gay extravagances? The impulse represented more than the "relaxation of an erudite humanist," the production of a jeu d'esprit like the *Praise of Folly* by Rabelais's idol Erasmus.[5] One way to begin to describe what was involved is to outline Rabelais's most basic institutional attachments; they had their negative as well as positive effects.

Son of a lawyer in the middle-sized town of Chinon on the Loire River, Rabelais entered adulthood as a Franciscan friar. After many years in a Franciscan monastery (ca. 1508–1524), he found it possible to shift his obedience to the Benedictine rule, where erudition was traditionally better received. In 1530 he left the monastery forever, receiving a medical degree at Montpellier and eventually becoming a secular priest. Rabelais was not endowed with a parish benefice until 1550, a few years before his death, and even then he was not a resident priest. His institutional attachment to the church expressed itself in both affirmations and denunciations. He hated monkery and yet felt great affection for many monastic habits and at least some monastic personalities; the prominence of Friar John, Pantagruel's companion, proves it. He believed in Christ and was continuously preoccupied with Christian

---

3. *Pantagruel,* chs. 11, 18, 19 in any edition of Rabelais's works.

4. The success of *Pantagruel* stimulated Rabelais to rewrite the chapbook stories of Gargantua and of course to invent more. When his two novels were printed together in the 1540s and afterward, *Gargantua* was placed first and *Pantagruel* second, as the time sequence of their episodes required. The date of *Gargantua's* first publication was either early 1535 or late 1534, judging from internal evidence. The title page of the only known copy of the earliest known edition is missing.

5. Michael Screech, *Rabelais* (Ithaca, N.Y., 1979), 13. Screech emphasizes Rabelais's Erasmianism here and in his other works on Rabelais.

teaching and practices, but he suspected Christ's church and especially its imperious, censorious elites. Even the sharpness and point of his attacks on churchmen, particularly those on ignorant Sorbonne theologians, were stimulated and made possible by the vast ecclesiastical leisure that this man of modest means enjoyed, especially in his early years in the monastery, as he acquired the prodigious learning exhibited on every second page of the novels.

The second institutional attachment permeating his writing was to the medical profession. After exhibiting his knowledge of the prestigious Greek physicians Hippocrates and Galen in the publications of 1532, Rabelais was appointed physician to the large and important Hôtel-Dieu hospital at Lyon. He remained at this post something less than three years but continued intermittently thereafter to practice medicine as an attending physician to the powerful patrons whom he acquired at Lyon: Jean and Guillaume du Bellay, diplomats and influential counselors of King Francis I.

With the du Bellays he traveled to the papal court at Rome, to the royal court at Paris, to Germany, and to many other parts of France and northern Italy over the next fifteen years. Through his connection to the du Bellays Rabelais was in regular contact with royal policy during this period when France was repeatedly at war with Emperor Charles V and on tenterhooks with the popes over France's support of those Protestant princes resisting the emperor in Germany. Rabelais's understanding of policy was sharpened by his comprehension of feudal and Roman law, acquired in the household of his lawyer father and apparently during an early period of university legal studies between 1500 and 1510.

Through his patrons the du Bellays Rabelais also gained some leverage on the fourth institutional system orienting his endeavors, the publishing world. He first entered this world at a late date, in 1532, at the age of forty-nine. One scholar has argued that Rabelais, working for the unknown firm in Lyon that first published the *Great and Inestimable Chronicles of Gargantua*, actually edited the latter work. That is why, Mireille Huchon argues, Rabelais praises these *Chronicles* so extravagantly—and then outdoes them—in his own novels.[6] However that may be, it is certain that he soon found good reason to work

6. Mireille Huchon, *Rabelais Grammairien* (Geneva, 1981), part 5, ch. 2: "La participation de Rabelais aux 'Grandes et Inestimables Cronicques.'"

closely with his publishers and his patrons, for his prodigious success as an author insured that his works would be imitated, pirated, and condemned.

Imitated: The anonymous chapbook versions of the tales of Gargantua that appeared after 1532 borrowed not only from the *Great Chronicles* but also from episodes in Rabelais's *Gargantua* or *Pantagruel*. In 1538 the anonymous *Disciple of Pantagruel* appeared, a little book that Rabelais in turn imitated in the *Fourth Book*, particularly in the Carnival episode.

Pirated: Rabelais's acquaintance Etienne Dolet, a daring evangelical humanist eventually burned for his beliefs, was a printer at Lyon in the early 1540s. In 1542 he published Rabelais's *Gargantua* and *Pantagruel* without the author's permission. Moreover, he combined them with the anonymous *Disciple of Pantagruel,* as if they had all been written by the same person.[7]

The disservice was not merely a question of combining Rabelais's words with non-Rabelaisian materials. Following upon a generation of Lutheran and other reformist propaganda against the papal church, *Gargantua* and *Pantagruel* had quickly acquired a reputation that was strongly anticlerical, if not heretical. Therefore Rabelais had decided to tone down a number of passages jibing at churchmen, in particular those making fun of the faculty of theology at the University of Paris (the Sorbonne). His expurgated edition appeared at Lyon in 1542, just as Dolet issued his unexpurgated version. Rabelais and his printer were furious.

Condemned: On June 25, 1545, a catalogue of censored books that included *Gargantua* and *Pantagruel,* drawn up by the Sorbonne and approved by the Parlement of Paris, was published by town criers in Paris. With the aid of Jean du Bellay, Rabelais secured on September 19, 1545, a royal privilege for his *Third Book*. Nevertheless, on December 31, 1546, only half a year after the *Third Book* was printed, the Sorbonne published a new list of censored books that included that volume.

Medicine, politics, clerical life, publishing: these areas chiefly engaged Rabelais's energies after 1532, when he began writing fiction. They guided his movements along the paths of their specialized inter-

---

7. The author's identity was by this time an open secret. Alcofribas [Nasier], the author announced on the title pages of both authentic and pirated editions at this time, is an anagram of François Rabelais.

ests and their routinized ways of doing things. But thoughts are free—
or rather they are relatively free.[8] Thoughts, however playful, can play
only with what is passed to them in the way of impressions, emotions,
and information acquired through the body's organs; what is thus
passed was already in Rabelais's time controlled in considerable degree
by vested interests, by "ideological apparatuses" like those institutions
that condemned Rabelais's books. Rabelais seems to have understood
this. The course of his life, insofar as we know something of it, seems
to have been calculated to frustrate or at least parry such institutional
grips.[9] He made life choices that maximized his personal and intellectual mobility, although this does not mean he desired to disengage himself from the pressing issues of his day. Avoiding both marriage and the
hunt for preferment in church, town, or princely court, he chose an
almost vagabond way.

The mind was—as far as Rabelais could manage it—free yet filled
with images purveyed by the body's attachments: ills of the physical
organism, ills of the body politic, ills of Mother Church; ills, or at any
rate irritations, in Rabelais's own aging body. When he took up his pen
again after the condemnation of his *Third Book* in 1546, he was a man
of more than sixty years. The book he wrote is his most fantastic and
most fascinating. The world he depicts has an intricacy and extravagance previously unplumbed.

8. "A private man has always the liberty, because thought is free, to believe
or not believe in his heart those acts that have been given out for miracles."
Thomas Hobbes, *Leviathan* (New York, 1962), book 3, ch. 37, final paragraph.
9. The reference is to Louis Althusser's essay, "On Ideology and Ideological
State Apparatuses," in his *Lenin and Philosophy* (Boston, 1972).

# ONE

# TEXT/CONTEXT

In the course of the strange odyssey, which Rabelais describes in his *Fourth Book,* Pantagruel and his friends sail along one morning "in high spirits"—until their guide Xenomanes points out Tapinos Island, where Quaresmeprenant rules.[1] Humanists among Rabelais's early readers would not have been surprised at the dampening effect the island's name seems to have on the company: *Tapeinos,* a Greek adjective describing something low, might refer to a low lying island or, more figuratively—and readers of Rabelais are amply conditioned to take things figuratively—to a miserable island, a base and paltry place. Humanist or not, Rabelais's readers might also have known the expression *en tapinois,* documented from 1480 onward, which meant to do something with dissimulation or like a sneak.[2]

Is it there that "Quaresmeprenant" reigns? French readers, humanist and nonhumanist, must have been very surprised at this, for to them Quaresmeprenant was a word referring to Carnival.[3] From at least the

1. François Rabelais, *Le Quart Livre,* ch. 29 (published 1552), in *Oeuvres,* ed. Jacques Boulenger (Paris: Bibliothèque de la Pléiade, 1955), 641. All quotations from Rabelais are from this edition, unless otherwise noted; page numbers, when relevant, will be given after book and chapter in this form: *QL,* 29, 641. Other abbreviations used with reference to this edition are: *G, Gargantua*; *P, Pantagruel*; *TL, Tiers Livre*; *CL, Cinq Livre*; *PP, Pantagrueline Prognostication*; Pr, prologues by Rabelais; DL, dedicatory letter in the *Fourth Book*; *BD, Briefve Déclaration d'aucunes dictions plus obscures contenues on Quatriesme Livre*; L, other letters by Rabelais; Pl. Bib., Bibliography compiled by Boulenger and revised by L. Scheler. Quotations from other works included in Boulenger's edition will simply give page numbers but will be identified by title in the text. English translations of Rabelais and other authors are mine throughout.

2. Xenomanes uses the phrase to describe Quaresmeprenant later: "De toutes corneilles prinses en tapinois ordinairement poschoit les oeilz" (*QL,* 32, 649). J. M. Cohen translates Tapinos Island as Sneaks' Island in his English translation of Rabelais, *Gargantua and Pantagruel* (Harmondsworth, Eng., 1955), 512.

3. Carnival will be capitalized when it refers to the festival preceding Ash Wednesday (see n. 1, Foreword). Mardi Gras also will be capitalized when referring to this festival generally; when it refers only to the day before Ash Wednesday, it will be lowercased.

...teenth century and perhaps in oral discourse for a long time previously, "Quaresmeprenant" rivaled "Caresmeentrant" and "Charnage" as a word designating either the personification of or the collective term for the revelry-filled days preceding Lent (*Carême* or *Quaresme*). "Mardi Gras," Fat Tuesday, the last day of Carnival before Ash Wednesday, was also occasionally used to mean Carnival time or its personification in general. Many other sixteenth-century writers—Clément Marot, Marguerite de Navarre, Henri Estienne, Etienne Pasquier, Agrippa d'Aubigné, and Michel de Montaigne—used Quaresmeprenant in this manner.[4]

What is Carnival doing as king of a miserable island, reigning perhaps as a sneak or over sneaks? From Xenomanes's subsequent description, this Quaresmeprenant is anything but a merrymaker. In fact, he behaves more like Lent than Carnival. He is, says Xenomanes, "a man of worth, a good Catholic, thoroughly devout. . . . He is a great fellow for breaking barrels . . . half a giant, fuzzy-chinned and wearing a double tonsure." Is this a member of the clergy, then, or is the phrase metaphorical, referring to someone doubly stupid, with even less wits than the proverbial doctor or lawyer "with a single tonsure?"[5] What kind of barrels does he break? Are they full of herrings—as has usually been assumed by commentators—or of wine, or perhaps of that ambivalent food, snails? What did he do with the broken barrels, empty them into his gullet or throw them away with abhorrence?[6]

4. See Edmond Huguet, *Dictionnaire de la langue française du seizième siècle*, Volume 2 (Paris, 1932), 98–99, article "Caresmentrant, Caresme-prenant," for quotations from the authors mentioned in the text. Estienne is particularly explicit, citing a "parish priest . . . speaking of mardi gras, in other words Quaresmeprenant or Quaresmentrant, [who] recommended to his parishioners Saints Big Paunch, Gross Eater, and Full-to-Bursting [Pansard, Mangeard, Crevard]."

5. *QL*, 29, 642. The "proverbial phrase, *docteur, medecin, avocat etc. à simple tonsure*" is quoted by Johan Gottlob Regis, ed. and trans., *Gargantua und Pantagruel*, Volume 2 (Leipzig, 1832–1841; reprint, Munich, 1911), 234. Regis also points to Rabelais's reference to "fol à simple tonsure" in *TL*, 38, 487, a phrase occurring in the comically antiphonal *blason* of the fool Triboulet by Pantagruel and Panurge. Panurge's "fol à simple tonsure" is his response to Pantagruel's "fol prétorial." Regis does not cite the source or derivation of his proverbial phrase. Does it come from the custom of furnishing university students with a single tonsure as a symbol of first entry into the clergy when they begin studies, but tonsuring them again when they enter higher faculties? In this case double tonsure could refer in an inversionary, satiric sense to someone of little wit.

6. *Caquerotier* seems to be composed of French *caque* with *-rotier*, from Latin *ruptor*, someone who breaks or strikes open. On *caque*, see Jean Nicot

Quaresmeprenant is a linguistic paradox, whose name is at once confirmed and denied by his actions. The man is full of contradictions. He dresses in a "joyous" manner both in cut and color, Xenomanes continues ironically: his clothes are "gray and cold, with nothing before and nothing behind, and sleeves to match." He spends his time manufacturing larding sticks and meat skewers—toothsome Carnival preparations—and yet "he weeps three parts of the day" and never attends a wedding. "He's the standard-bearer of the Fisheaters," declares Xenomanes, "dictator of Mustardland, a whipper of small children, a burner of ashes." Ashes were thrown about in Carnival-time, but a cross of ashes was also drawn on penitents' foreheads at the beginning of Lent. Mustard was consumed in great quantities with fish in Lent—and also with sausage in Carnival. Quaresmeprenant whips children and sits about weeping. Who is this fellow, whose appearances and activities seem so absurdly, violently irreconcilable?

Xenomanes soon mentions Quaresmeprenant's enemies, the "Zany Sausages who live on Ferocious Island" (*les Andouilles farfelues de l'Isle Farouche*). Although they might seem to be simple animations of Carnival fare—pork sausage was a favorite dish during Mardi Gras—these folk turn out to be as puzzling as the master of Tapinos Island. They behave, metaphorically speaking, less like sausages than like eels: Lenten food. The *andouilles* conduct themselves like *anguilles*, fishy and wriggling. As if to substantiate the point, a later chapter explains that they are the venerable ancestors of the mermaid Melusine and of the sly snake who tempted Eve.[7]

---

and Aimar de Raconnet, *Thresor de la langue françoyse, tant ancienne que moderne* (Paris, 1621), 101: "Caque, m. penac. Est une espece de futaille . . . et est à eau, à poisson salé." Randle Cotgrave's *Dictionarie of the French and English Tongues* (London, 1611), folio O, ii recto, translates: "Caque . . . a barrell, or vessell, wherein saults-meats, pitch, rosen, etc., are usually carried, or kept"; "Caqueroles: the shels of Snayles, Periwincles, and such like"; "Caquerotier: m. A catcher, eater, or owner, of shellfish." Hence "Un grand cacquerotier" is annotated in Rabelais, *Oeuvres complètes,* ed. Pierre Jourda, Volume 2 (Paris, 1962), 125, as "mangeur d'escargots (?) ou de cacques de harengs (?)." Snails are ambivalent food: In nineteenth- and twentieth-century Languedoc they were used, by varying the sauce in which they were prepared, to mark Carnival and Lent successively: "Ainsi l'escargot devint-il, entre les mains des cuisinières, une viande ou un poisson incarnant successivement les deux temps du calendrier alimentaire." Claudine Fabre-Vassas, "Le soleil des limaçons," *Etudes rurales,* nos. 87–88 (July–December 1983): 78. If the phrase refers to snails, the meaning of Quaresmeprenant's name and behavior become still more difficult to fathom.

7. *QL*, 38, 665.

The episode that describes the Pantagruelians' encounter with Quaresmeprenant and the Sausages is the longest in Rabelais's *Fourth Book*, the last work published before his death in 1553. I have indicated the larger interpretive reason for attempting to understand the puzzles posed by this unusually prominent episode: Bakhtin, who sees a "carnivalesque spirit" permeating Rabelais's text, deals with these chapters only in passing, although they would seem crucial to his hypothesis.[8]

Bakhtin is not alone in this. The most authoritative editors of Rabelais's text and most modern critics have argued away its paradoxes. Never mind the name, Quaresmeprenant *is* Lent, and the Sausages are just Carnival food, appropriately assaulted by Pantagruel's cooks. The Quaresmeprenant chapters are treated as an example of Rabelais's humanist, evangelical attacks on church practices, in this case fasting. The Sausage-people chapters, which involve a battle between them and Pantagruel's cooks, are seen as one of Rabelais's mock epic war stories. Such interpretations deal with what are considered the salient features of the text, not its troubling details. They construct an even surface, not a series of polysemic knots.[9] Separating the Quares-

8. In addition to chs. 29 through 42 of *QL*, there are two further episodes in Rabelais's novels, both in *G*, where Rabelais may be said to set the scene in Carnival time: the moment of Gargantua's birth (*G*, 4–6) and the visit of Master Janotus de Bragmardo to Gargantua (*G*, 18–20). But Rabelais says nothing about the nature of Carnival here, nor does he describe its relation to Lent. He merely alludes to several Carnival customs. Bakhtin, *Rabelais and His World*, 222–24, makes much of the birth scene and refers also at some length to Janotus's visit, but he mentions the Quaresmeprenant-Sausage episode in only a few scattered sentences: 177, 323, 346, 400, and 415.

9. For example, Pierre Jourda in his prestigious edition (the "Classiques Garnier") reproduces a seventeenth-century print, entitled "Le combat de Mardygras" (Rabelais, *Oeuvres*, ed. Jourda, Volume 2, unnumbered page following 126), mistitled as "Combat de Mardigras et de Quaresmeprenant": the verses written on the print identify the combatants as "Mardy gras" and "Caresme." Like Jourda, Boulenger (*QL*, 29, 642), Cohen, trans., *Gargantua*, 512, and Robert Marichal (ed. Rabelais, *Le Quart Livre, édition critique* [Geneva, 1947]) treat Quaresmeprenant as Lent. Marichal, whose edition offers the most complete and authoritative text of the full *Fourth Book* available at present, does not mention the conflict between allegorical figures of Carnival and Lent. Michael Screech does treat the Quaresmeprenant and Andouilles chapters as forming one episode, and he does point to the custom of Carnival-Lent battle as forming the background for the tale. But he calls Quaresmeprenant "the spirit of Lent," "the incarnation of the onset of Lent," or "Lent" *tout court* in his *Rabelais*, 371, 367, 373. He does not see any meditation on the nature of Carnival and Lent in this episode: Rabelais is for one and against the other, and so he con-

meprenant chapters generally from the Sausage-people chapters and treating Carnival-Lent conflict as little more than a vague formal framework for the episode has important consequences, for these moves lead one to wish away a third puzzle: Why do Pantagruel and his army, defenders of carnivalesque boozing and banqueting and hence the enemies of the Sausages' enemy "Lent" (that is, Quaresmeprenant), attack such presumably congenial folk as the Sausage-people while never confronting Quaresmeprenant, whom Pantagruel denounces as a monstrous "Anti-Nature"? Is there perhaps more to it than the obvious references to Sausages as Carnival food and to the Pantagruelians as gourmands?

The fact is that Quaresmeprenant meant Carnival in the sixteenth century, and Rabelais was no stranger to his times. He was strange enough, however, to find playing with commonplaces fascinating and perceptive enough to see that Quaresmeprenant, which etymologically seemed to mean "taking Lent," was a curious name for Carnival. Word games gave wings to Rabelais's fantasy. And what if the phonetic similarity between *andouille* and *anguille* were brought to bear upon the parallel obscenities clustering around their slippery, long, round forms? Once fantasy began its play, there was no stopping until meat merged with fish, man with woman, and humans with animals, or seemed to.

This episode of the *Fourth Book* largely dissolves the traditional moral difference between Carnival and Lent. Despite the conclusions about Rabelais's ambivalent or ambiguous position drawn by the few critics who have observed the variable overtones given to the protagonists in these chapters, Rabelais does not equivocate between the two calendrical moments. And although he hops and skips among etymologies and puns, he does not confuse the symbols traditionally associated with one occasion with those attributed to the other. He disseminates their meaning, rather than wobbling between two poles of

---

cludes, 377: "The Andouilles are not right but merry [Screech lays considerable emphasis on the contemporary religious meaning of the Sausages as Protestants]; Quaresmeprenant is wrong *and* repulsive." Other contemporary criticism of the episode is discussed in my chs. 3–5 and especially ch. 7 below.

Of course I am not arguing that Rabelais's chs. 29–42 can or should *only* be understood from the point of view of their allusions to Carnival-Lent customs. Important aspects of the text demand that quite different groupings of the chapters or subdivisions of chapters be considered, in accordance with interpretive goals different from the problematics pursued here.

traditional Catholic practice. The manner of this dissemination offers a general insight into Rabelais's enterprise in the most bizarre of his "Pantagrueline Books."

For nearly three hundred years Rabelais's reformulation of Carnival-Lent relations has been blatantly misinterpreted. Portions or all of this episode have been discussed by nearly every critic who has written about Rabelais since the seventeenth century. What is the reason for a critical tradition that has so long and so complacently argued away the contemporary meaning of Rabelais's words?

Rabelais's text has been misinterpreted because its context has been wrongly defined. The problem does not primarily arise from bringing wrong or inadequate information to bear upon the text. It is a question of redefining the relation of text to context. That relation is usually represented theatrically or cinematically: context is the background or stage scenery for text, which is front and center; alternatively the text is seen as a moving picture, a re-presentation or mirroring of the context. In recent decades semiotic critics like Roland Barthes, Julia Kristeva, and Michael Riffaterre have replaced the theatrical-cinematic model with that of a productive machine. Their key term is "intertextuality": every text is a product of other texts. Tracing the ties of one text with others, showing the linkages and transformations of the semiotic codes used in the whole group of texts, reveals the way in which the particular "machine" in question produces meaning.[10]

10. Julia Kristeva developed the concept of intertextuality in an essay on Bakhtin, "Le Mot, le Dialogue, et le Roman" (published in *Critique* [April 1967] and reprinted in her *Semiotiké* [Paris, 1968], 143–73); see especially 145–46 and also ch. 8, "La productivité dite texte," in the same book. Both here and in ch. 5, "Intertextuality," of Kristeva's *Le texte du roman* (Paris, 1970), intertextuality is related to what she calls "carnivalesque structure," whose verbal forms produce a "more flagrant dialogism [Bakhtin's term] than any other discourse" (*Semiotiké*, 161; see also my ch. 1, n. 56, below). Barthes's understanding of intertextuality is different: "By degrees," he writes in *S/Z, An Essay* (New York, 1974), 211, "a text can come into contact with any other system: the inter-text is subject to no law but the infinitude of its reprises. The Author himself—that somewhat decrepit deity of the old criticism—can or could some day become a text like any other . . . he has only to see himself as a being on paper . . . a writing without referent, substance of a *connection* and not of a *filiation*." Riffaterre's use of the term in *Text Production* (New York, 1983) is discussed in ch. 8 below. My labeling of intertextual criticism as mechanical refers to the ten-

The theatrical-cinematic metaphor reduces context to a scenic perspective that enhances or coerces writing, as the case may be, but in either case stands outside it. The mechanical metaphor supposes that context consists of other literary works, decomposable like the text in question into neatly separable literary units and reassembled for the purposes at hand. In this case context does enter into the text, and even seems to conjugate it, but only insofar as the context has been reduced to verbal forms.

Rabelais's text does not yield its meanings to such interpretive assumptions. To provide a more adequate model for analysis of the text/context relation requires an excursus to analyze some paratextual elements in Rabelais's works before we return to the puzzles of the Quaresmeprenant-Sausage episode.

---

dency of these critics to discern, behind the surface play of word and theme, the work of a definable set of operations that produce the text. In these writers the organicist metaphors of the "old criticism" to which Barthes refers are replaced by mechanical mathematical ones. "Any text is constructed as a mosaic of quotations, any text is the absorption and transformation of another. The notion of intertextuality replaces that of intersubjectivity" (*Semiotiké*, 146). Recent work by François Rigolot suggests that this association of intertextuality with mechanical mathematical models, much in vogue during the structuralist trend in the human sciences, is by no means necessary. Charles-Augustin Sainte-Beuve (1804–1869), Rigolot writes in *Le texte de la Renaissance* (Geneva, 1982), 19–20, anticipated the basic idea of these intertextual semioticians when he described "any text" in more traditional rhetorical terms "as the 'synecdoche' of another vaster, more complex text which remains to be written."

# I

# Paratexts and Printing

Context neither frames the text nor consists simply of verbal fragments that have been reassembled into a new text. How a text is interlaced with context is illumined and to some extent defined by paratext, a neologism that, like intertext, has value if used with other critical tools rather than as a sovereign methodology. Paratext refers to elements that frame the text, such as the title page, with its indications of title, author, and publisher, the table of contents, dedication, and preface; paratext includes elements scattered through the text such as illustrations, footnotes, and marginal indications or subtitles; it comprehends too a book's format: typeset, binding, size, quality of paper.[1]

Paratexts indicate the forces that have shaped a text: they show how contexts invade the text. But they are also an arena in which the author can, more or less openly, combat such forces. Precisely this is what Rabelais did with the paratextual elements most under an author's control, his dedication and prefaces. In the prologue to the *Fourth Book,* for example, Rabelais attempts to exercise control over how his book will be interpreted by representing the context in which the book is

---

1. Comparison of this brief list with the preliminary discussion of paratext by Gérard Genette, who seems to have invented the term, reveals some differences between his definition and mine; see his *Seuils* (Paris, 1987), 7–9, and his earlier *Palimpsestes* (Paris, 1981), 9. These differences stem from a theoretical disagreement: Genette sees the "literary work" as "consist[ing] exhaustively or essentially in a text," which is created by an author. Hence paratext for Genette is above all "defined by an intention and a responsibility [on the part] of the author" (*Seuils*, 7, 9). I assume, on the contrary, that neither text nor paratext are defined simply by an author's intentions and responsibilities but instead are the consequence of a series of compromises between the author and other persons involved in making a book, most obviously the book's editor and those representing the financial and other interests of a book's publishing house. This is true of "literary works" as of other printed publications. I have developed further this idea of collective creation and compromise in paratext in chapter 8. For a list of other studies of paratextual elements, some of them anticipating Genette's formalization of the concept, see the appendix to François Rigolot, "Prolégomènes à une étude du statut de l'appareil liminaire des textes littéraires," *L'Esprit Créateur* 27, no. 3 (Fall 1987): 15–18.

being received by his readers. The first words of the text treat readers as if they were being greeted physically by the author: "God save and keep you, worthy people! Where are you? I can't see you. Wait until I put on my glasses. Ha, ha! Lent is going by, well and fair! I see you!"[2]

With the use of a half-dozen interjections Rabelais transforms the text/context twice in three lines, from reading to looking to playing. The "Prologue of the Author M. François Rabelais to the Fourth Book," continues with a subtitle, "To Well-Disposed Readers" (*Aux Lecteurs Bénévoles*); title and subtitle identify this object as an element of written language, as one book among others available to a literate public. But the salutation, "God save and keep you," is an oral greeting. The shift from written to oral representation of the book's context is confirmed by the further words "Where are you?" The author looks where he cannot possibly look, and he claims to see.

His seeing is not like that of some omniscient deity. He does not say "I, Rabelais, see you, all of my present and future readers until Kingdom come!" The peeking the author-narrator pretends to do is human, even homely, given intimacy by reference to his glasses and playfulness by means of the words: "Ha, ha! Lent is going by, well and fair! I see you!" These phrases are associated with an old version of the game of "I spy."

The game, "Lent is going by, well and fair," is listed among those that Gargantua played as a boy in Rabelais's earlier book, *Gargantua,* describing Pantagruel's father. Presumably it was widely known, although historians have thus far not found other contemporary allusions to it. In the nineteenth century the game was played during Lent in Poitou, a region just to the south of the Loire Valley where Rabelais—and his fictitious giants—grew up.[3] There the game was called "capiote," from the Latin *capio te,* "I catch you," or "I take you." As Léon Pineau described it in 1889, it presupposed an agreement between the children or young people to play the game all through Lent. Morning, noon, or night, each one tried to surprise the other by shouting: "Capiote!" The person who had the lesser number of capiotes at the end of Lent was obliged to buy the winner a small cake on Maundy Thursday.

2. *QL,* Pr, 545: "Gens de bien, Dieu vous saulve et guard! Où estez-vous? Je ne vous peuz voir. Attendez que je chausse mes lunettes! Ha, ha! Bien et beau s'en va Quaresme! Je vous voy."

3. See *G,* 22, 88. Many place-names in Rabelais's fictions locate the scene in the countryside of the author's childhood around Chinon.

Antoine Oudin, an antiquarian writing in 1656 about "French curiosities," explained "Lent is going by" in terms parallel to Pineau, so the idea of the game seems well established.[4] But what does the phrase mean?

In the list of Gargantua's childhood pastimes the game listed just after "Lent is going by" is "I catch you without any green" (or "take you": *Je vous prens sans verd*), a May Day game in which one concealed a green leaf on one's person and produced it when accosted with this phrase. Gargantua played gargantuanly: Rabelais lists 216 games, and in the long listing one is often associated with the next. If this is why Rabelais thought of one after the other, then perhaps the phrase "Lent is going by, well and fair" has a seasonal meaning, as the green-leaf game on May Day certainly does: it heralds the change of weather toward fair and mild springtime. However, the phrase may refer ironically to the period of obligatory fasting, an obligation that was not a "good and fair" thing (*bien et beau*) in the opinion of many; but for such people, if Lent *is* passing along, that is well enough.

Rabelais's readers are not addressed from the distance of a writer's study. They are brought into the text as interlocutors, even as players in a game. The text is transformed into a public place, a place of encounter, as if the text's words were determined in some measure by the behavior of the audience. Rabelais creates a narrative frame as open-ended, as indefinite and inconclusive as the conversations of the Pantagruelians in the story, which are often broken into by some accident that interferes with their pursuits.[5] By using this conversational frame, Rabelais places readers in the position of politely responding in kind to his congenial warmth:

4. Léon Pineau, letter published in "Notes et Enquêtes" section, *Revue des traditions populaires* 4 (1889): 368. Antoine Oudin, *Curiositez françoises* (Paris, 1656) explains "Bien et beau" thus: "C'est une sorte du jeu où chaque jour du Caresme, celuy qui dit le premier ces mots à son compagnon gaigne le prix convenu." Oudin is quoted in Michel Psichari, "Les Jeux de Gargantua," *Revue des études rabelaisiennes* 6 (1908): 351.

5. Imitation of oral spontaneity and unplanned, inconclusive talk was developed by François Villon, to whom Rabelais frequently refers in the novels. Nancy Regalado analyzed Villon's techniques (breaking off phrases, inserting interjections and digressions, using frequent deixis) in her paper, "Speaking in Script: The Re-creation of Orality in Villon's *Testament,*" presented at the conference on "Oral Tradition in the Middle Ages," Center for Medieval and Early Renaissance Studies, State University of New York at Binghamton, October 22, 1988.

And so? Your vintage has turned out well, as I've been told, and I would never be sorry about that. You have found an infinite remedy against any kind of change, any kind of thirst. That's most virtuously done. You, your wives, your children, your relatives and households, are as healthy as may be? That's good, that's fine, that pleases me.[6]

This feigned warmth and closeness in the address to readers had first appeared in the prologue to the *Third Book*, published six years earlier (1546).[7] The attitude contrasts with that in the prologues of *Gargantua* and *Pantagruel*, where readers are more distantly, although still familiarly, praised and abused as if they were being harangued by a marketplace bookseller.[8]

The change is connected with a shift in persona: the "author" of *Gargantua* and *Pantagruel* was not indicated in the paratexts of those books. There the narrator calls himself Alcofribas Nasier, an anagram of François Rabelais. Few readers would have been able to unscramble the vaguely Arabian pseudonym and discover the notable doctor and editor of Hippocrates.[9] But "François Rabelais, doctor of medicine," is proclaimed as the author of the *Third Book* and the *Fourth Book* on the title pages, and the author's name is used again as part of the titles of the prologues: a certain distance is thus placed between author and narrator of the tales proper, who continues to be Alcofribas.[10]

Text is pulled away from paratext, as Rabelais makes more explicit his representation of himself as an author. There were several reasons

6. *QL*, Pr, 545.

7. The first lines of *TL*, Pr, 341, parallel the opening of *G*, Pr, 25, published long before (1534–1535). Readers are addressed with the same jocular praise/abuse and immediately introduced to a learned theme (an additional greeting, "Bonnes gens," added in 1552, will concern us in ch. 9): "Beuveurs très illustres, et vous goutteux très précieux, veistez-vous oncques Diogènes, le philosophe cynic?" This attitude of distant familiarity is exchanged almost immediately, however, for something approaching personal acquaintance; ten lines after the salutation the author pursues: "Vous item n'estez jeunes, qui est qualité compétente pour en vin, non en vain, ains plus que physicalement philosopher."

8. The marketplace-like settings have been frequently remarked. Bakhtin, *Rabelais*, 160–71, offers the fullest interpretation of their praise and abuse.

9. Moreover, the title page to *Pantagruel* refers to the author as "Feu M. Alcofribas," "the late Master Alcofribas": *P*, 187.

10. Alcofribas's name does not appear in the *Fourth Book*, but Panurge addresses him by his sobriquet "Monsieur the abstractor," and the book's narrator uses the collective "we" to refer to the Pantagruelians. For this and other reasons explained in ch. 8, it seems clear that Rabelais retained his fictive alter ego as narrator of the *Fourth Book*.

for the change; some involved the general form of the novels and others concerned particular events. Only the latter interest us at this point. Rabelais's first, second, and third novels had been condemned in 1543, 1545, and 1546 by the Sorbonne; the second and third condemnations had been endorsed by the Parlement of Paris; there was a risk that copies of the novels in bookstores would be confiscated and the booksellers fined if not imprisoned.[11] Reacting to this situation with some intrepidity, Rabelais issued a part of the *Fourth Book* in 1548 with a prologue in which themes and attitudes of the later 1552 prologue carried different overtones. In 1552 the prologue author feigns first not to see the "worthy people" whom he invites to conversation ("where are you? I can't see you"), but he then dissolves the pretense with his playful "Ha, ha! . . . I see you." The atmosphere of sedate ease thus engendered is quite different from that brought about by use of the same phrase in 1548 ("O worthy people, I can't see you!"), for no resolution of the tension introduced by this phrase follows. In its sixteenth-century context to say "I can't see you" meant to protest someone's absence, in this case presumably the absence of the kind of "worthy people" who could protect Rabelais's writings from attack.[12]

Rabelais lashes out with great verbal violence against those denouncing his writings in the prologue of 1548. Four years later his situation had changed. Having gained new support at the French court, Rabelais received a royal privilege to print all his works with the king's protection for ten years to come. The altered situation for his books is reflected in Rabelais's easy tone in the prologue of 1552. He asks about the health of his suppositious readers' friends and relatives and responds with an orotund Christian prayer: "Healthy as may be? That's good, that's fine, that pleases me. May God, the good God, be eternally

11. Francis M. Higman, *Censorship and the Sorbonne: A Bibliographical Study of Books in French Censured by the Faculty of Theology of the University of Paris 1520–1551* (Geneva, 1979), explains the sixteenth-century mechanisms of censorship and condemnation. For Rabelais's condemnations, not especially singled out for study by Higman, see 52, 62, 63.

12. As explained in ch. 9, the prologue is written with shifting ironic tones, so that even when one can be fairly certain about the text's referents, the meaning of such referents for the author represented in the text, let alone the real author, is not always clear. In *QL*, Pr 1548, 752, n. 4, editor Boulenger says that the contemporary writer Du Fail and later La Fontaine in his *Fables* also used the phrase in the sense of protesting someone's absence. Rabelais had already used it that way in *G*, 3, 204.

praised for it and, if such is his holy wish, may you long continue so." In 1548 the prayer is imploring: "Oh worthy people, I can't see you! May the great virtue of God come eternally in aid to you, and no less to me! There then, by God, let us never do anything without first praising his sacred name!"[13] The concluding declaration of orthodoxy seems almost tailored to belie charges of impiety.

On whom could Rabelais rely besides God? The royal privilege of 1550 was not the first he had received. The *Third Book* had been published in 1546 with a royal privilege that had not saved it from the Sorbonne's condemnation. Church authority was at least semi-independent from state authority; even the authority of Parlement was not always under the control of the king and his ministers. During the first half of the sixteenth century royal favor had waxed and waned toward those of humanist and evangelist persuasion like Rabelais. He could not feel entirely secure in royal patronage. Others—most signally the learned though impetuous Louis de Berquin and Etienne Dolet—had been burned for their humanist opinions and publications.

Rabelais's firmest source of support was not the king and his ministers but his anonymous readers. By 1552 it is probable that at least fifty thousand copies of Rabelais's first four books had been printed. The vogue of his books would continue after his death in 1553 until the end of the sixteenth century.[14] He was extraordinarily popular. Such massive although remote support was novel; it was due to the invention of printing a century earlier and to the inventiveness of publishers in exploiting new markets of readers.

The problem for Rabelais was how to use this new but anonymous power. Through printing the boundaries of literary influence and re-

13. *QL*, Pr 1548, 752.

14. The figure of fifty thousand copies is derived from multiplying the forty-six editions certainly published by 1552 (*NRB*, nos. 1–13, 19–51) by eleven hundred copies per edition. One thousand copies seems to have been the more or less normal printing for an author in Rabelais's time. But Aldus Manutius earlier in the century often printed three thousand copies of popular classical authors, and Reformation writings after 1520 also were published in printings much larger than one thousand. See Martin Lowry, *The World of Aldus Manutius* (Ithaca, N.Y., 1979), 257, 290. Rabelais was a popular author; at least some of the forty-six editions were probably published in runs of more than one thousand copies; there is always the possibility, too, that some as yet unknown editions existed, especially pirated editions of *Pantagruel* and *Gargantua*. Some persons also presumably bought single tomes of the multivolume editions among those listed in the *NRB*. The figure of fifty thousand is one-half the number of "Rabelaisian writings" estimated for the whole sixteenth century by

sponsibility, usual in the age of the manuscript book, were suddenly opened; given that, he was probably uncertain about the tactic to choose. There were as yet few conventions to follow. Authors derived little income from their publications. The only semblances of copyright were the privileges extended to favored authors or publishers by princes and city councils. Due to the still largely decentralized character of feudal-monarchical society, such privileges were ineffective in preventing pirated editions and even incapable of preventing condemnation by rival authorities. Yet Rabelais could be certain not only that he possessed power but also that this was recognized by those upon whom he otherwise depended. Luther's massively published writings proved that low and obscure men, capable of evoking popular response through the printed book, might move and even overturn church and state. The example of Erasmus's popularity was equally pertinent. The Dutch humanist, who unlike Luther was one of Rabelais's heroes, had both taught and demonstrated that writing seriocomically in a popularizing vein might through the new tool of the printed book be a leavening force.[15]

Printing was Rabelais's inspiration. "You have lately seen, read, and come to know *The Great and Inestimable Chronicles of the Enormous Giant Gargantua,*" Alcofribas Nasier declares in the prologue to Rabelais's first novel, *Pantagruel.* "You have often passed the time in the company of honorable ladies and maidens by telling them fine long stories from that book," he continues, and he urges that the *Chronicles* be committed to memory "so that if the art of printing happened to die out . . . everyone should be able . . . to transmit it to his successors and survivors, as if from hand to hand, like some religious Cabala." "Find me a book in any language, on any subject or science whatever,

---

Lucien Febvre and Henri-Jean Martin, *L'apparition du livre* (Paris, 1958), 415: "Les différents écrits rabelaisiens furent répandus dès le XVIe siècle . . . peut-être à plus de cent mille, compte tenu des éditions perdues."

15. Cf. Erasmus's clarion call in the *Paraclesis,* the paratextual introduction to his new Latin translation of the Greek New Testament (1516), where he states that his ambition is to make the biblical gospels and epistles so available and understandable through translations and commentary that farmers, women, weavers, and travelers might read it as they move about their daily tasks. See Desiderius Erasmus, *Ausgewählte Werke,* ed. Hajo Holborn and Annemarie Holborn (Munich, 1933), 142. Erasmus's *Praise of Folly, Colloquies,* and some other of his works are superb examples of popularizing elite culture, and, at least in the opinion of opposing authorities, they were ideologically effective. "Erasmus laid the egg that Luther hatched," the saying ran.

which has such virtues, properties and prerogatives, and I will pay you a quart of tripe. . . . For more copies of it have been sold by the printers in two months than of the Bible in nine years!"[16]

A few letters by Rabelais in Greek and Latin, published and unpublished at the time, remain from the years up to 1532 when this prologue was written. They, like the learned translations and commentaries he also published in 1532, exhibit correct but unexceptional diction. There is little sign of the audacious verve and ironic subtlety of expression that erupt in *Pantagruel*. Printing, because it was a mode of communication that widened the possible audience immeasurably, seems not only to have served Rabelais as a humanist but also to have suggested to him another, fictive avenue of verbal exchange with readers, calling upon a different level of mind and feeling from that with which he dealt in his scholarly productions.

Not so much a new group of uncultivated "popular" readers but the broadly mixed audiences made possible by printing proved the making of Rabelais as a writer; his audiences were literate and illiterate, serious and mocking, leveling and hierarchizing in feeling, idealist and practical, naturalistic and yet also religious in belief. Printing allowed communication with this varied and variable set of sensibilities. Rabelais pressed his readers to develop in themselves such variability by his paratextual tactics.

With the advent of printing a vast gray space emerged between composition and reception, between sending the text's messages and feedback to author and publisher about them; the prologue narrator's exclamation, "Where are you? I can't see you," carries this nuance, too. How different this was from the situation of pulpit preacher and jongleur, whose orally delivered texts necessarily involved audience encounter. Far from his readers, Rabelais represented his readers as paradoxically near, clustering around a bookstall in the prologue to *Pantagruel* as Alcofribas extols the exquisite virtues of the *Chronicles* about Gargantua and its sequel *Pantagruel*; sitting in some room with Dr. Rabelais himself in the prologue to the *Fourth Book* as that affable gentleman inquires about friends and family.[17]

16. *P*, Pr, 189–91.
17. After the opening salutations, as the "conversation" continues, Dr. Rabelais feigns to turn to his books, citing the New Testament and three medical treatises attributed to Galen. Hence one imagines him in some place, perhaps his study, with his books at hand: "Cl. Gal. . . . eust congneu et frèquenté les saincts Christians de son temps, comme appert lib. II, De usu partium, lib. 2

Text/context: paratextual elements like these prologues allow an author to represent his readers and hence to suggest to them how he would like his books to be read . . . and not read. For any representation implies a reality beyond it that differs from the representation. To represent author and reader in the obviously impossible forms of Rabelais's prologues requires the reader to reflect upon the identity of the author behind the simulacrum, to reflect upon his or her own identity in relation to these texts, and hence to separate in greater or lesser degree the reality from the representation. If Rabelais writes of Dr. Rabelais in his parlor or study, receiving worthy well-wishers of his books, one can be certain that he is asking his readers to imagine an author-reader connection that is something other than the one depicted in such a scene.

The manuscript book contained wide margins, filled with glosses. The physical space between the scribe or scholar who wrote and the theological, pedagogical, or otherwise interested reader who commented was broad because the intellectual space between them was assumed to be narrow.[18] The printed book had small margins, just wide enough for a word or two, an emendation, an exclamation, a notch or other sign to indicate interest. It was small because the physical distance between author and reader was large. Because it was large it stimulated authors to develop their manipulative powers, to inveigle readers, and to steer them in directions consistent with their textual purposes. The authors of the printed book had to imagine themselves and their readers in ways quite unparalleled in either oral or manuscript communication. They might move either to induce looseness and inventive digression or to insure compliance.[19] Whatever their tactics, the result

---

De differentiis pulsuum, cap. 3, et ibidem, lib. 3, cap. 2, et lib. De renum affectibus (s'il est de Galen)" (*QL*, Pr, 546).

18. See the first section, "Le temps du manuscrit," and especially the subsection in it by Paul Saenger, "Manières de lire médiévales," in Roger Chartier and Henri-Jean Martin, *Histoire de l'imprimerie française,* Volume 1 (Paris, 1983). Henry Chaytor, *From Script to Print* (London, 1945), also remains valuable as is Elizabeth Eisenstein, *The Printing Press as an Agent of Change,* 2 volumes (Cambridge, 1980). Rabelais's fictitious list of the books in the monastery library of Saint Victor at Paris (*P*, 7, 216–24) is from the point of view considered here less an image of monastic obscurantism and hypocrisy than a representation of the narrow, obsessively glossing mentality encouraged by the form of manuscript bookmaking.

19. Bakhtin's distinction between "dialogical" (loose, digressive) and "monological" (tight, authorially manipulative) texts, might be said to be re-

separated the represented reader from the reader beyond that representation, holding a real book in real hands.[20]

How did the real reader appear to the eyes of the real author? We
cannot be certain of course, but we have several clues. One clue consists
of woodcuts, showing scenes of reading, on the title pages of two pirated editions of Rabelais's *Gargantua*. Neither woodcut was influenced by Rabelais; they are presumably pieces of advertising chosen by
the publishers. The publishers, located in southern France, were familiar with the milieus in which Rabelais's books were selling so well: if
they chose to represent these reading scenes, it is because they were
commonly known and would beckon to the buyer. But because they
would have been commonly known, they may be assumed to have been
familiar to Rabelais as well and to have entered into his idea of his
readers.

The first woodcut, published by Etienne Dolet in the abusively
unexpurgated edition of 1542, shows a stout, long-robed gentleman
reading from a large book opened on a table before him.[21] His right
hand rests on the shoulder of a child of ten or twelve in front of him,
who is looking at the book. His left arm grazes the shoulder of another
child of the same age (both children seem to be male) while pointing
to a line in the book. Two large vessels, seemingly for liquid (one at
least seems filled), are placed to right and left of the book on the table.
Six men of varying ages crowd in upon the scene of reading, as if to
hear what the gentleman is saying. Two or three are represented with
open mouths, as if exclaiming in astonishment.

The second woodcut (see Fig. 1), published in 1547 by Claude La
Ville in a pirated edition of Rabelais, shows a cluster of people with
even more expressive facial gestures in a similar scene of reading. In-

---

lated to this difference. See the essays in Bakhtin, *The Dialogic Imagination*
(Austin, Tex., 1981). This is my suggestion; Bakhtin does not especially concern
himself with effects of printing.

20. These issues have been explored by, among others, Wolfgang Iser, *The
Implied Reader* (Baltimore, 1974), Umberto Eco, *The Role of the Reader* (Bloomington, Ind., 1979), Stanley Fish, *Is There a Text in This Classroom?* (Berkeley,
1980), Cesare Segre, *Avviamento all'analisi del testo letterario* (Turin, 1985), and
the authors in S. R. Suleiman and I. Crosman, ed., *Reader in the Text: Essays on
Audience and Interpretation* (Princeton, 1980). They are discussed further in chs.
7–9 here.

21. See the introduction above for reference to Dolet's edition. *NRB*, 48,
reproduces the woodcut.

# LA
# Plaisante, &
## I O Y E V S E
## histoyre du grand
## Geant Gargantua.

Prochainement reueue, & de beaucoup
augmentée par l'Autheur mesme.

## A Valence,
## Chés Claude La Ville.
## 1547.

stead of presenting the central figure frontally, here the reader is shown in profile, peering through spectacles at the open book. A cup or glass stands to the right of the book; is this a tavern scene? The five people listening to the reader crowd around him more closely than the people in Dolet's woodcut. They grimace or gaze with open mouths, bedazed or aghast at the words of the reader bending over his text. This representation shows more lower class and more eccentric people—note their bizarre hats—than that in Dolet's edition; these people express their reactions with toothy directness.

Rabelais mixed appeals to his readers, sometimes addressing "worthy people" like those in Dolet's woodcut and sometimes referring to "poor victims of pox and gout . . . their faces shining like a larder lockplate and their teeth rattling like the keys on the manual of an organ" as they listen to the *Chronicles* of Gargantua or crowd around a fellow in tavern or street like those on the title page of Claude La Ville's edition.[22] The complaints of other authors prove—and this is a second kind of clue—that scenes like those depicted in the woodcuts mixed the literate and illiterate inside or at shop doors and other gathering places in the towns. An anonymous prologue to a book about commercial ethics published in 1496 at the French city of Provins complained about "the useless novels and tales which people customarily read so assiduously at the workshops and stores of merchants, where many come to hear and listen to them for [purposes of] vain pleasure."[23]

Printing might be said to have paradoxically stimulated illiteracy no less than literacy because it increased the repertoire and means of entertainment at the disposal of oral performers, descendants of the courtly minstrels who still in sixteenth-century Europe told tales—and now might read them aloud—improvised songs, and broadcast the news in public places.[24] Printing glorified illiteracy, making it profitable both to imitate the modes of oral discourse in writing and to play variations on

22. "Worthy people": *QL*, Pr, 752. "Poor victims": *P*, Pr, 190.
23. Cited by Dominique Coq, "Les incunables: textes anciens, textes nouveaux," in Chartier and Martin, *Histoire de l'imprimerie*, 1: 184.
24. See Paul Zumthor, *La lettre et la voix de la "littérature" médiévale* (Paris, 1987), 67–80, who shows that the tendency of oral performers at court and in town to introduce written elements in their recitations begins almost with the first notices we have of their courtly existence in the tenth century. The mixture of oral with written elements, therefore, rather than the exclusion of one or the other, is characteristic of such performers, who continued to exist in some parts of Europe well into the twentieth century.

oral turns of speech, proverbs, and jokes.[25] The relation between oral and written forms of verbality both sharpened the distance between them (writing now passed through a more or less complex process of editing and printing before becoming public) and made it possible to recognize more easily their ultimate inseparability. Any written communication presupposes oral communications concerning the same subjects or using the same words in other connections. And vice versa: disconnecting oral from written forms of human exchange or giving priority to one over the other is in a philosophic sense a phonocentric or graphocentric illusion, depending on whether the oral or written side is accorded sovereign power. The sources of language do not lie on one side as opposed to the other but in the two sides' interplay, in utterance combined with inscription.[26]

Rabelais exploited the interplay by representing what was written not only as if it were taking place orally but also in a more general sense. "Rabelais writes prose which, when read, . . . gives the illusion of lis-

25. The inverse is equally true and has received more attention from scholars: Printing brought letters to the unlettered in new ways. Towns in particular were plastered with print, now that public proclamations of every kind could be cheaply reproduced. Those who could not read were in the presence of written documents at church, on the job, and in the streets in unprecedented ways, and this atmosphere of literacy formed their consciousness no less than that of the lettered. On this subject, see Natalie Z. Davis, "Printing and the People," in her *Society and Culture in Early Modern France* (Stanford, Calif., 1975), and Roger Chartier, "Stratégies éditoriales et lectures populaires," in Chartier and Martin, *Histoire de l'imprimerie*, Volume 1.

26. In a historical sense with reference to circumscribed communities one can of course often establish the priority of written over oral or of oral over written communication. The more general perspective alluded to in these sentences, developed particularly in the work of Martin Heidegger (e.g., *On the Way to Language* [New York, 1971]) and Jacques Derrida (e.g., *Of Grammatology* [Baltimore, 1974]) may serve to remind us that oral communication has frequently been accompanied, even in cultures "without writing," by inscriptive and mnemonic devices that resemble it, from the bone scratches that, Alexander Marshack supposes (*The Roots of Civilization* [New York, 1971]), represented Pleistocene humanity's way of calculating fertility cycles, to the mantic sticks that, Ferdinand de Saussure once suggested, were the means by which Sanskrit sages retained in memory their phonemically complex hymns; cf. S. Kinser, "Saussure's Anagrams; Ideological Work," *Modern Language Notes* 94 (1974): 1119–22.

During the time this study has been in gestation, the climate of opinion has already begun to shift from revisionism in favor of the claims of orality against literacy in art (Walter Ong, *Presence of the Word* [New York, 1967], Paul Zumthor, *Introduction à la poésie orale* [Paris, 1983], etc.) to arguments stressing the

tening to a supremely skilled oral performance."[27] In other passages, however, he reverses this procedure and wearies the reader's eyes with long lists of items whose significance emerges best from their visual presence in written rows over which the eye can rove back and forth, comparing and contrasting. The list of the books of the monastic library of Saint Victor in *Pantagruel* is one example; enumeration of the parts of Quaresmeprenant's anatomy in the Carnival-Lent episode of the *Fourth Book* is another.

I suggested that paratext is a linking place between elements proper to a book's composition and elements related to a book's reception. Investigation of this place of linkage will be helpful in explaining the misinterpretation of Rabelais's idea of Carnival and hence ultimately of critics' idea of the text as carnivalesque. Rabelais's paratextual elements constitute a series of feints and mixtures of tactics, favored by the relatively new character of printed book production. How did such feints and mixtures serve Rabelais's ends, which at the very least included that of being able to continue to publish? How did such tactics counter the attacks on him, attacks of which he took almost frenzied notice in the Carnival-Lent episode, denouncing the "maniac [Guillaume] Postels, the demoniacal [John] Calvins, the crazy [Catholic theologian Gabriel Du-] Puy-Herbaults . . . catamites and cannibals" who condemned his books?[28]

Rabelais was a dependent person economically and politically. Unlike the career-seeking, back-biting intellectuals in his time, he does not seem to have sought to rise above that condition. One might guess— but it is only a guess, an argument from silence more than from facts— that he even sought mediocre obscurity in arranging his life and career. Because he did not write from a position of power, he had to write from a place of concealment, almost like a guerrilla fighter whose allies are anonymous and changing, depending on circumstances. Rabelais

---

interaction of written and oral models of verbal communication in nearly all artifacts, artistic and nonartistic, whether performed in oral or written ways. See, e.g., Tony Lentz, *Orality and Literacy in Hellenic Greece* (Carbondale, Ill., 1988); and Carl Lindahl, *Earnest Games: Folkloric Patterns in the Canterbury Tales* (Bloomington, Ind., 1987).

27. Carol Clark, *The Vulgar Rabelais* (Oxford, 1985), 62.

28. *QL*, 32, 651. I follow the form of the name of the last-named person used by Eugenie Droz in her "Frère Gabriel DuPuyherbault, l'agresseur de François Rabelais," *Studi Francesi* 10 (1966): 401–27.

did not simply imagine this tactic; he was stimulated to do so by the newness of the printer's art. He drew upon the power of his numerous but remote readers by crossing boundaries made uncertain by the advent of printing.[29] Thus, we have noticed how he crossed the new gray space, removing reader from author through the printed book by representing readers in oral rapport with a series of authors—Alcofribas, Dr. Rabelais—who necessarily bear only an oblique relation to the real author writing about them. He crossed the frontiers between a number of genres of elite and popular literature by varying his rhetoric, mixing jokes with theology or medicine and Carnival topics with high seriousness. He also scrambled the boundaries between oral and written modes of writing. Let us briefly return to consideration of this third way of developing an anonymous popularity.

The new distance between author and reader imposed by printing stimulated recognition of the fact that writing like speaking never relies simply on words to communicate. Face-to face communication supplements the voice with gestures and clothes and bodily stance. In written communication various marks must be substituted for these supplements. Even in the medieval period of the manuscript book, separations between paragraphs and chapters, capitalization, punctuation marks, and other instruments irrelevant to orally oriented literature had been worked out.[30] With printing such aids were further elaborated by means of the paratextual elements mentioned earlier: title pages with identifying emblems, typeset, size of the printed page, paper quality, and so on. But for Rabelais's purposes all this seems inadequate. He seems to want to lean out of the page to accost readers with onomatopoeic, rhythmic, emotive utterances ("Ha, ha!" exclaims Dr. Rabelais), utterances that lead over the book's margins toward games and dances

29. "A 'tactic' [is] . . . a calculus which cannot count on a 'proper' (a spatial or institutional localization) [*sic*], nor thus on a borderline distinguishing the other as a visible totality. The place of a tactic belongs to the other. . . . Many everyday practices (talking, reading, moving about, shopping . . .) are tactical in character. And so are, more generally, many 'ways of operating': victories of the 'weak' over the 'strong' . . . , clever tricks . . . , joyful discoveries, poetic as well as warlike." Michel de Certeau, *The Practice of Everyday Life* (Berkeley, 1984), xix.

30. Paul Saenger's "Manières de lire," on the other hand, reveals the astonishing extent to which written literature in antiquity and the early Middle Ages remained wedded to oral models, ignoring the marks and distinctions mentioned in this sentence.

and popular theater. Then again he seems to withdraw into a medically professional anonymity, as in the descriptions of Quaresmeprenant in the *Fourth Book*. Rabelais's tactics acknowledge the otherness of non-verbal communication and seek to turn it to the printed text's profit by imitating those modes of everyday behavior with which he was especially familiar. The context is given opportunity to enrich the text throughout, not simply in its paratextual elements. Context permeates the text.[31]

The cumulative effect of these boundary crossings and mixtures is not simply to demand a great deal of knowledge and a nimble wit in order to seize an author's nuanced references; it is also to foster a kind of cunning. If readers are not prepared to shift and swerve with the feints of the author, they cannot apprehend the text. Printing brought immense new pressures to bear upon authors from state and church; these authorities were not interested in nimble wits, let alone cunning; they were concerned with security. The apparatus of the title page, indicating place, date, and printer's or publisher's name, was of course an economic advantage, telling buyers where to find the book; but it was also a means of political control, allowing the state to find and condemn suspicious books and booksellers. Printing increased the author's freedom by distancing him from official as well as unofficial readers. But printing also increased the pressures on the author to conform, on one hand to public opinion in order to sell and on the other to official opinion in order to avoid arrest of the books or oneself.[32]

To thwart these pressures Rabelais sought to stimulate cunning; he also tried something else. His gaiety of spirit, which comes from many sources and serves many ends, was at least in part a political attitude, if not at the beginning of his fictional writing in 1532, then certainly by 1545 or 1546 when he elaborated the *Fourth Book* after repeated condemnations by the Parlement of Paris and the Sorbonne. By means of laughter Rabelais sought to contact his readers in ways that would pry them loose from the demands of special interests and self-serving dogmatisms:

31. The attentive reader will have noticed that my use of the word "context" has varied—with the context. The word has unavoidably different meanings, distinguished in Appendix 1.

32. Judicial execution of printers and booksellers began in the 1520s in France in the name of religious conformity. It is a bloody tale. See the section, "Le livre et les propagandes religieuses," in Chartier and Martin, *Histoire de l'imprimerie*, Volume 1.

Amis lecteurs, qui ce livre lisez
Despouillez-vous de toute affection,
Et, le lisant ne vous scandalisez:
Il ne contient mal ne infection

. . . . . . . .

Mieux est de ris que de larmes escripre,
Pour ce que rire est le propre de l'homme.

Friendly readers, you who read this book,
Do strip yourselves of every predilection,
Do not find scandal, reading it,
It has no evil nor infection

. . . . . . . .

To write of smiles, not tears, is best,
For laughter is the proper quality of man.[33]

Rabelais's playfulness with readers, his digressive fables and tales, his obscenities, his scatology are frequently political in Bakhtin's sense of dethroning official pretentiousness; they are always political in the more general sense of thwarting orderliness with laughter.[34] Rabelais is a popular author not because he wrote for a certain class of people but because he wrote for a certain aspect of mind—an aspect given its due by nearly everyone some of the time. One of Rabelais's most effective feints was to represent his alter egos, Alcofribas and Dr. Rabelais, as if they were continuously in this state of mind, assisted by copious wine.

The Rabelaisian text is suffused with an atmosphere of leisure and pleasure: hence its relation to Carnival; hence the (limited) justice of certain critics' qualification of the text as carnivalesque; hence also Rabelais's recurrent imitation of oral communication. In the vagaries of talk, through the unforeseeable deviations of common language employed in common conversation, the spirit relaxes; it becomes pliable and receptive to excess, deviation, violation of norms.

Were these maneuvers politically successful? The *Fourth Book*, when it appeared, was immediately condemned. The royal privilege included in its paratext did not inhibit the Parlement of Paris from condemning the book on the advice of the Sorbonne on March 1, 1552. On April 8, 1552, the Parlement forbade sale of the *Fourth Book*, pending King Henry II's review of the case. That is all we know. About the time of

33. *G*, title page, 24: This "dizain" by the author occupies the reverse of the title page of *Gargantua*. Thus once Rabelais began publishing *Gargantua* and *Pantagruel* in order, with *Gargantua* first, these were the first words of the author's text.

34. For this aspect of Bakhtin's work, see the discussion at the end of ch. 1.

Rabelais's death in early 1553 the *Fourth Book* was published in several more editions in 1552 and 1553; the *Fifth Book*, probably based on drafts found among Rabelais's papers, was published in 1564. Thus just as in the case of other heretics (Rabelais's works were condemned one and all by the Roman Catholic Index in 1564), the conflicting jurisdictions of ecclesiastical, monarchical, and administrative bureaucratic powers seem to have allowed publishers by and large to print with impunity whatever they could sell.

It is too easy simply to look backward and take the represented author's side: Dr. Rabelais was the good guy and so the wise King Henry and his astute councillors supported him; the "demoniacal" Calvin, the "crazy" Catholic theologian DuPuyherbault and their ilk were wrong, evil-minded men. Such conclusions elide the context and make Rabelais's text ultimately less understandable.[35] Rabelais's support at court probably fluctuated less in accord with perception of his virtue or literary worth than in relation to political dangers from Rome, from Germany, and from rebellious, Protestant-inspired subjects. We have already suggested this by referring to the difference in tone between the two prologues that Rabelais published to his *Fourth Book*. The one published in 1552, with its Lenten game and calm prayer, was jovially sedate; the other, published in 1548 after the third condemnation of his books, was imploring in its prayerfulness and accusatory with respect to Rabelais's slanderers: "caphards, cagots, matagots . . . pope's parasites . . . pardoners, catamites," "some kind of monstrous race of barbarous animals," "black and white, domestic or private devils," "lunatic fools, bug-

35. Robert Marichal has done excellent work on the circumstances of censure and publication of *QL* in his edition of that book (Geneva, 1947) and in "Rabelais et les Censures de la Sorbonne," *Etudes rabelaisiennes* 9 (1971). But his conclusion in the latter study takes Dr. Rabelais too complacently at his own word and argues too positively from silence about the attitudes and power of his friends at court: "Il ne s'agit pas de méconnaître la puissance de la Sorbonne et du Parlement, mais François I^er n'avait-il pas trouvé, dans le *Tiers Livre* 'passaige aulcun suspect' et eu 'en horreur' ses calomniateurs? Les Réformés n'ont-ils pas, en avril 1547, fondé de grands espoirs sur Henri II? . . . Rabelais ne s'est donc pas trompé sur le crédit de ses protecteurs auprès du roi et sur l'étendue de leur pouvoir: ils ne lui ont pas plus manqué en 1546 qu'ils ne lui manqueront en 1552" (150). The words quoted by Marichal are from Rabelais's dedicatory letter to the *Fourth Book*, discussed at length in my ch. 9. Marichal's earlier conclusions about the censure of the *Quart Livre* were more tentative and more substantive. See his "Quart Livre: Commentaires," *Etudes rabelaisiennes* 5 (1964): 124–27, 132–33.

gers and bastards," let them all go "hang themselves" before the new moon rises![36]

The public scene between 1545 and 1548 provided justification for this near frenzy, whether feigned or genuinely felt.[37] In January 1545 a secretary to Cardinal Jean du Bellay, Rabelais's patron and protector, was burned for heresy, and the following year Rabelais's sometime friend, Etienne Dolet, was burned publicly at Paris for the same crime. The long-awaited Council of Trent began in a manner that augured little hope for Catholic liberals like Rabelais and Jean du Bellay. In the Smalkaldic War of 1546–1547 Emperor Charles V crushed the Protestant forces with whom the French king had been allied. On March 31, 1547, King Francis died, replaced by his young son Henry, whose political inclinations were not clear. He was closest to the conservative and peremptory Constable Montmorency. The iron age of force and orthodoxy of Francis I's last years threatened to continue.[38]

Then, as Rabelais perfected the *Fourth Book* between 1548 and 1552, the political atmosphere lightened. Montmorency showed himself no extremist and, in spite of his hatred of Lutheranism, remained committed to his family ties even with such religious liberals (and eventual Protestants) as the Châtillon brothers. One of these, Cardinal Odet de Châtillon, made himself responsible for a new royal privilege in 1550, protecting Rabelais's books.[39] Awareness of new support in 1549 or 1550 from the king's closest advisers contributed, according to the author in a dedicatory letter to Cardinal Odet, to the swell of novelistic energy and ingenuity displayed in the second edition of the *Fourth Book*.[40]

That swell of energy, like the towering anger that preceded it in the

36. *QL*, Pr 1548, 755–58.

37. Irony is never far from Rabelais's textual strategies. The question is further explored in ch. 9.

38. See Screech, *Rabelais*, 207–14, 293–303, 321–26, for a narrative of political changes in the late 1540s. Henri Hauser and Augustin Renaudet, *Les débuts de l'âge moderne* (Paris, 1956), 486–91, remains an accurate and more general summary of French policy in the 1540s. The eventual turn toward more rigid religious orthodoxy in Henry II's later years was not clear in 1547–1550. For one thing Jean du Bellay was on cordial terms with Montmorency, while Montmorency had political reasons to resist the influence of the repressive Cardinal Tournon over the king.

39. See the reference to this at the beginning of ch. 1.

40. For additional details about the censorship threatening Rabelais and the aid which Odet de Châtillon gave to him, see Rabelais, *Quart Livre*, ed. Marichal, x–xvi.

old prologue of 1548, had another source: the absence of institutions in the sixteenth century that could have coherently channeled response and interpretation of Rabelais's works to the author and to church and state authorities. Rabelais rehearses his good faith and innocence of all ideological wrongdoing in the old prologue by suggesting that his readers grant his writings total approval: "What? You say that you have not been irritated by anything in all my books printed up to now?" He attributes royal favor to himself: "Well, then, I shall certainly not irritate you either if I mention to you the saying of an ancient Pantagruelist, who says: 'It is no common praise to have been able to please princes.'"[41] Rabelais is able to construct an image of public opinion so entirely favorable because no one could measure what that opinion was. He constructed it gaily, of course, not only expecting that readers would recognize its exaggeration but also knowing that readers could not possibly judge just how exaggerated it was.

Nor could Rabelais himself. Printing, with its fundamental restructuring of the circulation of words and ideas, did not automatically create that complex network of critical reviews, authorial interviews, editorial analysis, and publishers' marketing research that over centuries has emerged to guide and constrain decisions to publish or suppress an author's work. Literary criticism had just begun to take shape as a discipline based on something more than moral or theological principles. Literature did not yet exist as a university subject separate from the study of grammar and rhetoric.[42] There were no research libraries, no scholarly gatherings,[43] no means of obtaining and consolidating opinion about any of the far-flung topics, political and scientific, professional and commonplace, to which Rabelais devoted attention. How could informed opinion about his polymorphic novels possibly

41. *QL*, Pr 1548, 754. The "ancient Pantagruelist" is Horace: *Principibus placuisse viris non ultima laus est.*

42. Literary criticism took on considerable sophistication with respect to the editing and exegesis of ancient authors. Philological and amateur enthusiasm cooperated to create some beginnings, too, in the analysis of modern authors, particularly with respect to their near or far imitation of the ancients. But this activity had as yet scarcely any conceptual unity and hence could call upon neither analytic norms nor institutional support.

43. I refer to conferences of otherwise distant representatives of a field of inquiry, like those for example that brought together theologians, and not to the more informal sodalities of local amateurs that flourished in the Renaissance and were the forerunners of academies.

emerge? All that existed in Rabelais's time were the two extremes of this eventual system of rationalization, normalization, invention, interpretation, and control: bookselling on one hand, and on the other inquisitorial committees dedicated to stamping out dissent from the official opinions of which they were the instruments.

If it was not wrong for booksellers to circumvent the decisions of the committees, by placing false names or none at all on their title pages, so also it was not evil of the committees to seek to suppress these circumventions and the—to them—pernicious originals disrupting public order. Books are social, not only cultural, tools, and they can cut deeply. All social fractions, including the governmental, therefore have a legitimate interest in what is published, and an author soon or late, consciously or unconsciously, takes a position in relation to them. Paratexts are the best clue to such assumed positions. Paratexts indicate at the very least how near or far a writer aspires to be from the social conflicts amid which and by means of which the text was composed.

On the other hand, by the very decision to give written and hence preservable form to words, a writer's work takes its place at some distance from social circumstances. Writers who give printed form to their words are especially distant because printing not only elongates the channel of communication between senders and receivers but also multiplies mediators between them, each with their own interests. In the case of a popular author like Rabelais this mediating position between author and public is not simply that of the collaborating patrons, financiers, printers, editors, licensers, and booksellers who bring the book to birth. It is also that of the offices of public opinion, formal and informal, that in the fifteenth and the sixteenth century were shaken to their foundations first by printing, then by Protestantism, and then by the two in conjugation.

These changes in the way words were circulated threw authors into confusion no less than their friends and enemies. Authors as they write inevitably imagine their readers, whether or not they represent that image, as Rabelais did in his prologue to the *Fourth Book*. The image is the response to a "conversation" with readers that goes on silently as one writes. Authors' attention is divided between fabrication of the message and those for whom it is intended.[44]

44. These points are raised in a different manner with respect to Rabelais by François Rigolot, *Le texte*, 138–44. My use of "represented" or "imagined"

The few messages received from Rabelais's early readers that we in the twentieth century have been able to discover seem, in the light of what we think about Rabelais's text, mostly ignorant or absurd.[45] The first to emerge emanated from Rabelais's literary friends and hence might be discounted as self-interested. Humanists were notorious for praising and damning each other in order to develop their reputations, a tactic encouraged by the absence of more regular institutions of criticizing and advertising.[46] In the short poem by Hugues Salel, which first appeared on the reverse of the title page of the eighth edition of *Pantagruel* in 1534, in a Latin poem by Jean Visagier, in a passing reference in one of Clément Marot's facetious versifications, Rabelais is a great poet, a laughing writer, a Democritus reborn.[47] Meanwhile the condemnations were already circulating; *Pantagruel* was gossiped about as an "obscene book" by learned men or ecclesiastics in autumn 1533, only a year after its appearance.[48]

---

reader corresponds to Wolfgang Iser's "implied reader" (*implizite Leser*: see ch. 1, n. 20) and to Rigolot's "'narrataire,' interlocuteur du narrateur," a term Rigolot (140) borrows from Gérard Genette.

45. I list five proto-critical attitudes here, based on the investigations of Lucien Febvre, *The Problem of Unbelief* (see esp. Book One, Part One), Marcel de Grève, *L'interprétation de Rabelais au XVIᵉ siècle* (Geneva, 1961), and Michael Kline, *Rabelais and the Age of Printing* (Geneva, 1963). The matter requires reformulation. Grève and Kline offer source listings without any model of the critical possibilities in the sixteenth century structuring these responses. Febvre's investigation of poetic, humanist, and theological circles to which Rabelais was related or in which Rabelais was discussed is less aimed at reconstructing the consistency or variability of the principles of discussion than at disproving the charge in some of these circles that Rabelais was seriously believed to be an atheist.

46. The absence explains the practice of publishing letters to and from famous and not-so-famous humanists, a practice that, together with the philological and editing activity referred to in n. 42, created the sense of a cultural community, the "republic of letters," with its own hierarchies of prestige. This system of mutual recognition was no adequate organ of critical analysis, but it should be mentioned, in addition to the widespread grammatical-rhetorical commentaries on "auctores" by humanist school teachers, as a third, relatively institutionalized mode of elaborating literary interpretation, along with the two extremes mentioned earlier: sales and inquisitorial committees.

47. Salel's poem is reprinted, *P*, 188. On Visagier's poem, see Febvre, *Le problème*, 34–35; and on Marot, see Grève, *L'interprétation*, 38–39.

48. Grève (*L'interprétation*, 16) cites a letter by Calvin to a friend, written in October 1533. Grève assumes that Calvin reports the opinion of Nicholas Le Clerc, a Sorbonne master; however, Calvin's phrasing is such that his reference to "obscene books which should be damned [like] *Pantagruel*" may reflect Calvin's opinion rather than Le Clerc's.

After such simplistic good and bad judgments came the more serious disrepute of Rabelais in fashionable circles, a disrepute popularized after Rabelais's death by persiflage in poems like Pierre Ronsard's comic epitaph depicting the writer wallowing amid spilt wine "like a frog in mud."[49] Such satire reinforced the rabid attacks of Catholic controversialists like Gabriel DuPuyherbault, who depicted Rabelais as a drunkard and glutton "who does nothing everyday but . . . sniff kitchen odors and imitate the long-tailed monkey."[50]

Already in the 1550s, however, other French writers and thinkers took Rabelais's works seriously and profoundly: the legist Etienne Pasquier, the poet Scévole de Sainte-Marthe, the thoughtful Protestant soldier and diplomat François de La Noue, even the Calvinist leader Theodore Beza.[51] Beyond all these there was the popular reaction to Rabelais's stories, not only in the massive sales of his books but also through occasional references in other popular literature. Rabelais here is understood less as good or bad, clownish or profound, than as simply interesting and engaging. The valet in "Mimin the Gouty," a Norman farce written in the 1530s, recommends *Gargantua* to his master as a remedy for his melancholic mood, for the book contains science "for the one who knows how to taste it." In 1541 the Carnival procession at Rouen included a float showing "Dead Commerce" (Rouen's citizens were complaining about the effects of royal taxes) with a placard reading: "Alcofribas said it well"; another float showed a person costumed as a hermit reading not the Bible but the "Pantagrueline Chronicle."[52] Within a few years Rabelais's characters had become popular paradigms. Such response was by far the most important, for it wove itself into turns of speech, festive habits, everyday understanding. It created a life for Rabelais's works beyond the libraries and bookstores, a life that always had a chance of sending people back to the books for another, perchance more careful, look at what he wrote.

Nevertheless these indications of early interpretations and responses reinforce the impression gained from Rabelais's paratexts and from

---

49. Febvre, *The problem*, 97. Febvre, 98, cites Joachim du Bellay's equally damning epitaph for Rabelais, a satiric exercise that followed and reversed his earlier praise for this "Democritus reborn," this "Lucian," this "Aristophanes." Joachim was cousin to Rabelais's patrons Guillaume and Jean du Bellay.

50. Gabriel DuPuyherbault, *Theotimus* (Paris, 1549), cited by Marichal, ed., in his Rabelais, *Le Quart Livre*, xiii.

51. See Grève, *L'interprétation*, 135–39, 158–59, 208–9, 209–10.

52. Ibid., 25, 50–51.

analysis of the largely lacking sixteenth-century apparatuses of public opinion: feedback was sporadic and incoherent, stimulating an author in ideological danger to develop as much protective covering as possible. But Rabelais's bobs and weaves, his resourceful representations of himself, his readers, and his patrons, had an ultimately catastrophic consequence. The superficial, prejudiced, falsifying metatexts developed in his lifetime and shortly afterward, shooting off as they did in diverse directions, went largely unchallenged. Rabelais was presumably too angry, too frightened, perhaps too bored, and certainly too subtle to reply directly. And so their worn, iconic plaster forms survived for centuries.

How is Rabelais the person related to his written personae? This has long been the most controversial aspect of text/context interpenetration. New-Critical and formalist thought in the twentieth century resolved the question by eliminating it, refusing to countenance any textual contamination by authorial intentions or inclinations because every retrospective reconstruction of such intentions or inclinations turns out to be so foreshortened as to falsify the text. For all its salutary effects this position is no longer tenable or indeed necessary. The author's person has something but not everything to do with the author's text, and yet everything is involved, everything with which the author has closely or remotely been in contact.

In confronting this problem it is wise to begin with an admission and to follow with several distinctions. Historians who strive to reconstruct past situations are obliged, late or soon, to throw up their hands: So many elements go unrecorded that reconstruction is bound to be tentative. So many elements of the reconstruction depend on the historian's insights—and corresponding blindnesses[53]—rather than on objective evidence that it will and should be replaced sooner or later. In the sentence using psychological language two paragraphs earlier to describe the reactions of Rabelais the person to contemporary metatexts, I have used the word "presumably" to express this admission.

Having said this, one may then at least divide the conundrums presented by the relation between life and art by distinguishing between short-term and long-term situations. Short-term situations create fluctuations in temper like that exhibited by the angry author of the 1548

53. The first requires the second as its precondition: Paul de Man, *Blindness and Insight* (Oxford, 1971).

prologue and the exuberant author of the 1552 prologue. Longer-term situations like the relation of ideological movements such as humanism, evangelism, and scholasticism to the pattern of political rivalries between France, the Holy Roman Empire, and the papacy stimulate more considered and complex authorial tactics. The author wrote the prologue to the *Fourth Book* in the name of that public person most professionally renowned in his time, Dr. Rabelais. That lent authority and prestige to the book and was presumably intended to do so, like the dedicatory letter to Cardinal Odet de Châtillon, the king's minister. But the book itself is narrated like preceding volumes by Rabelais's pseudonym, Alcofribas. Was this done simply for the sake of narrative continuity and because Rabelais was fond of his fictive alter ego? Or does it also indicate an authorial tactic, distancing the person beyond the text from the opinions voiced in the narrative, just in case the pattern of rivalries that seemed, in spite of short-term changes, to give public countenance to Rabelais's ideological commitments, should enduringly shift?

There are still longer-term situations that also affect the stance an author takes in relation to his text. One of these is central to the Quaresmeprenant-Sausage episode in the *Fourth Book*: the repercussion on Carnival and Lent customs of the success of Protestants in institutionalizing their reforms. Where reforming zeal led to founding Protestant churches, the practices associated with Lent disappeared: dietary rules, prohibition of marriage during the Lenten season, Ash Wednesday services with the ritual acceptance of an ashen cross drawn upon the body, and so on. Other internal, conscience-centered controls were substituted for the old ritually prescribed pieties. Carnival customs also changed, although there was no automatic correlation between repression of Lent and repression of Carnival. Many Catholic reformers had cried out against Carnival long before the Protestant movement achieved measured success, and they continued to cry out afterward. In parts of Catholic Europe Carnival disappeared between 1500 and 1700; in parts of Protestant Europe it still managed to survive. But survive or not, the manner of Carnival festivity in most places shifted toward state-organized spectacle and away from freewheeling popular participation.[54]

54. The decline and the survival are well described in chs. 8 and 9 of Peter Burke, *Popular Culture in Early Modern Europe* (New York, 1978).

Mikhail Bakhtin constructed his book around the idea that Rabelais's novels before all else opposed themselves to this long-term evolution. As forces gathered to create new internal restraints on personal
behavior and to substitute new supervised versions of festivity, the "carnivalesque spirit" was placed in jeopardy. It became dangerous to speak
in scurrilous, helter-skelter ways about "official culture," the institution-
ally sanctioned doctrines of church, state, and academy. Rabelais nevertheless took the chance of speaking out, Bakhtin maintains, and fulfilled
to perfection the role of affirming the culture of common people, "that
peculiar folk humor that always existed and was never merged with the
official culture of the ruling classes," that carnivalesque humor dedicated to bringing the high low.

> All the acts of the drama of world history [have been] performed before
> a chorus of the laughing people. . . . But not every period of history had
> Rabelais for coryphaeus [chorus leader]. Though he led the popular cho-
> rus of only one time, the Renaissance, he so fully and clearly revealed the
> peculiar and difficult language of the laughing people that his work sheds
> its light on the folk culture of humor belonging to other ages.[55]

Bakhtin's interpretation is inspiring but it is misleading if taken as
an accurate summation of the Rabelaisian text. There is certainly a relation between the carnivalesque spirit of this text and the very long-
term evolution, of which the evolution of Carnival and Lent is only a
part, which Bakhtin refers to as the "folk culture of humor." One dimension of Rabelais's work rejoins this tradition of scurrilous derision
of dogma, the officially endorsed and officially useful opinion which
pretends that proper, timeless understanding of the world can be apprehended, defined, and enforced by time-bound men. But it is only
one dimension. Bakhtin's view leads to subordinating some parts of
Rabelais's text to others in the same, although ideologically opposite,
manner as criticism that sees Rabelais as a high-minded humanist
whose comic writing pursues lofty goals above the political fray. In fact
Rabelais directs his writing toward diverse ends, some long- and some
short-term, some comic and some serious.

If Bakhtin is wrong, so are the critics who have generalized his discourse to the point of nearly inverting Bakhtin's theory. Rabelais did
not "carnivalize" his text so as to communicate ambiguous and unde-
cidable propositions concerning the subjects of his discourse, as these

55. Bakhtin, *Rabelais*, 474.

critics have suggested. If the many contexts of his work could be re-established with something approaching completeness, they would certainly *not* indicate that the text tries to propel itself beyond these contexts either by turning reality upside-down or by multiplying textually self-referential asides. Rabelais's fantasy intensifies rather than confuses references to reality.[56]

Aware of many levels of historical change, engaged by his experience in many facets of the social life of his time, Rabelais developed tactics of readerly manipulation and authorial disguise that became with each succeeding publication more complex. In this sense the last book pub-

56. Barbara Babcock's "The Novel and the Carnival World," *Modern Language Notes* 89 (1974): 911–37, explains how Kristeva conflated Bakhtin's ideas of "dialogism" and "polyphony" (developed by Bakhtin in writings other than the book on Rabelais) with his study of Carnival and Menippean satire (in the book on Rabelais). But because carnivalesque spirit in Bakhtin is subversively political, giving voice to the chorus of the people who laugh at official forms, it remains an assertion about the relation of text to context (see Bakhtin, *Rabelais*, 474, 8–12, on carnivalesque spirit and its relation to Carnival and "similar feasts"). Kristeva's carnivalism, on the other hand, refers to the development in prose narratives of polysemic, dialogical themes as opposed to narrative development of single, monological meaning. Politico-cultural contexts are then irrelevant: carnivalism becomes an intratextual phenomenon—and hence for Kristeva always also intertextual: see n. 10 to Part One above.

When Babcock concludes that Rabelais's "problem is to turn Carnival into the carnivalesque," she takes for granted the truth of Bakhtin's view and Kristeva's view of Rabelais, as well as the essential harmony of their views with each other ("The Novel," 926). Babcock further associates Michel Beaujour's *Le jeu de Rabelais* (Paris, 1968) with her idea of Rabelais's writing as "carnivalesque" (ibid., 927). But Beaujour's central analytic term is *jeu*, "play," not carnivalization. For Beaujour the power of the Rabelaisian text lies less in any reference to a semiotically limited form of playful practice like the inversionary tactics of Carnival or the carnivalesque, than in such verbal extravagance that the very project of meaningfulness, upside-down or right-side-up, becomes impossible. See Beaujour, *Jeu*, 126–28, for his commentary on the Carnival-Lent episode (he treats only the Quaresmeprenant section) and 171–77 for Rabelais's "rire noir de la négation."

The most valuable as well as potentially most misleading aspect of Beaujour's and Jean Paris's works on Rabelais is their use of twentieth-century cultural perspectives to confront the text ideologically. See Jean Paris, *Rabelais au futur* (Paris, 1970), and *Hamlet et Panurge* (Paris, 1971). Their works, like Bakhtin's—and also like Claude Gaignebet's, in quite another, equally embracing direction—attempt to understand what Rabelais has to say to us now without disregarding his historical otherness.

lished before his death, the complete *Fourth Book*, represents the culmination of a long-developing politics of communication. Rabelais manipulated readers and disguised himself so as to induce favorable reactions to his extraordinarily popular books. But it can also be argued that he did so in order to push readers toward critical awareness of the nature of literary composition. To that end he developed the prologue and dedicatory letter prefacing the *Fourth Book* in a particularly complex way, as we will see.

The absence of conventionalized, integrated networks for the exchange and elaboration of critical opinion, the inchoate conventions of paratext, the incoherent attempts of rival state and church apparatuses to control ideas forced as well as allowed Rabelais to be inventive in his tactics. This situation stimulated consciousness of the interplay among authorial assertions, their dissemination, and their interpretation that in more settled, conventionalized periods of the Age of Print tend to go unnoticed. Analytic use of the category of paratext brings this interplay to the surface.

Paratextual analysis makes clear that the printed book compels authors and readers to confront a double tension, a tension which expresses the manner in which con-text is truly with, not simply around or merely implicit in, the text. The fact that authors must supply some elements of paratext for their books obliges them and their readers to juxtapose the represented context in the paratext to the real context alluded to and displaced by that representation. Realization of this difference then may lead the self-conscious author and critical reader to think about the author's activity in creating this represented context. The author who writes is not the same as the person, only one of whose activities is writing; an author exists in tension with a person's other selves, which therefore affect but do not determine authorial gestures.

Text/context meet and clash at many points in a book, but most ostensibly in paratext. Paratextual analysis thus makes particularly perceptible the reactive as well as inventive activity of authors and makes relative the heroic or evil images that authors like critics are prompted to paint. Author/person meet and clash at every point in a book, but nowhere ostensibly. Or? . . . Perhaps this was Rabelais's most extraordinary move, his evident inclination to push readers toward consciousness of what lies beyond words and the printed page: physical threats, bodily joys, mental possibilities, social conviviality. He activated as well as manipulated the reader. Pretending to be close to tens of thousands of "benevolent" friends, he forced acknowledgment of the printed page's distance from the flesh-and-blood warmth of everyday living. He resorted to laundry-list enumerations, subverbal utterances, and neologisms without end in order to jostle and jar as well as explore the limits of verbality. Doing so, he intensified the effect of being more than verbally present to what he was saying, even while multiplying the masks of author, narrator, and heroes of his narration.

# 2

# Modes of Representation

Rabelais's play with the paratextual frame of the text prepares the reader to look for the same kind of swerving game in the narrative proper. In the *Fourth Book* this is facilitated by the magic voyage theme. The story line alternates between descriptions of the islands, interruptions in the manner of an oral teller of tales by Alcofribas Nasier, and reflections on the behavior of the islanders by Pantagruel and his friends. Thus, the comic-epic frame is broken into and broken down not only by the narrator but also by the meditations of Pantagruel, the ludic digressions of Panurge, the choleric interruptions of Friar John, and the learned explanations of Xenomanes. Although the travelers are ostensibly searching for the Oracle of the Holy Bottle, which will answer the questions posed by Panurge in the *Third Book*, nothing seems further from their minds. Pantagruel's fleet meanders through a series of seaborne allegories of sometimes political and sometimes cultural issues, drained of their contemporary violence by being projected upon imaginary islands. The body of the text thus nearly inverts the feint of the prologue: the movement of the episodes from island to island of talk creates a more verbally than physically active presence of the Pantagruelists to the objects along their passage. But in a deeper sense the textual strategy is the same as that in the paratext, transforming again and again a narration by represented authors into the semblance of a direct transcription of oral exchange.

Such is the framework established by the time readers arrive at chapter 29, the beginning of the Quaresmeprenant-Sausage episode. There they encounter the unnatural fellow on Tapinos Island who has Lenten habits while bearing Carnival's name. Friar John, a Carnival reveler par excellence, always eager to fight and eat, urges the Pantagruelians to go to the island and attack him. Would this fight—if it had occurred, which it didn't—have confirmed early readers' expectations? How did people in Rabelais's time conceive the opposition between Carnival and Lent? How was this opposition represented?

The tradition of Carnival-Lent conflict had some iconic and performative meaning for everyone. The contrast between the two was inseparable from Christian doctrine and liturgy as conceived in medieval Roman Catholic Europe. During the annual cycle of Lenten sermons Carnival behavior served the preacher as the obvious, proximate reason for repentance and contrition. Because this Christian attention was embedded in the calendar of springtime, the Church's sense of the Carnival-Lent boundary tended over time to fuse and become confused with lay people's celebration of the year's turning toward outdoor activities, warmth, and light. Carnival festivities, occurring in February or early March, grew up as a complex of Christian and non-Christian seasonal themes, in which masking and parading about as animals and wild forces of a reawakening nature were as important as banqueting, carousing, and having a last fling before Lent.

The festive ambience that grew up around the Carnival-Lent boundary produced literature and art from the early thirteenth century onward: poems, ballads, prose narratives, marginal illustrations in manuscripts, and eventually woodcuts and paintings inform us about the celebrations. From the late thirteenth century a subgenre of these festive representations emerged that must have been familiar in outline to the elite and literate and must also have been broadcast widely through hearsay, oral repetition, and incorporation into masking and parading practices. This subgenre depicts the difference between Carnival and Lent as a conflict between personifications of the two occasions. To this subgenre Rabelais's Quaresmeprenant-Sausage episode belongs. Some seventy texts and pictures, stemming from scattered parts of Western Europe between the thirteenth and the eighteenth century allow us to trace growth and change in this subgenre.[1]

The earliest pictures of a personified Carnival confronting a personified Lent are a lost oil painting by Hieronymus Bosch (d. 1516) and a Flemish tempera painting on linen noted in an inventory of the Medici palace in Florence after it was sacked in 1494. Four copies of Bosch's painting have been preserved, indicating strong contemporary interest in not only the artist but also the artist's theme.[2] The best known depiction is Brueghel's oil painting of 1559, *The Combat of Carnival and*

1. Martine Grinberg and Samuel Kinser, "Les Combats de Carnaval et de Carême, Trajets d'une métaphore," *Annales: economies, sociétés, civilisations* 38 (1983): 65. I have found other texts and illustrative materials since publication of this article, some of which are cited in notes below.

2. See C. G. Stridbeck, "'Combat between Carnival and Lent' by Pieter Brueghel the Elder," *Journal of the Warburg and Courtauld Institutes* (1956): 98—

*Lent,* based in part upon an etching by Frans Hoghenberg made in 1558.

Hoghenberg's work is situated in the Flemish countryside near a village (see Fig 2). Two groups of people, some masked and in costume and others not, advance toward each other from opposite sides, waving weapons. In the middle of each group is a wagon, one carrying Carnival and the other Lent. At the top of the print are the Flemish words: "Here comes Fat Carnival with all his guests to combat Lean Lent."[3]

Brueghel's painting transports the scene to a small town square into which merrymakers are crowded on one side and the devout and not-so-devout on the other.[4] Unlike Hoghenberg, who devotes more space to the bucolic ambience than to the festive figures, Brueghel's scene brims with people and their activities; iconic references to the town are pushed into corners and serve as props for the people's activities. Carnival is a fat young man seated on a wine barrel, like the Hoghenberg prototype. He has a sausage hanging from his lance and a chicken pie on his hat. Lent is a thin old woman wearing leeks and mussel shells. Instead of placing them in the middle ground of the picture, as Hoghenberg does, Brueghel locates the two toward its lower edge. Hoghenberg shows most people preceding or following their leaders; most of the people in Brueghel's picture pursue their own pleasures or concerns. Is the painting an allegory or a realistic depiction of Carnival in a Flemish town? If the bird's-eye view of the scene is accented, as the perspective encourages one to do, then the scene seems to be the latter, with some revelers pretending to be Lent and her followers and others

99, and Plates 30–31, for references to the tempera painting on linen and to the copies of Bosch's work.

3. On Hoghenberg see Adrien Delen, *Histoire de la Gravure dans les Pays-Bas,* Volume 2 (Paris, 1935), 91. Delen incorrectly dates Hoghenberg's work after Brueghel's.

4. On Brueghel's paintings, see Stridbeck, "'Combat,'" and also Gustav Glück, "Die Darstellungen des Karnevals und der Fasten von Bosch und Brueghel," in *Gedenckbock Vermeylan* (Antwerp, 1932), 263–68, both of which reproduce it. The original is in Vienna. The most thorough iconographic study of Brueghel's painting is Claude Gaignebet's "Le combat de Carnival et de Carême de P. Brueghel," *Annales: economies, sociétés, civilisations* 27 (1972): 313–45, although some of his identifications of popular customs are questionable (as are also those of Stridbeck and Glück). Obviously the fact that Bosch, if we trust surviving copies, dealt with the theme unrealistically does not preclude the possibility that he took actual Carnival-Lent processions as his point of departure.

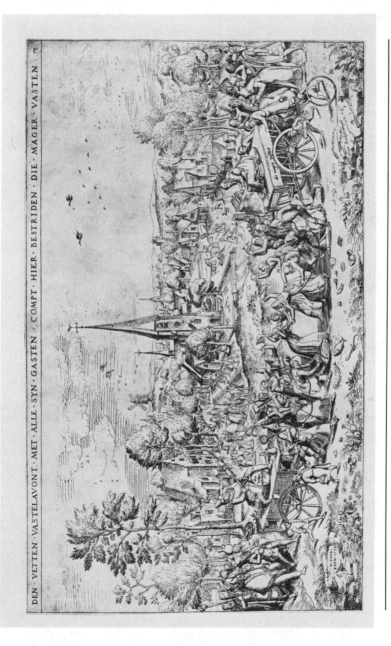

2. Frans Hoghenberg, Engraving, *Fat Carnival with all his Guests Comes Here to Quarrel with Thin Lent* (1558). Bibliothèque Royale Albert Ier, Brussels.

Carnival and his partisans, all of them proceeding lackadaisically toward confrontation. If a front-and-center view is taken, then the scene looks more like an allegory in which two unreal personages rule over a never-to-be-found collection of every possible whimsy connected with Carnival (on the left side of the painting) and Lent (on the right). There is no need to adopt one of these alternatives to the exclusion of the other. Like Hoghenberg, Breughel apparently combined some allegory with considerable realistic description. Both artists broke with Bosch's satiric, symbolic style, in which the figures were depicted generically and set in a vaguely surreal cityscape.[5]

Some light can be thrown on the degree to which these depictions reflected performances by looking at the scant records of the latter. At Norwich in 1443 a certain John Gladman, masquerading as "King of Christmas" and mounted on horseback, was followed by "Lenten," another horseman, who had draped himself with herring skins and his horse with oyster shells. These two were preceded by others representing "each month, disguised after the season thereof." In Norwich the New Year began on March 1. Hence the twelve maskers preceding the mock king and Lent represent the months of the old year, "in token that all mirths should end with the twelve months of the year," while Lent follows the mock king "in token that sadness and abstinence of mirth should follow and a holy time." Here Lent, part of whose forty-day fast always fell in March, symbolized arrival of the New Year. He is juxtaposed not to Carnival but to the King of Christmas, but the document of 1443 that I have been quoting refers the parade not to Christmastime but to "Fastengong Tuesday"—that is, mardi gras. At this season such parades, it is asserted, were customary "in any city or borough through all this realm." The whole period from Christmas to the beginning of Lent must have been considered a festive period in Norwich. Later documents show that it was so considered in other parts of Europe, especially in mountainous areas where winter's weather exempted people from work but not pleasure.[6]

5. The copies of Bosch's works are reproduced in Hanns Swarzenski, "The Battle Between Carnival and Lent," *Bulletin of the Museum of Fine Arts* (Boston) 49 (1951): 2–11.

6. William Hudson and John Tingey, *Selected Records of the City of Norwich*, Volume 1 (London, 1906), 345. I have modernized spelling. There are some problems concerning the exact date on which this procession occurred and its political implications. It is probable that, notwithstanding the affirmation of the defendants (Gladman was arrested; the document is legal) about the parade being customary on mardi gras, this parade in 1443 occurred in late January.

Rituals like that at Norwich are rarely documented. Literate people and officials did not find them interesting enough to record except when they caused trouble. But if the sparse notices are accurate, it would seem that although personifying Carnival and Lent and juxtaposing them in combat was a literary tradition dating from the thirteenth century, it was not a parade performed in the streets until the fifteenth or the sixteenth century. Even the Norwich example scarcely counts, because the King of Christmas, not Carnival, is personified vis-à-vis Lent. Combat between Carnival and Lent was developed as written allegory before it became a customary performance like those depicted by Hoghenberg and Brueghel.

By 1300 the two obvious outcomes of confrontation between customary feasting and fasting had been given literary form. In an anonymous Genoese poem written sometime between 1290 and 1320 Carnival meets Friar Friday on a highroad; each summons the other to give up his way of life. Carnival remonstrates with his opponent about the absurdity of his abstemiousness and suggests that they go off to drink together. The friar calmly disagrees, forecasts Carnival's evil end, and urges Carnival so vividly to repent that he does! An anonymous French poem written about the third quarter of the thirteenth century pictures Fleshliness (*Charnaige*) and Lent (*Caresme*) not as Christian travelers along the road of life but as rival barons, rich in fiefs and followers, who envy each other's power. A combat takes place in this case after negotiations between personified meats and fishes fail. The battle is long, invoking a vast array of vegetables, animals, fish, and fowl, as well as the two leaders themselves. Charnaige wins with the aid of his ally Christmas (*Noël*): here, as later in Norwich, the two festive moments are associated implicitly rather than directly. The spirit of Christmas comes to help the personification of meaty good cheer whose "life" is threatened by the caesura between Fat Tuesday and Ash Wednesday.[7]

In these literary versions of the conflict, attention to calendrical and agricultural functions of the opposition (Old Year/New Year; winter/spring; abundance/scarcity; fertility/famine) are less important than metaphoric and ideological exploitation of the comic difference between fat and lean. The boundaries of the calendrical occasion, acted out by Norwich's maskers of 1443, are loosened in the Genoese piece:

---

7. The two pieces are discussed in detail in Grinberg and Kinser, "Les combats," 66–71, 81–87. Friar Friday symbolizes the weekly fasting urged by the Church, not Lent.

the spirit of fasting and repentance, seizing Carnival, would in theory eliminate any need for the holiday at any time. The power of fleshliness in the French poem also expands beyond the calendrical bounds of the ritual occasion of Carnival. Charnaige rules over the whole year except for the six weeks he deigns to grant Lent. The literary medium frees these pieces from the constraint of fixing the meaning of the antagonists with reference to a particular calendrical occasion or particular ritual performance. Instead, the pieces develop their symbolism in accordance with the wishes and interests of certain social groups. The Genoese confrontation translates the desires of clerical elites, while the French poem reflects a secular and feudal ambience that took church imperatives lightly.[8]

Neither the Genoese nor the French text allows us to suppose that parades and processions like that at Norwich or the one depicted in Hoghenberg's print existed in the thirteenth century. But other features of Carnival celebration in the thirteenth century and following led in that direction. This time was chosen in many parts of Europe as the moment after winter's inactivity to recommence tourneys, ball games, stick-and-stone fights, and every other imaginable outdoor rivalry. Town governments and church councils legislated futilely against these practices (the clergy participated; there were many real-life Friar Johns who loved to fight). The combat between Pantagruel's men and the Sausages in the last part of Rabelais's episode was perhaps calculated to appeal to readers' familiarity with such fracases.[9]

At Nuremberg in the fifteenth and the sixteenth century the city

8. For an earlier literary depiction of the quarrel between personified Lent and Carnival (in this case *both* figures have the names that eventually became traditional in Italian, "Carnelvare" and "Quaresima"), see the account of the fictitious letters by Guido Faba written in the 1220s in my "Presentation and Representation: Carnival at Nuremberg, 1450–1550," *Representations* 13 (Winter 1986): 13–14. Faba, unlike the later Genoese and French writers, does not describe a face-to-face confrontation.

9. Hans Moser, "Städtische Fasnacht [*sic*] des Mittelalters," in *Masken zwischen Spiel und Ernst* (Tübingen, 1967), 151–56, provides examples of these confrontations in thirteenth- and fourteenth-century towns. Similar battles took place in the villages, called "behours" or "bouhours" in France. They usually occurred on the first Sunday in Lent, considered in many places as the last part of Carnival for complex calendrical reasons. Sometimes the fights were carried out not with sticks but around possession of a ball, in a rough ancestor of soccer called "soule." See Roger Vaultier, *Le folklore pendant la guerre de Cent Ans d'après les lettres de remission du Trésor de Chartes* (Paris, 1965), 45–52.

government seems to have encouraged development of a procession of the city's youthful elite called the *Schembartlauf* in order to drain off and redirect the informal violence accompanying Carnival. The policy did not entirely succeed. One feature of the Schembartlauf parade was a huge, man-drawn float called "the Hell," depicting castles, ships of fools, lovers' bowers, and so on. It seems to have been the practice to burn the Hell at the end of the parade. It may also have been customary for the patrician Schembart paraders to advance against the Hell and unman it before it was burned. Surviving records do not make this point clear. But an illustration of the procession in 1539 shows some patricians climbing ladders to assault the masked devils and clowns on the float designed as a ship of fools. On this occasion the fight got so out of hand that it spilled over into surrounding streets and led to a near riot.[10]

In 1506 at Bologna on mardi gras morning the first unification in performance of the three elements just traced took place. A spectacle organized for the reigning family on the public square in front of the cathedral included personifications of the two customary occasions, a parade, and a fight. Two men, each followed by a band of soldiers, advanced toward the center of the square, where a banner had been placed. One leader was disguised as Carnival, "a fat man on a fat horse," the other as Lent, "a rich old woman on a thin horse." The two groups struggled to carry off the banner to their "camp," presumably located at either end of the square. In this case, Carnival defeated Lent, implicitly defying the calendar's movement toward Ash Wednesday. But at the large east German town of Zittau in 1505, when Sausage battled Herring, it was Herring who won; Sausage was thrown into the river.[11]

The only other sixteenth-century performance of personified Car-

10. See Kinser, "Presentation," 19, on the procession of 1539. For a fuller discussion, see Hans Roller, *Der Nürnberger Schembartlauf* (Tübingen, 1965), 137–43.

11. See Grinberg and Kinser, "Combats," 65, for Bologna; for Zittau, see Heinrich Kämmel, *Geschichte des deutschen Schulwesens im Übergang vom Mittelalter zur Neuzeit* (Leipzig, 1882), 203, unnumbered note. So far as can be determined, no social-class or even guild rivalries were involved in these confrontations. The allegory could not have been ritually repeated if it had signified a traditional subordination in an era where class and guild relationships were very frequently contested. Guilds—especially butchers' guilds, appropriately—did have traditional rites of their own in Carnival, which sometimes led to impromptu fights and even murders.

nival-Lent conflict known at present was, like Bologna's, an elite and
official affair. Like Bologna's, too, it was anything but a stiff occasion. At Valencia in 1599, in honor of an approaching royal marriage,
none other than the young playwright Lope de Vega played Carnival
while a court fool disguised himself as Lent. Attached to the saddle
of Carnival's mule were rabbits, partridges, and chickens; attached
to Lent's mule were fish of various kinds. In addition, the buffoon
wore a hat fringed with eels and sardines. After an entrance parade
and salutation to the attending royalty (Lope made a long speech to
them in Italian and Spanish) they galloped about each other for a bit,
and apparently both fell off their mules. Then their accompanying cava-
liers joined in, engaging in somewhat formalized skirmishes "for more
than an hour." In this case, neither side seems to have been assigned
victory.[12]

Several separately developed elements of Carnival usage seem to
have coalesced around 1500 to stimulate the idea of acting out the opposition between Carnival and Lent. The towns with their crowds demanded spectacle, and their varied populations encouraged cross-
fertilization of diverging traditions and development of dramatic forms
of representation. So the variously described masked figures and literary
personages of late medieval times were standardized as the symbols not
of this or that aspect of Carnival or Lent—fasting or drinking, eating
or praying—but of the occasions as totalities. Giving an overall sense
to the occasion meant also sharpening the outcome. In the older literary versions of the combat the end of the battle was usually exile:
whether Carnival or Lent won, the other was sure to return in such
versions, as the seasons turned. But after 1490 texts appear in which
Carnival dies or is killed. A poem called "The Expiration of Carnival,"
depicting the old fellow on his deathbed, was written in 1493 by a Mil-
anese humanist. A "confession" of Carnival on the scaffold was published in 1516 at Bologna. In 1540 a French play on the combat theme
pictures Carnival, in defeat and at the point of death, bidding adieu to
his companions and pastimes.[13]

12. Henri Mérimée, *Spectacles et comédiens à Valencia* (Toulouse, 1913), 94–
97, gives an extensive résumé of the occasion, as described in an unpublished
manuscript.

13. Gaspare Visconti's *Il transito di Carnevale* was published in his *Rithmi*
(Milan, 1493). See Paolo Camporesi, *La maschera di Bertoldo* (Turin, 1976), 298–
300, on the *Processo e confessione del Squaquarante Carneval* of 1516. Jehan

Unifying, personifying, and dramatizing the occasion changed the focus of comic fun. Instead of being a passing panorama of human frailty and/or enjoyment Carnival's proclivities were individualized and given final, awful meaning by Lent, as in this Florentine play of 1554:

> O sad scoundrel, O iniquitous fellow,
> O sinner of sinners,
> You'll exchange your pleasures
> For anxious pains and suffering in Hell![14]

The issue turns inward. Instead of simply haranguing each other about bad habits, as in the Genoese poem (ca. 1300), Carnival's and Lent's behaviors are connected to psychic traits. In Hans Sachs's Nuremberg broadsheet poem, sold at Carnival time in 1540, Carnival becomes so conscience-stricken over the consequences of her behavior that

> the Carnival weak and pale
> climbed right upon the bridge's rail
> And jumped into the Pegnitz [a river at Nuremberg] . . .
> Then I went home all full of worries.[15]

I have argued elsewhere that popular no less than elite modes of representing festive behavior changed in three main ways during the Renaissance period. Instead of treating moral issues generically, according to schematized lists of vices and virtues, these representations concerned themselves with individual psychology, which meant among other things that empathy might be displayed, as in the last line of Sachs's verse. Instead of explaining human endeavors and their outcomes as part of the necessary cosmic frame of things, they embedded events, however sketchily, in the sociology of class and community. And third, they "embodied" the psyche and society; that is, they presented the human condition with its fleshliness, not as an aspect of reality that could be diminished or augmented by moral will and thus exchanged for a purely spiritual attitude, but as an inalienable attribute, a precon-

---

d'Abundance, *Le Testament de Carmentrant*, is edited by Jean-Claude Aubailly in his *Deux jeux de Carnaval de la fin du moyen âge* (Paris, 1978), 71–87.

14. "Rappresentazione e festa di Carnasciale e della Quaresima," in Luigi Manzoni, ed., *Libro di Carnevale dei secoli XV e XVI* (Bologna, 1881), 290.

15. Carnival is personified as a bestial woman in Hans Sachs, "Ein Gesprech mit der Fasnacht," in his *Werke*, ed. Adelbert von Keller and E. Goetze, Volume 5 (Hildesheim, 1964), 298.

dition of spirituality rather than alternative to it. Of course, none of these traits was entirely absent from medieval writings, festive or otherwise. But their preponderance and their conjugated force only emerged in the fifteenth and the sixteenth century.[16]

These traits, strongly exhibited in the Quaresmeprenant-Sausage episode, were neither Rabelais's creation nor his inheritance. He participated in their making. The poems, plays, pictures, and performances cited here, although they exhibit similar general traits, cannot be shown to have directed his pen in writing particular lines or chapters of his episode; they have thus only rarely and partially been cited by others in relation to it.[17] But they are part of the context of his work. They collectively constitute a set of influences. When they are ignored, Rabelais's writing appears more idiosyncratic than it is, and his ingenuity in using the theme cannot be measured.

One recent change in the old plot of Carnival-Lent enmity certainly interested Rabelais. The earliest example of a narrative in which a judicial process is substituted for battle between the two festive occasions seems to be a German play written in the 1480s.[18] Fifty years later Rabelais refers to the schema in his *Pantagrueline Prognostication for 1533*, written in late 1532. The little brochure parodies the pretensions of almanac writers to foretell the future. "Quaresmeprenant will win his lawsuit; one set of people will disguise themselves to fool the other and will run through the streets like fools gone crazy. Never has such disorder been seen in Nature." Rabelais describes the topsy-turvy triumph of Carnival here. He is not comically inverting calendrical order but simply predicting Quaresmeprenant's power during Carnival season. It will be noted that Rabelais in this earlier publication uses the word Quaresmeprenant unequivocally to mean Carnival. And in the long sentence just before the one quoted he uses Quaresme just as unequivocally to mean Lent, offering another comic prediction that states lean

16. Kinser, "Presentation," 16–18, 27–28.

17. A few critics have referred to two of the French literary texts, the thirteenth-century *Bataille* and sixteenth-century *Testament de Carmentrant*.

18. Hans Folz, "Ein Spil von der Fasnacht," discussed in Kinser, "Presentation," 1–41. In addition to two other Carnival plays from Nuremberg that use the lawsuit plot, we have the fragment of a play from a Tyrolean town written by Vigil Raber. In it Carnival is arraigned before the communal court for selling snow as salt, encouraging drunkenness and thievery, and seducing women. See Oswald Zingerle, ed., *Sterzinger Spiele nach Aufzeichnungen des Vigil Rabers*, Volume 1 (Vienna, 1886), 237.

facts: "Lard will flee peas in Quaresme; the stomach will go before, while the backside will take precedence in seating."[19]

Rabelais may have learned during his Italian travels of the lawsuit way of representing Carnival-Lent enmity. A comic narrative published in 1516 at Bologna was called *The Law Suit and Confession of the Scoundrel Carnival,* and a play published in 1544 at Brescia was entitled *Tragicomedy about the Scoundrel Carnival and My Lady Lent . . . and their Lawyers.*[20] Whether or not he himself saw a parade or play pitting one personification against the other, he did experience one element of such personae: their triumphal, larger-than-life quality. When Rabelais in the *Fourth Book* calls Quaresmeprenant "half a giant," he refers to a common feature of contemporary Carnival festivities: the grand and the menacing were of course spectacularly attractive. In sixteenth-century Nuremberg's Schembartlauf parades a recurrent figure was a giant wildman, depicted in the manuscript illustrations of this parade as nearly half again as tall as a normal person, carrying an uprooted tree over one shoulder with a normal-sized man bound to it.[21]

Some chapters after the Quaresmeprenant-Sausage episode in the *Fourth Book* Rabelais describes a Carnival giant that he had probably seen during the 1530s when he worked as a physician in Lyon. The giant, a puppet, was called Chewcrust (Maschecroutte). It was

> a wooden statue on a tall brightly-gilt pole . . . badly carved and clumsily painted . . . a monstrous, ridiculous, hideous effigy, a scarer of little children [Quaresmeprenant was called, in a similar phrase, a "whipper of small children"]. Its eyes were bigger than its belly and its head larger than the rest of its body. It had an ample pair of wide and horrible jaws, well provided with teeth, both upper and lower; and these were made to gnash horribly together by means of a little cord concealed in the gilt pole.[22]

19. *PP,* 2, 920–21. Of course, I am not denying that Rabelais might have invented the lawsuit idea himself, without knowledge that others had already used it.

20. See Grinberg and Kinser, "Combats," 91–92. It is possible that "avocati" in the title of the Brescia play, whose text I have not seen, means not "lawyers" but simply "advocates, supporters."

21. See the illustrations in Kinser, "Presentation," 9, 15. Why does Rabelais say "half" a giant (*QL,* 29, 642)? Is it because Quaresmeprenant, although depicted as larger than normal, is not superhuman but merely a frightening member of our own species? At the same time Rabelais's reference may be ironic: this person is not even a successful Carnival bug-a-boo, totally gigantic.

22. *QL,* 59, 722.

The description sounds similar to what is seen in manuscript illuminations of the *Kinderfresser* (Devourer of Children), a wickerwork giant that constituted the "Hell" float in 1508, 1511, and 1524 at Nuremberg. At Metz in 1498 a wickerwork giant was carried in carnival "with a huge head . . . and large rings in his ears." His eyes rolled in his head, while the latter moved from side to side, a thing "very terrifying to see" according to a contemporary writer.[23] Carnival monsters carrying to an extreme the voracity associated with Carnival were very much part of the sixteenth-century scene.

Into this relatively new framework of spectacularized conflict Rabelais poured his usual mix of allusions to contemporary events and ancient authors, merry tales, proverbs, and everyday pastimes such as the Lenten game referred to in the prologue. Particularly conspicuous in the Quaresmeprenant-Sausage episode are an excursus on the properness of proper names that burlesques the issues raised in Plato's *Cratylus,* references to several Old Testament terms, ample use of Erasmus's *Adagia,* and allusions to Lucian's *True History.* Such elite-cultural items are skillfully mixed with popular-cultural references. Barbara Bowen has described Rabelais's use of terms and images from French popular farces and proverbs in this episode, especially those concerning tripe sausages and eels (*andouilles, anguilles*).[24] The most extensive and literal use of a popular-cultural source in the episode comes from a book published anonymously in 1538 in imitation of Rabelais's best-seller *Pantagruel,* which was called *The Voyage and Navigation of Panurge, disciple of*

23. See the account by Philippe de Vigneulles republished in Martine Grinberg, "Des Géants au Carnival de Metz en 1498: innovation folklorique et politique urbaine," in *Etudes et documents du Cercle royal d'histoire et d'archéologie d'Ath et de la région,* Volume 5 (Ath, 1983), 320. Roller, *Der Nürnberger Schembartlauf,* 119, reproduces a sixteenth-century manuscript illustration of Nuremberg's *Kinderfresser.*

24. Screech, *Rabelais,* 362, 372–78, provides good indications of the elite-cultural sources and some popular-cultural sources for this episode. Barbara Bowen has written two complementary articles on the episode: "L'épisode des Andouilles: esquisse d'une méthode de lecture," in Halina Lewicka, ed., *Le comique verbal en France au seizième siècle* (Warsaw, 1981), 111–26, and "Lenten Eels and Carnival Sausages," *L'esprit créateur* 21 (1981): 12–25. Bowen sees a "mixture" of Carnival and Lent features in both of Rabelais's antagonists, Quaresmeprenant and the Sausages. She concludes, largely in accord with Alban Krailsheimer (see n. 27), that the episode as a whole is "a comment upon the doctrinal confusion which accompanies religious discord" ("Lenten Eels," p. 25).

*Pantagruel.* In this book Panurge leads a ship into a Sea of Ferocious Beings (*mer des Farouches*), where he and his men, landing on an island, encounter tripe sausages who swarm over the sailors, tearing off their noses. Panurge and his men repulse the attack of these castrating warriors, who would have all been killed except that they jumped into a mustard river that ran nearby. These incidents are used by Rabelais in his episode, as we will see.[25]

A number of incidents and terms in the Carnival-Lent episode refer to contemporary issues. In fact the conflict between Quaresmeprenant and the Sausages has sometimes been considered an allegory of the hostility between Catholics and Protestants. But if Quaresmeprenant represents Catholicism, he represents it only partially, as if he were drawn to the scale of the church's most bigoted leaders. If the Sausages represent contemporary Protestants, then Rabelais has chosen to portray only the most hot-headed and belligerent among them. Specific references to Swiss Protestants are certainly allegorized in some of the Sausage "tribes," as was already pointed out in the late seventeenth century by one of Rabelais's editors.[26] Alban Krailsheimer has suggested that the episode represents a closely worked-out allegory of the war of 1546–1547 by Emperor Charles V against the Protestant states grouped in the Smalkaldic League: Charles is Quaresmeprenant, and the Sausages are the Swiss and South German allies. There is no doubt that some reference to these events is included, but such references to contemporary affairs do not provide the basic pattern for either the episode's unfolding or its characters.[27]

Rabelais's mixed modes of representation and the broad range of his sources obviously correspond to and identify the mixed and varied au-

25. See the edition by Guy Demerson and Christian Lauvergnat-Gagnière, *Le disciple de Pantagruel* (Paris, 1982). When and how Rabelais first became aware of the book is not known, but it probably was not later than 1547, when the *Disciple* was published at the end of *Pantagruel* (i.e., at the end of volume 2 of a three-volume set including *G, P,* and *TL*) by Claude La Ville in Valence, France, thus pulling readers toward the false belief that it was by the same anonymous author as *Pantagruel.* La Ville is the publisher whose title page woodcut to *Gargantua* is reproduced in Fig. 1.

26. See "Remarques de Mr Le Motteux sur les Oeuvres," in *Oeuvres,* ed. Jean Bernard, Volume 3 (Amsterdam, 1741), 98. This interpretation and Le Motteux's Rabelaisian criticism generally are explored in ch. 6.

27. Alban Krailsheimer, "The Andouilles of the *Quart Livre*," in *François Rabelais; ouvrage publié pour le 4e centenaire de sa mort, 1553–1953* (Geneva, 1953), 226–32.

dience to which he wished to appeal. The pose of the author-narrator in the prologue is that of a jovial and benevolent Everyman, whose works are nonpartisan and therefore objectionable only to the narrow-minded. But how, with all this mixing, did he achieve not only coherence but also the narrative power that comes from pulling words and incidents together in accordance with an overriding theme and purpose?

# TWO

# MAKING IT STRANGE

Literary versions of the Carnival-Lent allegory generally include five segments: presentation of characters, preparation for combat, negotiations between the parties, a battle or lawsuit, and the consequences of the conflict. In Rabelais's episode nearly all the narrative is concerned only with the first two phases, and in this his work is similar to other sixteenth-century examples of the theme.[1] Beyond this, however, he parts company from everyone else by means of three devices that bend the old pattern to the breaking point.

The first deviation is to substitute a descriptive for a narrative approach to his characters. Instead of telling what Quaresmeprenant *does*—the usual staple of popular tales—Rabelais's narrator describes what Quaresmeprenant is *like* from different points of view, physical, moral, medical, and metaphysical. The narrator is always Xenomanes, the world traveler, and his audience is Pantagruel and his friends. After and during some of the descriptions the travelers make comments that, instead of unifying the different perspectives offered by each successive description, render those perspectives more perplexing. Bewilderment about the overall nature of Quaresmeprenant seems to augment rather than diminish with the addition of details. Meanwhile, because the monster is at a distance from those discussing him, remaining somewhere on Tapinos Island, which has already been passed by Pantagruel's ships, he becomes more and more imaginary, a creature in people's minds rather than an element of narrative action.

Second, Rabelais breaks the traditional pattern in two by separating his discussion of a Lent-like monster called Carnival from his account of carnivalesque Sausages who resemble Lenten eels. Between the two comes an account of Pantagruel killing a huge "physeter" (Greek, "spouter," adapted to Latin form by Pliny). Why does Rabelais introduce this incident? At the story-telling level it is an adroit move because

1. Grinberg and Kinser, "Combats," 66–69, 81.

it breaks the tension built up through the static, suspended descriptions of a figure whom one never sees. It is also appropriate to the tenor of the *Fourth Book,* one of whose dimensions is the comic imitation of voyages like those of the French explorer Jacques Cartier through whale-infested northern seas. Not only was an account of Cartier's search for the Northwest Passage to India published in the 1540s as Rabelais was composing his book, but Olaus Magnus published at Venice in 1539 an illustrated *Carta Marina* of northern Europe between Finland and Iceland. On Magnus's *Carta* a "sea-monster or spouter" is shown near the Faroe Islands which lie northwest of Scotland and southeast of Iceland (*pistris sive phiseter:* see Fig. 3). As Povl Skorup has pointed out, it seems clear that Rabelais associated Magnus's Faroe Islands (labeled *Fare* on the map) with Ferocious Island (*Isle Farouche*), which he adopted from another of his sources for the Carnival-Lent episode, the *Disciple of Pantagruel.*[2]

A spouter as described by Pliny, whose *Natural History* Rabelais read assiduously, was a large species of whale. In Magnus's sketch it has the appearance of a huge sea horse with two spouts instead of ears; the animal dwarfs in size a nearby ship. But this geographical and zoological shaping of the interlude does not explain its relation to the Carnival-Lent theme. If one looks at the passage in symbolic rather than story-telling terms, its relevance to the development of the Quaresmeprenant-Sausage episode becomes obvious. Below the "physeter" on Magnus's map is a huge fish-shaped creature with two spouts, volcanically emitting water like the other monster. It is labeled *balena,* the usual Latin word for whale. A third fish-shaped creature with the same two spouts and glaring eyes has been hauled up on the Faroe Islands where men hack away at its flesh. In the sixteenth century these giant spouters

2. Povl Skorup, "Le Physétère et l'Ile Farouche de Rabelais," *Etudes rabelaisiennes* 6 (1965): 57–59. On Cartier and his influence on Rabelais, see Abel Lefranc's well-documented if literal-minded book, *Les Navigations de Pantagruel* (Paris, 1905). Erik Gamby has republished Magnus's map and has translated the accompanying Latin text into Swedish and German: Olaus Magnus, *Carta Marina,* ed. Erik Gamby (Uppsala, 1964). Rabelais may have been inspired also by the whale episode in one of his favorite books, Lucian's *True History.* Certainly this text by Lucian plays a major role in the parodic voyage recounted in the *Fourth Book* generally, as Paul J. Smith emphasizes, *Voyage et écriture, étude sur le* Quart Livre *de Rabelais* (Geneva, 1987), 40. Smith also shows, ibid., 37–42, how the navigational references in the *Quart Livre* constitute a veritable pastiche of Cartier's *Brief Recit* of his voyages in 1534–1536.

3.  Anonymous, Engraved illustration in Olaus Magnus, *Carta Marina*, Venice, 1539. Section D: "Pistris sive Phiseter," and "Fare" (Faroe) Islands. Bayer. Staatsbibliothek, Munich.

must have seemed ambiguously fish- and animal-like. They were the most powerful creatures in the world, whose Biblical prototype was the Leviathan. Insofar as they were fishlike, living in the kingdom of the sea, spouters were in Carnival-Lent terms natural allies of Lent. In the late thirteenth-century French poem alluded to earlier, it is the whale among Lent's allies who takes the lead in the counsels of war at a critical point in the comic combat. In another piece, the "Marvellous Conflict Between Lent and Fleshliness" (i.e., *Charnaige*), an anonymous French poem published in the early sixteenth century, Lent summons a whale to come to his aid at the moment when his forces fail, but the whale refuses to "leave his domain" to fight on another's ground when his own life, he explains, may be in danger.[3] Thus when the monstrous spouter charges Pantagruel's ship after they pass Tapinos Island, sixteenth-century readers may have seen the action as an imitation of the traditional Carnival-Lent battles. Mental images of the outsized puppets pulled through public squares in Carnival parades would be reactivated by this fight between two giants; the mock battles that so delighted Carnival revelers would be evoked.[4]

The whale episode, like the descriptive approaches to Quaresmeprenant, breaks away from the usual narrative form of the conflict while preserving its symbols. And in terms of the kind of narrative that Rabelais is telling, the interlude serves well to disrupt but not to destroy the mold of the old conflict tradition. The interlude carries the reader away from the early chapters' obsessive focus on the minutiae of Quaresmeprenant's flaccid, monstrous body toward the more relaxed, narratively diffuse development of contact with the puffed-up Sausages.[5]

3. "Le merveilleux conflit entre Caresme et Charnaige," in Anatole de Montaiglon and James de Rothschild, eds., *Recueil de poésies françaises des XV^e et XVI^e siècles* (Paris, 1875), 125. For the whale in the thirteenth-century *Bataille de Caresme et de Charnage*, ed. G. Lozinski (Paris, 1933), see 8, 22.

4. Another source for the whale-killing episode may have been a scene in Teofilo Folengo's *Baldo*, in which Fracasso breaks the head of a whale as large as an island, as Louis Thuasne suggests, *Etudes sur Rabelais* (Paris, 1969), 251–52.

5. The unity of chs. 29–42 from the point of view of Rabelais's interest in Carnival-Lent customs, I reemphasize (see n. 9 to Part One), does not exclude their disunity from other points of view. Paul Smith, *Voyage et ecriture*, 109, pointing out that one of the "thematic constants" in the *Fourth Book* is the imitation of books recounting wondrous, supernatural voyages (he cites especially the medieval *Navigatio sancti Brendani*), sees the whale episode as part of this imitation: the whale as a preternatural animal is one of the typical "ob-

The belligerent encounter of Pantagruel and his friends with the Sausages is the third of Rabelais's innovations, for in his tale it is not only "Lent" who will be "Carnival's" opponent, as the whale interlude suggests, but also "Carnival" will fight "Carnival": Friar John and his cooks will confront the sausages. This anomaly is the culmination of Rabelais's plot to engage readers by puzzling them. Readers have already been confused, as I will show, by the difference between what they think they know about Carnival-Lent conflict and what the Pantagruelians seem to know. In the first chapter of the episode, Friar John tries to persuade Pantagruel to go fight Quaresmeprenant. Now with equal zeal Friar John fights the Sausages. Readers are thus summoned to abandon the conventional identifications they would have brought from festive experience. By this point Rabelais has compelled his audience either to reassess everything or to abandon hope of discovering the *substantifique moëlle*[6] concealed in the comedy. Yet substance there must be. If not, why does Rabelais end the episode, after the battle is over, with a dignified, didactic discussion between Pantagruel and the queen of the Sausages about the strange deity of these strange pseudo-people?

In larger terms the inherited combat pattern seems to fade in and out as the episode progresses, by pulling characters who at first act as mere spectators into the middle of the action and then shunting them aside again. The plot, too, instead of moving toward confrontation between the supposed representatives of Carnival and Lent, moves away from it. Chapters 29 through 32 deal with the monster Quaresmepre-

---

stacles que le héros [du voyage merveilleux] doit surmonter." From this perspective the association of the whale with the biblical Leviathan is one of "demythification" (ibid., 111–13). Smith does not connect the *physétère* with Carnival-Lent customs, nor does he find the connection to Magnus's map illuminating; among Rabelais's sources he emphasizes especially Pliny (ibid., 114–15). Smith's interpretation of the episode is also helpful on many points of detail (e.g., his demonstration of Rabelais's Pythagorean interests, 117, and his suggestion that Rabelais played on the phonic similarity of *physé[tère]* to [*Anti*]*physie,* 112; concerning that, see my ch. 4, n. 1). On the whale episode, see also Frank Lestringant, "L'Insulaire de Rabelais, ou la fiction en Archipel. Pour une lecture topographique du 'Quart Livre,'" *Etudes rabelaisiennes* 21 (1988): 264, who draws attention to another detail on Magnus's map that occurs in Rabelais's account (it does not concern the Carnival-Lent associations).

6. Alcofribas Nasier explains in the prologue to *Gargantua* that the apparently trivial exterior of his book conceals a "substance-stuffed marrow" of great worth (*G,* Pr, 26–27).

nant in isolation from his enemies the Sausages. Chapters 35 through 41
deal with the Sausages, their island, and their attack on the Pantagruelians in isolation from Quaresmeprenant. The chapters on the battle
activate the previously passive Pantagruelians. In the final chapter 42
they return to a passive role as their leader and the queen negotiate a
settlement that seems to have less to do with Carnival or Lent than with
feudal politics and religiophilosophic ideas. At the same time Carnival
symbolism is intensified in the chapter on the battle as Pantagruel's
cooks "fight"—that is, prepare for eating—sausages by the thousand.
Finally, however, no one eats anything. The Pantagruelians sail away.

A double tension is generated between the plot and the coherence
of the characters acting in it and between both of these and the symbolic level to which attention is drawn by using metaphorical names
for persons, places, and deities. The symbolic level evokes performances
and literary patterns loose enough to be familiar to most of Rabelais's
readers: there are spectacular figures of some allegorical value, there are
ritual battles, there are repeated references to Carnival and Lenten
foods. But the plot's dislocations ricochet on such symbolic references
to the point where the symbols themselves are placed in question.

# 3

# Who Is Quaresmeprenant?

Xenomanes gives his friends six descriptions of Quaresmeprenant that differ not only in what they say but also in how they are proffered. The first description generalizes about the "half-giant" in a relaxed, conversational manner. But the next three accounts move to doctor's chambers, abandoning the pretense of talk. Lists of anatomical and physiological traits succeed each other, mixing medical diagnosis with references to such a hodgepodge of objects that one seems to zigzag between hospital and junk shop. The fifth and sixth descriptions return to a more general style, but this time the tenor is one of philosophical reflection, speaking of the monster's behavior and speculating about the meaning of such a "strange case."

The first description revels in ambivalence.[1] Quaresmeprenant is called a "guzzler of dried peas," which would seem to identify him with Lenten meagerness. But dried peas were also carnivalesque. They were put in pigs' bladders and rattled by persons in fools' costume to suggest their empty heads. And they were a staple food during the winter and early spring seasons of Carnival *and* Lent, when fresh vegetables could scarcely be found. Then comes Xenomanes's comment that Quaresmeprenant is "the most industrious skewer and lardstick maker in forty kingdoms." What does he do with them? We are not told, except that we shortly learn that he is the "eternal" enemy of the Sausages. Does he use the skewers to torture and dispose of his prisoners of war? On the other hand, Xenomanes says that he presented a gross of the skewers to the butchers of Cande near Chinon. This detail reinforces the notion that Quaresmeprenant's name means what it usually did because butchers and their activities were for obvious reasons associated with Carnival.[2]

---

1. Quotations from the first description are found in *QL*, 29, 642–43. See the introduction above where I discuss some other ambivalent parts of the first description.

2. Jacob Le Duchat, ed., *Oeuvres,* Volume 4 (Amsterdam, 1711), 126, n. 16, explains Quaresmeprenant's activity in accordance with his interpretation of

Quaresmeprenant, Xenomanes continues, is a "great lanterner," descended from "Lanternland stock." A lanterner is a dreamer who passes the time to no purpose. Rabelais made fun of lanterners in a comically vituperative list of "persons of base estate" in his *Pantagrueline Prognostication for 1533:* lanterners will, along with adventurers, murderers, sergeants, counterfeiters, alchemists, and such, "make a killing" in the coming year (*feront ceste année de beaulx coups*).[3] Xenomanes uses the term almost accusingly in the conversation that follows his first description: that "big lanterner Quaresmeprenant" would like to "exterminate" the Sausages.

Lanterning is not necessarily, within the comic frame of the Rabelaisian text, a negative term. The Pantagruelians are sailing in the *Fourth Book* to Lanternland to find the Oracle of the Holy Bottle. The second ship in Pantagruel's fleet is named the "Lantern" and carries an image of a lantern on its stern. In an earlier chapter the travelers meet a ship returning from Lanternland where, it is learned, a general assembly of Lanterns is going to meet the following July. "From all the preparations it looked as if they were going to lanternize profoundly." This Lantern or "Lateran" council probably represented the coming sixth session of the Council of Trent, scheduled for July 1546.[4] Church councils had repeatedly been held in the Lateran palace of the popes in Rome, most

---

the monster as Lent: "C'est en Carême, et principalement sur sa fin, que les bouchers prennent leur tems pour faire des brochettes, et pour remplacer celles qui manquent à leurs Etaux. Les Cuisiniers et les Rôtisseurs choisissent le même temps pour cela, et pour faire nouvelle provision de lardoires, et de brochettes à retrousser la viande." Le Duchat's interpretation is corroborated by a statement in John Taylor's burlesque narration, "Jack A Lent: His Beginning and Entertainment" (1617), in Taylor, *Works,* ed. Charles Hindley (London, 1872), 12: "Civil policy [supporting Lent against Carnival] . . . causeth proclamations straight to be published for the establishing of Lent's government . . . [and so] the butchers (like silenced schismatics) are dispersed . . . leaving their wives, men, and maids, to make provision of pricks ["i.e., skewers": Hindley's note] for the whole year in their absence." Taylor's derisive reference identifies Lent as the customary time for preparing skewers, but it also associates this activity with butchers, the enemies of Lent. Quaresmeprenant's preoccupation with meat skewers is like that of the butchers' wives and servants and is anything but Lent-like.

3. *PP*, 5, 923.

4. See *QL*, 1, 561; 5, 574: This reference to the next church council session allows composition of ch. 5 to be placed with probability before July 1546; it does not seem likely that the passage was composed later because the session scheduled for July was postponed.

recently in 1512–1517, a council that Pope Julius II and Leo X used to counter French attempts to revive conciliar government in the church. Thus a punning reference to a Lantern council implied that at Trent the pope would probably try to carry further his pretension to rule over the church monarchically.

Such divergent references to Lanterners and lanternizing are Rabelais's way of communicating different perspectives upon one verbal sign by juxtaposing the points of view of author, narrator, and narrative actors. Is Rabelais the author making fun of the pious hopes of Pantagruel for a resolution to the questions of church reform at the long-awaited council? The Pantagruelians are portrayed as lanterners in the sense of seeking light and wisdom. But perhaps also Rabelais is suggesting that dreamy trust in light from human contrivances like lanterns or Lateran councils is vain. They beam forth not truth but merely the will and intentions of those using them.

The Pantagruelians and Quaresmeprenant share a tendency to dither around and lanternize. But lanterning also had a sexual meaning relevant to Quaresmeprenant. It was a slang word for the penis. In an obscene poem called the "Fricassée crotystylonée," purporting to record a rhyming game of Rouen children in the mid-sixteenth century, one question and answer goes:

> —What are you doing there?
> —I'm making lanterns
> To put in the ass [au cul]
> of the fellow asking for it.[5]

Lanterning seems to be understood here as something like the modern "fucking around," or "fooling around," the euphemism meaning the same thing. Panurge uses the word in a similarly aggressive male homosexual sense in the *Third Book* and again, offensively but heterosexually, in an early chapter of the *Fourth Book*.[6] When placed in parallel

5. Gaignebet, *Folklore obscène*, 167. The sixteenth-century rhyme also refers, according to Gaignebet, to a game that is played in present-day Carnivals in south France in which people try to attach a lighted wick to the lower posterior part of the costume of the person preceding them, as they dance single file through the streets. But Gaignebet does not cite sixteenth-century or other early sources to support this interpretation.

6. *TL*, 443: "Va (respondit Panurge), fol enraigé, au diable et te faiz lanterner à quelque Albanoys." Albanians like Bulgarians were popularly accused of

with some characteristics of the monster, which will be described later, this sexual meaning of Quaresmeprenant's Lanternland origin emerges as less than playful.

Quaresmeprenant nourishes himself on war: "his usual foods [les alimens desquels il se paist] are salted hauberks, casques, salted helmets, and salted sallets [salades sallées: punning on "salad"], on account of which he sometimes suffered a heavy hot-piss." Salty things stimulate the appetite: is this how the fellow excites himself for a voracious fight with the Sausages? However that may be, Xenomanes's first description, in spite of the ambivalences in detail, pulls the reader toward identifying Quaresmeprenant with Lent, not Carnival. The meaning of some seeming identifications of Quaresmeprenant with Lent only becomes questionable in retrospect. "He burgeons with pardons, indulgences, and altar prayers [*stations*]."[7] "I've found him in my breviary . . . after the movable feasts," declares Friar John. To what is Friar John referring? Has he concluded that Quaresmeprenant corresponds to Quadragesima (Lent) in his Latin breviary? If he has, should his conclusion be taken seriously by the reader, familiar with Friar John's tendency to jump to conclusions? If Quaresmeprenant is so clearly and simply Lent, why do his mortal enemies the Sausages have fishy characteristics?

The Sausages are identified in this first description merely as the dependents or perhaps the vassals of "noble Mardi Gras, their protector and good neighbor"; they are not equated with Carnival. These Sausages, Xenomanes explains further, are all "mortal women, some virgin and some not," yet they ardently make war. Lent was sometimes identified as a woman in the literary, iconic, and performative traditions of the theme, but only in Rabelais's text is it maintained that Carnival's allies are all female. Indeed the maskers of Carnival in Rabelais's time were in most parts of France all male. What can be the function of such sexual inversion?

---

sodomy. *QL*, 9, 587: "Le vent de Galerne (dist Panurge) avoit doncques lanterné leur mère?"

7. "Altar prayers" is only one possible translation. *Stations* might mean several things: the place within a church from which a preacher would deliver a series of sermons on some social occasion like the days of Lent; an altar before which one would halt to pray before an image (as in the "stations of the cross"); the ceremony in the course of which one would make such prayers; or the church designated for such prayers (as along the route of a pilgrimage).

Pantagruel asks Xenomanes to extend his account of Quaresmeprenant. The three long lists with which Xenomanes accommodates the giant describe first the creature's internal anatomy, then his external parts, and finally their functioning or physiology. Such a move from internal to external description was, as Marie Madeleine Fontaine has shown, common practice in the public dissections forming part of medical training in Rabelais's day. The items of internal anatomy are ordered vertically from the skull's contents down to the base of the intestinal cavity and then outward to muscles, ligaments, and invisible organs of the soul like imagination and intelligence. The items of external anatomy are ordered inversely, from the toes to the head, and then outward to skin and hair. The psychological list moves from upper bodily to lower bodily functioning and then to dreaming and worrying, that is, to a kind of invisible functioning.[8]

"As for his internal parts Quaresmeprenant has—or had in my time" (Xenomanes made a visit to the island some years earlier)—"a brain the size, color, substance, and vitality of a male cheese maggot's left testicle." What a superb example of what Bakhtin has called Rabelais's "grotesquely real" style, in which high, noble objects are debased by comparing human to less-than-human qualities and "high" areas like the brain to "low" ones like the genitals and intestines.[9] But the comparisons move sideways as often as up and down, always with the same unlikely vividness. "His [cerebral] membranes [are] like a monk's cowl ... his pineal gland like a bag-pipe ... his colon like a drinking-cup." Seventy-eight "internal parts" are explained in a series of terse analogies that corresponds stylistically to the dryness and lethargy of the creature being anatomized. The next chapter describes sixty-four external organs in the same way; the chapter after that, still maintaining the one-line style, catalogs thirty-six symptoms of sneezing, coughing, talking, and dreaming.

If one reads these lists at the same pace and with the same contextual framing of the text as one has done with respect to the description in the preceding chapter, most of their effect and meaning is lost. The continuity between one item and the next is frequently hard to see; a

8. See *QL*, 30–32, 643–49. Fontaine, "Quaresmeprenant: l'image littéraire et la contestation de l'analogie médicale," in *Rabelais in Glasgow*, ed. Coleman and Scollen-Jimack (Glasgow, 1984), 90–93, compares the ordering in the first two lists with those of contemporary anatomists.

9. Bakhtin, *Rabelais*, 19, 52–53, esp. 308–25.

sense of the whole is impossible to seize from a list of two hundred similes, read from beginning to end. At one level perhaps the reader's confusion is intended. Read apace, these lists create a strong general impression. Quaresmeprenant is, as one commentator puts it, "pulverised" by Rabelais's linguistic strategies, reduced to an image not merely of immobility but of disjointedness.[10] But how and why is this done?

Both the order and the vocabulary used in the lists follow commonplace anatomical practice in Rabelais's time. Sixteenth-century translations of Galen and of the fourteenth-century French physician Chauliac show the same mixture of Greek, Latin, Arabic, and everyday French nomenclature and also the same kind of comparisons to everyday tools and household accoutrements. But the doctors did not in their serious works animate the parts or offer concrete images of abstract functions: "His animal spirits [are] like fisticuffs . . . his consciousness like the fluttering of young herons leaving the nest . . . his understanding like a tattered breviary."[11]

Quaresmeprenant is akin, I have suggested, to the terrifying giants displayed in Carnival parades. Like these lumbering, lurid constructions, Rabelais's grammar urges the reader to peruse the monster part by part, enjoying each absurdly pseudo-human detail. Like the disconnected grammar, each organ and each organ's function operate as independently as the everyday tools and accoutrements, the commonplace insects and birds, to which they are for the most part compared.

The description of functions like memory and consciousness, which sixteenth-century medical science thought were related to what would now be called nervous and circulatory systems, produces magnificently comic effects of misplaced concreteness. Playing on the phonetic closeness of reason and resonance (*raison, résonne*[*r*]), for example, Xenomanes returns by means of the last item in this list to his opening com-

10. Floyd Gray, *Rabelais et l'écriture* (Paris, 1974), 184.

11. See Fontaine, "Quaresmeprenant," 111–12, n. 30, for quotations from the translations. Fontaine illustrates the points about nomenclature with rich details, 93–95. But her conclusion, 101, is questionable because it does not consider the differences from medieval texts of Rabelais's listing, occasioned by the latter's terse style and its inclusion of elements like young herons leaving the nest or tattered breviaries: "Un repertoire des analogies et comparaisons de Galien, souvent reprises par les médecins du XVIᵉ siècle, ou des analogies de Chauliac, aboutirait à un texte aussi grotesque que Quaresmeprenant. Il revelerait des zones de références absolument identiques à celles de Rabelais."

ment on the monster's stupidity by alluding to Quaresmeprenant's
hollow head: "His reason [is] like a little drum." Several ecclesiastical
references in addition to the ones about the tattered breviary and the
monk's cowl recall satirically Xenomanes's opening comment that the
monster is a "good Catholic, thoroughly devout." But they do not substantiate his Lenten identity, if such it is.[12] Quaresmeprenant's warmon-
gering is alluded to indirectly ("his stomach like a sword-belt . . . his
viscera like a gauntlet . . . his bladder like a catapult") and also rather
directly ("his repentance like the carriage of a double cannon"). The
metal and leather of his intestinal tract contrasts with his soft sexuality:
"his spermatic vessels like a *feuilleté* cake, his prostate gland like a
feather-jar."[13]

Quaresmeprenant's sperm, on the other hand, is like "lathe nails,"
and his progeny is even stranger: "His nurse told me," says Xenomanes,
"that when he married Midlent he begot only a quantity of locative
adverbs and *certains jeunes doubles*." The French words are a pun,
"double fasts" or "double young ones," double children, twins perhaps,
even Siamese twins, but singularly deprived.[14] As for the locative adverbs, a late sixteenth- or early seventeenth-century commentator, Perreau, refers this phrase to the vogue for indulgences among devout
Christians during the latter half of the Lenten season between Midlent
and Easter. Locative adverbs indicate the places where one is, where
one comes from and where one is going. Begetting locative adverbs
would then mean that Quaresmeprenant bustled from place to place at
this season, searching for ecclesiastic pardon.[15]

But Midlent in popular terms meant something far different from
churchly enthusiasm. Falling on the fourth of the six Sundays in Lent,

12. "His heart like a chasuble. . . . His mesentery like an abbot's mitre. . . .
His bum-gut like a monk's leather bottle."

13. A feather-jar, explained Rabelais's eighteenth-century editor Le Duchat,
is an old broken pot that is no longer useful as a container for liquids and so is
used to collect feathers for eventual use in bedding. Le Duchat, in *Oeuvres*, ed.
Bernard, 2: 78.

14. Fasts, *jeûnes*, would normally have been spelled *jeusnes* in the sixteenth
century. Would *jeusnes* and *jeunes* have been pronounced in exactly the same
way in Rabelais's time and place? Does the use of *jeunes doubles* also play on the
Church's classification of the Sundays in Lent as *fêtes doubles*, that is, as days of
special piety on which a "double office" is read?

15. See 156–57 for Perreau and the crooked history of this particular explication of Rabelais's text.

it was a holiday on which Carnival erupted anew. Parades, picnics, noisy musicmaking, masking, and bonfires marked the date. Here again Rabelais's description of Quaresmeprenant seems intended to puzzle: Does marriage pull the fellow toward or away from Lent? One ritual of Midlent Sunday, documented for later sixteenth-century Italy and presumably existing there earlier when Rabelais might have observed it, was for children to run through streets screaming "Saw down the old woman!" Wooden images of an ugly old female were carried about and then sawed in half to shouts of laughter as a sign that Lent was half-gone.[16] Does Quaresmeprenant marry an aged or even mutilated replica of Lent, or does he marry the Carnival spirit that violates Lent midway?

In either case the monster's action, viewed in its calendrical context, seems masochistic. Midlent was the only occasion between Ash Wednesday and Easter when in most parts of Catholic Europe a person was authorized to marry. But to marry on that day insured that there would be no prolonged celebration, for fasting must resume on Monday. To marry the personification of a day in Lent could only lead back to fasting, as the calendar insures that it does. Perhaps engendering double fasts simply means that Quaresmeprenant establishes a household in which the tendency toward asceticism is redoubled.

The similes used in the second anatomical description are again articles of everyday employment: slippers and cream cake, crossbows and bagpipes, chessboards and watering cans. Quaresmeprenant is a collection of commonplace things. Should one make a case for the preponderance of items forbidden or frowned upon in Lent, like musical instruments, sporting accoutrements (tennis rackets and billiard tables), and rich foods (drinking cups, dripping pans, cream cakes, butter-pots)? No. Reasoning from tennis rackets to anti-Lenten attitudes tortures the text as uselessly as concluding that Quaresmeprenant personifies Lent because he handles barrels sometimes filled with herrings.

M. M. Fontaine has argued that the ordering of the lists, choice of vocabulary, and especially the manner of argument in these descriptions

---

16. See, e.g., Giulio Cesare Croce's broadsheet poem, *Invito generale . . . per veder segare la vecchia* (Bologna, 1608) or Michelangelo Buonarroti's *Cicalata* (Florence, 1610), quoted in Lidia Beduschi, "La vecchia di mezza quaresima," *La ricerca folklorica* 6 (1982): 37.

indicate that Rabelais is making fun of Galenic medicine. Sixteenth-century anatomical science not only exposed a variety of particular errors made by Marcus Aurelius's physician but began to replace Galen's use of verbal analogies with the far superior method of visual illustration, most notably in the extremely meticulous representations of the dissected human body in Vesalius's *De humani corporis fabrica* (1543). Rabelais's tersely repetitious similes render the verbal analogical method ridiculous, not so much with the aim of satirizing Galenists or of directly taking part in the contemporary debates over scientific method, cautions Fontaine, but rather with the purpose of "experiencing the difficulties" encountered in practicing medicine at the time and indeed of experiencing them through laughter that objectifies rather than through satire that attacks.[17]

It is quite possible that one dimension of Rabelais's anatomical approach to Quaresmeprenant is a laughing critique of the use of verbal analogies in medicine. But it is certainly not true that, as Fontaine suggests, this critique forms part of a simple "logic" linking chapters 29 to 32 together by means of "several little syllogisms." For Fontaine these syllogisms are "rather easy to discern":

> Quaresmeprenant (Lent, its Catholic rituals and its folklore) inhabits Tapinos Island (the island of hypocrisy). Now, he is a "sucking babe of doctors" because the essential ritual of Lent, fasting, makes one sick. And what did doctors most busy themselves with at the time? With anatomies and descriptions of the structure of the body, and then with a diagnostic

17. Fontaine, "Quaresmeprenant," 90. This reasonable beginning is not always sustained in Fontaine's later argument. She claims that Rabelais in the *Fourth Book* refers at least by implication to an attack of the Galenist Sylvius on Vesalius, published at Paris in 1551, and also to Peter Ramus's criticism of Galen, since Ramus was appointed in 1551 to the Parisian Royal College (the present-day Collège de France) and Rabelais was resident that same year in Paris, just at the time Rabelais finished composition of the *Fourth Book:* "Il est impossible, puisqu'il en fait état dans son Prologue et qu'il est alors parisien, que ces implications soient inconnues de Rabelais, et notamment les aspects méthodologiques. Ce furent de durs temps de Carême!" (100). The only reference to Galen in the prologue has nothing to do with Galenic method, let alone with Ramus, Sylvius, or Vesalius (for the prologue reference to Ramus, which has to do with another affair, see ch. 8), and Rabelais's reference to Lent seems neither "dur" nor in any way connected to the issue cited by Fontaine (Fontaine, ibid., quotes the words discussed in ch. 1 above). Fontaine is not the first to point out that Rabelais's analogistic method in these anatomic chapters both repeats and enlarges upon contemporary medical practice: see Roland Antonioli, *Rabelais et la médecine* (Geneva, 1976), 289–90.

of the illness by means of studying the patient's "appearances" [contenances].[18]

From the first announcement of the name Quaresmeprenant and Friar John's comment on the presence of a creature like him in his breviary, Rabelais has led his sixteenth-century readers not toward the clarity of syllogisms but toward bewilderment. One of the author's strategies in this respect has been to juxtapose readers' knowledge to the knowledge of actors in the text. For although readers knew that the word Quaresmeprenant designated Carnival, the Pantagruelians, their guide Xenomanes, and their chronicler Alcofribas, the implied author of the tale, do not seem to know this. They also do not seem to know the inverse of this proposition, that Quaresmeprenant means Lent.[19]

Rabelais is encouraging his readers to distinguish between narrative and other levels of experience. After Xenomanes explains in his first description that the Sausages live under the menace of the monster, the friar wants to go fight Quaresmeprenant. Panurge exclaims: "*Quid juris*"—that is, by what right or in accordance with what legal judgment would we defend ourselves—"if we should find ourselves trapped between Sausages and Quaresmeprenant, between anvil and hammers?" If readers take narrative reality to be metaphorical play with behavior familiar to them, such as the mock battles on mardi gras, then Panurge's words correspond to readers' festive experience. If one or the other side in the battles should resort to law—as in the lawsuit farces of the day, and as in Rabelais's *Pantagrueline Prognostication*—then how could persons interfering in such an officially endorsed and customarily sanctioned fight legally justify themselves? But then why is a monster with so many Lenten traits behaving in such a Carnivalesque way, "fighting" sausages? Does fighting mean that he eats them, like his colloquial name, Carnival (Quaresmeprenant), would seem to require, or that he exterminates them, as so many of his Lentlike character traits would indicate? The Pantagruelians, existing at the level of narrative reality,

18. Fontaine, "Quaresmeprenant," 87. The terms of these so-called syllogisms were developed in anything but an easy and obvious way in the late seventeenth and early eighteenth century, as indicated in Part Three below.

19. The reasons for supposing that this is true even for Friar John, who finds Quaresmeprenant in his breviary, and for Panurge, who speaks of the contrast between Quaresmeprenant and the Sausages as a simple opposition in the passage quoted later in this paragraph, have to do not with the word's ambiguity but with its ambivalence, as we will see.

know nothing of such metaphorical puzzles. Nor can they be conscious of a second level of contextual reference in which the Sausages figure as Protestants and Quaresmeprenant as Charles V, leader in a Catholic war that had indeed "hammered" the German Protestants only a few years before the appearance of the *Fourth Book*. The French—that is, metaphorically, the Pantagruelians—were secretly allied with the German Protestants; they had in this sense "illegally" interfered in the German fight, in contravention of their alliance with Charles V in the Treaty of Crépy (1544).[20]

Such veiled allusions to contemporary politics cease during Xenomanes's descriptions of the monster's physiognomy. The Pantagruelians are entirely silent after each of the three lists. Alcofribas, the narrator, separates the lists, by beginning a new chapter for each of them. One by one, the *disjecta membra* of the lists dissuade the reader—and the narrative listeners, the Pantagruelians?—from identifying the monster as either traditional personification. During this section of the episode Quaresmeprenant loses his identity as Carnival without gaining that of Lent, and vice versa.

He also very nearly loses his identity as a human being. Although he has the organs and spirituous fluids thought to explain human physiology, the grammar used to enumerate them as well as the things to which they are compared make Quaresmeprenant seem more and more jerkily, discontinuously, mechanically connected in his parts. He assumes the dimensions of the gaping constructions that astonished merrymakers at Lyon, Metz, and Nuremberg. As with these puppets, the displacement and juxtaposition of the ordinary things used in Quaresmeprenant's fabrication are both horrifying and comic.

It seems possible—and the orderly sequence of now familiar and now arcane anatomical parts encourages readerly efforts in this direction—vaguely to imagine some such bizarre assemblage of tennis rackets and bagpipes, feather-jars and gauntlets.[21] But at the same time

20. *QL*, 29, 643. See ch. 2, n. 27. Krailsheimer, "The Andouilles," neither drew attention to this passage nor suggested that Panurge was speaking of French policy in veiled terms. But it is very probable that this level of allusion is present here because of Rabelais's personal connections with the policy. He was involved, directly or indirectly, with his patron Jean du Bellay's negotiations with the German Protestants while residing in Metz, 1546–1547. See Marichal, "Rabelais et les Censures," 138–41.

21. The modern reader has a difficult time of it in these passages, created by four centuries' distance from commonplace objects that are no longer common-

Rabelais is not describing something that could or should be seen as an entity at all. Part of the tactics of giving an emblematic quality to Quaresmeprenant is that in three of his six descriptions Xenomanes does not in strict grammatical terms describe but only compares the monster to an array of things to which his appearance and behavior are analogous.[22] Just as Pantagruel's fleet is in the process of passing by Tapinos Island without stopping, moving further and further away, so Quaresmeprenant, the more his characteristics are listed, the more remote from any coherent reality he seems.[23]

Having constructed the scarecrow, Rabelais wheels it into action. A

---

place. They have become exotic and unfamiliar or—potentially more distorting for understanding the text from a sixteenth-century point of view—objects of regret and nostalgia. This nostalgic and/or exotic framing of the descriptions accounts, perhaps, for Paul Eluard's extraction of these chapters from their context and their inclusion—as a surreal poem?—in his anthology of French poetry, *La poésie du passé,* Volume I (Paris, 1960), 273–79.

22. Fontaine, "Quaresmeprenant," 89–90, especially emphasizes Xenomanes's procedure by analogy. There are some significant exceptions to this generalization. The second description (ch. 30) consists of analogies except for the first characteristic, describing the size of the brain. The third description (ch. 31) also consists of analogies except for the first characteristic (Quaresmeprenant has seven extra ribs). The sixth description (end of ch. 32) consists of Pantagruel's extended metaphorical comparison of the monster to the children of Anti-Nature.

23. This point is established with many finely observed details by means of syntactic analysis in François Moreau, *Un aspect de l'imagination créatrice chez Rabelais* (Paris, 1982), 88–92, by means of stylistic analysis in Alfred Glauser, *Rabelais créateur* (Paris, 1964), 251–55, and at a philosophico-ideological level by Michel Beaujour, *Le jeu de Rabelais,* 127, 139. Michael Riffaterre concludes from syntactic and stylistic analysis that any attempt to "read it [the text of chs. 29–32] in search of a meaning, [by] trying to *see* Quaresmeprenant," is doomed to failure. "Quaresmeprenant is a monster not because he is formless, but because he cannot be expressed, because he is literally unspeakable" (*Text Production,* 20). In effect, Riffaterre carries to an extreme the thesis of Fontaine concerning Rabelais's satire of incoherent medical analyses based on analogical referents. None of these authors suggests the relevance of mechanical constructions like Carnival puppets to the passage. The tendency is rather to offer organic parallels: "Rabelais a vu toutes les possibilités du comique de raideur . . . indiquant par une accumulation de détails un arrêt de vie, une stupéfiante momification" (*Rabelais créateur,* 252); "On peut songer ici aux têtes grotesques d'Arcimboldo, composées avec des fleurs ou des fruits qui, si on les regarde isolément, sont très agréables à l'oeil" (Moreau, *Un aspect,* 92); "Rabelais décide à l'entrée du ch. 31, que Quaresmeprenant possède sept côtes et se moque ainsi du débat [between pro- and anti-Galenists; note the misreading; Xenomanes says Quaresmeprenant has seven *more* ribs than a normal person, *QL,* 31,

new syntax is employed in the third list (Xenomanes's fourth description, chapter 32).[24] Instead of using the anatomical form "Q's $x$ is like $y$," this list is diagnostic: if Q does $x$, then it means $y$. The $x$s in the third list vary between Quaresmeprenant's observable behavior (sweating, speaking, blinking) and actions that could only be reported by the patient to an inquiring doctor (defecating, worrying, wool gathering, dreaming, all grouped at the end of the list). The $y$s in the third list could be interpreted as having the same relation to Quaresmeprenant's behavior as implements, accoutrements, and animals have to his anatomy in earlier lists, but then why did Rabelais change the syntax? Perhaps simply because the "if $x$ then $y$" syntactic form is more apt to describe motions and actions than the "$x$ is like $y$" form.

Although the earlier lists give an impression of a body-as-machine with nearly all the parts there to see, high and low, inside and out, this inventory of bodily functions is heavily weighted in favor of movements of the head and actions of the brain.[25] Xenomanes in effect sketches the psyche. A few items concerned with invisible anatomy were already psychological in character (e.g., in the first list, "His intelligence, like snails crawling out of strawberry plants"), but now the emphasis is stronger and more continuous. A textual move toward psychologization of the creature also seems borne out by the following fifth description, as I will show. Interpreted thus, the $y$s in the fourth description careen between fear and nostalgia, reality and desire, boredom and wishes. Fear: "If he trembled it was large helpings of rabbit *pâté*; nostalgia: "If he blinked his eyes, it was waffles and wafers." Re-

---

646]. . . . Rabelais s'est ainsi donné un autre motif de rire: son Quaresmeprenant est un singe, et il retrouve ainsi la tradition médiéval de l'hypocrite, et du moine simiesque" (Fontaine, *Quaresmeprenant*, 97). Glauser's reference to the Quaresmeprenant descriptions in his more recent work, *Les fonctions du nombre chez Rabelais* (Paris, 1982), 144–46, develops his earlier idea of stylistic "mimesis": the "brevity" and "monochordal rhythm" of the items in the lists signifies "arrêt et mort de l'écriture, métaphore de Carême et inversement, car le personnage signifie le texte, autant que le texte signifie le personnage."

24. These and following quotations from the fourth description are from *QL*, 32, 648–49.

25. Twenty-nine of the thirty-six bodily motions in this list describe actions of the head and brain. Robert Groos has devoted an article to this particular description: "The Enigmas of Quaresmeprenant: Rabelais and Defamiliarization," *Romanic Review* 69 (1978): 22–33. But he constructs solutions to enigmas that exist only because he himself has created them, disregarding Rabelais's grammatical and rhetorical indications.

ality: "If he blew his nose, it was salted eels"; desire: "If he wept, it was ducks in onion sauce." Boredom: "If he yawned, it was pea-soup"; wishes: "If he sighed, it was smoked ox tongues."

In the opening description Xenomanes calls Quaresmeprenant "father and sucking babe of doctors." The enigmatic epithet is clear enough in the light of these lists. The fellow is a good Catholic, concerned with Lenten regulations, but the more he represses his impulses, the less he controls his appetites, and so he has fallen sick, and chronically. He sustains and stimulates the doctor's skills with his absurd mode of life. The monster's equal commitment to both rules and self-aggrandizement makes him all the nastier: "If he scratched himself, it was new regulations"; "if he dreamed, it was mortgage deeds."

Quaresmeprenant is a hypocrite and pathologically so. The aim of Xenomanes's lists is not to recapitulate the method of medieval authors developing the Carnival-Lent combat theme, in which material objects correspond to ritual rules, with fish and vegetables, meats and fowl, asceticism and self-indulgence, greed and generosity each fixed and distinguishable in their symbolism. In Quaresmeprenant any food, any everyday object may signify by turns a Lenten or a Carnival attitude, depending on the psychology investing it. Xenomanes's descriptions abandon pretension to any system of firm signs guaranteeing that behavior corresponds to belief. In Quaresmeprenant a certain psychology is merely *associated* with a certain physiology and physiognomy.[26] The congruence of one with the other could be illustrated with any sort of behavior, ad infinitum. Xenomanes's lists go on and on in order to develop that sense of congruence, not in order to arrive at a precise moral-theological definition of character like those in medieval representations.[27]

26. This distinction between correspondence and association is parallel to Michel Foucault's "resemblance" and "similitude" (this would be better translated as "similarity") in *The Order of Things* (New York, 1970). A brief and not unduly simplified discussion of Foucault's complex distinction is in the translator's introduction to Foucault, *This Is Not a Pipe* (Berkeley, 1983), 9–10, by James Harkness: "'Resemblance,' says Foucault, 'presumes a primary reference that prescribes and classes' copies on the basis of the rigor of their mimetic relation to itself. . . . With similitude, on the other hand, the reference 'anchor' is gone. Things are cast adrift, more or less like one another without any of them being able to claim the privileged status of 'model' for the rest."

27. I have discussed the medieval-modern contrast in "Presentation," 23–30. In medieval representations the significance of observable traits is deduced from general principles: "Stomachs like wine barrels, emaciated features like a

The congruence portrayed in Quaresmeprenant concerns the mental and bodily effects of routinely deferring and deterring the exercise of natural faculties. This Carnival puppet of a man is always moving toward Lent—but regretfully so, with his mind on the pleasures left behind. "If he mumbled, it was law students' farces" ( *jeux de la bazoche*); "if he was hoarse, it was the coming-in of Morris dancers" (the latter were as regular a feature of Carnival revels as the law students' farces).[28]

In addition to comically imitating Galenic modes of anatomical description, the use of material, humdrum elements to describe the monster moves readers to fill the imaginary space around that being with the everyday flotsam and jetsam used to describe his body and behavior. Not some place among churchly observances in the cleric's breviary but his obsessive desires and his feud with the people on Ferocious Island have shaped him.[29] This implication is in consonance with the etymology of the monster's name. The first part of it, *quaresme-*, is simply the

---

haggard face or scabby tail, hairy skin, and giant stature cannot change their moral meaning without pulling after them a skein of other symbols. Each is embedded in an elaborate framework of mutual reference, hierarchically organized. In the modern system this attachment of any particular symbolic feature to a hierarchic system has been eroded through such practices as the conversion of ritual into spectacle and the transfer of festive symbols to nonfestive contexts" (25). As traditional connections among Carnival symbols faded, new connections could be suggested, which were adapted to the expression of changing norms of political and psychological behavior rather than to the reflection, as in the medieval system, of the order of the seasons and their religious corollaries.

28. The *basoche* was an association of largely unmarried young men exercising legal professions in larger French cities.

29. Of course I am not suggesting that one should reconstruct the life of the monster beyond the text, as in the case of that school of Shakespearean critics that used to trace the supposititious biographies of the playwright's characters. Rabelais creates a semiotic, not psychosomatic, coherence between psyche and behavior. The concept engendering this coherence has more to do with the ancient idea of macrocosmic (natural)–microcosmic (human) correspondences than with any theory of medicine. As Roland Antonioli concludes in his surprisingly brief commentary on the Quaresmeprenant chapters in *Rabelais et la médecine:* "Pour l'anatomiste qui connait l'assiette et la conjonction des particules, le corps humain résume tout l'Univers" (290). In contrast to Antonioli's conclusions, the works by Anatole Le Double, *Rabelais anatomiste et physiologiste* (Paris, 1899) and Dr. Albarel, "La psychologie et le tempérament de Quaresmeprenant," *Revue des études rabelaisiennes* 4 (1906): 49–58, move to an opposite extreme of medical "realism," taking the text as a serious representation of actual maladies and praising Rabelais for the precision and clarity of his medical descriptions.

French contraction for the Latin name of the first Sunday in Lent, Quadragesima. The second part of it has been explained in two ways. The usual manner, adopted in the standard French dictionaries by Littré and Godefroy, derives *-prenant* from Latin *prehendere*. *Prehendere* means to take hold or pull to one's side, and so in this case Quaresme-prenant means to take hold of or begin Lent. The philologist and literary historian Leo Spitzer, however, suggests that the word comes rather from Latin *praegnans*: to be full of something imminent, not necessarily of a child but of this or that principle or reason.[30]

Quaresmeprenant, used with attention to its etymology in either of the two senses, would refer not to the season of revels in general but to its last days. What if Rabelais was thinking of Quaresmeprenant not as a fixed and determined object in the Christian calendar, but as a transition period? What if his purpose was to pry loose this personification from its medieval allegorical web of equivalences and oppositions and to offer instead a sense of what happens psychologically as Lent takes hold of the Christian soul?[31] The "pregnant" way of explaining the word would be particularly suited to developing this idea. It is abundantly clear from Rabelais's portrayal of Quaresmeprenant that in his opinion Lenten spirit fills the soul not with virtue but with contradictions. A former Franciscan monk, who must have sought to fulfill Lenten rules for years before he rejected monastic discipline and took up the profession of a doctor, Rabelais would have known something about the psychology and perhaps also the physiology portrayed in Quaresmeprenant.

This fellow represents neither Carnival nor Lent but the inversive logic that binds them together. Not ambiguity or confusion but the dynamics of ambivalence are the key to understanding Rabelais's monster. These dynamics are the psychic equivalent of the social inversions of Carnival time: men become animals, women dress like men, humans costume themselves as giants, Christians behave like pagans. The excesses of Carnival lead to the repressions of Lent, repressions known

30. Leo Spitzer, "Zu *carnaval* im Französischen," *Wörter und Sachen* 5 (1914): 194, n. 2, takes issue with Littré and Godefroy. Spitzer was puzzled by Rabelais's use of Quaresmeprenant in the *Fourth Book,* and he notes that Le Duchat was, too, but he does not pursue the mystery (195–96, n. 1).

31. See Appendix 2 for a delightful representation of the medieval mode in a poem by Charles d'Orléans.

and in some sense sought by every believing Christian. The pre-Lenten season is fat and full not only with feasting but also with what follows it. It is as pregnant with Lent as that ribald Midlent Sunday is pregnant with twin fasting and other obsessive ascetic practices, exercised with greater and greater fervor as the church year approaches its climax with Easter.

Carnival pregnant with Lent—an eminently carnivalesque idea and a commonplace one, as Claude Gaignebet and others have noted: male pregnancy is a fantasy recurringly played out in Carnival time.[32] Whether or not Rabelais had some sense of the second, pregnant way of explaining the word, he did in writing this episode intend to push his readers toward awareness of the word's roots, quite in contrast to the commonplace way in which he had used it twenty years earlier in the *Pantagrueline Prognostication*.[33] His emphasis in these lists is on the bodily emblems of contradictory desires. Quaresmeprenant is a monstrosity because he is torn between trying to live according to Lenten rules and wishing for Carnival foods, law students' farces, and Morris dancers.

Centering the question of Carnival-Lent difference not upon ritually selected aspects of behavior but upon the psychological consequences of such selection was not peculiar to Rabelais. Lent, talking to his captains in a *basoche* play presented at Tours called *The Battle of Saint Pansard* (1485), exhibits a similar susceptibility:

BRIQUET:  [*Greeting Caresme.*]
May Charnau [Fleshliness, or Meatiness, the personification of Carnival],[34] who's disputing with you, have cold teeth and a flat stomach,
A dry throat and nothing at all to fry!
And may Macaire [Caresme's cook], that excellent gentleman,
And Caresme, and all his empire,

32. Claude Gaignebet, *Le Carnaval* (Paris, 1974), 48–49. See, for the more ample context of the theme beyond Carnival as part of traditional popular tales, Robert Zapperi, *L'homme enceint, l'homme, la femme, et le pouvoir* (Paris, 1983).

33. See ch. 2 above. His concern here with the peculiar etymology of Quaresmeprenant is perhaps further indicated by the fact that he uses the word *carneval*, not *Quaresmeprenant*, elsewhere in the *Fourth Book* (*QL*, 14, 602; *QL*, 59, 722), to designate the period of revels.

34. *Charnau* is called *Saint Pansard* only in the title of the play, not in the text. The play is edited by Aubailly in *Deux jeux de Carnaval;* see 34–35 for these quotations.

Give them just such bits and pieces to gnaw
As will make their bowels do nothing but sigh
For eating and drinking.

CARESME:   O Briquet, Briquet, my sweet friend!
Your fine discourse makes me gurgle [me gourgoulle]
I experience such joy in listening to you
That my stomach churns [me triboulle] . . .

MARQUET:   There's no bristle on my butt which doesn't twist,
No gut in my groin which doesn't groan,
When I think of the great sausage blows
One [Carnival?] launches upon a naked head!

CARESME:   Marquet, you are most welcome.
[But] your words make me clutch my gullet
And I seem to be catching a fever
Which is stopping up my throat.

For all his susceptibility, however, Caresme in this law student farce remains Caresme, exhibiting no psychic ambivalence about his moral
identity or purpose. No one using the Carnival-Lent theme developed
anthropomorphosis of the old personifications to the pitch of psychic
subtlety found in Rabelais's episode.[35]

Xenomanes's fifth description, occupying the second third of chapter
32, returns to the sketchlike style with which he first spoke of Quaresmeprenant.[36] The monster's contradictions are developed so phantas-
matically that they no longer have much to do with either the Carnival-
Lent tradition or the larger literary and popular-cultural tradition of
grotesque realism. "Fasting, he ate nothing; eating nothing, he fasted.
He nibbled as if in suspicion, and drank in imagination. . . . He feared
nothing but his own shadow and the cries of fat kids." Each element in
the new description recalls at a more general level some part or parts of
the preceding lists. "He laughed as he bit, and biting, he laughed"; one
recalls Quaresmeprenant's teeth "like boar's tusks" and the remorseless
insatiability of his repressed appetites. He is both indolent and hyper-
active: "Doing nothing he worked, and working, he did nothing." "He

35. Similar embodiment of psychic properties is given by Hans Sachs to
Carnival in his poem, "Ein Gesprech mit der Fasnacht [*sic*]" (1540), in his
*Werke*, ed. von Keller and Goetze, 5: 295–98. See also Grinberg and Kinser,
"Les Combats," 84, on the theme of embodiment in a narrative poem by Giulio
Cesare Croce, *Processo overo esamine di Carnevale* (Bologna, 1588).
36. *QL*, 32, 649.

used his fist like a mallet"; his bodily parts are often like weapons. His mind twitches between the excessively soft and excessively hard, between regret and vengeance; he is, one recalls, a "whipper of small children" who nevertheless "weeps three parts out of each day."[37]

Contradiction, pushed to these extremes, is surreal: "He bathed above high steeples and dried out in ponds and rivers"; "He fished in the air and caught huge crayfish there."[38] Such features remove the creature still further from the reader and the Pantagruelians. The fourth description begins: "What an extraordinary case in nature" (*Cas admirable en nature*). The fifth begins: "What a strange case" (*Cas estrange*). Indeed, Quaresmeprenant has become stranger than nature: thus Rabelais prepares readers for his final move, in which the creature seems to vanish into the larger contours of a myth.

Pantagruel compares the monster in the sixth and last description to the children of Anti-Nature (*Anti-Physie*). "I am reminded of the form and appearance of Amodunt [glossed by editors as "Lack of Measure"] and Disharmony," declares the prince when Xenomanes finishes his fifth account. Quaresmeprenant's "strange and monstrous" psychophysiology shows a human being's natural parts thrown into such disarray that their combination engenders the opposite of Harmony and Beauty (the latter, says Pantagruel, are Nature's children). Anti-Nature's children are grotesque, although the elements of their bodies—like the things to which Quaresmeprenant's bodily parts have been compared in previous descriptions—are not themselves ugly, taken singly. But their assemblage has gone awry. Amodunt and Disharmony have heads and feet that are round, like bouncing balls. Anti-Nature interprets these spherical parts as evidence of divine kinship because the heavens are made in and move with circular tracery. Her children's arms have been joined to the torso so that they reach toward the back rather than front of the body. This, their mother explains, is an exceptionally well-made adaptation to defense; the front of the body is sufficiently defended by teeth. "Their eyes stood out of their heads on the end of bones similar to heels, with no eyebrows, and they were as hard as those of crabs. . . . They walked on their heads, continually turning cartwheels, tail over

37. See the beginning of Part One.
38. According to Screech, *Rabelais*, 368, these particulars come respectively from a "popular proverb" (no documentation) and from Erasmus's *Adagia* 1: 4, 74.

head, with their legs in the air"; all this to their mother was evidence of spherical perfection.[39]

Pantagruel expresses horrified disdain for such opinions and such creatures. These superb little Carnival machines are denounced by the hero in ways opposite to the gay and tolerant manner that Pantagruel favors on other occasions. Anti-Nature's "evidence drawn from brutish beasts" is absurd; her arguments are devoid of "good judgment and common sense." Pantagruel's amusing myth-tale is didactic in the usual manner of contemporary humanism; the place for functions like those lodged in heart and head is on high, while that of the limbs and their brutish, material functions is below. Mixing and inverting the two levels, head over heels, disgusts the prince, and prince he does seem to be here, defending the high as properly high and the low as forever low.[40]

39. *QL*, 32, 649–50. Stanley Eskin's description of the mythic tale by the Italian humanist Coelio Calcagnini (Rabelais's immediate source) in "Physis and Anti-Physie: The Idea of Nature in Rabelais and Calcagnini," *Comparative Literature* 14 (1962): 167–73, has been largely replaced by the more thorough analysis in Richard Cooper, "Les 'contes' de Rabelais et l'Italie: une mise au point," in *La nouvelle française à la Renaissance,* ed. Lionello Sozzi (Geneva, 1981), 196–98. Eskin, Cooper, and other editors of and commentators on this passage from the seventeenth century to the present have been puzzled by Pantagruel's comment that he found the story of Nature and Anti-Nature among ancient authors, since Calcagnini lived in the sixteenth century. Pantagruel's reference is probably to those aspects of Calcagnini's tale found in Plato's *Symposium,* where Aristophanes tells the tale of the originally eight-limbed spherical nature of the three sexes—male, female, and hermaphroditic (189A–191D). Aristophanes' humanity runs about turning cartwheels, and these queer beings are turned in opposite directions, just as in Rabelais's account. They are children of the sun, earth, and moon (hence their spherical shape) and are treated in Aristophanes' story as natural, although troublesome to the gods. Unlike Calcagnini too, and unlike the immediate Rabelaisian context, the Platonic story is explicitly comic.

40. M. M. Fontaine has discovered a marvelous visual parallel to the children of Anti-Nature in a series of drawings offered by Giovanbattista Braccelli to the Medici princes of Florence in the later sixteenth century. The drawings show geometrized assemblages of mechanical toy people with, indeed, legs and arms hooked on backwards in one case. See Fontaine, "Quaresmeprenant," 106–7, 112, no. 32. But Fontaine's assertions about Rabelais's mechanical-anatomical perceptions, again here drawn into parallel with Vesalian anti-Galenic method, both conflict with and move far beyond the Rabelaisian text: "Quoi qu'on en dise, on n'oublie pas que le corps de Quaresmeprenant forme une masse où tout fonctionne en rapports continus [*sic*]. . . . Le dessin imaginaire du corps permettrait de mieux comprendre la dénonciation de la comparaison et de l'analogie au profit d'une perception globale du corps, telle qu'elle se livre dans les images littéraires de Rabelais. . . . [Here intervene Braccelli's

Elevated in this way to the level of a metaphysical parable, the contrast between Nature and Anti-Nature may be applied to anything. In this passage it is applied with fine fury to Pantagruel's—and Rabelais's—pet hatreds. For Anti-Nature has continued to procreate, says Pantagruel. From her have come empty-headed barbarians (*Matagotz*), churchly bigots (*Cagotz*), hypocrites (*Caphars*), church-serving beggars (*Briffaulx*), and popemongers (*Papelars*),[41] and the zealots who have attacked Rabelais's writings: *les Maniacles Pistoletz, les Démoniacles Calvins, imposteurs de Genève, les enraigez Putherbes.* *Pistoletz* refers to Guillaume Postel, *Calvins* to John Calvin, and *Putherbes* to Gabriel Du-Puyherbault. These men, as I have mentioned, had denounced Rabelais's books in the 1540s.[42] They, like the other bigots and fools, like homosexuals (*Chattemites*) and like "misanthropes" (literally, *Canibales*) are all "deformed monsters, made in Nature's despite."[43]

The section of Rabelais's episode that served in traditional examples of the Carnival-Lent genre to introduce the hero and his adversaries ends here with an unexpected break in the fictive frame and a reference to the author's context of threatening religiopolitical fanaticism. The never-never story of Pantagruel and his friends is brought sharply back from the high seas of fiction to a society of jealously striving men full of vituperative suspicion. However unfamiliar readers might be with

---

illustrations; see also the analysis of Vesalius's mode of modeling the body, 102–4.] De telles solutions qui visent un corps entier dans ses gestes, dans ses volumes mobiles et ses activités propres, ne sont possibles qu'après Rabelais et Vésale" (104–6).

41. Many of these were banned in the same vituperative terms from Thélème Abbey in *G*, 54, 173; *cagotz* and *caphars* are attacked by Rabelais with the same comic excess in his own name at the end of the prologue to the *Third Book*, *TL*, *P*, 351. *Matagotz* seems to be invented from Greek *mataios*, empty, vain, foolish, and *Gotz*, the Goths, the humanists' synonym for barbarians. *Cagotz* is a synonym of bigot. A *caphar* seems to be a religious hypocrite (Rabelais uses it in *G*, 54, 173 with the adjective *empantouflez*, slippered). Demerson glosses *briffaulx* as "glutton" in a note to *G*, 54 (*Oeuvres de Rabelais*, 197, n. 9) but Le Double, *Rabelais anatomiste*, 410, n. 1, cites a pre-eighteenth-century poem and an ecclesiastical authority indicating that it meant a lay brother licensed to beg by papal brief; that is, a marginal religious person of low economic and social status.

42. See ch. 1. Screech, *Rabelais*, 209–11, 314, 325, 371, gives details about their publications. See L. Thuasne, *Etudes*, 404–13, 447–50, for the fullest account of Calvin's attacks on Rabelais and E. Droz, "Frère Gabriel DuPuyherbault," on the especially sharp attacks of DuPuyherbault. DuPuyherbault is often called "de Puy-Herbault" in older literature.

43. See Appendix 3 on *Canibales* and ch. 5, n. 8, on *Chattemites*.

Pistoletz as a reference to Postel or with Putherbe, a Frenchified version of the Latin form of the monk DuPuyherbault's name, they could scarcely be unaware in 1552 of the third person, a man whose name is not deformed and whose seat of power is announced without disguise: John Calvin of Geneva.

To the dedicated Pantagruelists among Rabelais's "well-disposed readers," those who had read the author's prologue to the short edition of the *Fourth Book* in 1548, this break in the text would have been even more striking. These readers would perhaps have noticed the deletion of Dr. Rabelais's violent attacks on his detractors in the 1552 prologue, only to find these same references to caphars, cagots, matagots, and catamites here, accompanied not only by the names of particular persons but also by an embracing philosophical denunciation.[44] Such readers, and still more Rabelais's modern critics, are forced by this shift from paratext to text to consider the meaning of the literary tactic. If Rabelais the real author, the person representing Dr. Rabelais and Alcofribas no less than Quaresmeprenant and Pantagruel, decides to name names in this way, what does it imply? Beyond its literary and eventually its philosophical sense, what are the moral and political implications of rending the symbolic fabric asunder in this manner?

In literary terms placing the denunciations here would tend to conceal them from nonliterary eyes, even while making the rhetoric sharper. Rabelais perhaps decided to make the shift from prologue to this part of the text because he supposed that inquisitorial committees would be less inclined to work their way through a comic depiction of Carnival-Lent customs in search of heresy than to peruse prefatory materials. The shift carried forward Rabelais's tactics of concealment. In political terms the particularized attack and its placement express new boldness and old shrewdness in facing adversaries. In moral terms they intensify the impression gained from many passages scattered through the novels. This gaily affable writer is irascible. Rabelais, as Michael Screech has commented, was a good hater.

Rabelais has sometimes been called a naturalist philosopher, a thinker who identifies man's destiny with his nature-embedded, material existence. For such interpretations Rabelais's myth of Nature's and Anti-Nature's progeny assumes special importance. It is one of the few places in the novels where such imputed naturalism is propounded in general although still humorous terms.

44. See pp. 34–35 above.

In Rabelais's Italian humanist source Nature pleads her cause against Anti-Nature before the council of the gods, the gods award their favor to Nature's children, and the latter then convert men to religious reverence for nature while Anti-Nature and her progeny vanish. But in Rabelais's version Anti-Nature's children show no sign of defeat or disappearance; perhaps, then, there will never be a lack of "brainless folk" and "fools" who accept with eagerness such confused arguments as Anti-Nature employs. If that is so, what does this ending of the fable imply? Does it present a philosophically open-ended view of the human scene or a somberly pessimistic idea of human nature as distracted in frightful and threatening proportions from the worship of Nature by the silly mechanisms of Anti-Nature? Or does it signify something else entirely? Should one say, moving beyond these futurological alternatives in the authorially self-inclusive manner suggested by Michel Beaujour, that Pantagruel's eruption of anger over the pullulation of Anti-Nature's children represents the snorting helplessness of someone who confusedly perceives an enemy more pitiless and implacable than even religious orthodoxy: the limitations of his own most far-reaching, metaphysical thought, thought that in Rabelais's case is, so far as his extant writings reveal, synonymous with literarily embedded thought?[45]

The Rabelaisian text is caught in its own toils, Beaujour maintains, caught in an endless babble of linguistic self-generation because it—the spirit incarnate in this text—cannot imagine a way of "perceiving culture and language as humanly founded, in spite of all its efforts to escape the alienations implied in the antithesis of Nature and Supernature." Rabelais recognized, as a Christian, the discontinuity between Supernature and Nature. The relation between God, on the one hand, and man and the world, on the other, was not a smoothly unfolding emanation like that proposed in Neoplatonic thought. The hiatus between Supernature and Nature seemed to Rabelais, according to Beaujour, so great as to involve man in inescapable alienations, the most

---

45. "Futurology" is not my neologism but that of certain present-day sociologists. It directs attention to an allied and more optimistic aspect of Rabelais's thought that has long interested scholars: his concept of human progress. See my "Ideas of Temporal Change and Cultural Process in France, 1470–1535," in *Renaissance Studies in Honor of Hans Baron,* ed. Anthony Molho and John Tedeschi (Florence, 1971), 710–11, 742–45, and Abraham C. Keller, "The Idea of Progress in Rabelais," *PMLA* 66 (1951): 235–43. See also Bakhtin's treatment of Rabelais's views of the future, discussed in ch. 10 below.

crucial of which was "Culture." "Culture (that which is no longer Nature yet is not Supernature) takes refuge with Rabelais in the practice of literature as satire." Man the maker of literature, disconnected from, yet finding no other ultimate source for Nature or Culture than Supernature, has no way of founding his activity in his own being, in an "anthropology" or science-art of the human, and so he is "the prisoner of anti-nature." His linguistic activity "cuts up the world, *anatomizes* it, but never succeeds in catching hold of the true thread of its coherence." In the end, therefore, "Rabelais's practice of language never lays hold upon Nature except as Anti-Nature does, delimiting objects so that they become *disjecta membra,* haunted by their nothingness: [this idea of] language is incapable of speaking about the world without drying it up."

Rabelais/Pantagruel, or rather the textuality their configuration procreates—is *that* who Quaresmeprenant/Anti-Nature is?[46]

46. The quotations are from Beaujour, *Le jeu de Rabelais,* 138–39, but they concern the problematic developed throughout the book and are stated with special clarity in the conclusion, 174–77. I have pulled Beaujour's affirmations in a certain direction and have perhaps extrapolated from them more than he would do. I offer the interpretation hypothetically, adopting a perspective posterior to Rabelais's own, the dangers of which were mentioned with respect to Beaujour in ch. 1, n. 56. The question is not whether such hypotheses can be "justified" by the text but whether the critic juxtaposes them clearly to the text, so that their contextual otherness can be seen and judged. In this connection one must admire the manner in which M. M. Fontaine (see nn. 23, 40) proposes her interpretation of Quaresmeprenant. Whatever one's reservations about the particulars of her exegesis, the open-minded, gaily ironic mode of presentation makes her article an intellectual feast in the best Pantagruelian sense.

# 4

# What Makes Sausage-People Fight?

After the long wrenching, dismantling, and finally mythicizing movement of the Quaresmeprenant section, the two-chapter interlude in
which Pantagruel kills a whalelike sea creature provides action-filled
relief.[1] Alcofribas resumes his narration, and the Pantagruelians behave
as they normally do: Friar John is brave, Panurge is cowardly, and Pantagruel dispatches the spouter with impossibly perfect marksmanship.
The whale-monster is hauled ashore on Ferocious Island where some
of Pantagruel's sailors carve it up "to gather the fat of its kidneys"—
just as the inhabitants of one of the Faroe Islands are shown doing on
Olaus Magnus's map (see Fig. 3). Faroe/Ferocious Island, we have already been told at the beginning of the episode, is the home of Farfelu
Sausages.[2]

1. Action-filled but not less richly symbolic: see n. 5 to Part Two and the
references to Paul Smith's analysis of the *physétère* episode. Because the *physétère*
appears immediately after Pantagruel recounts the myth of *Antiphysie,* and because Panurge at the approach of the sea-monster begins crying with fear,
Smith comments: "Tout se passe comme si Panurge se laissait tromper par
l'homologie phonique qui lie le physétère à Anti-physie." False or negligent
etymology: the sea-monster's name, from Greek *physeter,* means "the blower";
a whale blows out water from its spout; conversely, when Pantagruel's arrows
hit the monster in the right spots, the blower ceases to blow and is deflated.
Hence, concludes Smith, "La victoire de Pantagruel sur le monstre peut se lire
comme celle de l'Harmonie sur le Chaos, de l'Esprit sur la Matière, de Physis
sur Antiphysie" (Smith, *Voyage et écriture,* 112, 116–17; see further 120–21). Such
conclusions draw much metaphysics (and some hasty identifications of Pantagruel's significance generally) from a slight myth and its aftermath. But Smith,
like Beaujour and Fontaine, juxtaposes his conclusions clearly to the text (see
my ch. 3, n. 46). Smith, incidentally, identifies Quaresmeprenant in the traditional way with Lent (ibid., 120).
2. *QL,* 29, 643. *Farfelus,* "zany," is Rabelais's punning neologism, forged to
match Faroe/Farouche. Before Rabelais only *fafelu* existed, glossed in *Le Petit
Robert* (Paris, 1978) as "dodu," well filled-out, puffy. The group of words is
related to *fanfreluche* (see Rabelais, *G,* 1, 31), a bagatelle or light, floating thing
(from Old French *fanfelu,* twelfth century, and *fanfeluce,* fourteenth century);
see A. Lefranc, ed., *Oeuvres de Rabelais,* Volume 1 (Paris, 1913), 25, n. 48.

Rabelais's tripe-sausage tribes are a fusion of two groups described in a merry tale, anonymously published in 1538, called *The Disciple of Pantagruel*.[3] In *The Disciple* one group is called the Sausages (*les andouilles*): they are "about twelve feet long . . . [with] sharp, biting teeth"; they feed in herds on the Tuquebaralideaulx Islands, "like cranes or sheep." The other group is called "the ferocious people" (*les farouches*); they are "people who are hairy and colored like rats," and they live in caves at the bottom of the sea. Like the Sausages, they have "long sharp teeth." In Rabelais's *Fourth Book* the Sausages live on Ferocious Island and behave something like the scampering rat-people in *The Disciple*. But they have lost their sharp teeth and have acquired slightly more civil—and much more Carnival-like—customs.[4]

Pantagruel, eating lunch with his friends on Ferocious Island, asks Xenomanes what kind of animals are climbing up a nearby tree, "thinking they were squirrels, stoats, martens, or weasels." Xenomanes explains that they are Sausages, who are probably scouting to see if Quaresmeprenant has come. Rabelais's Sausage-people, then, seem at first to have the furry, small animal size of the *Disciple*'s ferocious people. They are just as unreasonably impetuous, too, as Xenomanes explains in giving an account of the latest stage in the war between them and Quaresmeprenant.[5]

Here is the place where Rabelais inserts references to the contemporary Protestant-Catholic war in Germany, clothing the actors involved in the traditional costumes of a Carnival-Lent combat farce: The "mountain Sausages" and "forest-dwelling Blood-puddings" (*Saulcissons montigènes, Boudins sylvatiques*) who are fighting Quaresmeprenant represent those Protestant Swiss and south German allies against whom Emperor Charles V took the field in the 1540s. Quaresmeprenant, says Xenomanes, has refused to make peace with these confederates—as indeed Charles V refused to make peace with the Protestants in 1546.

3. See ch. 2, n. 25.

4. Demerson and Lauvergnat-Gagnière, eds., *Disciple*, 23–27. The considerable inventive talents of the anonymous author may also have served to supply Rabelais with some bizarre associations developed in the description of Quaresmeprenant and with some names used in chapter 40, the list of cooks who fight the fierce Sausages. See *Disciple*, 60–61 (critical apparatus), 74, 77 (critical apparatus) for references to these possible associations.

5. Quotations concerning the introductory section about the Sausages and their war against Quaresmeprenant are from *QL*, 35, 656–58.

Alban Krailsheimer has pointed out, too, that Charles's well-known pious melancholy is similar to "the general idea of an unhealthy and gloomy monster" emblemized in Quaresmeprenant. But it would be a distortion to limit Rabelais's vast description to this particular meaning, just as it is illusory to expect to find historical referents for every symbol Rabelais uses in a context like this, especially in the case of those traditional to the Carnival-Lent combat theme like "Fort [Herring] Barrel" and "Brine-Tub Castle." In terms of contemporary French readers' perception of Rabelais's allegory, the mimesis of Carnival forms must have been more obvious than the political elements to all but the most internationally informed readers. Rabelais is as usual writing for several audiences here, one more political than others. The fact that the political dimension is there maintains the orientation to present-day events strongly affirmed with the references to Calvin, Postel, and Du-Puyherbault.[6]

But does not Xenomanes's account of the current stage of the war with Quaresmeprenant reinforce the old idea, at least for a less political audience, that all this is only an allegory of Carnival fighting Lent? Such an implication is bound to disturb readers who have closely followed the descriptions of Quaresmeprenant. They have concluded that Quaresmeprenant is both more and less than Lent. Regretful disciple

---

6. On the Swiss and Germans see Krailsheimer, "The Andouilles," 229. See also his 232: "What should be understood by the 'forteresse de Cacques,' which Quaresmeprenant refuses to surrender to the Andouilles? This . . . and 'le chasteau de Sallouoir' . . . were doubtless no mystery for Rabelais' contemporaries, and the violence of the language is surely provoked by some historical fact." If the "historical fact" can be found, its aesthetic integration and adaptation to the Carnival-Lent theme will appear all the more remarkable. Rabelais also vents his spleen against the Council of Trent in this chapter, referring to it obliquely in *QL,* 35, 658, as the "National Council of Chesil" (i.e., "Kessil," Hebrew for "fool" or "nitwit"): At this Council the Sausages, Xenomanes reports, were bullied and Quaresmeprenant too was threatened with denunciation as a "filthy, broken-down stockfish" if he should come to any agreement with the Sausages—all of which allegorizes nicely the Tridentine stiffening of Protestant-Catholic differences. As Robert Marichal has shown (cf. ch. 3, n. 20, above), Rabelais was especially well informed about the circumstances surrounding the Smalkaldic War and the negotiations of imperial moderates both at Trent and elsewhere with the German Protestants; he may himself have been used by Cardinal Jean du Bellay as an envoy to representatives of the German Protestants in Metz in 1546–1547. See Marichal, "Rabelais et les censures," 138–41, for the diplomacy, and 146–47, for some passages in the first edition of the *Fourth Book* influenced by this involvement.

of churchly injunctions, he is a pitiful invalid, sickened by contradictory allegiances. He is also the enlarged image of unnatural behavior, a par-adigmatically powerful figure who represents not simply the ill wisdom of observing Lent's prescriptions, but its looming, terrifying inhu-manity.

What then do the Sausages represent? Rabelais has already suggested that they, like Quaresmeprenant, do not incarnate Carnival; the role of incarnation seems to belong to their "protector and neighbor, the noble Mardi Gras."[7] The author thus frustrates readers' attempts to establish the allegorical identity of the Sausage-people just as he earlier did their attempts to categorize Quaresmeprenant. Delaying clear narrative meaning in this way is dangerous. Readers may become so exasperated that they abandon the text because it so frequently directs their atten-tion away from a linearly unfolding narrative that would carry them from an intriguing beginning to a satisfying end. The second half of the Carnival-Lent episode seems explicitly designed to court this disas-ter. Narrative progress here, even more than in the long lists describing Quaresmeprenant, is repeatedly deferred. In the first half the narrative seemed to grind to a halt as the symbols piled up. But even though in the second half direct action is equally in suspense, the narrative in this case gathers energy and dynamic thrust through the deferral of action because the delaying conversations of the Pantagruelians circle around and toward a coming battle.

The first delay occurs when Xenomanes recounts the past history of war between Quaresmeprenant and the Sausages, after Pantagruel sees some of the latter scampering up a tree. No sooner has Xenomanes finished than Friar John intervenes to say: "There'll be some asinine goings-on [*de l'asne*] here, I can see that! Those venerable Sausages may be taking you [Pantagruel] for Quaresmeprenant." Xenomanes seconds Friar John's warning with a pseudo-proverb: "Sausages are sausages, forever double and treacherous."[8] With the latter silliness we are launched in the same direction as that developed with Quaresmepre-nant, the Renaissance impulse to associate bodily with mental and emo-tional traits: such greasy, slippery tripe-people, who have furry hair and quick scampering movements like weasels, must be full of deceit.

I have translated Friar John's phrase "*Il y aura icy de l'asne*" in a

7. The statement is part of the first description. See ch. 3 above.
8. Quotations about the second and following delays are from *QL,* 36–40, 658–72.

minimal although still metaphorical manner. *De l'asne,* "some donkey" or "something of a donkey kind," is enigmatic. Did it mean behaving in a silly or obstreperous way, as in the English colloquial "horsing around"? Did Friar John, always the warrior, imagine some carnival-esque battle like those occasionally occurring on mardi gras between men in animal masks?[9] The butchers in fifteenth-century Nuremberg danced through the streets led by a hobbyhorse, hobby-donkey, hobby-ram, and hobby-unicorn. Did they, like the much later documented "Old Hoss" at Padstow, England, or the "Pony" at Pezenas, France, turn boisterous and belligerent, charging upon spectators? At Hof, Germany, in 1566 the butchers, led by a man dressed in raw oxhide and horns, ran and danced their way through the streets on Thursday after mardi gras, waving clubs and ringing cattle and sheep bells. Falling upon some textile workers who wanted to pass through the streets before them, the butchers drew knives and wielded their clubs. The textile workers pulled up paving stones. In the end one of the latter was killed.[10]

Rabelais's Sausage-people are like these revelers, half-animal, and bellicose. Wildmen in Carnival did not always pounce upon others. One has the impression that at Nuremberg they were objects of spectacle more than vehicles of aggression. Whether dancing about or wielding their clubs, however, they represented irrational, unpredictable behavior, and in this sense they were akin to the fool maskers in cap and bells.[11] Foolishness, wildness, and arbitrary assault are all illustrated by the Sausages in the *Fourth Book.* But their bodily shape and

9. Huguet, *Dictionnaire,* s.v. "âne," finds only one other sixteenth-century use of the phrase "de l'asne"; it occurs in d'Aubigné's *Baron Faeneste.* Huguet concludes lamely from both Rabelais's and d'Aubigné's usage that it meant "something bad, a battle, some blows."

10. See Kinser, "Representation," 2, for illustration of the hobby-animals in the Nuremberg butchers' dance of 1449. Violet Alford, *The Hobby Horse and Other Animal Masks* (London, 1978), 36–43, describes the two-man "Old Hoss" of Padstow, which has allegedly been charging into crowds and covering victims with oil and soot since the early nineteenth century. Alford, 94, also provides a brief description of the wooden-frame Poulain of Pezenas, France, documented since 1702 and usually carried by more than two men. For Hof in 1566 see Enoch Widman, *Hofer Chronik,* in *Quellen zur Geschichte der Stadt Hof,* ed. Christian Meyer (Hof, 1894), 202–3. The continuation of Carnival into officially Lenten days (here the Thursday after Ash Wednesday) was not unusual in some German locales for complex historical reasons. It was not considered an impiety but simply an age-old practice.

11. This fight is briefly described in ch. 2. Kinser, "Presentation," 9, includes a representation of the 1539 scene with fools and wildmen running about.

texture make their belligerence laughable: *andouilles* were sausages made from tripe and other fatty portions of the pig, cut in narrow strips, seasoned, and stuffed into a portion of pork intestine that had a phallic length and figure.[12] Constructing his protagonists in this way gave Rabelais a wide range of registers on which to draw, all of them characteristic of Carnival behavior and carnivalesque talk, with their emphasis on the irrational, emotionally dominated "bodily lower stratum," alimentary, intestinal, animalistic, and choleric, always ready to fight.[13]

The carnivalesque overtones to the name and character of the strange residents of Ferocious Island frame the conflict between them and the Pantagruelians. They are the text's festive context, supporting it more consistently and fundamentally than either politicoreligious references or the parodic literary allusions to epic warfare that emerge later in the episode. Rabelais interweaves one series of metaphors with another by means of this festive context.

From the Middle Ages, *andouille* and its equally boneless, slippery phonetic cousin, *anguille* (eel), referred in popular parlance to the penis.[14] Rabelais uses their similar sound to conflate the two phallic symbols, as Barbara Bowen has shown in a perceptive study. He conflates them by drawing on the derivation of *anguille* from Latin *anguis* (snake). The narrator Master Alcofribas explains sententiously that "the serpent who tempted Eve was Sausage-like" (*le serpens qui tenta Eve estoit andouillicque*).[15] The eel-like undertone to the Sausages brings out the slipperiness that makes them "two-faced and treacherous," as Xenomanes says. They are lively, sexy little creatures but not to be trusted.

---

12. J. M. Cohen's translation of *andouilles* as "Chitterlings" (*Gargantua*, 524) is hence incorrect, at least with reference to the present-day American meaning of chitterling. The translation has been repeated in all English translations since the first one by Pierre Le Motteux (1694); perhaps in his time and place it was correct.

13. See Bakhtin, *Rabelais*, 23, on the carnivalesque use of references to the bodily lower stratum.

14. See the examples in R. Howard Bloch, *The Scandal of the Fabliaux* (Berkeley, 1986), 52; Bowen, "Lenten Eels," 19, offers other examples.

15. *QL*, 38, 665. Bowen, "Lenten Eels," 20–21, makes the point about Rabelais's implied association of Latin *anguis* with French *anguille*. The *andouille/anguille* association may have been suggested to Rabelais from *Le Disciple de Pantagruel*, 50, which associates the two in passing; Bowen, "Lenten Eels," 18, also notes this reference. But the *Disciple* is not concerned with Carnival-Lent distinctions, so the reference does not carry the same associations as those in Rabelais.

The Latin root of *andouille* lends further support to these associations with eels: *inducere* means to put one thing into another, as is done in the manufacture of these sausages; *inducere* also means to lead one thing to, toward, or into another, and hence, metaphorically, to insinuate.

But all these verbal and proverbial associations do not mean that Rabelais is conflating the festive meaning of eels and sausages, nor that he suggests that Carnival and Lent themselves were becoming less ideologically distinct.[16] On the contrary, the larger context of this verbal play, the context that from the beginning of the approach to Quaresmeprenant leads readers to look for embroidery on the theme of Carnival-Lent opposition, insures that the difference between meaty Carnival food and Lenten fishy fare hovers over every mention of one or the other, pulling them apart in readers' minds even as the text pushes them together.

In a similar way Rabelais plays tantalizingly with readers' knowledge that as carnivalesque fare the Sausages should be eaten. In the nearly twenty octavo pages dealing with these juicy morsels, Rabelais never allows their ingestion. "Sausages will be sausages," Xenomanes declares. At the level of text, they are everything but that. Their alimentary dimension is suspended over the text, all the more hilariously.

Given the ribald associations brought by readers to any mention of sausages, the first direct view Pantagruel obtains of the Sausage-people en masse is a marvellous inversion of expectations. Just after Friar John's prediction of donkey business, Pantagruel jumps up to discover "a large battalion of huge and mighty Sausages marching toward us to the sound of bagpipes and flutes, sheeps' stomachs and bladders, pipes and drums, trumpets and clarions." Here come the same creatures who have been described up to now in small and sinuous terms, decked out as heroic fighters and marching uproariously along to sheep-bladder music. Did this idea too derive from Rabelais's perusal of Magnus's delightful map? There is a bagpipe player just above the whale being carved up on the Faroe Islands in Figure 3. Or is this one more reminiscence of Carnival spectacles? These are Carnival maskers, making rough music. "Their orderly movement, their proud step and resolute mien convinced us that these were no small fry [Friquenelles]."[17] The

16. See ch. 2, n. 24, on Bowen's conclusions.

17. *QL*, 36, 659. Boulenger, the editor, notes that *Friquenelles* also meant "femmes galantes." Because Xenomanes has said earlier that all Sausages are

low is mockingly portrayed as the high, as an army of well-disciplined fighters, as worthy of respect as would be any armed assembly of the nobility of Rabelais's day, whose claim to high estate was based on prowess in battle. In spite of this evidence of imminent attack, a second delay ensues similar to that which occurred after the Pantagruelians arrived on the island and Xenomanes recounted the latest incidents in their war with Quaresmeprenant. Pantagruel calls a council of his advisers, with which he discusses Greek, Hebrew, Roman, and modern French parallels to the uncertain situation in which they find themselves.[18]

It happens that among Pantagruel's followers are two soldiers named *Riflandouille* and *Tailleboudin,* "Maul-Sausage" and "Chop-blood-pudding." Pantagruel, taking this as an omen of victory, occasions a third delay by discoursing upon the prophetic properties of names.[19] As in the case of the preceding delay, during which Pantagruel speaks learnedly about affairs that have no practical bearing upon the matter at hand, the abstruse and superstitious absurdity of Pantagruel's examples proves to the reader the opposite of what Pantagruel proves to his listeners. These speeches occupy the same place in Rabelais's plot as the idle discourses of Carnival or Lent to their counselors in the traditional farces and narrative poems, just before the fatal invasion of the opponent. One side or the other in the combat schema is signaled to the reader at an early point as the eventual loser because of its vain activities and inattention to military preparation. In Rabelais's story, of course, these indications are belied. Although Pantagruel is portrayed as a wooly-headed carnivalesque leader, spouting classical *copia* at the most inopportune moments,[20] he is also shown taking proper precau-

---

women, their transformation into fierce fighters is all the more comical. Note the picture of a similar marching squadron of colorfully costumed pikemen with wildmen and fools gaily mingled among them in the Schembart parade of 1539 at Nuremberg reproduced in Kinser, "Presentation," 9, figure 2. On the "rough music" typical of Renaissance Carnival celebrations, see e.g., C. Marcel-Dubois, "Fêtes villageoises et vacarmes cérémoniels, ou une musique et son contraire," in *Les Fêtes de la Renaissance*, Volume 2 (Paris, 1975), 602–16.

18. *QL,* 36, 659–60.

19. *QL,* 37, 661–64. Calcagnini, whose work Rabelais used for the myth of Anti-Nature, was also the source of the stories of prophetic names, as Boulenger points out, 644n.

20. *Copia,* rhetorical copiousness; how to achieve it was a favorite topic of Renaissance humanists. The best-known handbook, familiar to Rabelais, was Erasmus's *De duplici copia verborum ac rerum.*

tions. All this is in consonance with another literary signal repeated in this part of the Carnival-Lent episode, mockery of the epic style. In the *Iliad* and the *Aeneid* leaders also take counsel and omens before entering battle. Pantagruel is a garrulous revivification of the heros of antiquity, a comic mirror of contemporary humanist ideals. Having concluded his discourse on names, he stirs up his two commanders' courage and gives them "mardi gras" as the password to be used in mounting guard. With the latter term Pantagruel assumes the mantle of Carnival for the coming fight. But why, then, are they fighting the carnivalesque Sausages, and why are the Sausages fighting them?

Rabelais has reached the high point in his dismantling of the traditional roles. After creating a personage carrying the usual name applied to Carnival, whose whole horrid force is devoted to traveling toward Lent, after sketching what seems to be the epitome of carnivalism in the Sausages, here come the Pantagruelians to take over the role of champions of Mardi Gras against the "treacherous" enemy. "You are making fun of me here, boozers! You don't believe that it was all in truth just as I have recounted it. I really don't know what to do about you. Believe it if you wish; if you don't, go see for yourselves. But I know what I saw. It was on Ferocious Island. I give you its name."[21] This marvellous turn of the narrator to what appears to be a set of auditors, not readers, refreshes the frame of oral narration that enters and exits from the Rabelaisian books in erratic counterpoint with the conventions signaling written discourse. The comic insistence of Master Alcofribas on the rule of eyewitness unimpeachability is patterned on the similar affirmations of Lucian in *A True History*. Lucian wrote his book in parody of Hellenistic historiography, in which it had become conventional to parade one's veracious closeness to the facts to be narrated, only to follow such principled beginnings by accounts of famous battles with invented speeches and sententiously fictitious discussions of strategy by the leaders. The habit was revived by fifteenth-century humanist historians like Bruni, Poggio, Giovio, and Polydore Vergil. Alcofribas's interruption, a parody of Lucian and perhaps also of these modern imitators of Lucian's targets, adds emphasis to the mockery of Pantagruel's pursuit of epic propriety.

Oral, apostrophic style—short sentences, direct address, personal af-

---

21. *QL*, 38, 665.

firmations, references to familiar time and place[22]—is maintained through chapter 38. But this fourth delay also introduces another shift in the fictive context. The Sausages are removed from the humble half-animal, half-alimentary contexts that served first to define them and are grotesquely draped in the finery of myth. The giants who piled Ossa on Pelion were half-Sausage in race, "good master Priapus" is nothing but a "transformed Sausage," the serpent tempting Eve was a Sausage, and so on. This mythologizing passage, which offers a noble pedigree to the Sausages, serves as a transition to the fifth and final delay before the battle.[23]

In chapter 39 written narrative style is resumed. Friar John argues, invoking classical and biblical parallels, that he and his cooks should fight the battle. Pantagruel agrees, although he later himself participates in the combat. Friar John addresses his subordinates as young knights about to win their spurs in battle. The *Iliad*'s Trojan horse episode is imitated, except that the cooks hide inside a war machine designed not like a horse but a sow.[24]

The words *Troye* (Troy) and *truie* (sow) are phonetically and graphically close in French, which is comic enough. But there are several other aspects to the joke. Such a war machine was used against the English by King Charles VI in the Hundred Years' War, so Master Alcofribas recalls.[25] Thus at the mock epic level of narrated action, Alcofribas asserts the authenticity of the absurd by historicizing it. Alcofribas also offers technical details that make the Pantagruelians' war engine seem the more real.[26] At the reader's level the reference appeals to

22. See, e.g., *QL*, 38, 665: "Si ces discours ne satisfont à l'incredulité de vos seigneuries, praesentement (j'entends après boyre) visitez Lusignan, Partenay, Yovant, Mervant et Panzauges en Poictou. Là trouverrez tesmoings vieulx de renom."

23. The grammatically ambiguous title to this chapter also helps shift the Sausages from low animal toward high human estate: "Comment Andouilles ne sont à mespriser entre les humains." "Among humans," in the phrase, "that Sausages should not be despised among humans," may be understood either as the human audience whom Alcofribas addresses in this chapter or as the human species to which Sausages, for all their divine and animal affiliations, are considered in this chapter to belong.

24. Marcel Tetel, *Rabelais* (New York, 1967), 71–73, indicates the points of mock heroic style used in this section.

25. The reference is correct, according to Boulenger, *QL*, 40, 668: Froissart recalls the use of such a "sow" in the siege of Bergerac in 1378. The king in question was Charles V, however, not Charles VI.

26. *QL*, 40, 668: "C'estoit un engin mirifique, faict de telle ordonnance que,

French pride in an English defeat during the Hundred Years' War. At the authorial level—that is, from the point of view of the author's representational activity—there is gentle irony about the manner in which the great victory over the English was won, with an iron pig. But the dominant level of signification is neither nationalistic nor mock-epic but popular-cultural. Erasmus notes in the *Adagia* that the phrase "Trojan pig" in "common parlance"—presumably in antiquity—meant a hog stuffed with all manner of living things, "just as the Trojan horse sheltered armed men."[27] Did the idea live on through medieval times? Was it combined in some manner with the Biblical story of Jonah living inside a whale? Whence derives that other spouting creature in Magnus's *Carta Marina,* northeast of the Faroe Islands, which looks for all the world like a seagoing wild boar (see Fig. 4) with two cooks inside its belly, tending a pot over a fire? In the sixteenth century as in antiquity the sow continued to be a symbol of fecundity just as it was a source of succulent nourishment. Rabelais combines ancient and modern popular-cultural meanings of the pig as womb-rich and men-sheltering and gives them a carnivalesque turn: the sow will be stuffed with food stuffers who will fight stuffed Sausages.

The comic idea of conflating juicy pig meat with hard fighting men had already been used in the Carnival-Lent literary genre before Rabelais. In the *Marvellous Conflict Between Carnival and Lent,* a French narrative poem published sometime between 1500 and 1530, Carnival's forces are led by "noble and courageous pigs." Here the idea is simply to symbolize Carnival by means of its most eminent food. In Rabelais's story, where Pantagruel's forces are led by "gay and noble cooks," the symbolic support of Carnival is less a category of food than the body's relation to food.[28] Listing the warriors' names is like declining the forms of a gourmand's fancies.

The names also describe the decline—comically—of these noble

---

des gros couillarts qui par rancs estoient autour, il jectoit bedaines et quarreaux empenéz d'assier."

27. Desiderius Erasmus, *Adagiorum Chilias quatuor,* reprinted in Erasmus, *Opera omnia,* Volume 2 (Leyden, 1703), 1176 (Centur. 10, Prov. 70): "Gulae veteres architecti et hoc commenti sunt, ut bos aut camelus totus apponeretur, differtus intus variis animantium generibus. Hinc et *porcus Trojanus* venit in populi fabulam, cui hoc nomen inditum est, quod ita varias animantium species utero tegeret, quemadmodum *Durius equus* texit armatos viros."

28. Cf. "Merveilleux Conflit," 121, with *QL,* 40, 672.

4. Section A of illustrations, Olaus Magnus, *Carta Marina*. Piglike Sea Monster near Iceland, north of Faroe Islands. Bayer. Staatsbibliothek, Munich.

fellows from the estate of warriors to that of greasy, clumsy kitchen help.[29] There are, for example, Sousecod, Porkfry, Master Dirty, Fatguts, Greasypot, and Swillwine. Then come a plethora of stuffing cooks and sauce cooks whose arts are indicated by their names, and some thirty bacon makers, plus Freepepper, Mustardpot, Greensauce, "and Robert, who invented *sauce Robert.*" In a third category are names full of kitchen humor, incarnating the praise-abuse combination characteristic of that carnivalesque mode of humor in which "all names tend to extremes."[30] So we are introduced to Blowguts and Tasteall, Smuttynose and Widebeak, Shittail and Smartster, Stickyfingers and Begging Bag, Coxcomb and Tittletattle. Rabelais's 161 names zigzag between physiological and psychological attitudes to food. They play with people's relation to nourishment rather than, as in the medieval farces, with food's relation to the ceremonies of Carnival.[31]

This lengthy final delay to the action, while the names are listed, effectively eliminates all reason for the old Carnival-Lent tradition's denouement in battle. The Pantagruelians and their opponents obviously belong to the same side, except from the culinary point of view. And so the words of Gymnaste, Pantagruel's herald, do no good, when he bows to the advancing enemy and loudly proclaims: "We . . . are at your service. We all hold [fiefs] from Mardi Gras, your old ally."[32]

When the fighting does come, it is over in a narrative twinkling,

29. Glauser, *La fonction du nombre,* 147, makes this point. The idea may have been developed by Rabelais from the *basoche* Carnival play to which we have referred, the *Battle of Saint Pansard* (1485), where Charnau's soldiers are Roasting Cook, Pastry Cook, Tripe-Stuffer, Egg-Cook, Butcher, and Scorching Cook (*Deux Jeux de Carnaval,* 16–17). The list of cooks is in *QL,* 40, 668–72.

30. Bakhtin, *Rabelais,* 460–63.

31. There are exceptions in the list, harking back to the medieval farces' personification of foods proper to Carnival: Goatstew, Pancake, Doughnut, Pigsliver. There is also a small group of names referring to physical "deformities": Scarface, Bignose, Hairy Prick, etc. See Lazare Sainéan's rather heterogeneous division of the list into eight categories, *La langue de Rabelais,* Volume 2 (Paris, 1923), 477–83.

32. *QL,* 41, 672–74, recounts the battle. In a feudal context like that depicted here, Gymnaste's words, "Tous *tenons de* mardi gras, vostre antique confaedéré" (italics added), are tantamount to affirming that the Pantagruelians owe homage and fealty to a lord named Mardi Gras. Perhaps Gymnaste asserts that the Sausages owe Mardi Gras homage and fealty also: "Tous" is ambivalent; it might refer to all the Pantagruelians or to Pantagruelians and Sausages. But the word *confaedéré,* ally, was more likely to be used between sovereign equals than between feudal unequals, and the rhetoric of the phrase seems to contrast "[nous] *tenons*" with "*vostre . . . confaedéré.*"

consisting of a mere thirty lines of text. The battle is a pell-mell free-for-all, like the rough-and-tumble fights on mardi gras by youths in rival village or town districts.[33] Pantagruel cracks Sausages over his knees,[34] and Friar John's soldiers jump out of the sow with dripping pans and cooking pots, wreaking havoc. All the Sausages would have died "if God had not intervened, goes the tale."[35]

Out of the north a "great, grand, gross gray pig" came flying. It had wide wings like the arms of a windmill, with crimson pink flamingo feathers. Its eyes were flashing and red, like great carbuncles: its ears were green and its teeth topaz yellow. The tail was long and black, like lustrous marble; the feet were webbed and diamond-transparent. Around its neck was fastened a gold collar inscribed with the words *hus Athenan* written in Greek. This means "a pig teaching Minerva," adds the narrator.[36] The pork bird dropped mustard on the battlefield and flew off screaming "Mardi gras, Mardi gras, Mardi gras!"

The Sausage-queen explains to Pantagruel that the flying pig is the "tutelary deity" of the Sausages in wartime, for it is the "Idea" of "Mardi gras." The word *Idée* is capitalized; it is glossed in the "Brief Clarification" with respect to Rabelais's earlier use of it in the *Fourth Book:* "invisible species and forms, imagined by Plato."[37] Ironic reference to Plato's concept of heaven-dwelling forms, which are the archetypal patterns for low earth-bound existences, is reinforced by the queen's further qualification of this anything but airy and spiritual pig-god as "the first founder and original [pattern] of the whole Sausage race." If this ideal form looks like a pig, that is simply "because Sausages are extracted from pigs."[38]

33. For instance, at Nuremberg or Hof.

34. Bowen, "Lenten Eels," 20–21, documents the phrase "rompre l'anguille" from 1509 onward as a comic proverb describing something impossible. Rabelais in 1552, like Noël du Fail in a work written only three years earlier, transfers the proverb to *andouilles*. Ch. 41, "Comment Pantagruel rompit les Andouilles aux Genoulx," gives prominence to this play with the proverb.

35. Tetel, *Rabelais,* 82, points out that divine intervention again mocks a usual feature of knightly epic.

36. This classical adage is given in Erasmus, *Adagia* 1: 1, 40.

37. Cf. *BD,* 761 (a reference to *QL,* 2, 565). The anonymous "Brief Clarification" is not always a helpful guide to Rabelais's usage, but it has the advantage of being contemporary, reflecting the reactions of a reader in the publishing ambience in which the author moved. It was added to some, not all, copies of the first editions of Rabelais's *Fourth Book.* See also Appendix 3.

38. *QL,* 42, 676: "Elle respondit que c'estoit l'Idee de Mardigras, leur dieu tutéllaire an temps de guerre, premier fondateur et original de toute la race

Friar John's Trojan Pig has been raised on high. The apparition confirms Gymnaste's cry: we like you owe homage to Fat Tuesday, for we are as loyal to the idea of mardi gras as you. But while the Sausages drop their weapons and raise their hands "as if they adored it [the pork bird]," Friar John and his men go on "smiting the Sausages and sticking them on spits" until Pantagruel gives orders to stop.

The pig has a heavy, hard body like Friar John's metal sow. Its limbs and organs of sense are like gems, like some glittering Biblical idol; one notes that the queen of the Sausages has a Hebrew name, Niphleseth, the language of the Chosen People. The pork bird is at once ugly and spectacular, one more comically riveting image in the series of strange visions the Pantagruelians have seen and will see in the *Fourth Book*.[39]

To worship heavenly pig is just what one would expect of the spirit of Carnival. What wisdom does this pig have to teach Minerva? Simply that in Carnival time the stomach instructs the head, the low dominates the high, and earth pretends to be heaven, screaming "Mardi gras!" and flying through the air like some noble Pegasus.[40]

The lighthearted audacity of this parody of misguided piety is astonishing. The mustard the pork bird casts down upon the slain Sausages on the battlefield "resuscitated the dead," for it was a "celestial Balm," indeed a "Sangreal." As Edwin Duval has recently shown, Sangreal seems to be a Rabelaisian invention, suggesting simultaneously Holy Grail (San Greal, more usually Saint Graal) and real blood (*sang réel*): both the holy chalice from which Christ drank symbolically consecrated wine at the Last Supper, founding the mystery celebrated in the Eucha-

---

andouillicque. Pourtant sembloit-il à un pourceau, car Andouilles feurent de pourceau extraictes."

39. Revelation 4:3, in addition to the Old Testament examples, conserves this gemstone concept of divinity with John's vision of Jehovah on his throne: "And he who sat there appeared like jasper and carnelian, and round the throne there was a rainbow that looked like an emerald." Was Rabelais influenced in his imagination of a pork bird deity by the Hebrew studies of which so many proper names in the *Fourth Book* give evidence? On this new importance of Hebrew in the *Fourth Book* see Screech, *Rabelais*, 391–92.

40. Pegasus is to Trojan horse as pork bird is to Trojan hog? Elizabeth Chesney, *The Countervoyage of Rabelais and Ariosto* (Durham, N.C., 1982), 89–90, suggests the Pegasus parallel to the pork bird, though not the rest of the equation. Chesney, 85, concludes more generally that Rabelais "blurs lines of demarcation [that is, the pig and its worshipers the Sausages]." Although she does not question the traditional identification of Quaresmeprenant with Lent (ibid., 82), she does emphasize the monster's internalized ambivalence.

rist, and the transformed wine of that sacrament, the very blood of Christ by which the Christian believer is resuscitated and saved.[41] Very lightly, very obliquely, Rabelais touches one of the most disputed points in early sixteenth-century theology: the doctrine of a saving immaterial grace mysteriously imparted by the "real" material "presence" of sacrificial "blood." Protestant reformers attacked the doctrine as an "idolatrous," "judaic" remnant of pre-Christian sacrificial practices, which ruined true faith.[42] It seems something less than an accident, therefore, that the Sausage-queen with a Hebrew name is the one who explains the "Sangreal" mustard to Pantagruel. The gross and gleaming character of the pork bird idolatrously adored by the Sausages disguises this satire of Catholic doctrine by means of its apparently appropriate excess, its perfect adaptation to the surface theme of Carnivalesque inversion.

The Sausage-people are strange beings. They are religiously hideous. They worship in the pork bird an image that in the classical adage to which the Greek words on its collar refer is one of ignorance and inca-

---

41. Edwin Duval, "La Messe, La Cène, et le Voyage sans Fin du *Quart Livre*," *Etudes rabelaisiennes* 21 (1988): 135–36, establishes the referents to which Rabelais's *sangreal* pertains. There is another earlier allusion to the word which Duval has not noted. In a letter of 1542 (see ch. 5, n. 22), Rabelais refers to the *bons vins* being kept for his friend's coming as *sang gréal*. Here the word is divided into two words and the "g" is double, making the word *gréal* closer to the frequently attested spelling *graal* (grail) and further from Duval's *réel* (and/or *royal,* as Duval also suggests). On the other hand, dividing *sang* from *gréal* places *sang* further from the familiar *sain(c)t* (holy), so often employed by Rabelais. Rabelais is writing in a loose and easy manner here; there can be no question of a serious, surreptitious attack on Eucharistic doctrine. However, he playfully invokes religious language at several points, and he uses literary language and allusions further developed in his novels. Among other things he signs the letter of 1542 with what might pass for an allusion to Alcofribas's profession as Pantagruel's cupbearer ("Vostre humble architriclin, serviteur et ami. François Rabelais, médicin"). I am inclined to think that this is an early articulation of the religio-literary neologism Duval has explicated, a neologism charged with satiric point from its eventual placement in the Sausage chapter. I disagree with Duval's explication only insofar as he makes this verbal play part of a consistent anti-Catholicism and indeed a surreptitious Protestantism, carried on from chapter to chapter and book to book (see Duval, ibid., 141, his conclusion).

42. Contemporary Protestant attacks on the Eucharist and the Catholic liturgy generally as idolatrous and judaizing are reviewed, ibid., 133–35. Erasmus's more cautious criticisms of the same kind are also indicated, an important link to Rabelais, whose ideas resemble those of Erasmus in so many respects.

pacity for learning, an "Idea" simply of great, gross eating.[43] They are like savages; indeed they are very much like those New World savages described by European travelers as a population indigenous to strange and wondrous islands in the north and south Atlantic seas. They are innocents, scampering about like squirrels and martens, "always double and treacherous" because they follow no rules.

Facing such barbarians, Pantagruel and the Pantagruelians do not let their common allegiance to a distant Mardi Gras interfere with their identity as Europeans. Like Cortez in Mexico, like Pizarro in Peru, like Raleigh in Guinea, they offer fair terms of greeting, but, when the natives resist, they annihilate them.[44] After the battle is over, a different political parameter intervenes. Unlike the medieval Carnival-Lent tales in which the feudal princes Lent and Carnival are merely the first and most honored among many powerful princes and vassals, from the sixteenth century onward the political context woven into the genre is monarchist, assuming a radical difference between sovereign and subject. Pantagruel negotiates peace with the queen of the Sausages, who possesses enough authority over her subjects so that she can offer without ado to ship him 78,000 "royal" Sausages each year to "serve" him during the first course of his meals. (Even here the reference to ingestion remains unspoken!) Master Alcofribas takes care to specify other terms of the proffered peace, which include the queen's becoming Pantagruel's vassal for herself, her successors, and all her subjects in the island. But Pantagruel graciously refuses the homage and pardons the

43. See the demonstrations of the "progressive devalorization of the alimentary theme in the *Fourth Book*" in Michel Jeanneret, "Quand la fable se met à table," *Poétique* 54 (1983): 163–80, and Jeanneret, "Alimentation, digestion, réflexion dans Rabelais," *Studi francesi* 27 (1983): 405–16, particularly 409, concerning the pig and its ignorance as connected with eating. Jeanneret is only concerned with the Carnival-Lent episode in passing, but his comments on it are acute and subtle, directing attention to the relevance of traditional Carnival-Lent combats and emphasizing Rabelais's negative presentation of both Quaresmeprenant and the Sausages. Like Alice Berry's "'Les Mithologies Pantagruelicques': Introduction to a Study of Rabelais' *Quart Livre*," *PMLA* 92 (1979): 471–80, Jeanneret emphasizes the generally darkened and negating tone of the *Fourth Book*, as compared to *Gargantua* and *Pantagruel*.

44. I am arguing not that Rabelais consciously satirized the beginnings of European colonialism but only that it existed as part of the general context of the tale. (Other islanders in the *Fourth Book*, almost as savage in behavior and certainly as strange, are not annihilated.) See on this point the collection of innovative studies in *First Images of America: The Impact of the New World on the Old*, ed. Fredi Chiappelli (Berkeley, 1976).

Sausages' aggression. The recent quarrel is expunged by introducing the forms of an idealized monarchic feudalism, in which two sovereigns treat each other as equals and dispose freely of the life and limbs of their followers. Because the two princes in question are idealized and the context is comic, everything turns out for the best. Even the shipped-off Sausages, although they "died" through lack of mustard, were honorably buried at Paris (there is a comic reference to the Rue Pavée d'Andouilles in the Latin Quarter, the modern Rue Séguier).[45] As is suitable in the case of a ritual opposition, where the purpose of confrontation is to mollify differences by expressing them, the very last word of the last chapter of the Carnival-Lent episode refers to the alimentary symbol to which both sides give allegiance, however different the style: "Pantagruel retired to his ship. All his good companions did the same with their arms and their sow."

45. Quotations concerning the events after the battle are found in *QL*, 42, 675–76. Marichal, *Quart Livre*, 181, n. 35, cautions that, in contrast to maps dating from after Rabelais's time, no map of Paris has been found from Rabelais's era or earlier that attests the *rue pavée d'andouilles* as the predecessor of the rue Séguier.

# 5

# Perversity and Patriarchy

Why is the leader of the Sausages a woman? Xenomanes has already reported that all Sausages are women. Strange island indeed! The queen's name is Niphleseth. In the *Brief Clarification of Some Obscure Expressions in the Fourth Book,* the glossary attached to some copies of the 1552 edition of the *Fourth Book,* Niphleseth is explained as "the virile member, Hebrew."[1] In fact the "double," treacherous, half-human, half-animal nature of the Sausages, played upon throughout the episode, is supplemented by their sexual duplicity. Melusine, ancestor of the people of Poitou, explains Alcofribas in his defense of the mythic grandeur of the Sausages, "had a woman's body down to the prickpurse . . . the rest below was serpentine sausage or perhaps Sausage-like serpent." Male-female ambivalence is insured in French by the gender of the words involved; sausage is feminine, and serpent is masculine, so that the phrase *"andouille serpentine ou bien serpent andouillicque"* jumps back and forth over the gender boundary. "The Scythian nymph Ora similarly had a body which was half woman and half sausage. But for all that Jupiter thought her so beautiful that he slept with her and had a handsome boy by her named Colaxes."[2] Food and sex are associated by means of the symbol of the serpent.

Association of *andouille* with the male member was commonplace. Playing the changes between male referent and feminine grammatical gender had of course been exploited before Rabelais, as for example, in the late fifteenth-century *Joyous Sermon of Saint Ham and Saint Tripe-Sausage.* Brother Ham and Sister Sausage were viciously murdered one day, so the bibulous preacher says in this comic monologue. One was salted, the other was hung, and both were put up for sale in the market by the murderers. Among those who decided to buy was a "silly girl, who for her part took Saint Sausage and put her in her lap." Saint

1. *BD,* 765.
2. *QL,* 38, 666.

Sausage of course is "propitious to females," for the "spirit" of this saint enters into the body of devout maidens with great alacrity and stays there, "piteously" returning to the flesh, until one day the girls have a baby.[3]

Women and also children are treated at several points in the Rabelaisian books as metaphorically equivalent to the male member. It is doubtful that Rabelais had anything more specific in mind than comic evocation of the generally accepted patriarchy of his time when he has Gargantua exclaim over the corpse of his wife Badebec, who dies in giving birth to Pantagruel: "Oh Badebec my darling, my friend, my little coney (*petit con*)—though hers was a good three acres and two rods in extent—my tenderling, my codpiece, my shoe, my slipper." The baby Pantagruel is similarly addressed in the same passage as "my little ballock, my potkin, how pretty you are!"[4] Women, like babies, are the decoration and pride of the male body. They are destined to serve male bodily needs through impregnation and child bearing. Pantagruel kindly offers Queen Niphleseth as his parting gift "a pretty little knife of Perche manufacture." Women, even when named for the male member, lack that little something.[5]

This is not very surprising in the male universe of the Pantagruelians, where Panurge's sexy stories and pranks and Friar John's obscene oaths are welcomed with giant laughter. But there seems to be something else involved than comic play with lexical gender for the greater glory of males in the emphasis on the Sausages' femininity at the beginning and end of this second half of the Carnival-Lent episode. (The middle part of this half does not mention the Sausages' femininity: the weasel-like Sausage spies and the fierce Sausage warriors are not treated as Amazons.) If such there is, it is probably not to be found at that psychophysiological level that is exploited in portraying Quaresmeprenant.

3. The text of the *Sermon Joyeux de Saint Jambon et de Sainte Andouille* (1460? published 1520) is edited by Jellie Koopmans, *Quatre Sermons Joyeux* (Geneva, 1984). I have excerpted from and paraphrased lines 178–84 and 197–206.

4. *P*, 3, 203. Another more complex equation of woman with the male member is played with in Rabelais's prologue to the *Fourth Book* where the peasant Ballocker's *coingnée* (*QL*, Pr, 548: literally, hatchet head and synecdochically the whole hatchet, head and handle) is explicated not only as "la femelle bien à poinct et souvent gimbretilletolletée" (*QL*, Pr, 553) but also, at a subtextual level, as Ballocker in erection. See ch. 9 for further comment on this example.

5. *QL*, 42, 675. "Knife," like "serpent," was probably used polysemically here. Knives were offered by Cartier to Canadian Indians. And gifts were usual among feudal sovereigns as a seal to negotiations.

The Sausages tend to jump to false conclusions. It would have been easy and comically effective to have added that such behavior is understandable because the Sausages are nothing but brainless women, thus associating psychology and physiology. But no one ventures the reflection.

The rationale behind the Sausages' femininity can be found in a different direction, when one considers the peculiar sexuality of Quaresmeprenant in connection with theirs. Only two references to his sexual behavior appear to the modern reader. When Quaresmeprenant daydreams, it is phalluses "flying and creeping along a wall." When he copulated with Midlent, he begot "only double fasts and locative adverbs"; whether this hints that he was at least fertile in piety or more darkly suggests that he was entirely sterile, Quaresmeprenant's reproductive activity can certainly be said to have produced strange effects. Several other sexual references were perhaps clear to Rabelais's contemporaries, or at least to doctors among them. According to Guy Demerson, the qualification of the monster as "fuzzy-haired and doubly-tonsured" indicates that his head and body hair had fallen out due to syphilis. Again, Quaresmeprenant's arsehole is "like a crystal mirror."[6] Anatole Le Double states that physicians in Rabelais's time gave the name "crystalline" to "anal syphilis" or "Ganymede's syphilis."[7] This trait would specify the monster as both syphilitic and homosexual. One recalls Pantagruel's furious denunciation of Anti-Nature's children as catamites or homosexuals.[8] However literally Rabelais meant his descriptions to be taken, his indications of Quaresmeprenant's sexual behavior categorize

6. The references to Quaresmeprenant's characteristics are in *QL*, 32, 649; 30, 645; 29, 642; and 31, 646. See Rabelais, *Ouevres complètes,* ed. Guy Demerson (Paris, 1973), 661, n. 8.

7. Doctor Le Double's *Rabelais anatomiste et physiologiste* is one of the strangest in the long history of Rabelaisian criticism. In the course of three hundred pages he painstakingly shows by means of words and superbly drawn designs how, with respect to the first fifty-nine internal anatomical parts and their analogies in *QL*, 30, the shapes of the ordinary things that Rabelais mentions correspond to the organs in question. The demonstrations require immense technical and antiquarian knowledge and are not always convincing. In the context of his often recondite associations, it is comical to read on 411 that Le Double decided against undertaking similar demonstrations for Quaresmeprenant's external anatomy because Rabelais's analogies seemed to him in this case so farfetched ("si risquées"). The information about Ganymede's syphilis is given on 412, n. 5, where Le Double cites a medical work published in 1612.

8. *QL*, 32, 651. French *chattemite* is derived from Latin *Catamitus,* which in turn is a corrupt form of *Ganymedes*.

it as obsessively phallocentric. In light of these details the reference in Xenomanes's first description to the monster's "Lanternland origin" probably symbolizes not merely his distraction of mind but also his sexual self-involvement, a trait that perverts the contemporary procreative ideals of patriarchy.[9]

Phallocentrism was typical of that century of codpieces; Rabelais's *Third Book* might be read as a psychoanalytic study before the letter of how phallocentric self-absorption—in this instance Panurge's—prevents commitment to marriage and marital reproduction. Does Rabelais mean to suggest that the Sausages' faithless impetuosity, their whimsical worship of themselves in the form of a jewel-like pig, is a corresponding female deformation, making procreatively stable marriage with them equally impossible?[10] In that case Rabelais points to the rule and the exception at once when he notes that the 78,000 females shipped off as hostages to his father Gargantua "died" without issue at Paris except for the queen's daughter, the "young Niphleseth," who was given in marriage to a man of wealth and worth, whereupon "she made several handsome children, for which may God be praised."[11]

The sexual level of symbolism is as appropriate to the festive context as are those levels that construct Quaresmeprenant as a terrifying puppet and the Sausage-people as comic fighters. People dealt with the ban on sexual activity during Lent by accenting it during Carnival.[12] At the level of character and incident, of course, the Sausages' femininity

9. See the account of Quaresmeprenant's first description in ch. 3.

10. Françoise Charpentier, "La Guerre des Andouilles, Pantagruel, IV, 35–42," in *Etudes seizièmistes offerts à V. L. Saulnier* (Geneva, 1980), 133–35, emphasizes the "double" sexual nature of the Andouilles-Serpens and concludes that their "matriarchy" represents a "bisexualité . . . close et stérile," in which reproduction is carried on without males, so that this kingdom represents a threat to male supremacy. But Rabelais's representation of the Sausages and especially of their queen hardly seems menacing. Moreover reproduction without the intervention of males is given positive meaning in Pantagruel's discourse on Nature and Anti-Nature: "Physis (c'est Nature) en sa première portée enfanta Beauté et Harmonie sans copulation charnelle, comme de soy-mesmes est grandement féconde et fertile" (*QL*, 32, 650). Anti-Nature copulates in the usual heterosexual way and produces disharmony.

11. *QL*, 42, 676.

12. Hans Folz's *Ein Spil* (ca. 1480–1490), for example, which claims to survey Carnival behavior among the different classes of people at Nuremberg, emphasizes licentious sexuality among all ranks. See Kinser, "Presentation," 10–13.

needs no such procreative rationale. Rabelais probably borrowed the idea of making the Sausages uniformly feminine from his farcical source, *The Disciple of Pantagruel*. There, although neither the sex of the furry "fierce people" (*Farouches*) is mentioned nor is that of the nose-biting sausages whom Panurge and his friends encounter next, the inhabitants of Lanternland are identified as female:

> We pushed on night and day until we arrived in Lanternland, the country . . . which Lucian mentions in his book of true histories. It was mid-May, the day when their queen gave a grand festival in honor of her birthday . . . for on that day all the lanterns of the world were assembled, rather like the Franciscans in their chapter-general, to treat of their business and affairs. . . . They [elles] all came in procession . . . two by two, singing so melodiously that one could not imagine hearing sweeter harmony.

The voyagers are invited to the queen's banquet. There they see the "noble" lanterns and queen dressed in fine clear ivory, while lanterns of less rank wear robes made of pork and beef bladders. Some are clothed in fabrics made from intestines, but still others appear in dresses made from ordinary cloth. The anonymous author makes no explicit comment on the lanterns' femininity (*la lanterne* is feminine in gender), but the details emphasize the traditional feminine perquisites of grace and beauty, a beauty by turns noble and grotesque, bizarre and ordinary.[13]

This passage was probably also the inspiration for Rabelais's use of "lanterning" in the nonsexual sense mentioned earlier. The Council of Trent will be a great and useless meeting of well-robed luminaries, similar to the Chapters General of Rabelais's former monastic order, the Franciscans. It will be very beautiful and very empty, glowing without substance, like women do from the patriarchal point of view.[14]

Textual and intertextual studies clarify the puzzles proposed by Rabelais's text. They also augment them. One sees more clearly, for example, the rhetorical contrast between the groups of chapters devoted to the two kinds of islanders. In the Quaresmeprenant section every new element adds from a different point of view to what is already suspected about the monster's ominous character. The meaning of the

13. *Disciple*, 29–33.
14. See the first description of Quaresmeprenant, as analyzed in ch. 3. The references to Lanternland in *CL*, 34–42, 878–99, with their emphasis on stonily glowing luminosity, owe much to this passage in the *Disciple* also (see esp. 30–31).

figure seems, through extensive enumeration, to approach full definition. In the Sausage section, however, each new perspective disrupts
the previous attempt to see, understand, and define. Are they animals
or human? men or women? food or warriors? friendly or fierce? In the
end this dissemination of meaning seems to be reversed by the philosophic conversation between Pantagruel and Niphleseth. The Sausages
are after all sausages, who through mustard and mardi gras achieve the
ends for which they have been created. The growing concentration of
meaning around the figure of Quaresmeprenant, however, does not
lead to any revelation. The last detail about him in the text is in consonance with his half-mad perverted sexual character, but it does not
wind up matters.

The Sausage-queen tells Pantagruel during their peace negotiations
that her spies have reported that Quaresmeprenant has landed on a
beach of Ferocious Island, not to make war, but to inspect the urine of
physeters.[15] Once more Quaresmeprenant is shown moving toward
Lent by associating with Lent's traditional allies, the fishy creatures of
the sea. But at the same time this report reinforces our sense of how
silly the Sausages are, for the inspection on land of the excretory prod-
ucts of seagoing whales hardly seems likely. Is Quaresmeprenant looking perhaps at the dead physeter that Pantagruel's men pulled up on a
beach of Ferocious Island? If he is doing something the Sausages suppose is the inspection of urine—playing the doctor of whom he is frequently in need—is he not looking at the Leviathan's sexual parts? Perhaps, or perhaps not. Even Pantagruel's identification of the monster as
one of Anti-Nature's children only renders him more powerfully enigmatic.

Rabelais's rhetorical strategy is to lead the reader to distinguish between the manner and the matter of his discourse. When he says something relatively simple, as with the Sausages, his manner is rhetorically
elaborate, delaying definition or offering ambiguous, incomplete perceptions. When he has something complex to communicate, he writes
with seeming sharpness, accumulating exact details. Matter and manner
conflict, or at any rate they seem to flow in opposite directions. Can
the reasons for the choice of such paradoxical rhetoric be found within
the text, or between the text and its textual sources and parallels? Yes,
at least some reasons can be found textually and intertextually by iden-

15. *QL*, 42, 675.

tifying the particular narrative modes used in the two halves of the episode.

In the case of Quaresmeprenant Rabelais considers the differences between Carnival and Lent as a kind of dialectic opposition. He examines this dialectic imaginatively, that is, in terms of concrete images and fictive representations, rather than philosophically, abstractly, or pragmatically as, for example, a rationalization of these occasions' rituals or as a set of suggestions about these occasions' proper celebration. Yet here as throughout the novels he inserts contemporary references into the fictive frame. The text is not didactic, but this does not mean that it does not judge and condemn and hence by implication—but only by implication—also admire and advocate.

The second half of the episode is not a dialectic exploration, imaginatively or otherwise. It is more simply and lightheartedly an arabesque on Carnival behavior. Its confusions and ambivalences conjoin rather than conflict as they did in the Quaresmeprenant section. One means of maintaining this harmonious rather than conflictual development of the latter part of the narrative, in spite of all its surprises and digressions, is clear maintenance of the Pantagruelians' human status vis-à-vis these islanders who are in turn furry animals, fishy serpents, brave warriors, and a one-sexed polity. By bringing the Pantagruelians into close and Carnival-prescribed contact with the Sausages, the latter are constantly being pulled back, in spite of all their changes, to what they epidermoidally are, food for men.

This basic reference to sausage food is why the symbols in the second half of the episode converge rather than grow in disharmony. Friar John's cooks employ not a Trojan horse but a sow in their struggles; the Sausages are saved by a motherly flying pig who casts down celestial balm. A big pig's "intestines" (the hidden cooks) fight against little pig tripe, and the pig tripe in turn is saved by heavenly pig essence. Just as was the case with the huge, composite body of Quaresmeprenant, the meaning of the Pantagruelians' visit to Ferocious Island is finally summed up in a sensuously concrete image, a gleaming transformation of Carnival food.

The difference between the two personifications around which Rabelais builds this narrative is thus maintained. Quaresmeprenant is the humanization, monstrous though it be, of an abstraction of a ritual occasion or rather transition between two rituals conventional among men. Sausages are humanizations, silly though they be, of something eminently concrete and essential to men, food. Aside from their formal status as parallel personifications, their similarity is only negative. They define something from which, in different ways and for different reasons, human beings—here the Pantagruelians—must differentiate themselves.

Carnival food, or more grandly, the place of food in human existence, its role in the body, psyche, and behavior, is the intellectual thread binding the two halves of the episode together. By the time the Pantagruelians arrive at Ferocious Island two narrative dynamics have been set in motion: on one hand the puzzles engendered by amalgamating, while not mixing, characteristics of Carnival and Lent in a single monstrous being; on the other the larger problem of relating Lenten rules and Carnival pleasures to human desires and human needs that flow right across the ritual boundary between Carnival and Lent and indeed expand through the whole year and through people's whole existence. How indeed should or can people deal with delicious, delectable, desirable, devourable food? At Carnival time men become so voracious that they may confuse themselves with the principle of eating. They may become very nearly like the Sausage-people, worshiping food as a deity, so that they too come to seem like nothing more than an intestinal integument, a skin stretched tight by stuffing.

The Pantagruelians begin their Carnival battle in this voracious manner: "But for God's special intervention the whole race of Sausages would have been exterminated by our soldiers"—exterminated, all chopped up, eaten or prepared for eating by the noble cooks.[16] But then they stop. The pork bird appears, the Sausages throw down their arms, and Pantagruel orders a halt to the piggish butchery by his men.

Is this intervention and halt just knightly grace, an inconsequential narrative incident, or is Rabelais suggesting that at least Pantagruel has a sense of proper restraint vis-à-vis food, even in Carnival? How are the Pantagruelians different from the Gastrolators, "worshipers of the belly," who are denounced by Pantagruel and by the narrator at the end of the *Fourth Book* for their savory sacrifices to their god Gaster? The long list of dainties that the Gastrolators shovel into Gaster's gullet would grace the best Pantagruelian table. But Gaster represents the principle of stomachic necessity, not alimentary enjoyment. The Gastrolators do him honor in the wrong way. Like the Sausages' reverence

16. *QL*, 41, 673.

for their gemlike pork bird, the followers of Gaster worship a part of nature as if it were divine: "Gaster confessed himself no god, but a poor, vile, pitiful creature." The Gastrolators, raising this creature on high, distort the significance of the lord of the belly in order to serve their own proclivity, which is—quite in contrast to Gaster's frenetic inventiveness—to do nothing. The Gastrolators fabricate a Carnival puppet whose mouth clacks open and shut, as if ever seeking food. They carry this image of a terrifying eater in triumphal parade in the mistaken idea that it represents the essence of Gaster.[17]

The parallel between the distorted worship of the Gastrolators and the idolatry of the Sausages for their pork bird sets off the Pantagruelians from both.[18] Pantagruelians eat pigs but do not worship them. Pantagruelians tipple and talk; they do not shovel dainty foods and fine wines into some ideational maw. Queen Niphleseth calls the pork bird a divine idea, but the narrator calls it a monster.[19] It seems that there is a proper limit to eating, and especially to preoccupation with eating, even in Carnival.

Within the terms of the Carnival-Lent episode the story of the pork bird sets this limit in one direction and the story of Nature and Anti-Nature sets it in another. Like the Gastrolators' puppet, the pork bird is a misrepresentation of the natural impulse to eat well and joyfully, just as Anti-Nature is a misrepresentation of the natural harmony and measure exhibited in conduct guided by "common sense and good judgment." Lack of the latter qualities, characteristic of the children of Anti-Nature according to Pantagruel, means that a creature like Quaresmeprenant is at odds with the way the natural universe is constructed. This monster with his voraciously meat-filled dreaming forever moves toward Lent because of his lack of natural sense—which

17. *QL,* 60, 729, and *QL,* 59, 722: this is the puppet the narrator compares to Chewcrust in the Lyon Carnival parade. Rabelais's unspoken equation of excessive eating with Carnival behavior is carried further by presenting the Gastrolators as maskers: "Rien ne faisans, poinct ne travaillans . . . craignans . . . le ventre offenser et emmaigrir. Au reste, masquez, desguiséz et vestuz tant estrangement que c'estoit belle chose. . . . Je vous asceure qu'en la vesture de ces Gastrolatres coquillons ne veismes moins de diversité et desguisement." *QL,* 58, 720–21.

18. The parallel sets off the Pantagruelians, but perhaps not the Pantagruelians' cooks or Friar John: I read into the text here when I assign this attribute to all Pantagruelians.

19. *QL,* 42, 676.

makes Pantagruel, Rabelais's personification of large girthed wisdom, so angry that he loses his temper.

Pantagruel's angry ill humor seems to violate Pantagruelism, explained in the Prologue to the *Fourth Book* as "a certain gaiety of spirit, pickled in scorn of everyday vicissitudes."[20] The Pantagruelians usually follow this rule, moving from one island to another in the *Fourth Book* not to judge and denounce, not to defeat the movement toward Lent or the distortion of Carnival, but to represent a mode of living. They depict not an alternative morality but another morale, another way of living that is embodied in their conversational camaraderie, bubbling talk, and bibulous eating. The prologue's gaily ambivalent greeting expresses the same embodied, active wisdom: *"Bien et beau s'en va Quaresme,"* how pleasantly Lent is passing by—and passing away!

Lent is accepted as a human convention, however unnatural—and indeed however unsupernatural—it may have seemed to Rabelais. Neither Carnival nor Lent, one realizes in retrospect, is attacked as such in the long episode that denounces their false idolators. But this does not mean that they are both affirmed. In the gayest and most Pantagrueline of his extant letters, Rabelais invites a friend to visit him during Lent of 1542: "You will arrive, of course, not when it pleases you to do so but when you are brought here by the will of the great, good, and merciful God who never created Lent." God did not create Lent, though he did create Lenten fare:

> salads, herrings, cod, carp, pike, dace, . . . stickle-back, etc.; also good wines, and especially the one . . . which we are saving here for your coming like a *sang gréal* [holy grail? royal/real blood?][21] and like a second, no, a quintessence. *Ergo veni Domine et noli tardare* [so come, sir, and don't delay].[22]

Both Lent and Carnival have their pleasures. Mardi gras, instead of standing as a regrettable boundary between them, is from this perspec-

20. *QL,* 545. Pantagruelism is discussed at length in ch. 8.

21. See ch. 4, n. 41.

22. "Or vous le ferez, non quand il vous playra, mais quand le vouloir vous y apportera de celluy grand bon piteux Dieu, lequel ne créa oncques le quaresme, ouy bien les sallades, arans, merluz, carpes, bechetz, dars, umbrines, ablettes, rippes, etc.; item les bons vins, singulièrement celui *de veteri jure enucleando,* lequel on guarde icy à vostre venue comme un sang gréal et une seconde, voyre quinte essence. *Ergo veni, Domine, et noli tardare"* (L, 1007). Note that Rabelais does not suggest defying the rule of no meat in Lent: vegetables and fishes are all the fare.

tive their common preserver. Indeed that is the role of noble Mardi Gras in Rabelais's tale. This lord never appears to fight for or against any combatants. How could Mardi Gras actively injure his namesake, Quaresmeprenant, or abandon those who take his idea as their god, however treacherous they may be? Mardi Gras stands symbolically outside the conflict because he stands temporally between its two poles. For him to exist, both poles, both kinds of ritual allegiance, must endure. Mardi Gras is there, like the Pantagruelians, to give distance and perspective to this human comedy. The Pantagruelians are Mardi Gras's vassals; they are not neutral in the fray, for only mardi gras's comedy, not Ash Wednesday's gravity, creates a space within which both Lent's and Carnival's pretensions can be satirized by placing on parade—as in Hoghenberg's print—the two sides' followers with their different kinds of silliness.

The interpretation of the Carnival-Lent episode suggested here affirms its festive frame, its popular-cultural representation of sociability, and its comic ideology. These things do not necessarily go together. Eminent Rabelaisian scholars dealing with this extraordinarily commented and interpreted group of chapters have affirmed or denied one, two, and all three of them. If, however, ideology, style, and form all do go together, then the reader must set to one side both commentaries that end by deriving high humanist truths from the episode and those that see it as linguistically self-enclosed and metaphysically somber. In spite of the garish and gruesome visions they include, these chapters are gaily written and antimetaphysical in tenor.

Carnival's rituals articulate the episode. The whole of this "performance" takes place on mardi gras, insofar as it may be supposed to be a burlesque translation of contemporary parades and games. Carnivalesque attitudes provide the basis of representation of most characters and activities in the episode. But Carnival is not affirmed morally. Quaresmeprenant's psychic excess is a horror while that of the Sausages is just silly, but both lead to catastrophe: the merry Sausages are always being caught by their old enemy, while Quaresmeprenant finds himself weeping ducks in onion sauce. Rabelais draws attention to the inversive logic binding each to each. Thus, although he transforms nearly every element of the old combat theme, he nevertheless preserves the schema. And although he derives the qualities of representation almost entirely from the Carnival, secular side and scarcely at all from Lenten, churchly views, the comic ideology supporting the representation affably accepts both kinds of institution, even with their common tendency to encourage excess. Both institutions are necessary to provide the dynamics driving either of them. The dynamics are not innately evil; they become so only when linked to a psychology of excess that has other foundations.

No study of the purely textual and intertextual aspects of Carnival-Lent relations is likely to discover this way of generating the episode. Literary scholars have for three centuries been more willing to twist verbal meanings to provide a semantically smooth text than to look beyond it for keys to its paradoxes. It is the changing behavioral context of Carnival *and* Lenten observance which allows understanding of its puzzling representations, and not anything discoverable on the printed page alone. Rabelais's pages pose themselves as part of that behavior, interacting with them as well as reflecting upon them. The Rabelaisian text is both centripetal in its energies, creating its own intratextual spirals, and centrifugal, reaching outward with a smile and sometimes with an oath.[23]

The passage listing the names of Friar John's cook soldiers is introduced by Pantagruel's disquisition about the accuracy of names in relation to things. It is a long parody of Plato's search in the *Cratylus* for a way in which to assure that words indicate the things they designate. "See the *Cratylus* of the divine Plato," recommends Pantagruel, when his men are discussing their chances of victory against the Sausages. "You'll see [in such books] how the Pythagoreans conclude from their names and numbers that Patroclus ought to have been slain by Hector, Hector by Achilles, Achilles by Paris, and Paris by Philoctetes. My mind is set in an utter whirl when I think of Pythagoras' amazing discov-

23. Shifts in the representation of Carnival in the sixteenth century were the main subject of the latter part of ch. 2 above. Rabelais's representations were intertwined with these changing representations, and both of them were in turn affected by nonfestive social and cultural conditions. The idea of three-cornered, reciprocal influence between social trends, cultural traditions, and specific texts (or other specific artifacts of art, science, or philosophy) is, I take it, at least one part of what is coming to be called the "new historicism" in literary studies. Contrary to the expressed fears of some, it has nothing to do with a rejection of textual and intertextual, let alone of semiotic and structural approaches to literature. See further comment on historicism in n. 4, Afterword.

ery."[24] The names of Friar John's cooks are all cratylic in this sense, truly designating what they do. Yet the episode as a whole enjoins the opposite lesson: the Sausages behave as if they were human . . . or animal . . . or eels . . . or women, and Quaresmeprenant, "Carnival," behaves like Lent. Language exceeds and rebels against the uses to which humans would put it: the writer's materials are chaotic. Rabelais's parody of the Carnival-Lent genre is simultaneously a parody of Pantagruel's cratylism, of the fashionable Platonism of contemporary humanists, and of the intellectualism which supposes that labeling processes could exhaustively exhibit the real.[25]

Instead of allegorizing human behavior, as medieval authors had done, Rabelais humanizes allegory. Did the gradual loss of transcendental surety, that system of cosmic correspondences between supernatural, human, and subhuman spheres, require this shift? Whether or not that is so, it is certain that among fifteenth- and sixteenth-century writers, the more they substituted concrete psychological and social description for allegorical typology, the more they sought to compensate for the consequent loss of religious authority with semireligious or frankly secular moralism.

A text communicates in a number of ways simultaneously. At the semantic level medieval texts tended to order their meanings like layers

24. *QL*, 37, 662. The examples Pantagruel mentions here are taken not from the *Cratylus* but from Cornelius Agrippa's *De vanitate scientiarum*, whose title might be paraphrased as "On the emptiness of knowledge-systems," a hilariously undermining fact in itself for anyone who recognized Rabelais's source.

25. Rabelais's concern with cratylism has been explored by Screech, *Rabelais*, 377–97; by François Rigolot, "Cratylisme et pantagruelisme: Rabelais et le statut du signe," *Etudes rabelaisiennes* 13 (1976): 115–32; and very briefly but with equal perceptiveness by Guy Demerson in "Les calembours de Rabelais," in *Le comique verbal en France au seizième siècle*, ed. Halina Lewicka (Warsaw, 1981), 88–90.

The same can be said for neither Vernon L. Saulnier's reflections on this cratylic interlude nor indeed for the other parts of his long disquisition on the Carnival-Lent episode in *Rabelais dans son enquête: étude sur le Quart et le Cinquième Livre* (Paris, 1982), 87–100. Saulnier treats Quaresmeprenant, the Physeter, and the Sausages in separate chapters of his book, devoting most space to the Sausages. By means of a remarkable series of circularly allegorical arguments, he concludes that the name of the Sausages, *andouilles*, is probably intended to evoke the Greek verb *endoiadzein*, to doubt, because this meaning of *andouilles* best unifies the politico-religious themes of German-Swiss war and Lantern "discipline" with Pantagruel's discourse about the cratylic character of proper names.

in a cake, each separated from the others—literal, moral, allegorical, eschatological, anagogical—all covered and made coherent by the frosting of theological postulates. In early modern times texts began to develop semantically as a set of perspectives, some consistent and others inconsistent with each other. None of these perspectives represents Truth, and, because they might be infinitely multiplied, defining truth as their totality would seem irrelevant. The perspectives these new fictions offer seem designed less to add up than to filter out dogma.[26] Alcofribas undermines the integrity of the plot with his parodic pose of reliable eyewitness authority, Pantagruel undermines his exemplary status with his credulity, his lanternism, and his humanist pedantry, and Rabelais, the author—can we trust him? Just as far as we are willing to believe the make-believe in the prologue, the *bonhomie* that greets readers as if they had just stepped in for a glass of wine during the current Lenten season.

The special advantage of festive, popular, comic modes of discourse and performance is that they thrive upon differences. Differences, not uniformity, provision the human comedy. Joining his writing to these modes, Rabelais multiplies perspectives. The truths this writer has to offer can only be seized obliquely and never quite clearly: they have more than one meaning. They are human truths, not divine, and so they shift their meaning with the human context—as Carnival revelers do, with their masks.

26. This generalization has been explored by a number of scholars in recent years, most interestingly with respect to Rabelais by François Rigolot in the conclusion to his *Les langages de Rabelais* (Geneva, 1972), 173–75, as well as in his *Le texte de la Renaissance,* and by Terence Cave, *The Cornucopian Text: Problems of Writing in the French Renaissance* (Oxford, 1979). Rigolot, *Langages,* 175, points out that this problematic was sketched in different form long ago by Jean Plattard in the introduction to his *L'oeuvre de Rabelais* (Paris, 1910) as a conflict between "artistic form" and "thought." Rigolot calls it "une perspective à la fois agonistique et encomiastique." I am suggesting here more numerous and more radical dissonances in Rabelais's text than these dichotomies define. Some of the most striking analyses of the Renaissance text as a set of dissonant, mutually filtering perspectives have been carried out with respect to Spanish works of fiction such as the anonymous *Lazarillo de Tormes,* Fernando de Rojas's *La Celestina,* and of course Cervantes's *Don Quixote.*

# THREE

# NORMALIZATION

By multiplying perspectives Rabelais suggested the seesawing psychology and tendency to excess that was nearly inseparable from Carnival-Lent customs. Did his rather intricate way of explaining the consequences of such customs, as European life assumed more secular, individualistic forms, help bring about the failure to understand the episode from the later seventeenth century onward? Exactly when and how did the misconceptions arise? What allowed them to flourish? We can answer these questions by pursuing the history of Rabelais's reputation and readership.

Rabelais died in 1553. Religious wars and the Reformation and Counter-Reformation ideologies feeding those wars rent France and Europe for the next hundred years. One might think that encompassing laughter of the kind urged by Rabelais would have become difficult. Yet during the first two generations after Rabelais's death (1553–1610) his novels were published and republished forty times in small formats that would seem to have encouraged reading by many more and varied audiences than elite and wealthy bibliophiles. Then quite suddenly the editions nearly ceased. Between 1610 and 1660 Rabelais was reprinted only twice (1613, 1626). During the following half-century, ending in 1710, his works appeared seven times.[1]

The 1613 and 1626 editions were probably published in France, but they gave either a false address or no address on their title page. Six or

---

1. The *NRB* ends with the edition of Rabelais's works in 1626. Pierre-Paul Plan, *Les éditions de Rabelais de 1532 à 1711* (Paris, 1904) ends in 1711. Jacques Boulenger (and Lucien Scheler, who in reediting the Pléiade edition in 1955 made some additions) extends the bibliography of all Rabelaisian printings to 1953. Although defective in details, the general proportions of the Pléiade bibliography—that is, the relative number of printings from one century to the next—are probably correct. They match those of the more exact *NRB* and Plan for the earlier period. Until the nineteenth century, printings of books like Rabelais's generally consisted of one thousand to fifteen hundred copies; exact statistics are impossible to obtain. See Pl. Bib., 1019–23, nos. 67–106, 107–9, and 111–18 respectively for the three groups of years mentioned in the text here.

perhaps all seven of the later seventeenth-century printings were published outside France. In the first half of the eighteenth century a new, fully annotated edition was prepared by the Protestant Jacob Le Duchat. First published at Amsterdam in 1711, it was reprinted four times between that date and 1732 and revised in a second edition published in 1741. Another Amsterdam edition, first published by the Elzevier firm in 1663, was reprinted four times at Brussels between 1709 and 1758. Two Catholic editors, Abbé Pérau and Abbé de Marsy, published differently expurgated editions in 1752. Thus between 1711 and 1752 twelve reprintings of the novels occurred.

What happened during that century and a half, first to diminish and then to revive interest in Rabelais?[2] The eclipse of publishers' willingness to print his works in France, at least openly, came after the Lyon editions of 1608, which appeared just before King Henry IV's assassination in 1610. During the regency of Marie de Médicis and the subsequent ministry of Cardinal Richelieu the government assumed a more publicly Catholic stance. From the point of view of Catholic reconciliation as well as of *bienséance,* Rabelais's texts were not suitable. Rabelais had been classified since 1564 in the Index of Prohibited Books endorsed by the Council of Trent as an author in the "first class," whose works were to be prohibited without exception and without hope of expurgation.[3]

Perhaps this very prohibition was responsible for Rabelais's posthumous fortune during the period of the sanguinary Religious Wars in France (1562–1596). The period was one of political no less than religious disunity. After the accidental death of Henry II in 1559 France was ruled by the queen mother of Henry's small sons, Catherine de Médicis. Great nobles seized the chance to resist the crown and frequently used religious revolt to that end, aiding the growth of Calvinism. What a revelation it therefore is to discover that all but five editions of Rabelais published in the half-century after his death can be shown to have been altered in their wording in such a way as to serve Protestantism!

The assertion is easy to prove. It is based on the superb new bibli-

2. See Pl. Bib., 1023–24, for the seventeenth- and eighteenth-century listings mentioned in the preceding paragraph. This survey is admittedly incomplete because it considers only Rabelais's works in French. By the end of the sixteenth century Rabelais had entered English and German literature. His polemic appeal to anti-Catholic audiences functioned there as well as in French-speaking areas.

3. Marcel de Grève, *L'interprétation de Rabelais,* 190, quotes the Index.

ography of Rabelaisian editions published in 1987 by Stephen Rawles and Michael Screech. To distinguish the often undated, anonymously published editions Rawles and Screech chose a limited number of passages that they discovered through comparison to vary frequently. One of these was the passage in the Quaresmeprenant-Sausage episode denouncing Calvin. In thirty of the thirty-five editions of the *Fourth Book* published between 1553 and 1610 this passage has been altered.[4] Of the five editions that did faithfully reproduce Rabelais's words here, four were published in the 1550s before Henry II's death.[5]

Rabelais's words concerning this particular species of Anti-Nature's children were: *Demoniacles Calvins, imposteurs de Geneve,* that is, "demoniacal Calvins, Genevan imposters." Rabelais's reference to his Catholic detractor immediately follows: *les enraigéz Putherbes,* "the crazy Putherbes," that is, Putherbius, the Latin form of DuPuyherbault's name. In five of the thirty editions the unknown editors contented themselves with simply dropping the reference to Calvin and Geneva, so that redoubled thunder fell upon the monk Gabriel DuPuyherbault: "the demoniacal, crazy Putherbes." But because these editions included no footnotes and the relation of the monk's Latin name and writings to Rabelais had perhaps faded by the 1560s, this slander was probably inconsequential, however injust.[6] The other variant of this passage, found in twenty-four editions of Rabelais published between 1564 and 1608, points Pantagruel's wrath unerringly at the wicked Catholics: "the demoniacal writ-servers," it reads, "rakers-in of benefices" (*les demoniacles Chicanous, aracleurs de benefices*).[7]

Calvinists like Lutherans made devastating use of the word against

4. Five of the forty editions published between 1553 and 1610 were of the *Fifth Book* only and hence did not include the passage in question. See *NRB,* nos. 53–57.

5. See *NRB,* no. 58 (1553); nos. 59, 60 (1556); no. 61 (1559). The fifth accurate edition was published in 1579 at "Antwerp" (*NRB,* no. 70: the printer's name on the title page is false; the place of printing is probably false, too).

6. *NRB,* nos. 52, 79, 88, 89, 90 (the wording varies slightly in nos. 52 and 79). E. Droz, "Frère Gabriel DuPuyherbault," esp. 418–19, has shown that, whatever DuPuyherbault's hatred of Rabelais's religious views and mores, he was by no means crazy but was rather a sincere and tireless proponent of Catholic monastic reforms. DuPuyherbault died in 1566.

7. *NRB,* nos. 62–69, 71–78, 80–87, 91 (nos. 75 and 77 are lost editions whose contents the editors reconstitute with plausibility). *Chicanous* is derived from *chicaner,* to serve with writs of justice; from its use by Rabelais in ch. 12 of the *Fourth Book* (*QL,* 12, 593), it is obvious that he considered writ-servers to be notorious for chicanery. *Aracleurs,* "rakers-in," comes from *racler,* "to rake." In

their Catholic opponents in the sixteenth century, not only the holy word of the Gospel but also the satiric words of controversial literature. However ill-received Rabelais was in Geneva, he was obviously welcomed among French-speaking Protestant zealots elsewhere and by printers and booksellers exploiting this public.[8] If Rabelais continued to be popular after his death, it was because he was of service in the acid atmosphere of the Religious Wars. His mirthful ambivalence can be and obviously was interpreted in two ways, especially during this early period, as humanist hatred of bigotry by moderate Catholics and as anti-Catholic satire by moderate Protestants. Except for the most devout or self-interested leaders of the two religious factions, most Frenchmen probably were moderates, at least most of the time, and sought only release from the bloodshed. Rabelais's raillery provided at least mental release.

Over the long term, however, the unannounced emendations of editors and the confessional ambience in which the texts were sold and read boded ill. Rabelais's low humor and high irony came to seem less evenhanded and less intricately Christian than they were. The second part of this study concluded with a generalization from the particular case of Rabelais's strategies in the Quaresmeprenant-Sausage episode: making the text strange meant to multiply perspectives in such a way that readers are obliged to filter their reactions to what they read. But most readers do not filter their reactions, whatever the stimulus to do so. Preoccupied with their own purposes—with their context more than the text's—most readers simply turn the pages to get the story.

At the surface of the text readers interested in the story without bringing to it any special confessional prejudice would be led by the later sixteenth-century adulterated editions to regard the story as anti-Catholic or, worse still, as godless. The meaning of Rabelais's text was normalized in the seventeenth century not as carnivalesque ebullience, let alone as multidimensional morality, but as irreligious excess.

---

some of these altered editions "benefices" is spelled "venefices," perhaps to suggest (as Protestants would) that the Catholic mode of acquiring and transferring ecclesiastical offices (benefices) was venomous.

8. *NRB*, 298, for example, speaks of a "Lyons/Geneva axis" to account for the large number of Protestant-oriented publications emanating from Lyon, the city in which most of the posthumous editions of Rabelais between 1553 and 1610 were probably printed; false title pages are numerous. They also document, ibid., 298–300, the continuing hostility of Genevan authorities to Rabelais.

# 6

## Post-Renaissance Metatexts

As religious controversy became more covert, Rabelais's public presence declined. In the new cultural atmosphere of peace and propriety, Calvinists could no longer hope for undoing Catholicism through disseminating ecclesiastical satire. The more general import of the novels, Rabelais's narratively filtered approach to all manner of public and private questions, from marriage and medicine to Carnival and chicanery, had already been lost in the later sixteenth century. The loss was inevitable, with or without the work of unscrupulous editors, for the cultural context in which Rabelais wrote had disappeared. His expressions came to seem more salty or more silly than they were when first published, in some places more incisive and in others more obscure. Rabelais continued to be read, but only by the cultivated. The popular audience disappeared as the popular ambience from which he had derived his locutions and the popular manner in which he had clothed his tales went its own way. Those who did read Rabelais read rather lightly. Whether condemned and shunned—as in Father Garasse's three fulminatory books against him in the 1620s and 1630s[1]—or passed from hand to hand, epigrammatized, and adapted to the subjects of court ballets, it was for the same reasons and among the same restricted elites. Rabelais was discovered as a wit; he was witty, indeed, to the point of wickedness.[2]

1. Of the Jesuit Garasse's three books concerning Rabelais (*Le Rabelais Réformé* (Brussels, 1619), *La Recherche des recherches d'Etienne Pasquier* (Paris, 1622), and *La Doctrine curieuse des beaux esprits de ce temps* (Paris, 1623), the third is, according to Abel Lefranc, the most violent. There Garasse writes: "Les libertins ont en main le Rabelais comme l'enchiridion du libertinage. . . . Il est impossible d'en lire une page sans danger d'offenser Dieu mortellement. . . . Je proteste en conscience que je n'en ay jamais leu quatre lignes de suite; mais à voir ce qui est rapporté de luy dans les oeuvres de maistre Estienne Pasquier . . . , j'estime que Rabelais est un très maudit et pernicieux escrivain . . . qui a faict plus de degast en France par ses bouffonneries que Calvin par ses nouveautez." Quoted in Abel Lefranc, "Garasse et Rabelais," *Revue des études rabelaisiennes* 7 (1909): 498.

2. A third factor causing Rabelais's public presence to decline was the in-

The atmosphere of official sanctimony, which in the course of the seventeenth century waxed and waned but deepened considerably in the later years of Louis XIV's reign, enhanced Rabelais's appeal as a daring satirist. So the uses to which Rabelais was put by *érudits, libertins, femmes savantes,* and *femmes galantes* reinforced the narrowing comprehension wrought by both time and the moralistic atmosphere of official propriety. As neoclassic norms in art and manners chastened and polished the language, taste for broad and grotesque humor shriveled. Rabelais's *gauloiserie* came to appear peculiar, if not intolerable.[3] As cultural boundaries were tightened, so were the social frontiers. Nobles and notables took less part in village or artisan fun. They avoided festive occasions like Carnival. They stared at such behavior from afar and lost the sense of its rhythm and articulation with the church year. Awareness of the relation of such occasions to Rabelais's text disappeared.[4]

The misunderstandings of Rabelais's text, which flourished from the moment of his death, could have been mitigated by paratextual elements like those found in modern editions of Rabelais: notes, indexes, interpretive introductions, critical apparatus. Such paratexts became usual for classical and Biblical texts during the sixteenth and the seventeenth century. But they were rarely perceived as necessary for modern authors until it was too late—too late to acquire first-hand information about the author's own ambience. Such belated recognition of lost dimensions of the text is nearly inevitable, especially with reference to popular customs or locutions that seem to their users to be age-old or so locally peculiar that they are of no general interest. Only when the

---

creased efficiency of state control over printers and booksellers during the prime ministership of Richelieu and during Louis XIV's reign. See Bernard Barbiche's demonstration of this in Chartier and Martin, ed., *Histoire de l'imprimerie,* 1:375–77.

3. See Marcel de Grève, "François Rabelais et les libertins du XVIIᵉ siècle," *Etudes rabelaisiennes* 1 (1956): 121–23, for further materials from Garasse, and Grève, "Les érudits du XVIIᵉ siècle en quête de la clef de Rabelais," *Etudes rabelaisiennes* 5 (1964): 41–43, for Rabelais's reputation at court and in the salons of the earlier seventeenth century.

4. The social process of noble dissociation from peasant culture and of mercantile "notables" from artisanal culture between the sixteenth and the nineteenth century has been little studied. Valuable initiatives in this direction can be found in Natalie Davis's "Proverbial Wisdom and Popular Errors," ch. 8 of her *Society and Culture in Early Modern France,* and in the works of Norbert Elias, *The History of Manners* (New York, 1978) and *The Court Society* (New York, 1983).

meaning of such items has begun to disappear en masse, leaving considerable sections of the text obscure, does the interest of their culturally conditioned quality appear.[5]

The first metatexts that concern the Quaresmeprenant-Sausage episode in particular were published in the 1690s. They were concerned with explaining and defending Rabelais's religious opinions. For Jean Bernier, a Catholic, as for Pierre Le Motteux, a French Huguenot refugee in England, Quaresmeprenant has become Lent, and the Sausages no longer have any performative, ritual relation to Carnival, let alone to a combative or parading performance on mardi gras.

Jean Bernier's *The True Rabelais Reformed,* published at Paris in 1697, responded to the hyperbolic attacks on Rabelais by persons like Father Garasse. It was a measured defense, for Bernier found "both bad and good in this book as in many others." A moderate Catholic with an immoderate enthusiasm for Rabelais, his purpose was simply to maintain that Rabelais was no heretic and no atheist.[6] Bernier's book is only the second publication to discuss all Rabelais's novels episode by episode; Le Motteux's English translation of 1694, filled with copious notes, was the first. Before the extensive comments of Bernier and Le Motteux only two guides to the Carnival-Lent narrative existed: a few notes in the "Brief Clarification" of 1552 and an alphabetic list explaining difficult words and phrases, published in 1663 in the first edition of Rabelais's work at Amsterdam.

The notes about chapters 29 through 42 in the "Brief Clarification"

5. The "Brief Clarification of Some of the More Obscure Locutions included in the Fourth Book" (*Briefve Declaration,* 759–68) is a good proof of this. Published in 1552 in some copies of the *Fourth Book,* it is the first attempt to annotate Rabelais. Of 178 items only 13 concern contemporary French customs or locutions; the rest try to explain Rabelais's references to obscure ancient (Greek, Roman, Hebrew) words and mores or foreign contemporary ones (esp. Italian phrases). See Appendix 3.

6. Jean Bernier, *Jugement et Nouvelles Observations sur les Oeuvres . . . de Maiter François Rabelais, D. M. ou Le veritable Rabelais Réformé* (Paris, 1697). Bernier's way of exculpating Rabelais was suggested by one of Rabelais's own statements in the dedicatory letter prefacing the *Fourth Book:* "meschantement l'on m'en a aulcuns [livres] supposé [qui sont] faulx et infâmes" (*QL, L,* 543). Bernier concludes on the penultimate page of the unpaginated preface to his book: "Rabelais étoit un bel esprit, et un sçavant homme pour son temps, qui écrivoit bien et qui avait du manège de Ville et de Cour. . . . Car quant aux hérésies et à l'Athéisme il s'en purge ce semble fort bien, accusant ses ennemis d'avoir ajoûté plusieurs choses à ses écrits." The quotation from Bernier in the text is from 501 of his book, the conclusion to his episode-by-episode commentary on the novels.

explain a few Greek and Hebrew words, two medical terms, and a term in geometry.[7] They make no reference to the puzzles preoccupying us here. The few allusions to the Carnival-Lent episode in the "Alphabet of the French author," as styled in the 1663 edition, are on the other hand fundamental. They were included in the reprints of that edition and studied by Bernier and Le Motteux for their commentaries. One allusion in the Alphabet indicates that Quaresmeprenant in Rabelais's text was still understood as Carnival at the time that the Alphabet was compiled, which was probably close to the time when the edition of 1663 was being prepared.[8]

The allusion of the Alphabet author explains the meaning of Tapinos Island, Quaresmeprenant's kingdom:

> Tapinos: An old French word which means secretly, and in hiding [en cachette]. Some people derive it from the Greek verb *tapeinoo*, that is, to lower or put on the ground, from whence one usually says *il s'est tapi*, that is, he has lain down to hide himself; the Greek figurative word *tapeinosis* means humility, abasement. Now since Quaresmeprenant flees after the moveable feasts (since from the time they have arrived there is no more news about Quaresmeprenant), as the author says in chapter 29 of Book Four—and it seems that by this means [lying down to hide: tapeinoo] he would like to hide himself, now advancing and now retreating—this is why he [the author] makes him inhabit Tapinos Island.[9]

The grammatically awkward last sentence of this explanation, which I have clarified by the use of dashes to set off the long parenthetical phrase, refers to Friar John's comment in chapter 29: "I pray you [to describe Quaresmeprenant], my ballocky friend, for I have found him

7. *BD,* 764–65.

8. The dating of the Alphabet author's work emerges from the date and manuscript history of another critic's work on Rabelais, which I discuss later in this chapter, Perreau's "Explanation."

9. This allusion is conveniently reprinted from the Elzevier edition of Rabelais's works (Amsterdam, 1663) in *Oeuvres de Rabelais,* ed. Esmangart and Eloi Johanneau, Volume 6 (Paris, 1823), 271, n. 3 (this edition is often called in Rabelaisian criticism "the Variorum edition"): "Viel mot français qui signifie secrètement et en cachette. Aucuns le tirent du verbe grec *tapeinoo,* c'est-à-dire abaisser, mettre par terre; d'où vient qu'on dit le plus souvent il s'est tapi, c'est-à-dire il s'est couché à terre pour se cacher, et la figure grecque *tapeinosis* signifie humilité, abaissement. Or, parceque Quaresme-prenant s'enfuit après les festes mobiles (parceque dès-lors qu'elles sont arrivées il n'est plus nouvelle de Quaresme-prenant), comme dit l'autheur au chapitre XXIX du libre IV, et semble par ce moyen qu'il voudroit se cacher, ores s'advançant et ores se reculant: voilà pourquoi il le fait habiter en l'isle de Tapinois."

in my breviary, and he follows(?)/flees(?) after the moveable feasts."[10] Modern commentators, supposing that Quaresmeprenant is Lent, apparently have no trouble explaining Friar John's phrase; after all, the liturgy for Lent is found in any breviary. But how would they make sense of the Alphabet author's idea that after the arrival of the moveable feasts there is no more news about Quaresmeprenant? The point is important to the argument developed here concerning the disappearance of the context in which Rabelais's text was written. It requires a fairly extended examination of different ways of interpreting Friar John's phrase.

Friar John's reference may not be a helpful clue to the monster's identity, not only due to the ambiguity of the phrase and the impulsive character of the man who says it,[11] but also for another purely material reason: Rabelais's text on this point is literally ambiguous. In the sixteenth and the seventeenth century the initial and medial *s* in words was printed in a manner that made it nearly indistinguishable from *f*; it was printed as *f*. The editions of Rabelais's *Fourth Book* made during his lifetime printed the word in Friar John's phrase sometimes as flees (*s'enfuyt*) and sometimes as follows (*s'enfuyt*). The only complete modern critical edition of the *Fourth Book*, that of Robert Marichal, "corrects" the reading of what he otherwise considers the two best of six editions of this chapter 29 published in 1552 and 1553. These two editions both read *s'en fuyt*, which Marichal changes to *s'ensuyt*.[12]

This tiny typographical difference may imply a large semantic shift, depending on how one interprets the meaning of Friar John's reference to the moveable feasts in his breviary. Many dates celebrated by the church, including Ascension, Pentecost, Corpus Christi, and Lent, are based on the date of Easter, a date that moves from year to year because it is determined by the shifting relation of the moon's phases to the spring equinox. The church year in Rabelais's time as in the twentieth century began with Advent, the Sunday on or closest to November 30;

10. *QL,* 29, 642–43.
11. See p. 72 above.
12. Marichal, ed., *Quart Livre,* 140. Marichal's edition, although it includes the complete *Fourth Book,* does not compare readings among all early editions. He compares only *NRB* nos. 46 (Marichal's "E") and 52 (Marichal's "I": ibid., xxxvii–xxxviii). The two editions of Rabelais most cited by scholars today adopt opposite readings, and neither offers readers any indication that a choice has been made: *QL,* 29, 643: s'enfuyt (Boulenger); *Oeuvres,* ed. Jourda, 2: 126: s'ensuyt.

so the beginning of Advent is also a moveable feast. The lay year began at various times, at some places on January 1 while at others on March 1, March 25 (Annunciation), or Easter.

The different ways of dating the church and lay year, taken in conjunction with the indeterminacy of *s'ensuyt/s'enfuyt* and the ambiguity of the phrase "after the moveable feasts," yield multiple modes of interpreting Friar John's phrase. The friar may be referring to where the word Quaresmeprenant literally occurs in his breviary, on such and such a page, in which case *s'ensuyt* would seem the most likely reading of the text. Or he may be referring to where the metaphorical equivalent of Quaresmeprenant—be it Carnival or Lent—appears in the breviary, in which case *s'ensuyt* or *s'enfuyt* would be equally possible readings. The ambiguity of Friar John's remark is further increased by the fact that the first effective standardization of breviaries took place after Rabelais's time. As a consequence of decrees passed at the Council of Trent, Pope Pius V issued a Roman breviary in 1568 whose order and substance were henceforth to be universally observed, as indeed they still are within the Roman Catholic church, although allowance for observance of local saints' days was and is admitted. When one examines the differences of breviaries before and after 1568, and one combines these differences with the uncertainty of the correct reading of *s'ensuyt/s'enfuyt,* one realizes how difficult it is to determine the meaning of what Friar John says with such easy definiteness.

In treating this problem three kinds of difficulty are best kept separate, that arising from the typographical ambiguity, that concerning possible differences of the breviaries Rabelais had in mind from those subsequently authorized, and that deriving from textual analysis, including the interpretation of Rabelais's purposes. With respect to the third kind of difficulty, a general conclusion can be stated in advance: Rabelais here as elsewhere offers a seemingly concrete detail that intentionally opens on an abyss of uncertainty. The means by which he produces this effect reside in the text's relation to context, as we will see.

The first difficulty also can be unraveled by reference to context. Typographical errors were very frequent in sixteenth-century printing, and indeed Rabelais used this fact in the dedicatory letter to the *Fourth Book* in order to defend himself from heresy.[13] The error involved here,

---

13. *QL,* DL, 543: Certain of his slanderers "fondoit mortelle haerésie sur un N mis pour un M par la faulte et négligence des imprimeurs."

whichever it is, is tiny. One can probably assume that Rabelais proof-read at least the first two editions of 1552, which read *s'enfuyt;* but this is no guarantee that *s'enfuyt* is correct, for Rabelais might easily have misread the word as its look-alike. He died in March 1553, only a year after the second edition appeared. Other editions of the *Fourth Book* in 1552 and 1553 seem to be piracies.[14] The printing history of the *Fourth Book* gives a presumption, but only slight, in favor of the reading *s'enfuyt*. If semantic reasons argued strongly in favor of *s'ensuyt,* they would outweigh typographical evidence.

The second kind of difficulty, that concerning the content and arrangement of breviaries, is of interest because the pages where anything resembling Quaresmeprenant might have been found before 1568 are not the same as those where it might be found since that date. This difficulty thus involves the main subject of this chapter, the evolution of readers' contexts away from Rabelais's context of writing.[15]

Long before Friar John claims to have found Quaresmeprenant in his breviary, readers have become accustomed to his phrase, "that's breviary stuff" (*matière de breviaire*). Insofar as readers bring this phrase to bear upon Friar John's utterance about Quaresmeprenant, they would tend to think that Friar John has found the monster as part of the contents of his breviary, perhaps even on a particular page or pages that he seems to designate, "after the moveable feasts." What pages would they be?

If critics have decided that Quaresmeprenant represents Lent, they have a strong motive at this point to read the text as "follows," not "flees." It would be strange for Lent to flee moveable feasts of which it is itself a prime example. If the text reads "follows," then critics equating Quaresmeprenant with Lent might read Friar John's phrase loosely, interpreting it to say simply that Lent comes along calendrically in the midst of all the pages concerned with the moveable feast days to which a breviary is, among other things, devoted. This is a possible reading. But it is not very likely for people of Rabelais's time; for reasons already explored, Quaresmeprenant as a word meant Carnival. There is a sec-

14. The two first editions of 1552 are further discussed in ch. 9. The statement on the title page of one printed edition, *NRB*, no. 52 (n.p., 1553), that this edition was "newly revised and corrected by the author" is false, as is shown in *NRB*, 262.

15. The following discussion of breviaries condenses conclusions explained more fully in Appendix 4.

ond reason why contemporary readers would have been puzzled by Friar John's phrase, as soon as they tried to associate it with anything they might know of breviaries. Nearly everyone knew at least that it would be impossible to find Quaresmeprenant materially or literally in breviaries, for the content of breviaries, which are devoted to performance of the church's liturgy, is in Latin. Friar John must mean that he finds in his breviary a Latin equivalent to the French word. If Quaresmeprenant signifies Carnival to Friar John, then he is hallucinating: *Carnisprivium,* the chief Latin word for Carnival, would scarcely be found in a breviary, nor would the Latin equivalent of Fat Tuesday. The only word resembling Quaresmeprenant in fifteenth-century or later breviaries is *Quadragesima.* This word was created to designate the Sunday, which in most parts of Europe before the year 1000 was the beginning of forty days' fasting for the laity, *Dominica Quadragesima,* "Fortieth Sunday." But at least as early as the ninth century it became customary to exempt from fasting all the Sundays in Lent, including Quadragesima Sunday; four days fasting from Ash Wednesday up to the following Quadragesima Sunday were then added, making the sum of forty days. At the same time the term Quadragesima by itself came to be used in breviaries and elsewhere to designate the whole term of Lent rather than the first Sunday in Lent.

Is this then the equation Friar John is using? It seems to be the one most modern commentators assume. They believe that Friar John is saying: I have found Quadragesima, the equivalent of Quaresmeprenant, in my breviary; this word "follows" (*s'ensuyt*) somewhere "after" (*après*), or perhaps among, the pages dealing with moveable feasts.

There were and are three main parts to breviaries, before as after 1568: a calendar and/or a series of calendrical tables with instructions as to how to calculate the varying dates of moveable feasts from year to year and indications as to when saints' days occur; a long section called the temporal, listing the liturgy to be read and chanted from day to day through the year; and a section called the sanctoral, indicating additions and alterations in the liturgy for saints' days. Saints' days are fixed feasts, occurring each year on the anniversary regarded as the day of the birth or martyrdom or other signal event in a saint's life. But the liturgy of the year is organized around the days leading up to and away from Easter, the summit of the ecclesiastical year. Hence use of the bulkiest part of a breviary, its temporal, required calculation of the moveable date of Easter from the calendrical tables so as to establish actual dates of Easter and all other liturgical performances and so as to be able to integrate the temporal and the sanctoral.[16]

Neither Quadragesima Sunday nor Quadragesima to mean Lent in general is found in those breviary calendars or calendrical tables, before and after 1568, that I have checked. In a breviary calendar made in Paris for Duke Philip the Good of Burgundy about 1450, as in modern tables of moveable feasts, there is no indication of Lent or Lent's beginning. These must be calculated from Septuagesima Sunday, the Sunday three weeks before Quadragesima Sunday; Septuagesima Sunday is indicated in both Duke Philip's calendar and in modern breviary tables.

If Friar John said "follows" after moveable feasts and if he meant by this that Quadragesima occurs on a page of his breviary after the pages devoted to a table or calendar of moveable feasts, then his statement makes sense. He could find Quadragesima in either the general or particular meaning of the word in the temporal, or at least he could find it in all breviaries after 1568 and in some before that date. But Friar John "died" in 1553, when Rabelais did. And if Friar John's breviary was like that of Duke Philip the Good, he could not have found Quadragesima after the calendar there because this calendar occurs in the middle of the breviary, *after* the temporal. I have not chosen this particular fifteenth-century breviary abusively. The modern editor of this breviary points out that the habit of putting the calendar in the middle rather than at the beginning of the breviary was customary in many places, including Rome, Paris, and Tours (the latter a town near where Rabelais himself served in a monastery).[17]

Hence the objections to this plausible interpretation of Friar John's phrase are that it would not apply to breviaries with calendars in the middle and so would confuse some readers, and, worse still, that it requires adding words to the text: follows after *a table of,* or *a calendar of* moveable feasts. If words are not added, then Friar John thinks he has found Quaresmeprenant after the end of the temporal section of the breviary, in the sanctoral. Maybe he did; considering his jovial proclivities, perhaps *his* breviary included Saint Pansart![18]

16. And also the moveable date of Advent, as noted earlier.

17. See Appendix 4. These calendars had columns on the left of the page devoted to each month with a system of letters and numbers allowing perpetual calculation of the shifting dates of moveable feasts.

18. What? You do not believe me, you boozers? Go look for yourself on p. 85. I have given you the name. It was at Tours, it was just the other year, "la

Perhaps Friar John, interpreting Quaresmeprenant as Quadragesima and uttering "follows," not "flees," merely meant that Quadragesima comes after the beginning of the pages in his breviary that are devoted to moveable feasts, whether Septuagesima or Advent. The first moveable feast in the church year is Advent, while the first one in the lay year, if it is considered to begin on January 1, is Septuagesima Sunday. In this case too one adds words to the text, something like follows after *the beginning of* or *the arrival of* the moveable feasts. The Alphabet author, adopting the reading "flees," added such words: "Quaresmeprenant flees after the moveable feasts (since *from the time they have arrived* there is no more news about Quaresmeprenant)."[19] As the Alphabet author saw, one must add words like arrival or beginning because Quaresmeprenant, whether it means Carnival or Lent or Lent-taking-hold to Friar John, cannot be said to have fled after the moveable feasts generally, which continue until Corpus Christi Day, occurring in May or June. Whatever Quaresmeprenant means to the monk, it falls in the middle of the moveable feasts, long before they are all over for the year. But if for the sake of making sense one adds such words as these after "flees," then one necessarily eliminates one of Quaresmeprenant's three probable meanings: Lent. The Alphabet author must have thought Quaresmeprenant meant Carnival or Lent-taking-hold, not Lent, because after the arrival of Quaresmeprenant-as-Lent there would continue to be news of him until Easter, when Lent ends.

The Alphabet author's interpretation envisions Quaresmeprenant as "now advancing and now retreating" in consonance with the passage of the liturgical year, very much in the festive manner in which Carnival and Lent advanced to do battle on Fat Tuesday, retreated to exile, and then advanced again as the seasons rolled around to a new year. The Alphabet author's comments presuppose a lay-calendrical point of view: the year begins with January 1, not Advent, so that the first moveable feast, Septuagesima, does not arrive for several months. Friar John, making his way from day to day through the breviary, arrives first at

---

dure et cruelle bataille et paix du glorieux sainct Pensart a l'encontre de Caresme." That's breviary stuff. (See also *P,* 1, 194: "aulcuns enfloyent par le ventre . . . et de ceste race nasquit sainct Pansart et Mardy Gras." Unlike the case in the *basoche* play, Saint Pansard is here merely associated with Carnival, not identified as its personification.)

19. Italics added. See the quotation from the Alphabet author on p. 134.

Septuagesima and then several weeks afterward at Ash Wednesday. From that time, the time when in a loose sense the "moveable feasts . . . have arrived," there is "no more news about Quaresmeprenant" because Lent has begun: the *advance* of that being is over. Can one push the Alphabet author's words further and say that he can only be thinking of Quaresmeprenant as Carnival because one may well regard the whole period from Septuagesima to Ash Wednesday as Carnival but not all of this two and one-half weeks as a transition period, Lent-taking-hold? The psychologizing and etymologizing conclusion to the Alphabet author's comment seems to argue in precisely the opposite sense: Quaresmeprenant, lowering himself in accordance with the meaning of the Greek verb from which his island's name is derived, "would like to hide himself." Carnival *desirous* of hiding during Lent? Possibly. Carnival as Lent-taking-hold, desirous of hiding after the arrival of Septuagesima, with its increased tension over the ambivalence between desire and duty as Ash Wednesday comes closer? Quite plausible.

The disadvantages of the Alphabet author's interpretation are obvious. He carries anthropomorphosis so far with his psychological interpretation that the monster loses much of its looming half-human, half-puppet aura. He disregards Friar John's clerical identity and attributes to him a lay way of thinking about the relation of the beginning of the year to the moveable feasts, precisely when Friar John is talking about a clerical book, the breviary.[20] And like those who read the text as *s'ensuyt*, he adds words to the text.

Of all the critics writing about this particular phrase, the Alphabet author was closest in time and space to Rabelais's context. But he still wrote, it seems, a full century after the first publication of the *Fourth Book;* readers' contexts had radically changed. To return to the typographical question, the reader must conclude that semantic reasons for one or the other are not overwhelming. A slight presumption in favor of *s'enfuyt* remains, for the evidence of early editions is also more in consonance with the expectations of readers who recognized the au-

---

20. If one begins the year with the moveable feast of Advent, as clerics were taught was proper, then the moveable feasts arrived too early—that is, immediately, and more than three months before Carnival-Lent—for Quaresmeprenant plausibly to flee after their arrival. If one begins the year with January 1, as had become a much stronger custom for everyone by 1650, lay or cleric, then the first moveable feast is Septuagesima.

thor's references to Carnival-Lent combats. The end of the plays and poems depicting the victory of one or the other typically described the departure of the defeated. If Carnival was defeated, he or she fled, was banished for the duration of Lent, or was exiled for an entire year until the return of Carnival time. If Lent was defeated, he or she was given forty days to leave or, as in the thirteenth-century French poem about the victory of Fleshliness over Lent, the latter was granted an annual return of six weeks and three days.

Sometimes Lent fled and sometimes Carnival. Knowledge of the conventions of Carnival-Lent combat reinforces the idea that Friar John's sure and easy identification of Quaresmeprenant is a comic snare: he may mean either party. In fact, in the light of what one is eventually led to understand about Rabelais's ideas of Carnival and Lent as the episode unfolds, it seems probable that he wished readers to consider Friar John's statement just enough to be thrown into confusion.

The Alphabet author's explanation of the Greek root of Tapinos, taken together with his psychological interpretation of Quaresmeprenant's fleeing so as to mean that the monster desired to hide himself, was destined for a long life. It attached itself tenaciously to Rabelais's text, inspiring false readings of this passage by Bernier and Le Motteux, which became influential in their turn. Bernier writes:

> Some wish that Tapinos Island should be interpreted as the land of hypocrites because of its name, for *tapinosis* means humility (*tapinoo*, I lie down on the ground [these words, in Greek and Latin, are printed in the margin]). It is said that Quaresmeprenant reigns there because Lent [*sic: le carême*] disappears after the movable feasts.

Quaresmeprenant reigns on Tapinos Island because it is the sort of place where *carême* can "disappear"—that is, neither flee nor follow after but lie down and even hide under the ground.[21]

What does it mean for Lent to disappear in this underground sense after the moveable feasts? Bernier, who attributes to some unnamed person this reading of Friar John's words, does not himself explain it. The unnamed person was almost certainly Pierre Le Motteux, a Hugue-

---

21. Esmangart and Johanneau, ed., *Oeuvres de Rabelais,* 6: 267, reproduce Bernier: "On veut que l'île de Tapinois soit le pays de hypocrites *a notatione nominis;* parceque *tapinosis* signifie humilité, *tapinoo, in terram decumbo;* et que Carêmeprenant y règne parceque le carême disparoit après les fêtes mobiles."

not refugee in London since the revocation of the Edict of Nantes in 1685, whose English translations and annotations of Rabelais's *Fourth Book* and *Fifth Book* appeared in 1694. How he rationalized the equation of Quaresmeprenant with *le carême* is ingenious.

"The Sneaking Island which Pantagruel sailed by," writes Le Motteux, "is the dwelling of Shrovetide, by which we must understand Lent." Thus at the very outset the ambivalence that remains liminally present in Bernier's account is abolished from Le Motteux's Rabelais. Quaresmeprenant personifies Lent, in spite of the monster's name. The name was chosen not to express ambivalence but to hide Rabelais's intentions. One well understands how this seemed plausible to not only Protestants but also those who saw Rabelais as generally anti-Christian. Rabelais, writes Le Motteux, wished to "expose the Superstition of the Papists about Lent." But he was obliged to do it in such a way as to "secure himself from the informations of his prying enemies." This is how he did so.

"The Ecclesiasticks of the Church of Rome," Le Motteaux explains, "begin their Lent before the Layety; Shrove-Tuesday is to them a Day of Humiliation; and is properly the time when men are shriven. Our author calls it Quaresmeprenant, that is, the Beginning of Quadragesima; in opposition to Mardi Gras, Shrove-Tuesday."[22] Le Motteux nearly admits that Quaresmeprenant might have two meanings, depending on whether one is lay or cleric. For if Quaresmeprenant means Lent-taking-hold or Carnival-full-of-Lent and one is lay, then Quaresmeprenant means one last fling, Shrove Tuesday as mardi gras, the time of feasting; if it means the same things but one is of the clergy, Quaresmeprenant signifies Shrove Tuesday as the beginning of Quadragesima, a time of shriving and fasting. Something of the ambivalence Le Motteux wants to eliminate from Rabelais's intentions remains in the way he reasons about the text. But he does not reason enough, for we have seen that the text shows the word has at least four meanings to persons aware of its French and Latin, ecclesiastic and lay dimensions: one thing etymologically (moving toward, taking up, being pregnant with Lent), another in popular parlance (Carnival time generally, and espe-

22. *The Works of François Rabelais,* trans. T. Urquhart and P. [Le] Motteux (in English editions "Le" was dropped), Volume 2 (London, 1708), 210. (Thomas Urquhart had earlier translated the first three books of Rabelais's novels about Gargantua and Pantagruel.)

cially Carnival's last day or days before Ash Wednesday), and a third and fourth when its French form is related to Latin Quadragesima (Lent generally; or alternatively the first Sunday in Lent, Quadragesima Sunday, and hence the first days of Lent).

Le Motteux ranks and reduces the word's meanings; having done so, he easily explains the name of Quaresmeprenant's residence, Tapinos Island. Quaresmeprenant hides himself because he, like the "ecclesiastics of the church of Rome," has already begun his Lenten fasting, perhaps as early as Septuagesima.[23] The approach of Ash Wednesday is shameful because it is preceded by Shrove Tuesday, which, although it should be a "day of humiliation," is in fact a time of gaiety. He therefore flees underground on Tapinos Island after the moveable feasts have begun—for him—*before* Shrove Tuesday. Apart from the intentionalism that moves Le Motteux to tie the meaning of Tapinos so closely to a name reductively regarded as signifying only Lent, Le Motteux's interpretation is useful because it highlights the difference between lay and clerical points of view and thereby directs attention, if only inadvertently, less to Carnival and Lent as fixed and separate entities than to the zone of transition between them.

It is difficult in the anthropologically oriented late twentieth century to recapture the mentality prompting these exegetic twists and turns of argument. Their essential character is their confessionalism, their inwardly oriented understanding of religion as credal belief and moral codes more than as everyday activity, in which belief, morality, and behavior are more reflexively intertwined. Rabelais's sensitivity to the ambivalences of religious observance in daily life was, like that of many of his contemporaries, quickened by participating in the humanistic and evangelical movements of his time. For him the mixture of secular and sacred custom and creed, derived from fifteen hundred years of Christian battle with ethnic and antique ideologies, was a richly conflictual matter of daily experience, which prompted delight, humor, and despair by turns. For Le Motteux and Bernier such fullness of response had receded. But it had not yet disappeared or become—as in the twentieth century—part of a primarily intellectual effort to understand the

23. To repeat points made earlier, Quadragesima as Lent in general is especially ambiguous with respect to a beginning date, which was rarely Quadragesima Sunday, often Ash Wednesday, but frequently still other dates, depending on geographical area, the custom of the ecclesiastical order to which one belonged if a cleric, and so on.

text. Both Le Motteux and Bernier find the significance of the Carnival-Lent episode worth arguing about.

The details Rabelais offered about Quaresmeprenant, however, scarcely engaged Le Motteux's attention. He found them "odd." They seemed irrelevant to Rabelais's general purposes, which to him were grand and unambiguous:

> His Design seems rather to expose the Superstition of the Papists about Lent, and how much the practice of it, their way, shocked good sense: This made him run on for two or three chapters with an odd description of this ridiculous Monster; and probably also to secure himself from the informations of his prying enemies, by this mixture of Carnival seeming Nonsense. For as in the time of Luther, the Superstition, Grimaces, and Hypocrisy of the Papists are most observable, and they look on it in a manner as the basis of the Christian Religion, twould have been dangerous to have attacked them openly in Point [*sic:* presumably for "in Print"].[24]

How extraordinary it is that Le Motteux sensed the spirit of Rabelais's episode, "this Carnival seeming Nonsense," even while introducing an interpretation of Quaresmeprenant that did much to confirm erasure of the passage's context. Le Motteux's influence on Rabelaisian criticism, although indirect, was great. His commentary became the "cornerstone of historico-allegorical exegesis" until the early nineteenth century.[25]

Le Motteux's reference to the "Hypocrisy of the Papists" in the passage just quoted is probably the phrase that led Bernier to say that "some" affirm that Tapinos Island is the land of "hypocrites." For Bernier such an attitude toward Catholicism on the part of Rabelais is not cunning but surprising:

> The rest [of this chapter 29], down to chapter 30 is nothing but raillery about Lent made by libertines, if they are not by Rabelais. . . . But if all that is by Rabelais, I am the more surprised since, being a capable man, he must have known that Lent is a holy and ancient institution.[26]

Bernier is surprised at the raillery. But what bothers him is not that the enigmas posed by the text are sheared away by such an interpreta-

24. Le Motteux, *Works of Rabelais,* 2: 210.

25. Lazare Sainéan, *L'influence et la réputation de Rabelais* (Paris, 1930), 73. Le Motteux's notes were translated from the 1708 English edition for the French-language 1741 Amsterdam edition by J. Bernard and thence became a part of French Rabelaisian criticism.

26. Quoted in Esmangart and Johanneau, ed., *Oeuvres de Rabelais,* 6: 267.

tion. Like Le Motteux, Bernier is thinking in confessional terms. The question has become whether Rabelais is pro- or anti-Catholic. For this episode at least the confessional question has so stripped away the other dimensions of Rabelais's writing that, confronted with what he, following Le Motteux, views as sharp and prolonged satire of "a holy and ancient institution," Bernier turns to the possibility that the text may be corrupt. Rather than abandon his notion of Rabelais's Catholicism and the *bienséance* it implies, he is ready to assume that chapter 29 may have been written by "libertines" without Rabelais's authority.

Few people in the 1690s could have known how much Rabelais's text had varied in detail over the previous century and a half, due to both the author's attempts to quiet his censors during his lifetime and the vagaries of his many editors. Bernier's suspicion that the text might have been changed was verified by Le Duchat, who pointed out that in three unspecified Lyon editions the phrase referring to the "demoniacal Calvin" was changed to the "demoniacal writ-servers, rakers-in of benefices," which I have already discussed.[27]

Jacob Le Duchat's edition, made in exile at Berlin by the émigré French Protestant and published in 1711, was the first to offer readers some awareness of the variant readings. His view of Rabelais's work was less militantly Protestant than Le Motteux's, and his scholarship was impressive. Double-column annotations in small type occupy one-third or more of nearly every page of his five-volume edition. Although he is, like Le Motteux, aware of the everyday meaning of Quaresmeprenant, Le Duchat also decides that the word refers to Lent or Ash Wednesday: "Ordinarily one refers to Carnival and in particular to Mardi Gras with the name of Quaresmeprenant. But here it must be Ash Wednesday or even Lent in person, since Quaresmeprenant is put in opposition to Mardi Gras, protector of the Sausages." In spite of his use of a logic of dichotomous pairs to conclude that Quaresmeprenant must mean Lent, Le Duchat further understands the references in the

27. Le Duchat, 4: 142, n. 17, writes: "On a retranché cet endroit dans l'édition de 1596, mais dans les trois de Lyon on a substitué ces paroles: Demoniacles chiquanous et racleurs [*sic,* for: chicanous, aracleurs] de benefices." A Protestant-inspired equation of Quaresmeprenant with Lent was of course easier to make before Le Duchat restored Rabelais's denunciation of Calvin. Once the equation of Quaresmeprenant with another of Anti-Nature's children, Calvin, was brought to light again, it became difficult to imagine Rabelais as a secret French Protestant.

"grotesque portrait of Quaresmeprenant" in chapters 30 through 32 as normally applying to Carnival masquerades. To make this observation compatible with his previous conclusion, he decides that the grotesqueness cannot refer to anything other than the bizarre qualities of mistaken Catholic custom:

> Since the grotesque portrait of the figure of Quaresmeprenant made here by Xenomanes cannot be related to the extravagant masquerades of Carnival, this portrait must on one hand refer to the bizarreness of monkish customs generally, whose rules prescribe a perpetual Lent, and on the other refer to the error of those who make a good part of Christian religion consist in the observance of Lent and its devotions.[28]

For Le Duchat there is even less ambivalence—because less deception—in the figure of Quaresmeprenant than for Le Motteux. He does not refer to Le Motteux's interpretation of Tapinos Island, annotating it bluntly: "Tapinos Island. The home of monks, whom Rabelais calls *Taupetiers* [molelike folk] in Book 3, chap. 46 and in the Prologue of Book 4. . . . Lent [*sic:* le Carême] is said to have chosen his dwelling in their convents, where abstinence from meat is the rule."[29]

In spite of their knowledge of popular customs and their occasional historical details about them, the confessionalism of their interpretative position led Le Motteux and Le Duchat also to see the physeter episode and the Sausage-people chapters as essentially distinct from the chapters about Quaresmeprenant.[30] The monster makes war against the "zany Sausages," writes Le Motteux, "because in Lent all kinds of flesh, or at least dead flesh, are prohibited for people." The Sausages are, as far as their relation to Quaresmeprenant is concerned, just a category of food that has its ritual role; they are not a representational form of

28. Le Duchat, 4: 128, n. 1: "*Quaresmeprenant etc.* C'est ordinairement le Carnaval, et en particulier le *Mardigras* qu'on désigne sous le nom de Carême-prenant; mais ici, ce doit être le jour des *Cendres,* ou même le Carême en personne, puis qu'il est mis en opposition avec le Mardigras Protecteur des Andouilles. Ainsi, le portrait grotesque que fait ici Xenomanes de la figure de Carême-prenant ne pouvant se rapporter aux extravagantes Mascarades du Carnaval, il faut que d'un côté ce portrait regarde la bizarrerie de l'habit des Moines en général, à qui leurs Règles prescrivent un Carême continuel, et de l'autre l'erreur de ceux qui font consister une bonne partie de la Religion Chrétienne dans l'observation du Carême et de ses Devotions."

29. Le Duchat, 4: 124, n. 1.

30. Theodore Fraser's study of *Le Duchat, First Editor of Rabelais* (Geneva, 1971), 90–94, 162–73, emphasizes Le Duchat's elucidations of popular customs, proverbs, and "bawdy" turns of speech.

Carnival, let alone part of Rabelais's reflections, in this and other episodes of the *Fourth Book,* about alimentary habits. But when he treats
materials connected with the third enigma in the episode, the war between two allies or vassals of Mardi Gras, Le Motteux develops Rabelais's occasional references to the Swiss Protestants and the German war
of 1546–1547 into a full-blown allegory, elucidated with a mass of details. "The French Protestants, if my conjecture is true," he concludes,
"would be represented by Pantagruel's men, while the Sausages would
represent the Swiss or the Germans."[31]

Le Duchat does not develop this historicization of the second half
of the episode with the allegorical luxury of his predecessor but he
accepts its main contention, while modifying the particular identities
involved:

> I do not doubt that these Sausages [Andouilles] and mountain-dwelling
> Sausages [Saucissons montigènes] refer to the English, principally those
> in the mountains, whom Mary [queen of England 1553–1558, Catholic
> daughter of Henry VIII] had burned for the religion which they pro-
> fessed. The intrigues of some cardinals to bring these people [the En-
> glish] back into the Roman communion are well known. . . . Down to
> the Council of Trent they did not entirely give up hope of succeeding,
> but [finally] they proceeded to anathematize these people formally. This
> is what, in Rabelais's style, renders Lent [*sic:* Le Duchat writes Carême
> for Quaresmeprenant here] *breneux, halbrené,* and *stocfisé,* that is, without
> any allies and excommunicated, in case he were to form a friendship or
> alliance with the Sausages of Ferocious Island.[32]

The hallucinations brought about by reducing the context of the text
to religious controversy could not be better illustrated. In such a situation perhaps it was wisest to treat the Sausages as just sausages, as the
Abbé de Marsy insisted on doing in his expurgated Catholic edition of
1752. To pretend that they are mountain-dwelling English Protestants
like Le Duchat or Swiss Protestants like Le Motteux, he writes, is to
"lose oneself in vague ideas" and to "entangle Rabelais rather than clarify him." But de Marsy did not avoid another kind of allegory, spiced

---

31. These quotations are taken from their reprint in Esmangart and Johanneau, ed. *Oeuvres de Rabelais,* 6: 269, 327. I have used this French translation of
Le Motteux's notes and their reprints of the notes of some other eighteenth-
century editors because of the difficulty of repeated access to the originals in
rare book collections. In cases that I could check, these editors' reprints have
been accurate.

32. Ibid., 6: 335, n. 17. Le Duchat's note to this effect is found only in his
second edition, published in Amsterdam in 1741.

with nationalism. In this passage the Pantagruelians wage war against "foreign-made saveloy," he writes, particularly against those "made at Bologna in Italy"![33]

Caught as he was in his own confessionalism, de Marsy saw himself compelled to accept the Protestant commentators' idea of Quaresme-prenant, even though he too was bothered by the clash of that idea with the word's colloquial meaning:[34] "Rabelais . . . gives to Lent the name of Quaresmeprenant, which ordinarily refers to the last days of Carnival. Xenomanes, who represents Luther [!], goes on to explain Lent with the same temerity as that reformer. According to Luther, Lent and many other austerities of that kind are useless practices. . . . Rabelais thought like Luther on this matter."[35]

If the process of elision of Rabelais's context were merely a tale of ideologically motivated misreading, it would be superfluous to have pursued it in this detail. I have sought to illustrate a more general principle: understanding the history of a text's interpretation is part of understanding the text itself. Readers' contexts are not merely different from those of authors because they concern different times and places; they should be categorically distinguished from authors' contexts because they evolve indefinitely, unlike authors' contexts, which cease to evolve with authors' last revision of their texts. The distinction makes—or should make—readers aware that their understanding of the closed set of authors' contexts is of necessity open-ended and indefinite. The means readers have of achieving closer understanding of a text are thus two, not one: reconstructing the text/context through study of the text and its sources, and reconstructing the always unfinished evolution of the interpretation of the text, with its revelations of readers' always too finished conceptions of text/context. The sum of one and the other kind of reconstruction constitutes a text's metatexts.

Metatexts include interpretations and exegesis, editorial apparatuses and critical analyses. I use the term in loose analogy to Louis Hjelmslev's and Rudolf Carnap's references to metalanguage as language de-

33. Ibid.
34. Was he also bothered by the ambivalences in Rabelais's text? Whatever Quaresmeprenant is, it is hard to read Rabelais's descriptions of him as a straight condemnation of Carnival, as required by a strict allegorical schema.
35. Esmangart and Johanneau, ed., *Oeuvres de Rabelais*, 6: 269.

scribing or commenting on another language. Metatexts are as inevitable an element of communication through print as are paratexts.[36] But they do not intertwine themselves with the text in the same manner as paratexts do.[37]

Paratextual elements—such as prefaces, typeface, and footnotes, created tacitly or explicitly by joint decisions of authors, publishers, and editors—are physically adjacent to and inseparable from text. They cooperate with the text to bring it into being. Metatexts juxtapose themselves to text. They are only partly and never necessarily adjacent to or inseparable from the text physically.[38] Some metatexts—Calvin's and DuPuyherbault's, for instance—are even dedicated to annihilating a

36. Umberto Eco is right in his controversy with Claude Lévi-Strauss, *Role of the Reader,* 4–5: A text exists as a result of the mingling of author's context with readers' context. (I would add that in this mingling a third element, the representation of readers and their context by the author, plays an important role.) "To postulate the cooperation of the reader does not mean to pollute the structural analysis with extratextual elements. The reader as an active principal [*sic*] of interpretation is a part of the picture of the generative process of the text. . . . There is no text escaping such a rule. . . . Open texts are only the extreme and most provocative exploitation—for poetic purposes—of a principle which rules both the generation and the interpretation of texts in general." Except for its omission of the processes of evolution in readers' and authors' reactions, the statement and the passage in which it occurs is very useful in probing the problematic addressed in this chapter, the relations between texts and metatexts.

37. The dividing line between metatext and paratext, however, is not clean-cut, as will be indicated. The term metatext came into vogue in the later 1970s. After Claude Duchet's use of it in "L'Illusion historique. L'enseignement des préfaces (1815–32)," *Revue d'histoire littéraire de la France* 75 (1975): 249, and Eco's passing reference to it in *Role of the Reader* (1979), 256, Gérard Genette gave it a more powerful, although ultimately passing place in his literary theory in his *Introduction à l'architexte* (Paris, 1979), 87. The term, defined by Genette, differs from my use of it here. Genette has since abandoned the term metatext and incorporated in his definitions of paratext those elements of the former concept that interested him. See my ch. 1, n. 1.

38. Genette, *Seuils,* 11, distinguishes two parts of paratext, the "peritext" and "epitext." As I have noted in ch. 1, n. 1, this gives too physically local meaning to paratextual elements that may crop up anywhere in a book (e.g., Rabelais's "demoniacal Calvins") and of course filter it throughout its pages through the choice of typefaces. Moreover, those elements Genette calls "epitext" (chs. 12 and 13 of *Seuils*) have, it seems to me, as much metatextual, interpretive meaning as they have peripherally textual meaning: interviews of authors, their participation in colloquia, their conversations, their private journals concerning their texts are means of taking distance from the text no less than means of presenting it.

text. It would be well for the text if metatexts were always clearly situated beyond the text, as one way of interpreting the Greek proposition *meta-* suggests. Readers would then have a better chance of judging their intent. Instead of this, metatextual elements only too often weigh *upon* the text, which indeed may be just as good a way of translating *meta-* in this and some other cases. Metatextual ideas produce critical introductions, footnotes, and commentaries like those I have been considering. They encourage tampering with the text and emending it with the best of intentions. Thus Robert Marichal in the only complete twentieth-century edition of the *Fourth Book* which deals systematically with at least some of the editions published in Rabelais's lifetime, explains his impeccable, impersonal rules:

> Our criterion has been as a general rule to consider as a typographical error in E [the second edition of the *Fourth Book* in 1552, apparently made under Rabelais's supervision], anything which violated sense or grammar and in addition had been corrected in I [published in 1553, falsely advertised by its publisher as a second edition reviewed and corrected by Rabelais[39]]. We have violated this rule only three or four times and corrected readings obviously false which were found in both E and I.

One of those times corrects the "obviously false" reading "flees," found in both E and I, to "follows."[40]

A critical edition like Marichal's allows readers to judge matters for themselves if they will take the trouble to consult the critical apparatus. "Obvious" emendations can then be rejected or at least made problematical. This example is useful because it shows how difficult it may be to discern the metatextual biases determining editorial decisions (why did this emendation seem so obvious?). It is also useful because it shows the interaction of these two forms of mediation between text and reader. The evolution of paratext has made the instrument of critical apparatuses customary in the twentieth century, and so paratext in Marichal's case here parries his metatext. In the eighteenth century the instrument was not customary. Le Duchat, like Marichal, went to great trouble to compare editions of Rabelais, but his paratextual customs led him simply to note the variants in cases that struck him as

39. See n. 14 to this chapter.
40. Rabelais, *Le Quart Livre,* ed. Marichal, xxxviii, 140. See my references to the variant readings of the word in early editions at the beginning of the discussion of *s'enfuyt/s'ensuyt* in this chapter.

critically important, whereupon he wrote an explanatory note about that case.[41]

Classical texts like Rabelais's are deformed, compared to the way they looked in the author's day, when printers' and publishers' customs and technology evolve. But they are bound to evolve, and, when they do, the changes induce altered perceptions of the text, quite independently of any interest in changing the text on the part of new editors or publishers. Paratextual participants like editors are always in fact interested, commercially if not ideologically. The function of paratext is to facilitate the communication of the text. In so doing, the paratext also interprets it.

The early editions of *Pantagruel* and *Gargantua* were printed with clumsily lettered, cluttered title pages and set in a typeface called "bastard gothic," an altered version of the writing hand used in fifteenth-century manuscript books.[42] About 1544 Pierre de Tours of Lyon published, apparently with Rabelais's agreement, a new edition of *Gargantua* and *Pantagruel* set in roman typeface and prefaced with more elegant and less crowded title pages than previously employed (see Fig. 5). The cherubs, garlands of leaves and flowers, and classicizing architectural elements turn aside the popularizing bombast of the long title of *Gargantua;* they suggest instead that the reader take a light, ironic attitude to the text that follows.[43] What is the reason for this shift? Has the author changed the audience at which he aims, or has the publisher? It is likely that both Rabelais and his publishers had changed their ideas of their readers after ten years of sales, the condemnation by the Sorbonne of 1543, the praise of Rabelais as a Democritus reborn, and so on. Paratext is compromise. Paratext will always reflect in some degree the author's context, a context that in the case of new editions by the

41. The case of *s'enfuyt/s'ensuyt* did not so strike him. See Rabelais, *Oeuvres,* ed. Le Duchat, 4: 126: *s'enfuit* (a modernized spelling) is printed without comment. Critical apparatuses did exist in the eighteenth century, and they were occasionally employed for sixteenth-century authors. See the very fully developed one in the sumptuous folio edition by Thomas Carte of Jacques-Auguste de Thou (1553–1617), *Historiarum sui temporis libri CXXXVIII,* 7 volumes (London, 1733).

42. See the reproductions of title pages and text pages in *NRB*; e.g., 65, 76, 84, 135, 142.

43. See *NRB,* 161–65 (no. 27) for details and other reproductions of the pages of this edition. This edition, which bears no date, was published after 1542 and before 1546.

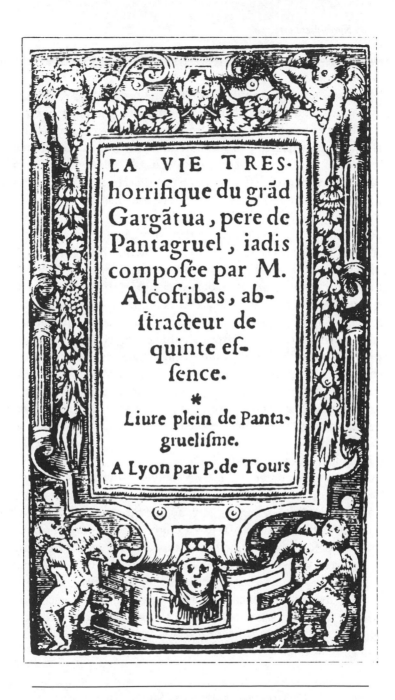

LA VIE TRES-
horrifique du grãd
Gargãtua, pere de
Pantagruel, iadis
compoſée par M.
Alcofribas, ab-
ſtraƈteur de
quinte eſ-
ſence.
*
Liure plein de Panta-
gruelifme.
A Lyon par P. de Tours

5. Anonymous, Title page, Rabelais, *Gargantua* (Lyon: Pierre
de Tours, n.d. [ca. 1544]). Phot. Bibl. Nat. Paris.

author in his lifetime includes representing the metatexts of which the author is aware.[44]

Metatexts, existing essentially beyond the text, do not compromise. They emend the text (Marichal), assault it (DuPuyherbault), or laud it (Bakhtin) in ways that only too frequently turn out to be falsifying. This is appropriate, for the function of metatexts is less to communicate the text than to make it interesting. Metatexts define what is at stake for us in what we read. They are always as reflective of the critic's context as of the author's. That is no less inevitable than the evolving paratext's deformations of the text's physical form.

Metatexts are divisive. Whatever their objectifying pose, in fact they ask readers to take sides. Critics write for coteries. However broad the synthesis they attempt, they always favor some things over others, and they cultivate some kinds of readers over others. If they did not, they would not bother to write. Metatexts excite us: they tell us how and why the text is related to who we are. They also tell us how and why the text is differently written from anything that we or our contemporaries might write. This is the double function of criticism and editing: to make the text accessible and to place it at a distance, to expose its limits as an artifact, complete and finished only in relation to a certain state of opinion, a certain cultural context, and at the same time to reveal its unexpected relevance to something in our times which connects us to that particular past. Metatexts are interpretations; they are also insights.[45]

To their double salutary effect corresponds, with the passage of time, a double distortion. Metatextual insights collect like barnacles on specific passages of text, passages that were, for the critic or editor, points of access to their insights. What was a source of revelation for one critic cannot be so for others. Others' contexts are different, for times and critical coteries evolve. The points of entry to the text become barnacles (Le Motteux's Tapinos Island; Kinser's *s'enfuyt/s'ensuyt*) because they eventually obstruct apprehension of the text's general character. They interfere with one's sense of the text's structure. They need to be scraped off, and they are when new seawaves of opinion sweep in.

44. See point 3 of Appendix 1, Contexts, concerning this matter. In the case of posthumous editions the very decision by editors and publishers to republish an author reflects metatextual ideas of some kind.

45. Hence the hedging statement about metatext as interpretation on the first page of the Foreword.

The other distortion that follows from metatexts' hold upon a text is generally rather than specifically located. When the critics' context disappears from a cultural milieu, replaced by other fashions, the general concepts to which the critics' context gave rise do not disappear with it. They remain like a residue, orienting succeeding studies and editions of the text, largely because—unlike barnacled points of opinion—they cannot readily be seen. The diffuse, often unwritten presence of critical principles passes unnoticed unless, as in the case of the criticism of Homer, Dante, or Rabelais, a long-term history of metatext becomes possible, which makes visible the slow staining of the text's colors through the collection over centuries of such residues of critical insight.

The socioreligious commitments of Rabelais's seventeenth-century critics are so easy to discern at three centuries' distance that they seem absurdly prejudiced. But they are no more so than our own obscure proclivities. "You" here—you people who have received the *Fourth Book* with vinous affability in the spring of some fortunate year—receive it with critical notes, indexes, introductions, and bibliographies which in various ways deliver to you not exactly Rabelais's words but a colored and accented version of them.

Time-space and sociocultural change elide context and secrete metatext. But criticism can be used against its own thickening substance to restore context and modernize metatext, when the history of metatext is pursued at the same time. Criticism excavates the text/context relation, while the history of metatext explains the accumulation of debris around such mining sites and offers counsel about what to clear away. Carried on jointly, critical and historical work offer defense against the tendency to translate anachronistically and to annotate inertially, as contexts of communication continue to change.

During the seventeenth and the eighteenth century the double process of contextual elision and metatextual secretion around Rabelais's text went unperceived in the case of Rabelais's *Fourth Book.* Four types of annotation developed: the philological work on difficult words and phrases by the anonymous author of the Alphabet published in 1663, which left open the import of episodes like the one in Book 4; the confessional allegorism and biographism of Le Motteux and Bernier in the 1690s, which integrated single episodes into overall interpretations; the far more developed critical method of Le Duchat's 1711 edition, which took some account of variant readings in previous editions and buried Le Duchat's mild Protestant confessionalism in a plethora of nearly phrase-by-phrase footnotes, thus returning to the more open-ended metatextuality of the Alphabet author; and the repressive confessionalism of de Marsy's edition of 1752, which, based upon Le Duchat's work, could for the first time expurgate Rabelais with thoroughness and authority.

The Alphabet author's kind of interpretation was not first attempted in the mid-seventeenth century. The Alphabet was adapted from the earlier work, apparently unpublished until the twentieth century, of a person named Perreau who wrote in 1611. His alphabetically ordered list of words and phrases can be considered the earliest example in Rabelaisian criticism of a philological allegorism. We do not know for certain who this Perreau was, except that he was familiar with medical terms and with folk customs in Poitou. The signature of one Franciscus Perrellus has been found in Rabelais's copy of Galen's medical writings. Is it this François Perreau who wrote the "Explanation of some Sayings Taken from the Works of François Rabelais"? The date 1611 as the time of composition can be determined from internal evidence in the manuscript. Perreau's "Explanation" came into the hands of the Parisian scholar Jacques Dupuy, who sometime before his death in 1656 made a copy that is the only presently existing manuscript of it.[46]

46. The "Explanation" is printed in full in Grève, *Interprétation*, 275–93. Grève does not say where or how the "Explanation" is attributed to a person named Perreau in the manuscript; he simply states that no first name is included in this attribution. Grève, 254–55, follows the work of another scholar, Henri Clouzot, who in "Les commentaires de Perreau et l'alphabet de l'auteur français," *Revue des études rabelaisiennes* 4 (1906): 60, n. 3, mentions the François Perreau who possessed Rabelais's Galen. Neither Grève nor Clouzot decides between F. Perreau as author and one Jacques Perreau, who wrote a book published in 1654 (this book was cited in turn by Bernier as having been inspired by Rabelais: ibid., 60), because neither critic noticed Perreau's entry "Turelupin" where the author states that he is writing 237 years after 1374, that is, in 1611 (see Grève, *Interprétation*, 293). The date 1611 makes it nearly impossible that Jacques Perreau, whose work was published in 1654, was the author of the "Explanation." But we cannot say certainly that François Perreau was the author because we have no further information about him than his undated signature in Rabelais's Galen. As Jacques Boulenger shows in *Rabelais à travers les âges* (Paris, 1925), Rabelais's Galen belonged at one time to Cardinal Duperron, who died in 1621. The Franciscus Perellus who owned it would have possessed it after Duperron, according to Boulenger, although he does not explain the evidence for this assertion.

Perreau's "Explanation" includes no entries for Quaresmeprenant, the Sausages, or Tapinos Island. Was this because Perreau assumed that readers understood the festive references of these names? Perreau was interested in festive customs; he clarifies Rabelais's term "pamyle" (not a term used in the Carnival-Lent episode) by explaining a Carnival parading custom in Poitou, which was no doubt his native region.[47] It is Perreau, too, who explains Rabelais's reference to Quaresmeprenant's children, "locative adverbs," as a Lenten search for indulgences because such, it seems, was the practice in his time and place. Neither this entry nor one or two others dealing with terms in the Carnival-Lent episode show any sign that he supposed Quaresmeprenant to represent Lent or the Sausages to represent Carnival, or vice versa.[48]

The Alphabet author whose work was published in the 1663 Elzevier edition had little interest in folklore. He borrowed Perreau's explanations of Greek terms and dropped much of the rest. The difference between Perreau's sense of Rabelais's text in the early seventeenth century and that expressed in the Alphabet author and other readerly aids in the Elzevier edition seems due less to changes in Carnival-Lent customs than to destruction of the mixed social and cultural milieus characteristic of Renaissance France. The separations of elite and folk, of high and low culture that took hold after Henry IV's death (1610) shifted perception of popular customs.[49] In addition to obtaining or financing the Alphabet author's adaptation of Perreau's "Explanation,"

47. Grève, *Interprétation*, 288.

48. Locative adverbs are discussed in my analysis of the first anatomical description of Quaresmeprenant in ch. 3. Clouzot, "Les Commentaires," 62, prints the Alphabet author's foreshortened version of Perreau's entry concerning locative adverbs side by side with the latter. The difference is an excellent illustration of how the discovery of one critic becomes such a platitude for another that it loses its meaning and appears as a metatextual barnacle: one can scarcely understand what the Alphabet author means to say without Perreau's fuller text.

49. We assume here that the Alphabet author wrote closer to 1663 than to 1611 and that his work was perhaps specifically adapted from Perreau's text for the Elzevier edition. This is a mere hypothesis in the absence of other information. What is not hypothesis is the difference in tenor between Perreau's metatext and the ensemble of metatexts in the Elzevier edition. I write "shifted perception," not "erased interest," in popular customs. It is well to recall such antiquarian works from the middle and later seventeenth century as Oudin's *Curiositez françoises* (1656), quoted earlier in this study to show the proverbial existence of Quaresmeprenant-as-Carnival at the time of the book's publication.

the Elzevier editors republished the "Brief Clarification . . . of the Fourth Book" and two others aids: "A Clarification of Some Difficult Places in Rabelais" and a "Key to Rabelais." These aids make the Elzevier edition not only abusively allegorical, as in the exegesis of Tapinos Island, but simplistically positivist in its understanding of allegory. The Key identifies Gargantua as Francis I, Pantagruel as Henry II, and the land of the Sausages, for example, as Rabelais's home province of Touraine.[50] Even if they were courtiers and *beaux esprits,* people in the mid-seventeenth century no longer possessed through personal or family memory the knowledge of Rabelais's political and social ambience that Perreau in 1611, it seems, still took for granted.

The new cultural milieu that took shape in the early seventeenth century (moralism, neoclassicism, and the separation of elite from popular classes) was seconded in Rabelaisian criticism by the sheer historical distance between 1550 and 1650. Even though something of Rabelais's embracing exuberance continued to be apprehended by persons like Madame de Sévigné and her cousin Bussy-Rabutin as late as the 1670s, such readers needed clarification of the profuse topical references in Rabelais's text.[51] That clarification was offered in the form of keys and alphabets dealing with individual words and characters because editors like those who made up the Elzevier edition assumed that they and their readers knew what Rabelais was generally about. Meanwhile, however, a third factor to which I have already referred was eliminating that general knowledge: the successful efforts of French authorities in church and state to prevent open publication of Rabelais's work in France. From 1613 to 1783 no edition appeared with a French place name on its title page.[52]

50. The "Brief Clarification" (*Briefve Declaration*), first published in some copies of the *Fourth Book* in 1552, is included in the Elzevier edition only in a mutilated form, from which all the terms also clarified in the Alphabet have been subtracted. The "Key" is printed at the end of both volumes 1 and 2 on two unnumbered pages. The "Clarification" (*Eclaircissement de quelques endroits difficiles du Rabelais*) is written with the same historicizing positivism as the Key. Grève, "Les érudits," 45–46, quotes some excerpts from it. The Alphabet, Brief Clarification, and Clarification are printed at the end of volume 2, just before the Key.

51. On Madame de Sévigné and Bussy-Rabutin, see Boulenger, *Rabelais à travers les âges,* 42–43.

52. See Boulenger's listing of editions, Pl. Bib., 1022–24. Boulenger's no. 128 seems to have been published at Paris in 1732. If Boulenger has been consistent

Another aspect of this political factor, the resurgence of officially endorsed Catholicism that culminated in the revocation of religious and civil rights to French Protestants in 1685, pulled interpretation of Rabelais's text toward simplified religious alternatives. It concentrated readers' attention on the text's ideological implications and on how to match particular passages with the religious image of a man called— sometimes approvingly, sometimes contemptuously, but always irrelevantly—"the priest of Meudon."[53]

This combination of forces made possible and perhaps inevitable the allegorizing mistakes in interpreting Rabelais's Carnival-Lent episode by the 1690s. The rebirth and extension in the late seventeenth century of the philological method initiated by Renaissance humanists occurred just when an ill-informed, confessionally inspired allegorism completed the dissociation of the text from its context. The misunderstandings that had grown in the hollow places left by seventeenth-century arrogance toward and ignorance of Rabelais were systematized. An industriously Protestant critical tradition acted in combination with the defensiveness of Catholic scholars to reduce Rabelais to bits and pieces. In this setting La Bruyère's mixed reaction of puzzlement and disgust was representative and would continue to be so for another century:

---

in his punctuation, however, Paris was not indicated openly as the place of edition. Boulenger's no. 134 was ostensibly printed at Geneva but actually at Paris in 1777, as was de Marsy's "Amsterdam" edition of 1752. Grève's two excellent studies of seventeenth-century Rabelaisian criticism, "Les érudits" and "Les libertins," neglect the influence of this changing climate of opinion. To him it was a grave mistake to comment upon Rabelais's works in 1663 because it stimulated a stream of partial and wrongheaded keys to particular passages. But the censorship stimulating such keys was more important than wrongheaded editorial policy. As indicated later in my text, the development of critical philological method in the late seventeenth century (Mabillon, the Maurists, the Bollandists, Bayle) was equally important in stimulating the historico-allegorical approach to Rabelais.

53. Rabelais was given the benefice of the parish of Meudon near Paris in 1551, two years before his death. He seems neither to have resided there nor to have otherwise occupied himself with parish duties. Boulenger, *Rabelais à travers les âges*, 67, quotes Voltaire in a passage that shows the way this biographically marginal fact could be pulled out of context: "Rabelais fut curé de Meudon, et [Jonathan] Swift fut doyen de la cathédrale de Dublin: tous deux lancèrent plus de sarcasmes contre le christianisme que Molière n'en a prodigué contre la médécine et tous deux vécurent et moururent paisibles, tandis que d'autres hommes ont été . . . mis à mort pour quelques paroles équivoques."

"Rabelais is incomprehensible . . . inexplicable . . . a monstrous assemblage of fine, witty moralism and foul corruption."[54]

Le Duchat's dutiful scholarship, because it embalmed the partitive approach to Rabelais, had a double effect. It contributed to the continuing disregard of Rabelais's literary qualities during the Enlightenment and early Romantic era because it was concerned to explain Rabelais's ideas, not his language. But it also contributed to the gradual disappearance of simplistic, alphabetized "keys" to his "satires." As early as 1737 John Ozell, an English editor of Rabelais, praised Le Duchat "because we now see that Motteux is wrong in many things."[55] Silently the mental space was cleared for the nineteenth-century discovery of a Rabelais once more made whole, this time as a genial embodiment of Humanity.

Others have traced the manner in which the eloquence of Balzac, Michelet, and above all Hugo apotheosized Rabelais.[56] The exaltation did little to aid understanding of the Carnival-Lent episode, which, as it lost its confessional color, became an amusing but rather long-winded and opaque farce. The conservatism of scholarship—sometimes a synonym for its inertia—combined with the disappearance of the ritual value of Lenten as well as Carnival customs in a lay society to insure that the passage's enigmas rarely even existed sufficiently to be footnoted except in repetition of what had long ago been said.[57]

Rabelais's textual tactics proved a failure. His welcoming-in has shut most readers out. His repeated shifts in representational strategy may fatigue the most diligent *rabelaisant*. What Rabelais could not foresee,

54. Jean de La Bruyère, *Les caractères et moeurs de ce siècle* (Paris, 1941), 82.

55. John Ozell, eds., *Works of François Rabelais,* Volume 1 (London, 1737), xiv–xv.

56. See Boulenger, *Rabelais à travers les âges,* 100, and Lazare Sainéan, *L'influence et la réputation de Rabelais.* As with other forceful metatextual constructs, Victor Hugo's was not only important as a counter to neoclassic particularism, but his vision of the text also seizes one of Rabelais's essential values and mysteries: "Rabelais que nul ne comprit . . . / Et son éclat de rire énorme/ Est un des gouffres de l'esprit."

57. The grandest monument of uninventive antiquarianism that resulted from this is Esmangart and Johanneau's Variorum edition of Rabelais (1834: see nn. 9, 21, 26, 31, etc., above). The inventive exception that nonetheless proves the antiquarian rule is Anatole Le Double's book (1899: ch. 5, n. 7).

of course, was the way in which the climates of opinion affecting his book would change. But he seems to have taken little account of future readers. Aware as he was of vast cultural changes in the past, he apparently had less interest in what the future might think of his book. Perhaps he assumed that everyone, if they possessed good will and common sense, would understand.[58] This idea of several simple and unchanging qualities that Rabelais was apt to attribute to the community of his readers has affected his commentators. Critics have seen the necessity of situating the text historically, but they have assumed that the period stretching between them and Rabelais is essentially a fixed and stable duration and thus that their clear eyes, good will, and common sense suffice to penetrate Rabelais's era directly, without taking account of the echelons of intervening cultural change.

It is as if the very ambiguity of the text provoked its opposite, those two mirages that glimmer, now one and then the other, before the mind's eye of every enthusiast for Rabelais: the mirage of some unifying meaning to this large and diffuse text, caught in the amber of a past dead and gone, the glamorous European Renaissance; and the mirage of a past in continuity with the present, the sixteenth-century beginning of modern times, so that Rabelais's meaning is our meaning, and Rabelais's invitation to step in for a chat is indeed addressed to us.[59]

These fond visions are only that. Sooner or later they dissolve to reveal the fretful double truth: Rabelais's times are in continuity and discontinuity with our own, and hence his words have both the same and different meanings from ours; which words are the same and which are different is also something that changes.

58. See in chs. 8 and 9 the analysis of Rabelais's new theory in the *Fourth Book* of partial audiences.

59. The reader will have observed that I have shifted in the last few paragraphs from seventeenth- and eighteenth-century to nineteenth- and twentieth-century attitudes toward Rabelais's times.

# 7

# Semiotics and Criticism

After the seventeenth century the words comparing Rabelais's Carnival-Lent episode scarcely corresponded to what readers and critics experienced during Carnival. Changed contexts led critics to interpret the signs in the first part of these chapters so that they would refer to Lent and to separate them from the rest. If this version of the signs' referents still survives today, it is not only due to the tendency of metatextual elements to turn into barnacles and discoloring residues;[1] metatexts of course adhere to texts because of the somnolence with which a text is received, once it has been normalized by some prestigious editor. But the version also adheres because the way in which a text has been meta-textually constructed makes it impossible to perceive many particular passages in any other way. Only a general reconstruction of the text will unveil its lost meanings, for the more powerfully a certain kind of critical instrument cuts into the text the more threads of meaning are severed, which can only be apprehended by dissecting it in another way. Paratextual constructions are conservative: the integrity of the inherited text tends to be respected as far as is economically and technologically convenient, out of allegiance to codes of impartiality and out of interest in profiting anew from modes of textual realization that have worked in the past. Metatexts may be conservative or not: that depends on the critic's situation, which in turn depends on general cultural conditions. But whether conservative or innovative, metatexts are always antago-

1. John Ozell, Rabelais's eighteenth-century English editor, although he disagreed with the excessive allegorism of Le Motteux's notes to Rabelais and eliminated many of Le Motteux's notes, retained Le Motteux's translation of the *Fourth Book*. Later English editors have done the same, modernizing the style but not the sense. Thus the Modern Library editions of Rabelais in the 1940s and 1950s translated Tapinos Island as Sneaking Island and Quaresme-prenant as Shrovetide without annotation. So does the currently published "Great Books" edition of Rabelais (Chicago, 1984). Cohen's Penguin edition of 1955 exchanged Le Motteux's barnacle for Le Duchat's in one case (Quaresme-prenant is translated as King Lent; no annotation), while retaining the others (Tapinos Island is Sneaks' Island; no annotation).

nistic. Consensus rarely lasts long, for critics must criticize, and they have ample impulse to do so: the Age of Print has steadily augmented the number of intersecting, competing cultural milieus.

A complex text that has become a classic text thus will have solicited over time the application of many kinds of tools. Discovery of the severed threads will always occur if interest in the text continues. What, then, is the nature of the sharp tools in use today? How has the play of interpretive antagonisms now arranged itself so as to buttress or hollow out inherited attitudes toward Rabelais's use and critique of Carnival-Lent customs?

In 1923 C. K. Ogden and I. A. Richards wrote a book about semantics called *The Meaning of Meaning.* They used a simple triangular model to illustrate their ideas, which were adapted from those of the American philosopher C. S. Peirce, a founder of the present-day disciplines loosely grouped under the name of semiotics, the study of sign systems. Ogden and Richards call the three points of their triangle "symbol," "thought," and "referent." The triangle represents the semantic process, the coming into being of meaning. This process is described by them as a single action made by one individual to another. A person uses some symbolic means, such as words, gestures, or facial expressions, to convey a thought to another person about some condition or thing.[2] The terms Ogden and Richards use to describe their model possess long histories; they are words more useful for their polyvalent suggestiveness than for their precision. The word "symbol" is particularly fraught with meanings at variance with Ogden and Richards's use of it, and I have sometimes substituted the phrase "linguistic vehicle" for it. Ogden and Richards's schema is pragmatic rather than theoretical, and I propose to adapt it in turn for pragmatic reasons. They ask how someone talking to another, for example, grasps the meaning of what the other person is saying. I ask how readers, and a fortiori critics, analyze a text viewed as a set of signs and conclude that its meaning is one thing rather than another.

Pluralizing the elements of Ogden and Richards's triangle, one might call it a simplified semiotic image of a text.[3] One could call em-

2. C. K. Ogden and I. A. Richards, *The Meaning of Meaning* (London, 1923), 11.

3. The image is oriented toward the semantic side of semiosis. The relation of semantics to the grammatical, phonological, rhythmic, and other more physically localizable and measurable aspects of linguistic semiosis remains controversial. Indeed, nearly every term and every system of terms proposed by schol-

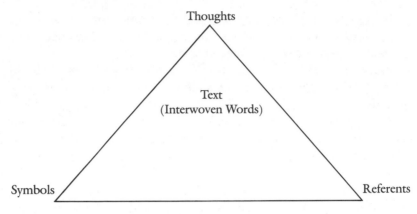

Thoughts

Text
(Interwoven Words)

Symbols                                    Referents

6.   The Mixed, Alternating Stresses of Textual Meaning

phasis on one or another of its three angles a critical tendency and then ask how the development of a particular school of Rabelaisian criticism might be related to analysis of one aspect or angle of such a textual sign system at the expense of or even in polemic opposition to analysis of other aspects. (See Fig. 6.)

Texts, and above all fictional texts, are sign systems that create what W. H. Auden once called "secondary worlds."[4] The passage of a text's signs to readers is not taken up in the kind of immediate action-reaction-action chains that distinguish exchange of sensory signals and signs as one performs daily tasks and responds to one's environment in practical, short-term ways. Understanding a text presupposes some removal from such practical exchanges and tasks and demands complex and sometimes lengthy absorption in its artificial universe.

Once caught up in and fascinated by the secondary world of a text, readers are apt not simply to absorb what it says but to wonder about it. How did such a world come to be created? What were its ingredients? One wants to know, late or soon, not simply what but why Rabelais wrote what he did, and this questioning sends one in two directions, to his experience and to his skill. One wonders about Rabelais's place and his possibilities in the world to which he belonged, and one reflects upon how he wrote, as opposed to what he said, about this

---

ars working in the new disciplines of semiotics are highly controversial and have drawbacks. The problematic broached here will be better conceived in a future era.

4. W. H. Auden, *Secondary Worlds* (New York, 1969).

experience. Readers are sent by the complexity and power of the whole text back to its parts to study the author's techniques; they are equally sent beyond the book to the "first" world of society, human history, and human culture to which it pertains. Critics, formalizing these tendencies, tend to produce metatexts that philosophize, historicize, or aestheticize.

When the relation between the Rabelaisian text's world of *thought* and that of the critic seems of most importance, metatexts are written that emphasize the author's ethical, religious, metaphysical, or otherwise philosophical message. When the text's *referents* to social, political, cultural, or other circumstances of its composition are most ardently pursued, metatexts have a strongly biographical or literary-historical character. When analysis of the writer's skills is pursued, the text's specifically literary or symbolic qualities begin to separate themselves from more general philological concerns. This last trend has emerged in Rabelais's case primarily in the twentieth century; it has arisen especially as part of the vogue of formalism and of the movement sustaining Ogden and Richards's enterprise, semiotics.

Formalist and semiotic emphasis on the symbol, the written vehicle of thoughts and referents, has been carried on a wave of anticontextualism, a salutory reaction to the excesses of late nineteenth- and early twentieth-century historical realism. Those who have sought to isolate what Russian formalist critics called "literariness," the specifically literary qualities of a text, have been the most exciting recent explorers of the text.[5]

> It is Rabelais' use of language to obtain a total, complex emotional response which is essential. Yet the bulk of Rabelaisian scholarship is concerned with his "philosophy," his religion, his legal and medical authority, his humanism and his Christian-Stoic wisdom rather than with the words on the page. . . . Rabelais is a writer in love with his medium. His inspiration is primarily literary.[6]

Such has been the tenor of the battle cries (against philosophy, against moralizing criticism, against history) and such, often enough, the new biographic intentionalism (Rabelais in love with his medium), no less

5. Victor Erlich, *Russian Formalism: History-Doctrine* (Paris, 1965), 175–78, discusses the development and importance of "literariness." Shklovsky initiated the phrase, along with the idea of art as "making strange" stereotyped language, in an essay in 1919: "Art as a Device."

6. Dorothy Coleman, "Language in the 'Tiers Livre,'" in Coleman and Scollen-Jimack, ed., *Rabelais in Glasgow*, 39.

tendentious in its way than those of earlier days concerning the priest of Meudon or the hero of humanity.

Perhaps the tendentiousness has been necessary. The task, in any case, is enormous. It has been no less than the definition of the aesthetic dimension of Rabelais's work, a task scarcely even thinkable, let alone possible to perform, in terms of the neoclassical norms dominating French literary judgment until the twentieth century. Even Sainte-Beuve, although he both attacked the absurdity of the biographically positivist approaches to Rabelais, which asserted one-to-one relations between life experiences and textual expression, and suggested that the roots of Rabelais's aesthetic lay in linguistic inventiveness, never formalized his intuitions and elaborated a methodology that could be used to extend his observations.[7]

Everyone interested in Rabelais has their own version of the Picrocholean Wars, which pit good interpretations against bad, frivolous, irresponsible ones. But I have proposed the trichotomy above for analytic not judgmental reasons, and I would urge that analysis be carried on in the mood of Epistemon's cry: "We all hold [fiefs] from Mardi Gras!" For in spite of the many differences between Spitzer, Lefebvre, and Saulnier; Glauser, Febvre, and Beaujour; Bakhtin, Demerson, and Gaignebet; Rigolot, Screech, and Defaux, none of these *rabelaisants* (pace Spitzer)[8] is so one-sided as to use none of the insights of his or her antagonists. Just as in Rabelais's Carnival-Lent combats, selecting one enemy seems to attract another antagonist who often turns out to be a confederate. Defining literariness demands, as Dorothy Coleman suggests, deliverance from historicizing philosophy, but in most cases it soon urges conciliation with some other brands of history to support one set of literary standards rather than another. Historicizing critics, concerned with establishing as full a context for the text as possible, find the ahistorical pose of strictly literary appreciation of the text prone to elementary misconceptions about the limits of the author's universe of discourse. Yet few such critics fail to comment on the more than historically predictable power of Rabelais's verbal magic. Philosophically inclined interpreters are often the most difficult treaty partners;

7. See the discussion of Sainte-Beuve's criticism of Rabelais in Rigolot, *Le texte de la Renaissance,* 12–18.

8. Leo Spitzer's "Rabelais et les rabelaisants," *Studi francesi* 4 (1960), reprinted in his *Etudes de style* (Paris, 1970), 134–65, is among the most famous (or infamous) pieces of polemic in the history of Rabelaisian metatextuality.

they are usually ready to acknowledge historical and literary qualities as long as they remain the arbiters of those qualities' place in the whole, that is, of their subordination to some overriding implication of the text.

A moment's reflection about the communicative process, the means by which words are transferred from authors to readers, makes obvious the complementarity of the five or six major schools of criticism that have emerged or maintained themselves with force in the twentieth century.[9] It is not a person, Rabelais, who fabricates the message subsequently printed as a book, but rather a sign maker, one whose primary relation to the book is his literary behavior, his written manipulation of words. Whatever an author otherwise does, says, or suffers while making his text is only mediately connected to his text, and the nature of this mediated connection is sufficiently complex so that it remains forever opaque to both the author and others, however much authors themselves may feel certain about its nature and however copiously they leave behind them materials that seem to substantiate this view.

A printed text exists for its author, if it reflects with accuracy the manuscript he wished to be printed, as a set of words with their three aspects in a certain ordered relation to each other, but for readers that ordered relation is necessarily unclear. The readers' text is present first as symbols, a set of black marks upon the page, which can be decoded enough to be read if one is literate and knows the language in which the text is printed. The text is present secondarily as a set of referents with which readers are more or less familiar, depending on how his or her information matches that of the author. It will be tertially, and most obscurely, present to readers as an attempt to match the author's thoughts. Readers assemble meaning from their sense of grammatical, syntactical, phonological, rhetorical, and stylistic markers in the text, from their information about the representations in the text, and from

9. Five or six major schools: Historicizing critics are generally divided between those who connect biography to matters of political and especially national political import and those who connect the author's life to matters of literary history and other cultural affairs. Those philosophically interested in the text tend to split between metaphysically and morally concerned critics. Those inclined to limit Rabelaisian criticism more strictly to analysis of the linguistic vehicle, Rabelais's "symbols," are divided between those adhering to the important and continuing tradition of philological criticism and those cultivating the newer semiotic methodologies.

their knowledge of "intertexts" containing signs that seem to them related to the signs in question in any of the three semiotic ways.[10] Reaching out toward the three sources of textual understanding of course occurs with near simultaneity in complex feedback fashion, and any conclusions reached are constantly revised as readers pursue the text. But no matter how readers try, they cannot match with exactitude the way the author's intertextual awareness and contextual concerns led to his or her verbal arrangements so as to achieve meaningfulness. An author's behavior establishes the material aspect of a text; it does not by itself determine the meaning of the text, as Ogden and Richards's schema suggests. The relation of the text's linguistic vehicles to its thought and referent patterns is so opaque that readers are bound to substitute thought and referent patterns of their own for those they do not clearly see.

Linguistic behavior is accessible: the symbolic aspect of words codifies it for any particular book or other deposit of language made by the author. Authorial representation of people, experience, and events is semiaccessible: the referential aspect of signs can be apprehended as constituting a certain universe of things, but information about the referents available to the author when he fabricated his representations can only be onerously and approximately discovered. Hence the relation between referents that exist outside the text in the social, psychological, and natural worlds with which the author was in contact, and the author's sketches, recombinations, and fantasies of and about these referents—his textual representations—not only is initially but also will remain opaque.[11] Unlike French words, which exist in such massive quantities that it is at least hypothetically easy to compare other au-

10. "Intertexts" are parts of other texts by either the same author or other authors. Other parts of the same text as the word or phrase in question are not treated as intertexts. See Appendix 1, esp. point 2.

11. The context of analysis here remains that of fiction. Objects represented in fiction may exhibit especially strong differences from the real objects to which they are in some ways related. Neither represented nor real referents are elements of some ultimately true universe beyond the human instruments of knowing; both are perspectives on reality. Represented referents map a world particular to a specific text, while real referents are, as defined here, objects and experiences of the author-as-person, and not, for example, Kantian "things-in-themselves." Real referents will be idiosyncratic in some respects due to unique personal experience, but they are to a large extent characteristic of the person's milieu. Particularly helpful in distinguishing the parts of the author's world of represented referents are ch. 7, "The Stratum of Represented Objects," and ch.

thors' ways of using them with Rabelais's way, only a few sixteenth-century representations of Carnival puppets exist similar to that which may be one dimension of the description of Quaresmeprenant. I have found no representations, except for Rabelais's own description of Chewcrust, of Carnival puppets that Rabelais himself saw. But if authorial referents are therefore often difficult to interpret, authorial thoughts are nearly inaccessible to precise codification. An effort to mind read an author and to match exactly his or her semantic associations is possible, but it is no more likely to succeed than perfect telepathy.

In fact all three angles of the text's meaning are impossible to measure with exactitude. The words on the page are there, but their linguistic significance is no clearer than their ideational or referential character because each compositional decision by authors represents a set of rarely perfect compromises. Intratextual linguistic patterns adjust themselves to intertextual influences and possibilities. The world of ideas proper to the text, stated and implied, exists in tension with the not necessarily vaster but certainly more varied and conflictual world of all possible ideas characteristic of an author's time and place. The universe of objects, beings, and actions, stated and implied, determining the parameters of the work is erected against, no less than in consonance with, the universe of all possible objects, beings, and actions found in the author's time-space. The patterns, worlds, and universes upon which authors draw cannot possibly be enumerated by readers, let alone articulated in their word-to-word relations to the text's meaning; but it is true that the less inventive a work is, the closer one may come to an exhaustive listing.

One probes the limits of the possible meanings of a text by reading comparatively and by looking at all manner of documentation from the author's locale, archaeological no less than artistic, economic no less than ideological. The further distant from the author in time, space, and sociocultural condition the readers are who conduct such probes, the more they will need help in decodifying the diverse aspects of sign. Literary, philosophical, and historical modes of criticism are equally

---

10, "The Role of Represented Objectivities in a Literary Work of Art and the So-Called Idea of a Work," in Roman Ingarden, *The Literary Work of Art* (1930; trans., Evanston, Ill., 1973).

necessary. We cannot unravel literary manners without expert aid, still less references to cabbages and kings four hundred years gone, and least of all can we correct the ideological preconceptions ordering twentieth-century semantic associations about the text without initiation into the very different modes of sixteenth-century thought, the swirl of meanings amid which Rabelais lived and moved.

When the three kinds of criticism function interdependently, they do much to prevent metatextual barnacles and much to reveal the staining of the text by limited and limiting critical principles. When they function separately, they allow these critical encumbrances to accumulate. The main encumbrance acquired from the labors of seventeenth- and eighteenth-century critics was historico-biographical: because they assumed a double equation (the author *is* what his narrators narrate—never mind his other writing—and what his narrators narrate *is* the meaning of the text's representations), they tended to believe that author and person were one and to bequeath that belief to others in the form of a growing body of biographical tales. This encumbrance did not disappear when legends about Rabelais, the jolly drunkard or exemplary priest, were dispelled. It continued to inspire the "realism" of Abel Lefranc and continues to undergird the allegorism of Claude Gaignebet.[12]

A secondary encumbrance acquired from early critics like Le Duchat and Le Motteux was politico-moralistic. The slippage from Rabelais's antimonastic barbs to his secret Protestantism was nearly inevitable because these critics' historico-biographical equations were seconded by what seemed to them obvious corollaries: an author is as sovereign over his text as a king over his subjects, and hence the author's personality, his beliefs, commitments, and proclivities, determine the relative importance of different parts of his text. For critics with a judgmental turn, the approach to the text through its thought patterns means distinguishing between good and bad, good and less good meaning. The text's significance lies neither outside the text, as it does for thoroughgoing historical "realists," nor at the surface of the text, but just beneath

---

12. On Abel Lefranc, dean of *rabelaisants* in the early twentieth century, see Lucien Febvre, *The Problem of Unbelief in the Sixteenth Century, The Religion of Rabelais* (1942; trans. Cambridge, Mass., 1982), an extended polemic against Lefranc's tendency to regard Rabelais as a modern realist and rationalist. The massively documented *thèse de doctorat* of Claude Gaignebet, *A Plus Haut Sens,* 2 volumes (Paris, 1986), presents a Rabelais devoted to learned magico-mystic theories of the universe and man.

it. For those whose concerns are politico-moralistic it is easy to slip into the place of the sovereign, which they attribute to the author. The hidden unity of the text that an ideologically insistent philosophical critic discerns with the unerring eye of a severe judge authorizes him to privilege parts of the text over others. But Rabelais, for all his humanism, populism, Platonism, evangelism, and any number of other things, did not argue for one or several of these at the expense of the others; to rank their importance merely reveals how the insights of philosophical critics entail blindnesses to which they cling as tenaciously as historians cling to their "facts."

What encumbrance, then, arises from literary or linguistic critics' insistence that the surface of the text is the *whole* of the text and that any move to classify some parts as more important, let alone to explain the text by reference to arbitrarily chosen contexts, forgets the basic reason for the text's continuing appeal to readers, its specifically verbal qualities? This emphasis on "literariness" engenders a new kind of positivism scarcely less reductive than older forms. Michael Riffaterre, we recall, understands the anatomical descriptions of Quaresmeprenant as a series of signifiers designed to make the monster "unspeakable." Refusing to explore the dimension of thought patterns as a domain of textuality with its own relative autonomy, he ignores the relation of Rabelais's words, for example, to contemporary medical practices and controversies of the kind explored by Fontaine: "We should not read it [the text] in search of a meaning, trying to *see* Quaresmeprenant, but . . . instead we should go with the flow of the words."[13] Eliminating investigation of referent patterns, he seems to deny any usefulness to knowing, for example, how Carnival puppets in Rabelais's time might have appeared:

> *The referent has no pertinence to the analysis.* No advantage is to be gained by comparing literary expression to reality. . . . Critics have found themselves at an impasse whenever they have turned to an outside norm to define literature. So this leaves us with only signifiers and signifieds. . . . From my own perspective, which is phenomenological, the signified is deduced from the text. . . . The very way in which the score of the text is deciphered totally subordinates the signified to the signifier. Everything happens at the level of the signifier.[14]

13. Michael Riffaterre, *Text Production*, 15. See the discussion of Fontaine's metatext in the first sections of ch. 3.
14. Ibid., 15. Riffaterre's critical terminology is derived from that of Ferdinand de Saussure, who regarded language as "a system of signs in which the only essential thing is the union of meanings and sound-images"; thus texts are

In my discussion of the identity of Quaresmeprenant I also referred to Floyd Gray's view—similar to Riffaterre's—that each additional detail of anatomical description subtracts from the monster's organic, real existence. "Since few of the comparisons are brought about by phonemic play [amenées par la voie des phonèmes], Rabelais might have been determined in the writing of these litanies by the search for a new language which is caught up in looking for and exploring itself, and which tends to reproduce pure privation."[15] For Gray the *Fourth Book* generally unfolds in the direction of representing a purely verbal existence. Gray does not deny the relevance of "signified" and "referential" aspects of signs in polemic terms like Riffaterre, but like the latter his interpretation subordinates such aspects to the development of relations among the text's linguistic vehicles or symbols. The *Fourth Book*'s ostensible theme of a questing voyage is seen as essentially a verbal device, a stereotype by means of which the divagation of the text toward grammatical, rhythmic, phonemic, stylistic play becomes more visible.

Metatextuality of this kind is extremely valuable. But it is not the whole of criticism. Its exclusionary totalism, isolating the text from the vagaries of biography, ideology, and history, ends often enough in presentmindedness. If we see *our* world as desperately ambiguous, and envisage no happy or at any rate happily executable end to its polyvalence, we may easily find Rabelais's linguistic virtuosity forecasting this dilemma. "Behind the giant-hero [Pantagruel] and his opponents"—Terence Cave is speaking of the Sausages and other characters found in the *Fourth Book*—"lurks a more radically Protean figure—that of the discourse itself. . . . The medium of language might be said to contend gratuitously with itself."[16] Thus, more generally, concludes Cave:

---

combinations of words, which in turn are composed in analytic terms of binary pairs called the "concept" and "sound-image" or, more technically, the "signified" and the "signifier" (*Course in General Linguistics* [New York, 1959], 15, 67). There is a rough correlation between what Riffaterre calls the signified and the referent and what I call thought patterns and referent patterns, but the similarity is only approximate. I am not concerned with the correctness or usefulness in some contexts of Riffaterre's theory, but only with its effects on literary criticism as an evolving body of thought about literary texts in our time, as exemplified in the case of Rabelaisian metatexts.

15. Gray, *Rabelais et l'écriture*, 183.
16. Cave, *Cornucopian Text*, 213–14.

Rabelais, Ronsard, and Montaigne are all caught, in their different ways, in the same problem: the resistance of alien fragments within a new formal context tends to disrupt the movement of the text towards a stable meaning, and thus draws attention to the mode of operation rather than to the product of the writing system. . . . Written in the shadow of an impossible ideal, they proliferate in order to question themselves and to lay bare their own mechanisms. Thus they inevitably represent *copia,* or the cornucopia,[17] as a centrifugal movement, a constantly renewed erasure of their origins.[18]

The *author* is caught? inevitably?—or the modern critic, so obsessed with text-as-text that he or she ignores the communicative mode that frames the *Fourth Book,* the author's offer to readers of a draught of wine and an exchange of amusing stories, and so ignores also the temporally and spatially embedded referential patterns such an offer presupposes?[19]

Over and above their specific historical forms in Rabelaisian criticism three recurrent kinds of metatextual encumbrances may thus be discerned. Philosophico-ideological: the text is an intellectual pattern explained by ideas outside the text that offer a consistent measure for subordinating some parts of it to others. Aesthetico-semiological:[20] the text is a stylistic pattern explained by the coherence of the relations among the text's linguistic vehicles; facts and circumstances, ideas and feelings beyond the text provide only the set of commonplaces and verbal clichés against which the text erects itself. Historico-biographical: the text is a museum exhibit that reflects in a manner deter-

17. On *copia* see ch. 4, n. 20. Cornucopia, as Cave uses it, means fullness to overflowing; that is, overabundant verbality.

18. Cave, *Cornucopian Text,* 182.

19. It is true, as Cave emphasizes here and as Beaujour shows more generally in his *Le jeu de Rabelais,* that Rabelais by means of his verbal explorations entered with gusto into something twentieth-century thought is prone to call, with the dark wisdom of hindsight, an epistemological debacle, that metaphysical indeterminacy that has constituted the power and the snare of modern mentality. But Rabelais did not rest there, confounded. The impossible tangle of faith and reason and of nature and eternity remains for Rabelais an embodied reality. The way to deal with this tangle, Rabelais seems to say, is to act.

20. I use the word "semiological" to denote versions of semiotic criticism that analyze texts as the product of structured oppositions that themselves form or in any case imply a complete and closed logical code. Other kinds of semiotic criticism, not making this assumption, may allow for incoherence in coding and may admit that a verbal text cannot be utterly sealed off from nonverbal elements.

mined by the life and thoughts of the author the times and places in which it was composed.

These metatextual attitudes establish a relation between text and context, but the relation is one-sidedly dominant-subordinate, prescribing critical movement from outside toward or into the text or conversely urging the priority of the "inside" of the text against everything outside.[21] But con-text means what it says: it denotes combination with the text, participation in it in a variable way that can only be exemplified in detail, not by precept. The only general characteristics of the text/context relation are variability and involvement as opposed to the falsifying characteristics of textuality-as-sovereignty and of textuality-as-slavery, that is, the text's total domination over, subordination to, or autonomy from the context.

Even if Rabelaisian critics pursue complementary, mutually limiting approaches in an effort to avoid their metatextual heritage, the text when it arrives before the reader will always include some superfluous glosses and some empty critical space where metatextual aids should have been applied. This happens because the lapse of time and the distance of space between sending and receiving the text does not simply cut away the context of a text definitively, but rather shiftingly. Although no context ever remains exactly the same for long and none is ever revived in its entirety, some social circumstances involved in a text's context may disappear and then reappear, reproducing elements of understanding long vanished. Petrarch's letters to Cicero are an obvious case: elements of empathy became possible within the framework of Italian fourteenth-century city-state life that were not available to a monastic scribe at Monte Cassino in the sixth or the seventh century,

21. The priority of the "inside": given this priority, the crucial issue for critics like Riffaterre and Stanley Fish (see my ch. 1, n. 20) has been the question of whether texts contain sufficient encoded directions to indicate one kind of reading as preferable to all others, as the best reading, as a paradigmatic reading. If one supposes instead that the inside is not hermetically sealed off from the outside, that text and context are intersecting rather than closed spheres; if one supposes further that some parts of the text's context emerge only by contrast with critics' contexts that develop long after that text's context, then *any* reading of the text—even for those whom Susan Suleiman calls "author-centered critics" or "hermeneutic absolutists"—can only be tentative and approximate. Some can be classed as more perceptive or more complete than others but none as more authoritative or definitive. For a review of this critical debate, see Suleiman, "Introduction" in Suleiman and Crosman, *Reader in the Text,* 118–20.

although the scribe read Cicero's letters at a time and in a place physically nearer to Republican Rome. The usefulness of metatextual commentary is not stable.

Metatext also falls out of date because, even as the text/context relationship disappears from critical view with respect to the particular circumstances involved in each section of a text, it begins to appear to the critic in the sense of large contours. The context of sending—planning a work, inventing it, contacting readers by means of a more or less complex mode of publication, receiving feedback on the text—is revealed by new and contrasting ways of doing the same things. The larger parameters of writing and publishing may not emerge until they become problematic.

Readers who try to understand a text whose context is not their own—a text, let us say, written more than two generations ago, or in another country, or in a sharply different social milieu—will construct a metatext, wittingly or unwittingly, if it is not offered to them. Even when metatexts are offered, readers will modify them because their angle of vision differs from anything anyone else writes about the text. Such personally constructed metatexts have the same deficiency as most professionally constructed commentaries; they juxtapose the writer's here-and-now to Rabelais's there-and-then as if it were a single opposition. But in fact we read Rabelais's text in relation to a sequential series of theres-and-thens, the series that has formed our cultural consciousness.

For example, if we use a metatext constructed in our time and geo-social environment, we acquire help from minds that have passed through the same or related contexts as we have. We find such metatextual commentaries from our time more relevant and insightful than older ones, not always because of what they say about the text but because they share our context. Writers of the best metatexts, conscious of this, assault our shared cultural proclivities instead of assuaging them. They draw attention to the ways our perceptions and conceptions of the semiotics of Rabelais's time have changed and to the fact that they have changed in an uneven manner. We read the text with the eyes of people who live and think as we do because of an irregular cultural passage from the sixteenth- to the twentieth-century West, full of bumps and hollows, with moments of high consciousness of Rabelais's messages followed by others where the text has been largely replaced by unlikely icons. Little of this irregularly shaped cultural evolution constituting Rabelais's readerly contexts may be conscious knowledge in any given reader, but it is virtually there because the reader's twentieth-century sense of words stands in evolutionary relation with the words in the text. The falsehood of our reading is predictable, and it is seconded by the biases of a text's metatexts, insofar as we accept these metatexts unreflectively. If we know something of the history of and mutual relations among a text's metatexts, on the other hand, we may discover the incompleteness of our reading, and some of the reasons for it.

Maintaining and extending the relevance of metatext to text is the professional critic's accomplishment. If criticism can be described as the agon that goes on between the inertial, blinding power of critical tradition and the fresh power of new insights prompted by the evolution of readers' contexts, then it has a parallel in the irreducibly dual nature of the text's context. A text emerges from the context of composition not as the unclouded victory of linguistic power over recalcitrant materials but as the unstable and often externally prompted result of struggle between desire and possibility.

Desire, possibility: It is difficult—and finally dehumanizing—utterly to avoid the vagueness of psychological terminology when speaking of the text/context relationship. Critics who have warned against the intentional fallacy have too often been taken to mean that any exploration of the mental life of authors is irrelevant to understanding the text. The intentional fallacy emphasizes the absurdity of psychologism, not of psychology, the absurdity of the Romantic notion that the creative process is a simple movement from inside the brain and heart to outside on paper, of a flow from intention to achievement. If, however, psychological processes are understood as the mental work of sorting out and arbitrating between socially created alternatives, ideal or actual, then one may set aside the strict opposition between social and cultural work existing in the public world, and psychology, existing apart from the world in a wholly private place. Just as the context of the literary work of art should not be described as "outside" the text, so also should it not be described as "inside" the author.

The context of composition is conflictual and processive. The author works with physically existing but not always physically accessible means, some of them in the body, like the nervous system, and some outside or on the body's edges, like the pen that scratches paper or the eyelids that flutter in dreams. This processively developed context has three aspects corresponding once again to the angles of the textual triangle. From the point of view of thought the author struggles to accommodate his experience to his vision, his vocabulary of ideas and feelings to his goals. From the referential point of view the author moves between his knowledge of the world as it is represented in his time, its natural and supernatural, historical and mythic, animal and human elements, and his intuition and feeling for what lies beyond the represented world, reality as it is not yet schematized by percepts and concepts, the world beyond signs, even though imagined solely by means of their representations. From the point of view of linguistic vehicles or symbols the conflict is between the verbal codes an author absorbs from family and society, the clichés that expedite everyday discourse, and the horizon of all possible linguistic play. At each moment of composition, too, whatever the semiotic angle to which primacy is given, the author envisions audience. Composition is directed toward certain kinds of readers always and everywhere, marginally or centrally, consciously or unconsciously; of course, the aim is not usually at the same kinds of readers throughout a text.

Desires, expectations, ideals on one hand; possibilities, practicalities, efficiencies on the other. The issue is a universe of ideas peculiar to the work, a special representation of the world, and a literariness, a linguistic strangeness. No solution is perfect, because each results from conflict between the field of perfection and the field of the practicable and realizable.

Each of these large battles presupposes dozens of minor skirmishes, for the fields of perfection and practice are infinitely divisible. The practicable is a closed space in theory, but its components are poorly known; they must be explored. The main component of the realizable is experience, that which has been tried, obtained, or lost: matters must be sorted out and some of them tried again. The ideal also has a limit, but it is like a horizon rather than a closed space: one knows that reaching for it, redefining it even in part, will reveal another horizon beyond.[22] Every writer hesitates—adds, subtracts, and substitutes. How

22. I am adapting the binary pair used by Reinhard Koselleck in "'Space of Experience' and 'Horizon of Expectation': Two Historical Categories," in Ko-

then does an author decide, with so many relations and conflicts to pursue, to join final battle and wrest away a text? "Nothing was ever created except in haste."[23] The context of the achievement of text is more often that of something like printers' deadlines or personal crises than of leisured achievement of goals, let alone of supernally or genially inspired surety. The struggles of the context of composition are impossible to resolve with satisfaction. Even when the author supposes their solution peacefully acquired, the result may appear provisional in retrospect. The posterity which gazes upon works of art as if they were perfectly realized merely exhibits its ignorance of and unwillingness to imagine the context of composition.

Which semiotic aspect of words is given primacy by the author from passage to passage and even from phrase to phrase, then, is a result of sometimes delicate, sometimes brutal, sometimes negligent compromises taking place during composition. And just as the text may well veer at each point of its unfolding along now one and then another of the connecting lines in the textual triangle, so also does readerly attention change its focus. A book is never read as it seems to present itself, linearly, from beginning to end. We pause before we begin, as the horizon of our expectation spreads out above the printed page; we muse about what went before in relation to what we are reading now, and we fill in the spaces above, below, between each phrase with interfering memories, verbal and nonverbal, associating code to code, narrator's message with our experience, author's purposes with our desire.

The desire of readers to understand writing and not merely to enjoy its virtuosity points to the indissolubility of text/context. Analytically we would do well to separate the written from the writing, just as we should separate critical instruments from their object. But these are

---

selleck, *Futures Past* (Cambridge, Mass., 1985). Koselleck's purposes are more general and theoretical: "In brief: it is the tension between experience and expectation which, in ever-changing patterns, brings about new resolutions and through this generates historical time" (275). As his translator points out in the book's introduction, xvii, n. 17, the term "horizon of expectation" has a previous critical history. It had earlier been developed by Karl Mannheim in *Man and Society* (London, 1940), and by Hans R. Jauss in *Untersuchungen zur mittelalterlichen Tierdichtung* (Konstanz, 1959) and in Jauss's later works.

23. Jacques Lacan's aphorism, as quoted by Anthony Wilden, *The Language of the Self* (Baltimore, 1968), xxviii, n. 7, is characteristically more complex in its context: "Rien de créé qui n'apparaisse dans l'urgence, rien dans l'urgence qui n'engendre son dépassement dans la parole."

counsels of perfection. As metatext tends to cling to a text because readers insist on props, which reassure them that by and large their normal verbal context is sufficient for reading purposes, so an author's context tends more and more to be disregarded. Thus context disappears not only because of lapse of time and critical ignorance but also and above all because readers, including critics, lose or refuse awareness of the text's status as a delayed, highly reflexive and reflective message.

A text represents a secondary world at some remove from daily practice. This fact, enshrined so nobly in the stateliness of print, obscures the text's existential origin. A text was first and so ever and again shall be an attempt to communicate a lengthy message from an author who writes with certain cultural equipment, while living in a certain social complex under certain now vanished bio-ecological conditions, to readers equally specifiable and also equally moving along in the course of change. Identifying the shifting relationship between two sets of communicative aspirations—one which evolved and ended, the other ever shifting, as a book passes from hand to hand and from age to age—is in the largest sense, the critic's charge.

FOUR

# TEXT, SUBTEXT, COUNTERTEXT

From Rabelais's time to Victor Hugo's the writers of metatexts agreed on one thing: an author's verbal power lay in his or her text's relation to an ultimate source, an origin. In the Renaissance this origin was most often construed as inspiration and related ultimately to divinity; in the Romantic era inspiration was historicized and related ultimately to humanity.

The rupture of twentieth-century metatexts with this tradition is extreme. Texts that traditionally represented singular discoveries of truth and original constructions of beauty now appear, less loftily, as crossroads: of opinions, of experiences, of other texts. The author is a point of concentration, not of revelation.

What an author writes seems today less expression than communication. It is part of a conversation with companions, known and not known, contemporary and not so; it can rarely be construed as a cry of enlightenment. But if that is so, is not a text simply one case among many of the signifying activities that mark all human endeavor? Writing is talking, and talking is communing, and communing is the exchange of information and feeling and sympathy without which human life withers and dies. Although Rabelais lived in the sixteenth century, not the twentieth, his conception of literary composition, as of verbal behavior generally, is remarkably similar to this contemporary vogue. A communicative conception of bookmaking is the theme of all his prologues, that place among paratexts where authors deal most directly with readers.

In Part One, I emphasized that Rabelais was able to develop an extraordinarily complex politics or strategy vis-à-vis readers because his writing took place near the beginning of the age of printed books, when the limits of communicative possibility invited by that innovation were not yet conventionalized. He played with readers' awareness of widening places and modes of reading—publicly, privately, together, and alone—and of broadened kinds of reading materials—elite, popular, and any mixture of the two—by representing readers and himself in multiple guise. Dispersing the narrative function, designating readers ironically with many names, he focused attention upon the writing process and its inevitable duplicities in a situation in which the channel of communication, the printed book, removes senders from the receivers of messages and renders them mutually unknowable.

Paratexts are Janus-faced. They not only pull attention toward the text that follows. They also show—they *must* show—solicitude for the lives and opinions of the unknown many whose eyes may touch them. From the very first example of Rabelais's novelistic inventions the stance of the imputed author in the prologues capitalized on this necessity, turning attention outward, beyond writing to the readers' lives, as well as to the author's life. Rabelais's books present themselves as means to an end, as precious medicines for mental and physical grief. The medicine offered is conviviality. In this perspective the fracturing of the narrator and the representation of readers in many different masks serves moral rather than literary ends. Humane living is no solitary self-discipline; it requires the exchange of words. It treats verbal exchange as restorative, as mutually inspiring and vivifying, like a shared draught of wine.

Merry books are good for the spirits of authors no less than of readers because they signify an ambience of convivial exchange. Rabelais's notion of how to write "Pantagrueline" fiction thus posits a certain context for its execution. That context seemed to him to disappear in the 1540s. The slanders of certain "cannibals" were so sharp, he wrote some years later, that he had decided not to write another jot. Rabelais's jovial sense of communication with like-minded persons shriveled. He began to change the concept of his readers and his relation to them. An altered sense of audience appears in the prologue to the *Third Book* (1546) and in the prologue to the incomplete *Fourth Book,* hastily published in 1548.

Then in 1552 the author seemed to beam again. The complete *Fourth Book* published that year, which includes the Carnival-Lent episode, is introduced by renewed declarations of ease and happiness: "Freed from all intimidation, I let my quill-feather take to the wind." "Shake your ears and you shall hear marvels of the good and noble Pantagruel."[1] If

---

1. The last quotation concludes the prologues, *QL,* Pr, 559. The two preceding quotations are from *QL,* DL, 542–43.

Rabelais regained a certain equanimity about the time that he published the full *Fourth Book,* it was because he had finally succeeded, it seems, in formalizing a new way of dealing with his readers, a way that I have in my turn formalized in the title to Part Four.

This concluding section returns to the problems broached in Part One, those of the author's relation to his text/context. As in Part Three, the chapters of Part Four are roughly chronological, proceeding from the early system of author-reader relations to its crisis in the 1540s in a first chapter and then exploring the new method of 1552 through examination of several sections in the *Fourth Book.* The new system did not imply utter rejection of conviviality as a prescription for good writing and good living. Gymnaste can still declare that the Pantagruelians are enfeoffed to Mardi Gras, that prime paradigm of conviviality. But this very Carnival-Lent episode in the *Fourth Book* of 1552 marks, like the other examples to be examined, the limits to the ideal.

What does such a recognition imply about Bakhtin's theory of Rabelais's carnivalesque text? It urges us to reread Bakhtin's text, like Rabelais's, from another angle.

# 8

# Communalism

In the sixteenth century most people's lives were socially articulated; their membership and participation in the communities into which they were born determined most of what they did. At the same time these communities themselves were loosening, enlarging, and subdividing as a result of commercial enterprise, political centralization, military expansion, religious debate, and a dozen other European developments following upon the socially and biologically more difficult fourteenth and fifteenth century. If "Renaissance individualism" has seemed an important theme since its historicization by Burckhardt and Michelet, this is due perhaps more to its burgeoning importance in these authors' nineteenth-century environment than it is to the typicalness of Leonardo da Vinci, Ambroise Paré, or Martin Luther. It is less, in any case, the actual behavior of people than their thoughts, feelings, and aspirations that become themes in Rabelais's fiction.

To quantify the relative power of communalism or individualism to guide people's ideas and desires in Rabelais's time is impossible. We know that individualism in this sense is dominant in the twentieth century, that communalism was similarly dominant in the tenth century, and that the sixteenth century offered persons reasons to believe in either. But if there were many reasons to believe in individualism, there were fewer means to live so. People's homes—rural, urban, or royal—grouped family, servants, relatives, and often friends for long periods; in the towns the home also housed the master artisan's workmen. Small nuclear families of three or four persons living in separate homes were rarely the norm and scarcely the reality. Unmarried persons did not live alone unless they were old and widowed. Courts, ecclesiastical or secular, and convents for monks or nuns were, like the workshops in the towns, places where groups of people lived together, sharing the whole range of daily life rather than retreating to the privacy and isolation of "residential communities" at the end of the workday.

The relation among different kinds of communities was loose or tight, depending on changeable circumstances. Everyone belonged to many interacting groups—religious, occupational, political, familial. Each membership involved some shared patterns of living together, not merely attendance at an occasional meeting. Religious lay brotherhoods passed days and weeks together in group prayer, festive meals, charitable practices. Town citizenship carried similar obligations of service, with none of the mechanizing facilities that render modern political and administrative life impersonal and routine. Above all, the scale of communities was small. Fewer than a dozen cities in all Europe, including Balkan Turkey, possessed more than one hundred thousand people. The primary tie in a technologically primitive age was neighborhood; the primary social sense in a politically decentralized age was mutual dependency.

This is the kind of society represented in Rabelais's books, an unsettled society full of monarchic, entrepreneurial, rural, religious thrusts toward greater power and centralized control, thrusts that are ever and again swallowed up in a sea of localized communities. This society is neither the rigidly articulated one of local feudal-manorial dominance, which made the social typologies of allegory feasible and insightful, nor the anticommunal one of later days that requires literary entry into the details of individualized choice. But it is one in which enough rips and tears have opened in the network of local communities, and enough grand opportunities for individual talent have emerged due to the expansion of European society generally, so that an illusion of fully individualized choice could arise and the ideal could be fabricated of a life lived purely for the sake of the self's fulfillment.

Enter the picaresque hero, enter the humanist. The rogue lives in society's interstices, pursuing his own profit like the military mercenary Jack Wilton, for example, Thomas Nashe's first-person hero in *The Unfortunate Traveler:*

> About that time that the terror of the world and fever quartan of the French, Henry the Eighth (the only true subject of chronicles) advanced his standard against the two hundred and fifty towers of Turney and Turwin [the campaign against Tournai and Terouanne, 1513] and had the Emperor and all the nobility of Flanders, Holland, and Brabant as mercenary attendants on his full-sailed fortune, I, Jack Wilton, a gentleman at least, was . . . [there intervenes more cheerful bombast, which finally winds down to] winnowing my wits to live merrily, and by my troth so I did. The Prince could but command men to spend their blood in his

service; I could make them spend all the money they had for my pleasure.[1]

The humanist was no more capable than the roguish vagabond of
establishing a stable foundation for his grand dreams in a century when
copyrights, royalties, and professional posts in the humanities scarcely
existed. The international community of scholars clogged sixteenth-
century printing presses with their self-seeking letters, always written
with an eye to publication, protesting admiration for the addressee and
his friends and disdain and disgust for nearly everyone else. Perhaps
even Rabelais's letter to Guillaume Budé in 1521, the first of his extant
works, only deviates from the genre because he is so anxious about his
own obscurity that he scarcely dares backbite.[2]

Panurge represents the Rabelaisian concept of deviant freedom; Epistemon is an incarnation of the humanist ideal. These men are not
individualists, and perhaps they do not even dream of being so. They
are Pantagruelians, members of a young men's confraternity of joyous
travelers who share allegiance to and the bounty of a grand feudal
prince. Pantagruel, who is drawn as the most self-sufficient, both physically and mentally, is the most communally minded of the group, never
failing in his feudal, filial, or religious obligations. He is also a humanist
and a rogue, boon companion of Panurge and given to expressing himself exaggeratedly, gigantically, in the learned and pedantic rhetoric by
which humanists distinguished themselves. Pantagruel shares the life of
his fellows even while presiding over it. He is communal in ethos.

There is only one *practicing* individualist in Rabelais's books:
Quaresmeprenant, who hunts at the bottom of the sea, bathes above
the steeples, and hangs around the streets, alone. Quaresmeprenant's
monstrosity is in the largest sense his lack of capacity for community.
Throttled perpetually by his simultaneously Carnivalesque and Lenten
conscience, he seems to be forced to live alone, incapable of sharing any
desire with others for very long. But Quaresmeprenant is only half-
human. It is too much to say that Rabelais attributes an ethic of individuality to him. All we learn about him in this respect are his individualistic habits; relevant to our theme here is the author's apparent

---

1. Thomas Nashe, *The Unfortunate Traveller* (Harmondsworth, Eng., 1972),
254–55.
2. *L,* 959–61.

association of individualistic behavior with monstrosity. Quaresme-prenant's idiosyncrasy is larger than life, worse than anything actual, perhaps because actuality, still so communal, made a self-isolating mania—something which for twentieth-century persons is almost the norm—seem possible to represent only in fantasy. Quaresmeprenant is a mental projection, an imagination of mind-torn self-absorption that balloons in the psyche to create a somatic freak, a child of Anti-Nature like those critics who led the author to brood with mythifying intensity on the excesses of censure.

In Rabelais the representation of action is usually undertaken collectively and shared communally. Heroes may recount adventures undertaken individually elsewhere—Panurge most conspicuously—but they do so for the benefit of sharing the account with Pantagruelians and with Pantagruelist readers.[3] The politics of communication *within* the narrative—who narrates to whom, for what purpose?—are constructed so as to urge a certain kind of communication *beyond* the narrative, between the text and its readers. Tracing the devices by which one kind of communication urges the other reveals the communal ethos.

The novel between the seventeenth and the early twentieth century depended upon representing highly individualized narrators. The novel's construction was based either on presenting everything from the point of view of a character involved in the action, the first-person narrator, or on presenting everything from the point of view of an omniscient observer capable of entering into each character in turn, such that overall unity emerged from the assembly of individual views. After and before the period of the classic novel, however, the narrator's voice is split. There are discontinuities between one or several narrators' comments, and the actions to which they refer are not resolved by an omniscient voice.[4] But the reasons for splitting narrators and disrupting the unity of signification are not the same in the twentieth century as they were in the sixteenth. Discordant narrator-voices in Joyce's *Ulysses*

3. I use "Pantagruelian" to designate Pantagruel and his fictional companions. "Pantagruelist," as used by Alcofribas and Dr. Rabelais, refers to those in all ages, past and future, real and fictional, who profess Pantagruelism: Horace, the "ancient Pantagruelist"; Dr. Rabelais; the Pantagruelians—and you too, "gouty ones."

4. Of course there were and are exceptions to this schema. In the very heyday of the classic novel, for example, Laurence Sterne wrote *Tristram Shandy* and Denis Diderot wrote *Jacques le fataliste*.

correspond to split subjectivity, to the discovery of gaps and disjunctions within as well as between private, individualized psyches. The split narrator in Rabelais's books is another matter. Here narrative voices interact with each other. They repeat, overlap, and participate in each other's mentality.

Rabelais's narrator Alcofribas enters into the action; he is part of the Pantegruelian troop on shipboard. The personage standing on the margin of this narrative report, the "author Master François Rabelais" who writes the prologue to the *Fourth Book,* is revealed by the character of his discourse to be an alter ego to Alcofribas, especially for those readers who have read the prologues to *Gargantua* and *Pantagruel* "by the author" who is not François Rabelais but "Master Alcofribas," as stated on the title pages to these earlier volumes. In the case of the *Fourth Book,* still another figure writes for all to read: "Dr. François Rabelais," the signer of a letter of dedication to the "Most Illustrious Prince and Most Reverend Lord Odet, Cardinal of Châtillon." This narrator dons the mask of a leisured doctor who knows many "great persons" like Odet and writes both for his own amusement and, like Alcofribas, in order to give some "relief" to the "sick and unhappy."[5] Because the title page states that the *Fourth Book* is written by "Master François Rabelais, doctor in medicine," readers over the cardinal's shoulders would have concluded that Rabelais was a metaphorical and also a real doctor who claimed skill in the arts of both words and medicine.

Perhaps the narrator's presentation of himself as a well-off doctor-writer is less a mask than a costume suitable for a man of middling estate to present himself to a courtier. Most readers would probably have slid easily from title page to dedication letter to prologue, scarcely troubling themselves to differentiate among narrative personae to reflect upon Rabelais's device of using an anagram of his name, Alcofribas, to tell his tales. That is no accident. Merging of the narrators is as encoded as their separation because the context of these narrations in dedication, prologue, and text is the communal framework shared by real author and real readers. That framework establishes identity not through a sense of inimitable selfhood but through calculation of the relations among life's many memberships.

5. *QL,* DL, 539, opening paragraph. Alcofribas's parallel words as a writer who cures physical ills are in *G,* Pr, 28, concluding paragraph, and especially in *P,* Pr, 190.

Rabelais's many selves, including the selves peopling his imagination, were interconnected with each other and with those of other members of contemporary society: stated thus, I simply affirm the obvious. It is the way a communal consciousness interplays with political tactics and formal subtlety that is interesting. The interplay is most developed in his last publication before death, the *Fourth Book* of 1552. It develops so far, in fact, that it ironically undermines the communalism.

It took time for Rabelais to arrive at the chastened, curtailed, and sometimes negative visions of community in the *Fourth Book*. The development is easiest to trace in the paratexts and clearest in reference to two issues that, in Rabelais's usual way, are fictionally represented rather than openly discussed: the issues of author-narrator interplay and of readerly reactions to his tales.

Until 1546, when the *Third Book* was published, Rabelais avoided coupling his own name with title page, prologue, and text. Perhaps because he received a royal privilege in September 1545, he published his name on the title page in 1546. But he changed the title of the prologue: instead of "Prologue of the Author," as in *Gargantua* and *Pantagruel*, it reads: "Prologue of the Third Book." The fiction that prologues have been written by Alcofribas is not belied.[6] The same is true of the incomplete *Fourth Book* published in 1548: "Rabelais, doctor in medicine" is on the cover, but the prologue is entitled simply "Prologue of the Fourth Book [of] Pantagruel."[7]

From 1532 to 1552, when the final form of the *Fourth Book* appears, Rabelais labels his works ever more subtly. Why, for example, did he undermine a straightforward claim to authorship on the title page of the *Third Book* (1546) and incomplete *Fourth Book* (1548) by not only qualifying himself as "Doctor in medicine" but also as "Calloier of the Hieres Islands"? "Callo-ier" is an adaptation of Greek *kalos hieros,* handsome (or appropriately looking) priest; *kalos hieros* was a common Greek Orthodox Christian term for monk. The Hyères Islands, situated off the Mediterranean Coast near Toulon, France, were desolate, rocky places that would have served well for the cenobitic life of many Orthodox monks; a Cistercian monastery was founded there in the twelfth

6. Cf. P. Plan, *Bibliographie,* 35 (*Pantagruel*) with *NRB* 130 (*Gargantua*) and *NRB* 174 (*Third Book*).

7. Plan, *Bibliographie,* 140.

century. By Rabelais's time this group of three islands had also become a refuge for pirates.[8]

Rabelais, whose books celebrate conviviality, seems to identify himself in 1546 and 1548 as a doctor *and* self-isolating ecclesiastic on a rocky, unsavory isle. Was it simply that he could not resist the approximate phonic reduplication of the word calloier's *loi-er* in (is)*les* (H)*ier*(es)? Obviously not. I have commented on the fury with which Rabelais attacked his censors in the prologue to the incomplete *Fourth Book*.[9] At the end of the prologue of the *Third Book* he already raged in the same manner:

> As for those padded big-wig brains, haggling critics, don't bring them up, I beg of you, by the name and by the reverence you bear to the four buttocks that begot you and the life-giving peg that coupled them. . . .
>
> Back off, you mastiffs! Out of my way, out of my sun![10] Cowls, to the devil with you! So you'd come here to buttock around and article my wine before you piss on my barrel? . . . Get packing, *cagotz!* Off to your sheep, mastiffs! Out of here, *caphars,*[11] get the devil away! You're still there? I'll give up my share in Papimania if only I can nab you![12] Grr, grrr, grrrrrr. Away, away![13]

The misanthropic anger of this prologue writer is anything but communalist in spirit. The cantankerous, individualistic persona of an island-dwelling monk, full of rocky, rough crotchets like the islands of his supposed origin, is appropriate.[14]

8. Frank Lestringant, "L'insulaire de Rabelais," 269–71.

9. See pp. 34–35.

10. The prologue author, having assimilated himself to Diogenes, refers here to the incident in which the Cynic philosopher, seated in his humble barrel upon the public square, is visited by the world conqueror Alexander. Diogenes tells Alexander, shadowing his barrel, to step aside; he does not yet own the sunshine.

11. On *cagotz* and *caphars,* see ch. 3, n. 41.

12. In 47–54 of the *Fourth Book* the Pantagruelians visit Papimania, island kingdom of papal devotees.

13. *TL,* Pr, 350–51. *NRB,* 45, explains the mistaken reading of "Grr," etc., as "Gzz," etc. in *TL,* Pr, 351.

14. Lestringant, "L'insulaire de Rabelais," 268, points out that "caloyer" was also a term used in Italian, Dutch, and French navigational atlases to mean rocky island. Rabelais's "calloier" is polysemic, as Lestringant emphasizes. Screech, *Rabelais,* 298, suggests further, for example, that the use of calloier is meant to designate Rabelais's current ecclesiastical status in 1548 as a priest rather than to refer to his past identity as a monk: the fatherhood of priests, not the brotherhood of monks, is supposed to be emphasized; this seems doubtful.

In *Gargantua* and *Pantagruel* author and narrator seem to be the same persons, but this is only an appearance: Alcofribas Nasier is an anagram, a mask for the author who is never mentioned. In the *Third Book* and incomplete *Fourth Book* the author Rabelais is explicitly separated from the narrator Alcofribas but implicitly unified with him because the reader is now given the means to decipher the relation between Master François on the new title pages and Master Alcofribas on the title pages of the first two books. But no sooner has the true author's name appeared than it is falsified by a mystifying attribution: Rabelais, the monk from pirate islands near Toulon.

With the subterfuges of the *Third Book* and incomplete *Fourth Book*, the dispersion of the narrator has been developed so far that Rabelais the author and Rabelais the doctor, instead of standing dimly at the edge and beyond the books, are folded into its structure as two more of its overlapping images. The dispersion of the narrator semioticizes the participation of the writer in his writing, of the doctor in the writer, and of the monk in both of them. I mean by "semioticize" what was established in chapter 7: Rabelais's words develop their power by combining with each other sometimes in a primarily "symbolic" manner, as mutually conditioning linguistic patterns, sometimes in a primarily ideational manner, as words directing attention to thought patterns, and sometimes in a primarily referential manner, as words referring to persons and states of action in and beyond this fictional universe.

Then in 1552 the complete *Fourth Book* is published, and the *Third Book* is reissued with corrections. Rabelais's monkish identity is deleted from the title pages; on both of them he is introduced as simply a "doctor in medicine."[15] Moreover, the prologues are now identified in both the *Third Book* and the *Fourth Book* as by the "author"; given the adjacent title pages, they can only be by Rabelais, not Alcofribas. The narrator represented in the text is therefore eliminated from the paratext. But even as narrator and author are more explicitly separated, even as the author's profession is simply stated without fictive adjuncts, the author's personality, as exhibited in the fictional masks and costumes of the paratext's parts, takes on a new complexity: the prologue narrator in the new prologue to the *Fourth Book* of 1552 seems at first to be a very

15. Rabelais, *Oeuvres,* critical edition by A. Lefranc, 5: 1, gives the details of the title page in the *Third Book* in 1552. *NRB,* 231, reproduces the title page of the *Fourth Book* in 1552.

proper gentleman, however playful (the Lenten game of "I spy"), but he soon drops this role for the more familiar one of priapic storytelling, only to switch from that to the role of preacher. The dedicatory author is by turns very proud and very humble, very anxious about and very loud in praise of his books.[16] The character of the source of these fictions becomes more convoluted with each publication; Rabelais's paratexts become more elaborate and add new parts.

Paratexts are stitched all around and into texts; they expose the indefiniteness of a text's edges, the *literal* impossibility of cutting an author's words neatly from their context and exhibiting them as an icon. As I suggested in Part One, paratexts seem to be chiefly interesting at times of swift, disruptive change in the conventions of written communication. At other times they tend, far more than texts, to become standard in form and content. Perhaps because twentieth-century readers are now entering a period of major dislocation in the communication of lettered words, the possibilities inherent in the paratext-text relationship appear more clearly to present-day critics; in the case of Rabelais, as in the case of Montaigne and Cervantes, they appear to have been exploited with virtuosity.[17]

Paratexts are inescapable in printed books for at least four reasons: the print has an edge, it has a beginning, it has parts and subdivisions, large and small, and it has an end. To this physical character of printed books correspond psychological and economic necessities. The printed book maximizes an impersonal tie between the senders and the receivers of its messages; I say "maximizes" because manuscript books of the later Middle Ages already developed this impersonality. As impersonality develops, so does a commercial relation: senders and receivers are less related as client and patron or master and student and more as seller and buyer. The writer must find readers; they are no longer known in advance.

The paratext-as-edge is the first approach to unknown readers; book cover, title page, table of contents, and the colophon at the other end of the book in the early days of printing make this approach. The pub-

---

16. These narrative feints are studied in detail in ch. 9.

17. See on Montaigne and Cervantes, Randa Sabry, "Quand le texte parle de son paratexte," *Poétique*, no. 69 (February 1987): 85, 94. On Rabelais's narratological play generally, we refer again to François Rigolot's chapter, "Narratologie: Vraisemblance et illusion référentielle," devoted to *Gargantua* and *Pantagruel*, in his *Le texte de la Renaissance*, 137–53.

lisher's influence over an author is great at these points, but both publisher and author realize that it is in their mutual interest to confer and compromise on such elements: neither of them knows certainly how readers will react to their choices, and each knows that the other possesses expertise of which they have need.

The paratext-as-beginning follows upon the book's greeting to its readers: readers are ushered into the text by dedication, preface, epigraphs, frontispiece, introduction. Paratext-as-edge maximizes the seller-buyer tie and is as attractive—even deceptively attractive—as possible. It does not hesitate to exhibit titles and show chapters that may contain far less than they promise. Paratext-as-beginning has other functions that are in part defensive. It is a question not only of acquiring readers but also of insuring understanding of the text that follows. These parts of paratext try to guard against misreading just as much as they try to stimulate sympathy for the writing project. Authors deal here more directly with their public than at any other point: the sender-receiver tie is primary.

The paratext as a set of signals of subdivision in the text does not arise primarily, like the earlier two parts, from concern with the book's readership but from concern with the book's readability. A book is long, ordinarily too long to read at a sitting, and so it has parts that allow for pauses in its enjoyment and understanding. Chapter titles, intertitles, notes, chapter epigraphs, illustrations, graphs, diagrams, and tables point and summarize the arguments and the flow of narration. They give rhythm to the verbal energy, articulating its rise and fall. They bring out hidden connections in a verbal medium that, although necessarily linear in its acquisition by readers, is nonlinear in its understanding. The longer a text is, adding words to words from page to page, the more its contrastive levels appear, evolving in varied directions, and the more its reflexively stitched form comes to readerly consciousness. Paratextual signals of subdivision orient readers toward these realizations.

Paratextual forms are finally used to make an end of the book, to mark its conclusion, summarize it, and in some cases reevaluate it. The end of a book stimulates the critical function in authors as it does in readers; this is all there is: What was said? What should have been said? What was not said but nevertheless implied? The paratext-as-end tries to guard against the menaces of metatexts and, often enough, to offer its own in postfaces, endnotes, and appendixes. It tries to facilitate reuse of the book with indexes of greater or lesser complexity.

The critics who in the last few years have renewed and broadened our sense of paratexts have stressed the difference between text and paratext as one between stasis and movement, although not always in the same way. On one hand the text is regarded as a solid, unchanging monument, while paratexts are seen as parade wagons that convey the monument from authors to their public; they activate the text and render it performative. On the other hand the text-paratext relation is formulated as the difference between textual attention to polysemic openness and paratextual concern for fixity of sense, such that interpretation of the text is oriented by paratext toward the historical, psychological, and social particulars of the text's production.[18]

These dualist contrasts are illuminating, but they may obscure the ways in which text and paratext function together; they may diminish awareness of books as jointly created by authors, publishers, editors, and readers' responses. Paratext renders the text more supple but also more definite in its contextual assumptions. The text reveals both the meaning and the limits of the overly measured and overly grandiose claims held out by paratext. Text and paratext belie each other. Their disjunction is not only inevitable but also enjoyable. Doesn't everybody already know this game anyway?—I see you! Now you must join me in a toast to the monk.

Rabelais's repeated revisions and reeditions of his works, together with his frequent changes of publishers (he was sued by one of them in early 1546)[19] offer rich materials for a study of the novels' paratext-as-edge. Complete study of it or other aspects of paratext is not my purpose here.[20] The different dimensions of the text-paratext relation have been indicated primarily in order to focus more clearly on parts of Rabelais's paratext-as-beginning. I want now to clarify the implications of the addition of a dedicatory letter to the *Fourth Book* beyond its obvious political function. Adding this letter caused the author not only to re-

---

18. These alternatives are considered in Rigolot, "Prolégomenes." See, e.g., 11–13, his use of the text/discourse distinction to throw light on the difference between text and paratext as fixity and flow, versus 13–14, his reference to a Kristevan distinction between sign and symbol, the former (primary in the text) allowing for verbal variability and the latter (primary in the paratext) "oriented to a precise sense."

19. See *NRB,* 172, concerning the lawsuit brought by Chrétien Wechel. Original documents stating the cause of the lawsuit have not been located.

20. Much fuller study of paratextual and textual responses in the form of revisions and reeditions of a Renaissance French author's works is included in my *The Works of Jacques-Auguste de Thou* (The Hague, 1967).

vise the function and narrative personae depicted in the prologue to
that book but also to tinker with the prologue and title page to the
*Third Book,* which was reissued at the same time (1552).

Some of the most difficult problems in Rabelaisian interpretation are
thereby broached. Analysis of the relation between dedicatory letter
and prologue clarifies a general shift in narrative voice, noticeable in the
*Third Book* and obvious in the *Fourth Book*. This shift specifies Rabelais's
communalist assumptions in writing and why he felt they were in jeopardy in the 1540s, which in turn will allow us to guess why Rabelais
impersonated himself as an angry ecclesiastic from the Hyères Islands
and why he at the same time gave a new nuance to Pantagruelist philosophy.

The shift in narrative voice must have slowly matured during the
long silence of this writer between the publication of *Gargantua* and
*Pantagruel* in 1532–1535 and that of the *Third Book* and *Fourth Book* in
1546–1552. Linguistic virtuosity deserts the previously dominant narrator (Alcofribas) to place itself after the silent period in a more diversi-
fied way among the Pantagruelian actors and those they encounter. In
the *Third Book* the eloquent anxiety of Panurge and sententious wisdom
of Pantagruel orient while doing little to integrate this scattering. In
the *Fourth Book* rhetorical dominance is a three-way and four-way tussle
among Pantagruel, Xenomanes, Alcofribas, and the occupants of the
islands.[21] Especially in the *Fourth Book* the fusion of the narrative functions with that of acting in the narrative—Alcofribas is present on shipboard; Xenomanes offers advice about the ship's route—reinforces the
representation of writing as a translation of collective, oral contexts.
Meaning emerges from an ongoing, open-ended, social process.

21. See Rouben Cholakian's analysis of these shifts and tussles, established
by calculating who tells the stories in each of the four books in his *The Moi in
the Middle Distance: A Study of the Narrative Voice in Rabelais* (Madrid, 1982).
To some extent it is falsifying to give Xenomanes the same narrator status as
Pantagruel, Alcofribas, or the inhabitants of the islands. As a guide to the Land
of the Lanterns who has already traveled this route, his information is given
special status, somewhat similar to that of the omniscient narrator in the classical novel. What he says is not subject to the seesaw of comic-serious allegory
that puffs up and deflates the words of Pantagruel, Friar John, Panurge, and
Alcofribas. But even Xenomanes is no exception to narrator dispersion and
narratee confusion; he is not hierarchically set off to occupy an author-reader
box of communication. Xenomanes, like his shipboard companions and unlike
the putative author and readers, is presented as experiencing these fictive islands as real.

From this point in chapters 8 and 9 readers will be asked to cope with some movement back and forth among four topics that are interwoven in order to show how, alongside the continuing representation of collectively created verbal meanings, a narrative counterflow emerges in Rabelais's later texts that changes the character of the author's communalism. The four topics are: the authorial strategies shared by all four books published by Rabelais; Rabelais's defenses against misinterpretation in his first two books; Rabelais's development of new defenses in 1546 and afterward; and finally, the formalization of these new defenses into altered author-reader relations in the *Fourth Book* of 1552.

First, then, a further word about authorial strategies in all four books. The ragged, intercepting, overlapping form of author-narrator-reader representations was a useful strategy at a time when storms of religious war were ominously gathering, for who could say which narrative voice designates the opinion of Rabelais the person? But the assumption that people's normal mode of existence is that of participants in a number of cross-cutting communities also played a role in Rabelais's authorial strategy. The shifts among narrators confirm the idea that authorial meaning should be seen as scattered over the whole field of actors and actions in a book rather than be understood as concentrated in a hero. This is not to say that there are no hillocks and hollows in the field but only to emphasize that such varied landscape takes its shape from the whole. To suppose that Alcofribas or Pantagruel or any one else speaks consistently for the author, so that his voice runs like a mole's burrow of half-hidden meaning through the whole field, is to mistake parts and whole and to ignore Rabelais's communalist assumptions about communication. One should look not for what Rabelais intends to say but for the variation in the groups and members of groups to which he lends his voice.

The place of the narrator is not yet, like the place of the king in Velasquez's painting *Las Meninas,* a space beyond the reach of the communities filling Rabelais's tale. It is not yet a space beyond the chessboardlike partitioning of social orders each from each, the generalized, overspreading, almost invisibly located space of the sovereign who designates the places of his subjects. In the sovereign-centered "classical episteme" both senders and receivers of messages stand outside the action and the actors in it; each element inside the narrative frame has its appointed, separate space, as the author-king urges his partners in power, the readers, to see.[22] The postclassical novel of the twentieth century undoes this narrative clarity in the name of a centerless text representing unorderable reality. Senders and receivers of such dissipating messages are even more separate in the postclassical novel than in the model it assaults. The Rabelaisian text-paratext, on the other hand, represents narration as a meeting ground rather than as a means of assessing the separation of author, actors, and audience.

In Rabelais's prologues this sense of meeting and mixture of narrative fields and personae is not merely represented; it is thrust upon the reader. The scenes that are sketched and the actors in them are manipulated in such a way as to demand that readers understand the novels only in such mixed and flexible ways. If readers therefore begin Rabelais's prologues expecting to be ushered into the text in the manner of an introduction or preface, they are soon baffled. The prologues present conflicting images of the author then or subsequently. Their conflict suggests that they must be read for what they imply as well as for what they say.

The locus classicus of this suggested double reading is the prologue to *Gargantua*. Referring to Alcibiades's praise of Socrates as a Silenus box in Plato's *Symposium*, Master Alcofribas declares that his books are like these ancient Greek playthings, comically ugly on the outside but packed inside with pharmaceutical rarities and other precious things. Hence while you the readers will find "in a literal sense" some joyous matters here, you must not remain at this level but "interpret in a higher sense what you perhaps thought was said in gaiety of heart." These words urge readers to seek high meaning beneath a low and negligible surface. But the following paragraphs seem to turn against this impulse:

> Do you faithfully believe that Homer, when he was writing the *Iliad* and *Odyssey,* thought about the allegories which Plutarch, Heraclides Ponticus, Eustathius, and Phornutus plugged into him [lesquelles de luy ont calfreté; literally, which have stopped up the chinks in, or caulked, him] . . . ? If you think so, you do not come within hand or foot of my opinion, which is that those things were as little dreamed of by Homer as the Gospel sacraments were by Ovid in his *Metamorphoses*.[23]

22. The reference is to Michel Foucault's analysis of Velasquez's painting in *The Order of Things,* ch. 1, and to his definition of the classical episteme in chs. 3–6.

23. *G,* Pr, 25–27.

The seeming contradiction of these words to Alcofribas's allusion to Silenus boxes with their precious inner meanings has been dispelled by Edwin Duval. The prologue to *Gargantua* does not concern the choice of allegorical over literal readings or the inverse. It is about both readerly and authorial perceptions of the text: one may find in my books, as others have found in Homer, says Alcofribas, meanings that I never dreamed of as I wrote. But that does not imply that the meanings are not there. I wrote while eating and drinking and "that is the proper time to write about these high matters and profound sciences, as Homer, paragon of all philologists, knew well how to do . . . according to Horace."[24]

Neither the relative value of allegorical and literal reading nor of learned versus naive interpretation but the inevitability of false consciousness is Alcofribas's theme. Homer never imagined the things Plutarch saw in the *Iliad* and the *Odyssey* because Homer's context was different from Plutarch's. Both Plutarch's and Homer's other commentators saw some meanings that were true and others that were false to Homer's words. How can one know which are which? How should one read? In the same manner as one should write, while eating and drinking. Drinking is emphasized in all the prologues as the manner in which and indeed by means of which author and readers may best meet. "Most illustrious boozers," the prologue to *Gargantua* begins, and they are also the first words in the prologue to the *Third Book;* the *Fourth Book*'s prologue begins by praising last year's vintage and assuring readers that they have in wine a sure remedy for every difficulty.[25] *In vino veritas:* drinking inspires not simply good companionship but true understanding. Drinking inspires that loosened framework of semiotic suggestiveness and empathetic receptivity which discovers matters not consciously known. It leads readers, as it has led writers, to intuit matters unconsciously written about by authors.

These ideas are implicit in the very choice of Alcofribas's exemplum.

---

24. *G*, Pr, 27. Edwin Duval, "Interpretation and the 'doctrine plus Absconce' of Rabelais' Prologue to *Gargantua*," *Etudes rabelaisiennes* 18 (1985): 1–17, shows that in the case of this prologue, much as in the case of the misreading of the passages concerning Quaresmeprenant, simple mistranslations have led scholars to false conclusions and illusory controversy.

25. *G*, Pr, 25; *TL*, Pr, 341; note that the first words appearing here, *bonnes gens*, displacing *beuveurs très illustres*, were added in 1552, for reasons to be discussed later.

Alcibiades's comparison of Socrates to a Silenus box occurs in Plato's *Symposium*, which is the representation of a banquet. Alcibiades makes his comment in this convivial setting, being very drunk. Alcrofribas makes his reference to Plato the philosopher's representation of drunken truth in a comic prologue that offers serious arguments in a comic, convivial manner parallel to Plato. Most humanist readers would have been aware of this replication at a subtextual level of Alcofribas's seemingly outrageous assertions. To humanist readers these assertions would scarcely have been surprising for other reasons, too.

In distinguishing between literal and allegorical readings, humanists insisted that a text should first be read for its literal sense, which meant establishing the historical setting of the words, the text's linguistic and social context.[26] In this sense Alcofribas refers to Homer as the paragon of philologists. The word philologist in Rabelais's day meant not a scholar equipped with the complex and precise methodologies elaborated by linguists in the nineteenth century but more simply and generally a lover of words.[27] Homer probably seemed to Rabelais a philologist because he indulged in words as much as he was said to indulge

26. *QL*, Pr, 545. In their insistence on the primacy of the literal-historical sense, humanists polemicized against theological interpretation, which prescribed a fourfold approach to words in which the anagogical, mystical sense of words, for example, was to be given equal weight with the literal.

27. In Rabelais's day philology, in spite of the new critical instruments developed by humanists like Lorenzo Valla and Guillaume Budé, was still generally interpreted, in accordance with its etymology, as the learned orator's and writer's love of language, as the pursuit and practice of eloquent, learned discourse. Budé, the very person from whom Rabelais borrows the list of Homer's commentators (as Duval points out, "Interpretation," 7, n. 10), was responsible for popularizing the term among French scholars (*De Philologia*, 1532), and he did so in this broad, embracing sense. Of course, even if Budé, like Rabelais, did not distinguish clearly between philology as a technique for restoring texts and philology as a rhetorical ideal, a vision of perfect reading, writing, and discourse, this does not mean that the former did not exist at all. On this point see Donald R. Kelley, *Foundations of Modern Historical Scholarship: Language, Law, and History in the French Renaissance* (New York, 1970), 19–25, 55–65: the reasons for the emergence of philology as a critical science, separate from or superior to its meaning as a rhetorical ideal, have to do with the growth of historical mindedness (1400–1600) and with the changing materials, above all legal, to which humanist modes of textual restoration were applied. Emergence had begun, but clear separation of scientific from rhetorical ends for philology lay in the future, beyond Rabelais's times. Thus, Boulenger, *G*, Pr, 27, n. 15, and other commentators on this prologue passage explain philology anachronistically, which is part of the cause of persistent misinterpretation.

in wine; it was certainly not because he studied words technically. Taking words literally and letting them flow, Homer gave them, drinking, other meanings high and low without necessarily knowing what he did.[28]

Rabelais's alter ego Alcofribas asserts, then, that readers need inspiration in order to read well, and that the best, most word-loving writers possess that virtue. Inspiration guides writers' and readers' thoughts beyond their conscious knowing. But although such inspiration accompanies eating and drinking according to Alcofribas, it is not derived from them but instead comes from on high, infers Edwin Duval. The deeper meaning of Homer's vinous verbal richness is that the poet is a vessel of divine wisdom. Duval admits that belief in a divine source of poetic power is only implicit in Alcofribas's argument; the inference seems warranted, he believes, because it is nearly as commonplace an idea among humanists as their emphasis on the priority of literal meaning. The inference is not warranted. The inspiration that comes from food and drink transforms writers not into "inspired . . . *vates*" but into boon companions.[29]

Rabelais was a doctor; his idea of a writer's inspiration was physiological no less than philosophical. He speaks of it with the voice of Dr. Rabelais in a most telling place, at the end of the dedicatory letter to Odet de Châtillon prefacing the *Fourth Book:* "For you with your most honorable exhortation have given me both courage and inventiveness, and without you my heart would have failed me and the fountain of my animal spirits would have remained dry." Heart and courage (French *coeur, courage*), animal spirits and inventiveness: the psychophysiology is Galen's and is explained in two passages in the *Third Book*, once by Panurge and once by Pantagruel. Food and drink, transformed into blood in the stomach and liver, flow to the heart. The heart is the "fountain" of animal spirits because its left ventricle so "subtilizes"

28. The allusion of Alcofribas to Horace for this concept of Homer is from Horace, *Epistles*, Book 1, epistle 19, vv. 1–6: "Learned Maecenas, no lyric poems live long or please many people . . . which are written by drinkers of water. . . . By lavishing praises on wine, Homer shows that he was a drinker." See Duval, "Interpretation," 2, on the humanists' literal sense, and 9, n. 14, on the common reference to divine inspiration as the source of poetic wisdom.

29. Duval, "Interpretation," 9–10. I am not asserting that Rabelais nowhere expresses belief in a divine source of poetic power, explicitly or implicitly. I am only saying that such belief plays no role in the interpretative system proposed in the prologue to *Gargantua*.

the blood "that it is called spiritual"; then the heart sends it through the arteries. Animal spirits "spring up" in this arterial blood "refined to a pure state in that admirable network [retz admirable] which lies beneath the ventricles of the brain," so that we "imagine, speak, judge, resolve, deliberate, reason, and remember."[30] Pantagruel adds in his description of the process, as one would expect him to do, that fasting is not a good thing for the animal spirits, for hunger will "pull down the roaming spirit, making it neglect its nourisher and natural host, the body."[31] The process is circular, from matter to mind and back again; it is naturalistic, involving no supernatural intervention. The stimulus to which Rabelais refers as so essential in renewing his animal spirits, the exhortations of Cardinal Odet, has a social character like Alcofribas's plea at the conclusion to the prologue of *Gargantua:*

> To be called and reputed a good fellow and good companion is for me nothing but honor and glory, and with such a name I am welcome in all good companies of Pantagruelists. . . . Interpret therefore all my words and deeds in the most perfect way; hold in reverence the cheese-like brain which feeds you with these pretty, puffy-bowel trifles[32] and, as far as you can, keep me always merry.

Writing feeds fellowship; words are inseparable from deeds; sociability is the soul of honor. The "most perfect" interpretive effort no less than the body's most material profit flows from and back into convivial merriment:

> Now be cheerful, my dears, and gaily read the rest for your body's ease and intestine's profit. But listen, you donkey-dongs (may an ulcer lame you!), remember to pledge me likewise and I'll drink to you in just a minute.[33]

Is this the appeal to the benevolent nature of Christian humanist readers of which Duval speaks? "The prologue to *Gargantua* is quite simply

---

30. *TL*, 4, 367–68, and *TL*, 13, 395.

31. *TL*, 13, 396.

32. *Belles billes vezées:* Lefranc's edition of Rabelais, *Oeuvres,* vol. 1, 17, n. 121, says that *beillevezée* means an empty bowel in Poitevin dialect but does not document or date the observation. *Vezé* is translated by Nicot and Raconnet, *Thresor* (1621), 659, as "Ventrosus," that is, wind-filled, puffed-up, pot-bellied. *Billes vezées* is translated by Cotgrave, *Dictionarie* (1611; no pagination; see under *billes*) as trifles or trash, presumably considering "windy bowels" to be analogous to air-filled fools' bladders.

33. *G*, Pr, 28. Part of the uncouth, rustic air for which Rabelais strove in this passage (he used Gascon and Poitevin dialectical forms) is lost in my translation.

a *captatio benevolentiae* in the strictest sense of the term. It represents an effort on the part of the author to disarm the reader by overcoming his initial skepticism, to make him want to read on by winning his confidence in the value of the book. . . . Christian benevolence of the kind defined at the end of the prologue [*sic*] is in fact a crucial element of the 'doctrine plus absconce' [the 'more recondite teaching' Alcofribas suggests lies 'inside' the lighthearted exterior of his words] . . . promised in the prologue. . . . The 'doctrine absconce,' in other words, is nothing more nor less than the moral virtue required to seek it."[34]

Every critic selects some words of the text at the expense of others in order to give point and power to his or her ideas. The key words for Duval at the "end" of the prologue are "Interpret . . . my words and deeds in the most perfect way" (*Interpretez . . . mes faictz et mes dictz en la perfectissime partie*). These words, he suggests, refer to the "special kind of benevolence" in interpreting others' behavior which is urged upon Christians by Rabelais's contemporaries Desiderius Erasmus and Jacques Lefèvre d'Etaples.[35] I have quoted the rest of the sentence after the semicolon that follows "most perfect way," a remainder that refers once more to eating. The eating is not just anything: it refers to tripe— let me be outrageous and say sausage-tripe, the tripe proper to Carnival.

Conviviality is animality is spirituality for Rabelais. The three are blended, not elevated by their equally divine sanction. "God never gave us Lent but certainly the good things we will enjoy together," he wrote to his friend.[36] Duval: "The truly unique importance of the prologue to *Gargantua*, then, is the way in which it transposes the entire issue of 'interpretation' from a literary to a strictly moral plane, from a question of exegesis to a question of *caritas*." Rabelais: "But listen you donkeydongs . . . I'll drink to you in just a minute." The last words of this prologue are not Christian and moral but Dionysian and phallic.[37]

Criticism concerned with the manner in which readers are related to the text by authorial strategy has been in vogue for several decades.

34. Duval, "Interpretation," 12 (for the first two sentences), 17 (remainder of quote).

35. Ibid., 15.

36. See the quotation from Rabelais's letter of 1542 in ch. 5, n. 22.

37. Duval, "Interpretation," 17. Gérard Defaux's "D'un problème l'autre: herméneutique de l' 'altior sensus' et 'captatio lectoris' dans le Prologue de 'Gargantua,'" *Revue d'histoire littéraire de la France* 85 (1985): 195–216, follows Du-

Rouben Cholakian's book on the narrative voice in Rabelais, Dorothy Coleman's chapter on Rabelais as an "Olympian author," and Rigolot's chapter on "narratology" in Rabelais deal with many of the same materials and problems discussed here. But these critics understand Rabelais's procedures within the individualizing terms of a generically designated "implied reader" or "narratee."[38] As suggested in a variety of ways here, neither narratee nor narrator is generically designated by Rabelais. The readers envisaged by the text shift their identity in such a manner as to stimulate recognition that they belong to varying groups whose differences—at least in the first two Pantagruelian books— count for less than their common sociability.

In the last as in the first books, Rabelais's implied readers crowd around the text like the grotesque group pictured on the 1547 title page of *Gargantua,* readers whom one might suppose, on the basis of addresses made at various points in the text, to be merchants, artisans, servants, nobles, officers of the king, bespectacled scholars, and mere passersby (Fig. 1). Nothing in the text or in the text's sixteenth-century context forces us to think that Rabelais's readers remained the same from one chapter to the next or that Rabelais thought they did. The oral overtones of parts of the discourse, the extraordinary shifts of mood between "high" humanism and "low" scatology, and the episodic patterning of plot, would rather seem to imply an in-and-out participation like that of people on the edges of a crowd watching an entertainer.

---

val's essential syntactic distinctions and concludes, similarly to my suggestion here, that for Rabelais a text's meaning includes not only what the author wished to say but also what he said without wishing it explicitly (214). As for Defaux's ideas of the implications of this point of view for Rabelais's text generally, we differ on many issues, as readers of his sharply polemic article may judge.

38. Cholakian's *The Moi in the Middle Distance* (Madrid, 1982), extending the work of Floyd Gray and Abraham Keller on storytelling in the novels, is especially revealing in showing how often and in how many varied ways the characters in the novel take over narrator functions. He is not directly concerned, however, with what Rigolot calls the varying designation of the "narratee" (i.e., *narrataire,* cf. Rigolot, *Le texte de la Renaissance,* 140). There is little difference between Rigolot's *narrataire,* Wolfgang Iser's "implied reader" (*The Implied Reader*) and Dorothy Coleman's "envisaged reader" (*Rabelais, a Critical Study in Prose Fiction* [Cambridge, 1971], 46). On the vogue of reader-oriented criticism and its several varieties, see the helpful anthology and introductory essay by Susan R. Suleiman in *Reader in the Text,* ed. Suleiman and Crosman.

Rigolot, Cholakian, and Coleman analyze Rabelais's procedures in terms appropriate for the individualized and privatized world of the classic novel developed in the seventeenth, eighteenth, and nineteenth century. Many authors even before the seventeenth century, of course, wrote in terms that individualized and at the same time gave generic qualities to implied readers. But Rabelais was not one of them. He moved rather in the direction of merging readers into a group that included the author and described readers' collective interest and common enjoyment. The invention of Alcofribas is Rabelais's chief narratological device here, Alcofribas the narrator who is also one of the Pantagruelian actors, a faithful servant of Pantagruel, and yet anagrammatically none other than Rabelais the real author.[39]

The attitudes attributed to Rabelais's author-narrators, Dr. Rabelais as well as Alcofribas, are participatory and political rather than Olympian and manipulative. Thus the examples of the "trick[s] of the Olympian author," which Coleman gathers from the *Fourth Book,* for example, "elevating us to the right hand of the god who is controlling the scene," seem quite to the contrary to emphasize the inseparability of narrator from the narrated and to encourage the participation of narratees in the fictive fun.

Coleman cites the second chapter's description of the mythical "tarand" that Pantagruel purchases on the island of Medamothi as an example of this Olympian movement: "The *nous* [we] device is a witness to all the things happening on board ship; it is able to observe details which any of the company can see and also to comment on them from a superior perspective."[40] Here is the passage in question:

> [Pantagruel] also commissioned the purchase of . . . a tarand which a Scythian sold to him. . . . A tarand is an animal the size of a young bull. . . . It changes color according to the variety of the places where it grazes and lives. . . . Indeed I have seen it change color. . . . What we found especially marvellous about that tarand was that not only its face and skin but even its hair took the color of its surroundings.[41]

The text moves from description of the exotic animal to the intrusion of Alcofribas the narrator into the text to give ironic realism by means

39. Gérard Defaux, "Rabelais et son masque comique: *Sophista loquitur,*" *Etudes rabelaisiennes* II (1974), 89–135, studies Alcofribas's narratological significance in *Gargantua,* emphasizing the sophistic rhetorical model on which Rabelais drew.
40. Coleman, *Rabelais,* 71.
41. *QL,* 2, 566–67.

of his eyewitness testimony. Then the theme shifts from "I" to "we," from Alcofribas to the group of which he is a member. Far from elevating readers above the scene, this move plunges them into it by multiplying the ironic realism: not to believe what is said about the tarand would mean rejecting the veracity of not only the narrator but also those who, by the device of Alcofribas's membership in the group of narrative actors, have become coguarantors of the narrative's reality. The passage proceeds to exploit this condition by next describing the changing colors of the tarand as he was led from Panurge to Pantagruel to the ship's captain.

The point emphasized here is not how this comic verification of incident affects the truth value of the narrative but how it makes truth depend on group witnessing and participation. The groups that witness and participate are presented by Rabelais in such an interlocking manner that the passage from purely fictive to nearly real persons is almost imperceptible. Alcofribas's move from "I" to "we" in this passage is narrated in the same conversationally sociable style as his address to readers about the noble ancestry of Sausages in the Carnival-Lent episode. Dr. Rabelais's authorial address to well-wishing in the Prologue and even the doctor's dedication letter to Odet de Châtillon are couched in orally derived, publicly oriented terms. What allows this series of moves among actors, narrators, implied authors, and implied readers to slide along so easily?

Ever since the title page of *Gargantua* (1534–1535) announced a "book full of Pantagruelism," readers of the novels must have asked themselves about the meaning of this name-turned-abstraction. Surely it has something to do with the qualification of Alcofribas on the same title page as an "abstractor of quintessence"; surely, too, it is related to Alcofribas's assertion in that same preface that there are deep meanings within the Silenus box of his writings. At the end of the first chapter of *Gargantua*, Alcofribas explains that to "pantagruelize" means to drink when it pleases you and to read about the dreadful deeds of Pantagruel.[42] This early definition retains some link with the non-Rabelaisian farcical figure of Pantagruel as a thirst-making devil. But already in an addition to the very end of *Pantagruel*, which was published in a new edition of that book in 1534 at the time Rabelais finished work on *Gargantua*, the term "Pantagruelist" is defined not simply as a mode of

42. *G*, I, 31.

reading and drinking but as a way of life.[43] To be "good Pantagruelists" people should "live in peace, joy, and good health, always making good cheer."[44] The most abstracting reference occurs in the prologue to the *Third Book*. Pantagruelism is a "specific form and individuating property . . . by means of which those who possess it never take in bad part any things whatever which they recognize as springing from a good, frank, loyal heart."[45] In the *Fourth Book*'s prologue, also, the somewhat briefer reference to Pantagruelism relates an abstract definition to the behavior resulting from possession of this character trait. Dr. Rabelais, the "author," explains that he is, "thanks to a bit of Pantagruelism (that is, you know, a certain gaiety of spirit pickled in the scorn of fortuitous things) well, strong, and ready to drink, if you will."[46] Pantagruelism is Rabelais's name for that virtue that makes conviviality possible. It describes not merely a tolerance of matters beyond personal control but a positive empathetic desire to appreciate others' intentions as more important than their actions.

But why did Rabelais invent this quality? What was it about the developing form of his novels that led him to give it regular prominence at paratextual points of contact between author and reader? To ask the question is almost to answer it: Pantagruelism identifies an attitude that Rabelais regards as essential in the author-reader relationship. He therefore represents his authorial personae as possessing it, and he represents his chief actors, the Pantagruelians, as bonded together by it.[47] Pantagruelism insures conviviality in advance and at a distance; it reaches beyond the narrative frame to embrace author and readers unknown and unknowable, everyone who manages to accept the unforeseeable circumstances of life gaily and with spirit.

By giving the word "Pantagruel" a substantive form at the paratextual beginnings and ends of his books Rabelais places this element at once inside and on the margins of textuality. Pantagruelism plays over

43. See introduction, n. 4, on the date of publication of *Gargantua* in 1534 or 1535.

44. *P*, 34, 335.

45. *TL*, Pr, 349.

46. *QL*, Pr, 545.

47. Louis Thuasne long ago pointed out that Rabelais had a model for purposely confusing the personae of author, narrator, and actors in Teofilo Folengo's *Baldo*. But nothing in Folengo's work corresponds to Pantagruelism, a concretized abstraction that deepens and alters this masking play. See Thuasne, *Etudes sur Rabelais,* reprint, 177ff.

the text as well as being incarnate in Pantagruel. This allows the books' hero to take the voice of the masked author on occasion, just as the author of the prologues does; if the prologue author growls at the "caphars" and "cagots" who beset him and his writing, Pantagruel does too.[48]

Pantagruelism is Rabelais's idea of social wisdom. It derives from two simple assumptions, humanist and communalist. People possess common human reactions that incline them to laugh at many of the same things, regardless of class and cultural differences. These class and cultural differences are related in overlapping and intersecting rather than sharply divisive ways because people are simultaneously members of many correlative and adjacent communities; their sense of connection is thus as easily or more easily summoned than their sense of separateness. Yet this simple, clear basis on which Rabelais stakes his ability to hold the attention of a disparate, unknown readership is belied by the outcry against his books—an outcry which mounts almost as steadily as the sales. Readers there are many, but not all of them laugh, and even fewer, perhaps, sense much communal identity with each other.

There are readers who are positively committed to twisting the author's words, writes Alcofribas in the new conclusion of *Pantagruel* in 1534: "false cenobites, *cagotz,* snails, hypocrites, *caffars,*" they pretend to be absorbed in devout contemplation when in fact they spend all their time reading Pantagrueline books, "not as much for a joyous pastime as for the purpose of wickedly doing someone mischief." Here is the first sketch of the refrain that becomes in the *Fourth Book* the myth of Anti-Nature. These bad readers do nothing but "article,[49] monarticle, twist their necks, buttock, ballock, and diaboliculate, that is, calumniate." Flee, abhor, and hate such folk "like I do," exclaims Alcofribas, and then he adds the definition of Pantagruelists in the very last phrase of this amended book: "And if you wish to be good Pantagruelists (that is, to live in peace, joy, and good health, always making good cheer), never put your faith in people who watch through peepholes."[50]

48. Cf. the terminology and the anger in *TL,* Pr, 351, with the terms Pantagruel uses to denounce Rabelais's enemies in *QL,* 32, 651.

49. See the quotation from the end of the prologue to the *Third Book,* in ch. 8, no. 13, for another use of this word. It means to list as part of a condemnatory or other potentially injurious inventory. Does "monarticle," then, mean "to single out"?

50. *P,* 34, 335.

When the attack is mounted against the "haggling critics" who are once again berated as *cagotz, caphars,* hypocrites, and so on at the conclusion of the prologue to the *Third Book,* the context is once again that of apprehension about the reception of the novels, and the books are once again called Pantagrueline.[51] But this time the prologue author goes much further in dealing with those who read his books wrongly. Calling his books a kind of wine, he invites "every true boozer, every true gouty fellow," to come and partake freely of as little or as much as they wish. However, he adds that "I have broached my cask *only* for you gouty freeholders and drinkers of prime vintage" (italics added).[52] Then follow the vituperative references to bad readers that culminate by calling them dogs and in which the narrator imitates—or hears?— their growling.[53]

The hyperbole of the passage insures its oblique, ironic interpretation. The writer Rabelais, beyond his fictional persona, knows that he can do very little about bad reading and biased metatexts. But does this ironic undercutting of the text's violence extend so far as to cause, and intend to cause, doubt about how nefarious Rabelais's detractors really are? Hardly. Even supposing that Rabelais wants readers to think less ill of his enemies than his narrative personae do, his text gives readers

---

51. *TL,* Pr, 348.

52. *TL,* Pr, 347–50.

53. See the discussion and citation of this passage near the beginning of ch. 8. The context is particularly convoluted in the *Third Book* Prologue. First, one must remember that the prologue is entitled in 1546 the "Prologue of the Third Book" and hence should be considered to be written by Alcofribas, in line with the two previous prologues. In 1552 the title is changed to "Prologue of the Author" and hence would seem to be attributed to the author mentioned on the title page, who in turn has shifted in 1552 from being Dr. Rabelais, monk of the Hyères Islands, to being plain Dr. Rabelais. The shift is possible because this prologue, unlike *Gargantua* or *Pantagruel* or the later *Fourth Book,* makes no mention of the profession of the prologue narrator. All the reader knows is that he is a Frenchman, a writer, a drinker, and an ironic imitator of Diogenes. As a patriot wishing to do his bit for a nation preparing for war (the context is the recurrent threat of war with Charles V in the 1540s), the prologue narrator declares that he is about to open his "cask" again, as he has already done in two earlier volumes. Thus not simply the composition of Pantagrueline books is accomplished while drinking (*Gargantua* prologue) but the result of composition is, as stated in the text, a kind of wine: "Envers les guerroyans je voys de nouveau percer mon tonneau et de la traicte . . . leur tirer du creu de nos passétemps épicénaires un gallant tiercin et consécutivement un joyeulx quart de sentences pantagruelicques." (*TL,* Pr, 347–48.)

no means to do so except that of encouraging a generalized skepticism about anything these personae say.

The critical situation was, in a way, impossible to treat otherwise than in this ambivalent fashion, which on one hand asks for naive trust in all the authorial personae's intentions and on the other develops an ironic stance toward those same personae's affirmations. Rabelais could not in his paratexts openly debate Sorbonne theologians, papal devotees, Calvinist zealots, and assorted moralists; the ideological stakes were too risky and Rabelais's own moral and intellectual sentiments were too complex to make open ideological confrontation anything but a travesty. But Rabelais must bear the consequences of his unwillingness to state in detail how he disagreed with those attacking him. When the authorial personae affect moral and doctrinal purity, when Dr. Rabelais or Alcofribas protests that the sole intention of the stories is to cheer people up, readers are forced to conclude one of two things about the attitude of the real author: either such affirmations are subterfuges, or the real author is very muddleheaded about the implications of what he writes in the text proper. The latter is most unlikely, and so Rabelais's ranting harshness in calling others hypocritical makes it hard to avoid invoking the same adjective about his writerly strategies.

"The slander of certain cannibals, misanthropes and agelastes,"[54] Rabelais declares in the dedicatory letter of 1552 to Cardinal Odet, "was so outrageous and beyond all reason that I lost all patience and decided not to write another iota." They said my books were full of heresies, he continues:

> Gay fooling there is in plenty, offensive neither to God nor the King: such is the sole subject and theme of these books. Heresies there are none, unless one were, perversely and against all usage of reason and common language, to interpret [them] in such a way that I would a thousand times rather have died, if it were possible, than to have thought so. It is as though bread meant stone, fish serpent, and egg scorpion.[55]

54. These three words mean the same thing: men who cannot laugh. See Appendix 3.

55. *QL,* DL, 542: "Car l'une des moindres contumélies dont ilz usoient estoit que tels livres tous estoient farciz d'hérésies diverses . . . ; de folastries joyeuses, hors l'offense de Dieu et du Roy, prou: c'est le subject et thème unicque d'iceulx livres; d'hérésies poinct, sinon perversement et contre tout usaige de raison et de languaige commun interprétans ce que, à poine de mille fois mourir, si autant possible estoit, ne vouldrois avoir pensé." An agitated spirit, it seems, coupled with a rhetoric modeled on officious oratory, produces convoluted grammar in this long sentence.

The references in the last sentence are biblical; did Rabelais also want to begin suggesting here the association amplified in the shortly following chapters about fishy, serpentine, eel-like Sausages? Rabelais continues, reversing the easy irony of earlier paratexts in which prologue authors vowed to defend the truth and worth of everything in the Pantagrueline books "up to any point short of [a heretic's] burning."[56]

> For I have said openly to you, complaining of these [slanders], that if I did not deem myself a better Christian than they portrayed me, and if in my life, writings, words, or even thoughts I detected a single spark of heresy . . . I would myself, imitating the phoenix, pile up the dry wood and light the fire in order to burn myself in it.[57]

Between 1546, when the Diogenic author of the *Third Book*'s prologue denied his book's "wine" to slanderous readers, and 1552, when this prefatory letter was written and published, Rabelais abandoned the method of establishing rapport between author and readers whose features we have traced. In the prologue to the incomplete *Fourth Book* of 1548 and in the prologue and dedicatory letter of 1552 Rabelais developed the difference between good and bad readers so far that he imperiled the communal-humanist code on which he had based understanding of his writing. Central to that code had been, as Rabelais explained in the prologue to *Gargantua,* a collective, cumulative sense of words' meaning; neither author nor any particular set of readers was supposed to possess, let alone express, full metatextual truth about the text. But in 1552 Dr. Rabelais does claim to possess his text's meanings; moreover, he claims that he can interpret the words of his slanderers as perfectly as his own, by employing his knowledge of the uses of reason and common language.

56. *P, Pr,* 190. The formula is repeated several times in the course of the *Third Book* and in the prologue to the incomplete *Fourth Book* of 1548: *QL, Pr* 1548, 755.

57. *QL, DL,* 542.

# 9

# Mockery

The prologue of 1552 is the first introductory paratext that unambiguously proclaims François Rabelais the author.[1] The proclamation is reinforced by its association with the dedicatory letter and its details about the author's reaction to his critics. Taken together, the two seem to offer as straightforward a portrait of François Rabelais as he was capable of presenting in a fictional context. As the author changes, so do the readers. For the first time the prologue carries a subtitle or salutation that qualifies the readers to whom Rabelais the author addresses himself: To well-wishing—or benevolent—readers (*aux lecteurs bénévoles*). The earlier prologue-writers' invitation to readers of every stripe is abandoned.

To the moral distinction of the subtitle Rabelais adds a greeting that carries social overtones: "worthy people" (*gens de bien*), he begins, and several lines afterward he asks after their wives and families and comments on the produce of their vineyards. These are not the same folk as the "illustrious boozers" and "precious poxy fellows" (*Gargantua*), the "chivalric and illustrious champions, nobles, and others" (*Pantagruel*), and "illustrious boozers" and "precious gouty fellows" (*Third Book, Fourth Book* of 1548) summoned to the threshold of earlier publications. Cross-cutting indications, ironically heightening and lowering terms of pseudo-camaraderie and social status, are abandoned in favor of a uni-dimensional address to comfortably situated men of means. In the re-issued *Third Book* of 1552 Rabelais takes care in the prologue to alter his

---

1. That is, introductory as opposed to framing paratexts. See the early pages of ch. 8 and ch. 8, n. 17, on the difference between paratext-as-beginning and paratext-as-edge (title pages affirmed Rabelais as author from 1546). I have drawn heavily in what follows here concerning the 1548 prologue and 1552 dedicatory letter and prologue on Jerome Schwartz, "Rhetorical Tensions in the Liminary Texts of Rabelais's *Quart Livre*," *Etudes rabelaisiennes* 17 (1983): 21–36. Although my conclusions differ in details, I agree with his general conclusions and methods in arriving at them.

readerly addresses at the same time as he clarifies his authorial persona; he adds the words "Good people" (*bonnes gens*) to the beginning, before the salutation to boozers and gouty folk, and he inserts "worthy people" (*gens de bien*) near the end of the prologue, when he identifies those for whom alone he intends to broach his wine cask of new stories.[2]

The dedicatory letter indirectly reinforces this impression of an intended shift in the social status of Rabelais's represented readers: the author addresses himself effusively to one of the highest men of worth in the land, and in the course of the letter he vaunts his connection to the very highest:

> The late King Francis of eternal memory was informed about these slanders and, having heard and comprehended these my several distinct books . . . as read aloud with the voice and pronunciation of this kingdom's most learned and careful [royal] reader . . . had found no passage suspect. . . . His son . . . King Henry . . . also had [heard the public reading], so that he granted to you [Cardinal Odet] for me a privilege and particular protection.[3]

The causes of such paratextual shifts in 1552 were both short- and long-term. We have discussed the short-term causes in another connection: within months of its publication in 1546 the *Third Book* was condemned, in spite of its royal privilege, and King Francis died, rendering the political future for evangelical and humanist reform uncertain.[4] Rabelais reacted with shocked anger. The hasty publication of a portion of the *Fourth Book* in 1548 with its bitter satire of royal politics and its concluding vituperative misanthropy documents part of his reaction.[5] In 1550 Rabelais was introduced to Cardinal Odet, and in August a new royal privilege for all Rabelais's works was granted in the presence of

2. *TL*, Pr, 341, 350.
3. *QL*, DL, 543.
4. See pp. 35–36. As suggested in this earlier discussion, not only Rabelais's personal fortunes affected his mood during these years, but also in October 1547 the infamous Chambre ardente ("Burning Chamber") of Parlement began its repression of heresy, passing 450 sentences, including 60 for capital punishment, in 1548–1550. A system for carrying out effective persecution for belief was set in place in France, and both there and abroad the power of humanist Catholics and other reforming liberals within church and state hierarchies declined.
5. Schwartz, "Rhetorical Tensions," 23–25, emphasizes Rabelais's "violence" in the 1548 prologue. See esp. his analysis, 22–23, of the satiric references to royal politics in Rabelais's tale of the magpies and jays.

the cardinal, who had been entrusted by the king with responsibility for book censorship. The conjuncture of Rabelais's publishing fortunes thus veered sharply from nadir to zenith within four years. The tone of the dedicatory letter in 1552 reflects the rebound.

Publication and its protection was one thing; readerly misunderstanding was another. The longer-term cause of the paratextual changes culminating in 1552 is Rabelais's slowly matured recognition that he could never expect to win over with laughter whole sectors of opinion, represented by the negative metatexts that had persistently attached themselves to his novels. Rabelais by 1552 seems to have recognized the enormity of the enemy; instead of moving to encounter and convert, praise and abuse, welcome and then make fun of one and all, he chooses his ground and reserves his wine. Offering the latter to one and all had done little or nothing to discourage the partial and distinctly un-Pantagruelist reading of his books. In 1548 the prologue narrator salutes his illustrious drinking companions in the usual way at the outset, but the fictional ambience that he then sketches is unprecedented in the prologues, mixing a law court case with the exchange of ambassadorial gifts between unspecified authorities. The context is that of patently arbitrary judicial and administrative proceedings similar to those satirized in the text proper of the first three books. In 1552 the fictional ambience of the prologue is equally unfamiliar, as we have seen: the semiprivacy of a house well equipped with books and wine and the complacency of familiar, well-off friends who know and share each other's tastes are substituted for the earlier helter-skelter street or tavern context. Is Rabelais then moving toward the world of the classic novel with its individualistic ethos and sharp caesuras between public and private?

A new surface appears in the texts of 1552, a surface sketched in 1546 and 1548 but brought to more regular form in the full *Fourth Book*. The subtext, that is, the text's metaphorical prolongations and half-conscious intentions, correspondingly shifts as well. Juxtaposed to both the surface of the text and its implied extensions (its "substance-stuffed marrow" of current philosophical, religious, and social issues)[6] is a third element, the countertext, which allows more play, more flexibility

6. In the prologue to *Gargantua, G,* Pr, 26–27, Rabelais compares the inner meaning of his Silenus-box text to a bone's marrow, difficult to obtain but infinitely nourishing and delicious, *la substantificque mouelle.*

in the way text and subtext are related. This is because the central rhetorical device of the countertext is mockery.

Rabelais's old notion of text was set forth explicitly in the prologue to *Gargantua;* the new notion is not formulated in any particular passage. I do not assert that it was consciously substituted for the earlier system; it is there, I would argue, in the same sense that Rabelais allowed for the existence of unconscious meanings in Homer. Although not a consciously deployed system, it is a consciously employed and repeatedly invoked stratagem in the *Fourth Book.* It is present here as a regular part of the kind of reading the author solicits from readers; it was present in earlier books only spasmodically. In *Gargantua, Pantagruel,* and the *Third Book* irony is met, supported, or overwhelmed by the exuberant faith expressed by the invention of Pantagruelism. In the *Fourth Book* mockery overtakes any and all affirmations, including those pertaining to Pantagruel and Pantagruelism.

Irony floods the narrative. Curiously enough, the regular adoption of a way of countering the surface of the story and its implications allowed Rabelais to preserve something of his humanist-communalist principles at the very point in his text where he seemed to abandon them. Contrary to the conclusions of some interpreters of the *Third Book* and the *Fourth Book,* populist sentiments are not abandoned in these late publications. Folkloric and antiofficial allusions do not disappear. They are stated obliquely; they are also critically and ironically evaluated along with other partitive social stances.[7]

The idea of a Rabelaisian countertext is proposed and tested in this chapter as a hypothesis. It requires further application both within and beyond the *Fourth Book,* as well as comparison with other authors, before its usefulness as a way of reading the text can be confirmed. It certainly clarifies some puzzles which interpreters of the *Fourth Book* have encountered. That has been demonstrated already in this study in dealing with the Sausage War and its outcome. Beneath the surface

---

7. Richard Berrong, *Rabelais and Bakhtin* (Lincoln, Nebr., 1985), objects to Bakhtin's interpretation because Bakhtin attributes populist views to Rabelais from beginning to end of the novels. Berrong believes the popular elements in Rabelais's writings were progressively abandoned, beginning with *Gargantua.* Berrong borrows a binary view of culture—learned and popular, the "great tradition" and the "little"—from Robert Redfield, via Peter Burke's *Popular Culture of Early Modern Europe,* which is too simple a conceptual tool to deal with Rabelais's multiple and shifting cultural proclivities.

representation of Carnivalesque battle and voracious alimentary enjoyment is the mock epic subtext with its national pride in an iron sow
once used to defeat the English. But the pride is comically, countertextually undercut by the piggish, massacring manner of the Pantagruelians' victory. The subtext's construction of battle as a realization of fecundity (the soldiers are carried in a succulent animal's "womb") is
undermined by the character of the cooks who stick fingers and tongues
into nearly everything and drop the rest before getting it to table. The
Sausages appropriately adore a pig as their deity, but this propriety is
countertextually undone by constructing the deity's form as a biblical
idol that secretes mustard; the Sausages' worship rhymes with what was
seen by evangelical reformers as a materialistic deformation in the sacrament of the Eucharist.

Even more telling examples of the way countertextual techniques cut
across and against surface and subtextual meanings were observed in
Rabelais's chapters about Quaresmeprenant. The strategy used toward
readers in these chapters starts by encouraging their curiosity and then
swerves toward forcing them to admit bewilderment, as Quaresmeprenant becomes not only less like Carnival but also less like Lent. Rabelais slides this personage from Carnival toward Lent and back again,
not once but many times, as if intent on assaulting every effort at clear
identification.[8] These moves, I have suggested, do not produce ambiguity but rather stimulate attempts to read the text perspectively.[9]

Perspectival readings in the *Third Book* and the *Fourth Book* become
more and more often ironic readings. Did this signal that the secondary
world of the novels had come to seem entirely out of harmony with the
primary, pragmatic world, even though Rabelais continued to represent
in the paratexts an embodied connection to it through the wheeling

8. The ineffectiveness of Rabelais's textual tactics is dramatically demonstrated by the tenacity with which seventeenth- and eighteenth-century critics,
ignoring any idea of countertext, sought to maintain text-subtext clarity and
consistency through the impossible equation of Quaresmeprenant with Lent,
even at a time when actual linguistic usage and Carnival-Lent customs belying
the equation were still relatively strong and integral parts of these critics' cultural awareness.

9. See the conclusions to ch. 5 and to the introduction to Part 3 on oblique
and perspectival readings. The examples given in these chapters of the arrangement of text such that readers are directed to hold two meanings in mind when
a certain object is invoked (the Sausages as meat and fish, penis and woman,
etc.) are examples of how countertextual irony leads readers to consider more
flexibly the relation between the text's and the subtext's meanings and train of
development.

and dealing of the prologue narrators? At least we can conclude the following: ironic countertexts gave Rabelais's fictional universe somewhat more autonomy from other worlds—social, practical, natural, and supernatural.

It is useful to remember that fiction, like literature generally, had in the sixteenth century still no generally admitted functions or status separate from those of serving to amuse and adorn on one hand and of instructing or offering moral encouragement on the other. The lack of adequate vehicles to develop reasoned and sophisticated metatexts, noted earlier, reflected the more general absence of ideologically sanctioned ways of thinking about cultural endeavor in terms of its own ends. Michel Beaujour suggested that Rabelais's lack of an anthropological theory of culture was due to his inability to find a place for culture which, while not utterly subordinated to the commands of Supernature, would also be more than the reflection of Nature's impulses—any place, that is, other than "the practice of literature as satire." But the problem facing Rabelais was not just that or primarily that; after all, an adequate concept of human culture requires some idea of independence too from the exigencies of society. It seems likely that Rabelais practiced literary satire not primarily to combat the overbearing claims of God and Nature on human existence but because it allowed him to deal effectively with—and finally by means of his countertextual strategies to wriggle away from—the threats of church and state condemnation.

Rabelais founded his solution not on the alienated autonomy of the writer of fiction but on reformulation of the connection between culture and society.[10] In the earlier books the communalist ideal was based upon the humanist presumption that everyone possesses a good nature and potential generosity to which convivial appeal can be made: the harmonization of social groups may be possible, at least in leisure time. People may be at least temporarily restored to health from their folly through gaily communicated and exchanged experience. From shared cultural enjoyment positive social effects will flow.[11] Having experi-

10. Beaujour's views, which I have found most helpful in specifying my slightly differing ones, are briefly discussed at the end of ch. 3. His idea of Rabelais's rather desperate belief in the power of literary invention is stated with particular eloquence at the conclusion of *Le jeu de Rabelais,* 174–75.

11. As suggested in ch. 8, Rabelais's communalism was not a description of actual social relations but rather one of the ideal form of those habits of shared living characteristic of most everyday behavior in his time.

enced the steady enmity of certain critics over twenty years, Rabelais recognized that some people wanted no restoration from their folly. There is discontinuity between culture and society: good effects do not always flow from good causes. Although Rabelais never says so, he may have realized that one major reason for this is that cultural communities—theological readers for one, courtiers for another, humanists for a third, the hoi polloi gathered around shop doors for a fourth[12]—do not normally have the kind of close communicative contact with each other that the intersecting social groups of his time did. Thoughts are relatively free—and idiosyncratic—because they are relatively distant from the body's involvements and quite far indeed from the thoughts of other people in different cultural milieus. That freedom has its consequences, one of which is ideological rigidity.

Rabelais's friends were his readers, but few of his readers had close contact with each other's ideas. He drew the conclusion: the prologue to the *Fourth Book* addresses itself to a community existing in scattered, physically unknowable form, united by an invisible and socially ineffective trait, that of wishing the author of the Pantagrueline tales well. Elaboration of the countertextual strategies to be analyzed in this chapter was the joint creation of a literary inclination (it is obvious that Rabelais had a flair for satire), an at least half-conscious sociology, and a most assuredly conscious political reaction to the threat to his books. It had the unexpected and, I think, unintended consequence of contributing to the construction of a cultural realm, that of literature, which has its own criteria of value and which has over centuries gradually come to be recognized by the very powers so often threatening it as possessing a peculiar but inevitable, dangerous but essential, autonomy from everyday life and its sanctions.[13]

We will limit analysis of Rabelais's countertextual mockery in this chapter to its use in the *Fourth Book* at the most sensitive point of his text, the point at which contact with and defense against readers is normally strongest: the introductory paratexts. We begin by looking again at the prologue to the incomplete *Fourth Book* of 1548 so as to establish a comparative means of measuring the more formalized strategy of 1552.

12. See p. 28, the anonymous quotation from 1496, and Fig. 1.
13. As I write, the scandals over D. H. Lawrence's "obscene" *Lady Chatterley's Lover* and Ezra Pound's "fascist" *Cantos* are being played out again, in even more personally threatening terms, around Salman Rushdie's "sacrilegious" *Satanic Verses* (New York, 1989).

"Illustrious boozers and you my precious gouty friends, I have seen, received, heard, and understood the ambassador which the Lordship of your Lordships has sent to my Paternity." Sometime in 1547 Rabelais traveled to the Roman See for the third time: the unctuous gravity of the curial setting inaugurates the 1548 prologue. The "Lordship of your Lordships" presents the prologue narrator with a "breviary" that contains not the liturgical texts which a monk from the Hyères Islands should chant at prescribed times but instead a bottle or bottles inscribed with rules for drinking:[14] "So you wish that at prime I should drink white wine, at the third, sixth, and ninth hour, the same; at vespers and complin, claret. . . . I grant the request." The reference to breviary here does not lead the reader to an abyss, like that in the description of Quaresmeprenant in the later *Fourth Book*. The satire of ecclesiastical complacency and self-interest is sharp and direct, concealed just enough to be called a subtext. At the surface is ambassadorial protocol, requiring the taking of wine according to rule. Just below the surface is a monastery drunk who drinks, perhaps, alone. No convivial suggestion to share in the wine and to toast each other intervenes, unlike the case in previous prologues. However, a convivial exchange does take place—words for wine—however official and however physically remote. The motif remains but is significantly transformed.

"You say the wine of the *Third Book* was to your taste. . . . And you copiously invite me to continue the Pantagrueline history, allegating the utilities and fruits received from its reading by all men of worth [gens de bien]." The separation of good from bad readers in partly moral and partly social terms proceeds:

> Responding I say and maintain, up to the point of burning [at the stake] (you understand: for obvious reasons), that you are exalted men of worth [grandz gens de bien], all descended from good mothers and good fathers, and I promise you, with the word of a commoner [literally, foot soldier, foi de piéton: inversion of foi de chevalier, as in the English proverbial phrase, "word of a gentleman"] that if I ever meet you in Mesopotamia . . . you shall receive a fine Nile crocodile [in return for the breviary].[15]

14. The identity of the prologue speaker in the prologue of 1548 (entitled "Prologue du Quart Livre") is not stated (contrast the prologue of 1552, entitled "Prologue de l'autheur"), but, because the title page identifies the author as "François Rabelais, doctor in medicine and monk from the Hyeres Islands," presumably it is he.

15. *QL*, Pr 1548, 755.

The prologue of 1548 hops and skips between this aping of ambassadorial custom and that of a law court hearing the narrator's case against the slanderers of his books. Among the prologue's many fine inventions is maintenance of the fiction inaugurated by the narrator when he says, "O worthy people, I can't see you."[16] The flow of discourse is interrupted five times in fifteen paragraphs by seemingly confused queries to the narrator's interlocutors, as if the narrator were hard of hearing as well as poor of eyesight: "You say what? That you have not been irritated by anything in all my books . . . ? You pronounce judgment. What? To whom? All the old quarters of the moon to the caphards, cagots, matagots."[17]

The law court reference is of course to the Parlement of Paris, which in 1545 and again in 1546 had confirmed the Sorbonne's censure of Rabelais's books. The narrator's imaginary law court inverts the behavior of the real one, finding Rabelais's books blameless and the slanderers guilty. "I pardon them," declares the narrator, but not "their malignities and impostures." Toward the latter, "I shall employ the offer made by Timon the Misanthropist to his ungrateful [fellow citizens] the Athenians." Converting himself into a hanging judge, he concludes—in parallel with the anecdote he recounts about Timon but in seeming contradiction with his "pardon" just a paragraph earlier—that "these diabolic slanderers shall all have to hang themselves during the last quarter of this moon. I shall furnish the nooses. . . . Once the moon renews, they'll not be accommodated so cheaply and will be forced to buy cord and choose a hanging tree on their own."[18]

This conclusion, like the prologue generally, has been called contemptuous and uncompromising with respect to Rabelais's opponents, an "inflammatory text" whose irony is "acid sharp, not urbane and witty."[19] It is indeed uncompromising and acidic but it is also urbane with its ambassadorial aping and witty with its law court inversion of Parlement's attack; most interestingly, it is implicitly self-critical by reason of the absurd hyperbole of its first fumbling and then forgotten pardons, its condemnations, and its modification of the condemna-

16. See the opening pages of ch. 1 on this phrase and the contrasting ways it is used in 1548 and 1552.

17. *QL*, Pr 1548, 755. This denunciatory passage and its context is discussed at greater length on pp. 34–35 above.

18. *QL*, Pr 1548, 757, 758.

19. Schwartz, "Rhetorical Tensions," 25.

tions. Just as Rabelais in the *Fourth Book* exalts in new ways the sovereign command and philosophic wisdom of Pantagruel and at the same time pokes fun at the fellow's digressive vagueness, so also the author hangs out his anger to dry in this windy new-model prologue.

When Rabelais wrote the new prologue to the *Fourth Book* in 1552, his animal spirits revived, the acerbic quality had evaporated. This is the most buoyant of all his prologues, the most complex in its storytelling, and the most ironic in its doubly undercut narration. We have discussed its opening salutation, its Lenten game, its description of the author's happy state due to a pinch of Pantagruelism, and its ready invitation, so different from the 1548 prologue, to share a glass of wine.[20] The subject then turns with a pious flourish to the doctor's preoccupation with health and so moves to a theme that structures the remaining thirteen of its fifteen octavo pages: it is best to wish in moderation.[21]

The subject is ostensibly homiletic: If your wishes are moderate, worthy people, God will reward the modesty. The Stoic-Christian lesson is illustrated with the story, adapted from Aesop, of a poor woodcutter named Ballocker (*Couillatris*) who loses his hatchet and clamors to the gods for it. Jupiter offers him a choice between a gold, a silver, and his own homely wooden-handled one; he chooses the latter, whereupon he is given all three and becomes rich. A corollary is added: Ballocker's neighbors, hearing his story, throw away their hatchets, too, but when they are offered the same choice they choose the gold-headed hatchet; for that they are, by order of Jupiter, beheaded.

Into this moralistic mold Rabelais pours all manner of other materials which so digress from it that its point is obscured and overwhelmed. The guiding thread in these distractions is the phallic theme announced with Ballocker's name and amplified in the ambivalent meaning of *coignée*: the word means "hatchet," but also "hatchet head"; the latter refers metaphorically to the female genitals, and as such is in

20. See the end of ch. 1 and the middle of ch. 8.

21. The theme of men's health is introduced immediately after the opening salutation and Lenten-game greeting. Dr. Rabelais states that his own health is good at both the beginning and the end of the prologue, but the considerable space given this theme in the 1552 prologue and the ironic turn given to each story about famous ancient doctors who thought they could maintain health through their art, makes one wonder if Rabelais's affirmations may not be an inversion of something worrying him, something that may have led the following year to his death. See also note 23.

common parlance juxtaposed to the hatchet handle, which doubles as the penis. The theme is emblazoned in tall red letters, so to speak, when the deliberations of the Olympian gods about Ballocker prove to be dominated by Priapus. Priapus sings bawdy songs, explains in ample detail the meaning of *coignée,* and tells a tale about a fox and a dog that itself digresses from the heaven-storming difficulties with which Priapus's sovereign, the great god Jupiter, is preoccupied. Jupiter is particularly troubled by the ruckus raised at Paris by two fellows called by Priapus "little testicle-shaped self-admirers," the logicians Peter Ramus and Peter Gallandus, who in the 1550s discussed with great hue and cry the significance of Aristotle for their discipline.

The verve of the narrative outruns all possible didactic point. The prologue is a careening mixture of ancient and modern, profane and sacred topoi that swerve away from and then unexpectedly collide with each other. Its zigzags are prescribed by the techniques of Menippean satire, as André Tournon and Jerome Schwartz have demonstrated.[22] Two of these techniques were especially useful in developing the altered mode of contact between the represented author and readers of the text, initiated by Rabelais in 1548. One device gives examples and draws out the implications of a precept so that, instead of confirming the precept, subsequent discourse obliquely suggests its falsity.[23] The other device inserts what seems to be an aside in a story, a passing comment that so develops as to displace the whole universe of discourse. The two techniques are alike in the sense that they both depend on exploiting the polysemic and eventually contradictory character of seemingly unexceptional commonplaces.

22. See André Tournon, "Le Paradoxe ménippéen dans l'oeuvre de Rabelais," *Etudes rabelaisiennes* 21 (1988): 309–17. Tournon, like Schwartz in "Rhetorical Tensions," emphasizes Rabelais's acquaintance with such techniques through his study of Lucian.

23. Schwartz, "Rhetorical Tensions," 28–30, gives examples of this from the first part of the prologue. Galen was "completely healthy," Rabelais begins and then moves sideways: he had, of course, some "passing fevers," was "none of the healthiest by nature," and "evidently had a weak stomach." Asclepius, too, was never sick right up to an extreme old age, so that he was indeed "triumphant over Fortune"—except that he died by falling from the top of a rotten staircase. The reader is prepared for these attritions by Rabelais's displacement of a quotation from Luke (4:23–25), in which Jesus himself displaces the proverb, "Physician, heal thyself." Another demonstration of examples undermining precepts occurs in Schwartz's analysis of the Ramus-Galland digression in the prologue of 1552, ibid., 32–33.

The main example of the second technique has been mentioned: the story of the lost hatchet is developed so as to displace the theme from that of the wisdom of moderate desires to one of the necessity, for a man, of his hatchet handle. The phallic theme is overtly proclaimed everywhere in the story of Ballocker (the nickname means "testicled"; the woodcutter is immediately identified as well endowed) except at the moment of his choice of the restored hatchet. There the reader must drop below the surface of the text to read along lines only metaphorically indicated. In Tournon's paraphrase:

> He "lifts the golden hatchet . . . he finds it rather heavy . . . That one is not mine. . . ." That is understandable: how is he going to "go to work," poor fellow, with that golden "hatchet," so heavy to lift? It's his own he wants, his "hatchet of *wood*," says Rabelais, since it is especially the handle which counts. . . . When it is given back to him, he "attaches it to his *leather belt,* placing it *under the backside* [sous le cul] . . ."; equipped with his tool at last . . . happy Ballocker can pronounce his "little word" of triumph: "Have I got it? [En ay-je?]" . . . Don't ask me to explain things more clearly.

Tournon's commentary terminates by indicating the unspoken relation between this story of lost and found erection and the prologue's first theme, men's health and how to safeguard it: To wish for the means of subsistence that insure health is natural; to desire those things that directly affect the body—one's "physical integrity, the exercise of one's vital energies, pleasure, and fecundity"—is still more so. Thus it is that the "priapic equivocation" of the text suffuses with "erotic joy" the totality of text.[24]

Erotic indeed. The sense and sentiment of male physical vitality wells up and replaces the theme of sober desire without ado when the scene shifts from Dr. Rabelais's study with its medical books and Bible to the heavens of Olympus. The sexuality evoked by the prologue's piquant language is as male-centered as in the Sausage War episode or the talk of the Pantagruelian company generally.[25]

The sexuality is male, and so are its discursive effects. The prologue

24. Tournon, "Le Paradoxe ménippéen," 313.
25. Priapus concludes his second commentary on Ballocker's predicament with a song: "'If hatchets unhelved are quite useless / and tools without handles no use too / Let's make one then fit into the other / I've a handle. Let the hatchet be you,'" at which words, continues the prologue author, "all the venerable gods and goddesses burst out laughing," and "Vulcan with his twisted leg did three or four pretty little jigs for love of his mistress," *QL*, Pr, 555.

springs from subject to subject like a young buck. The sedate beginning is forgotten; Rabelais's rabble-rousing readers return:

> They [Ballocker's neighbors] chose the one of gold . . . but as they lifted it from the earth, bent over and stooping, Mercury cut off their heads, as Jupiter had decreed. . . . There you have it, that's what happens. . . . Take warning from that, you scabby fellows from the flat country,[26] who say you wouldn't forego your wishes for ten thousand francs a year.

Faith in the Lord God, invoked with pious conventionality at the beginning, returns with onomatopoeic gusto at the end:

> Hey, there, hey! And who taught you to prattle and talk of the power and predestination of God, poor people? Peace! Sh, sh, sh! Humble yourselves before his sacred visage and recognize your imperfections. It is on this, gouty ones, that I found my hopes.[27]

Reference of any sort to predestination in the vexed theological ambience of the mid-sixteenth century in France was touchy business. The word carried a wide range of meanings whose nuances, Calvinist, Catholic, or other, all involved the reconciliation of God's omnipotence and omniscience with some version of human freedom. A loose interpretation of the words of this suddenly appearing preacher on the prologue scene would paraphrase it so: what people get in the way of wealth is fixed by almighty God, and so it does no good to talk about it. One should be as sober in religious talk as in one's desires. The subtext of such a clear and easy surface text answers the question of the preacher: Who taught you to talk of predestination? The heresiarch Calvin, of course.

A stricter and, as it happens, countertextual interpretation of the preacher voice would be: of course, what you get is fixed by God, but so indeed are wishes. To urge moderation in wishes is irrelevant because wishes like rewards are predestined. The moral of this story is that its moral is pointless. If this pointless point is indeed the one aimed at by Rabelais the author (as opposed to Dr. Rabelais, the author represented as narrating the prologue), then it is only the final turn in slowly undermining the prologue's ostensible theme.

26. "Gualliers" in the epithet *gualliers de plat pays* refers to persons afflicted with galls, skin sores caused by rubbing. The epithet derives from Rabelais's medical experience, but at the same time signifies return to the motley, unsightly readers of earlier prologues, the poxy fellows infected with syphilis who are welcomed to his books.

27. *QL,* Pr, 558–59.

Ballocker got back the "tool" he needs to "labor." He also became rich, while his greedy neighbors were killed. This is the point at which the unexpected preacher voice comes forward, scolding an audience of equally unexpected hecklers, unsavoury fellows full of scabs; the "worthy people" first greeted have disappeared. Yet is it not "dubious morality to excoriate materialism"—as seems to be done in Jupiter's execution of Ballocker's greedy neighbors—"by showering material gifts upon the simple Couillatris [Ballocker]"?[28] From this perspective perhaps Ballocker's "little word" has another meaning, as he parades around his parish with the gold and silver hatchets slung around his neck: "En ay-je" can equally well be translated, "Haven't I got some?"[29]

He has. The following paragraph dwells with delectation on Ballocker's canny conversion of his two superfluous but precious hatchets into coins and then into farmlands, farm animals, mills, forests, ponds, and much else. No wonder, then, that his neighbors threw away their hatchets and yelled to the heavens for Jupiter's help. But their destiny, pursues the prologue author, like that of anyone who wishes for too much, is cankerous, consuming sickness and death.[30]

The preacher, in fact, promises nothing else. "Wish, then, for mediocrity [médiocrité: a middling, modest situation]," the preacher pursues. "It will come to you, and even better duly [deuement: in due time?] if meanwhile you labor and work." The "it" refers not to wishes, as a careless French reader—and many readers of unclear English translations—might think, but to mediocrity.[31] When he continues "and even better duly," this laconic phrase is overtranslated—and so it is in many English translations—if it is taken to mean "and even better

28. Schwartz, "Rhetorical Tensions," 34.

29. The useful French "en" takes its precise meaning from linguistic context. To translate as literally as possible, one would write: "have I of it?" But even such a literal effort is not really literal, making four words out of three. *Traduttore, traditore.*

30. Rabelais in *QL,* Pr, 558–59, adds other examples of people with excessive wishes and warns of the illnesses that often then ensue, thus rejoining the theme of health. Schwartz's interpretation of the preaching attributes a somewhat too Protestant moralism to the prologue author, "Rhetorical Tensions," 33–34. The prologue author is not preaching against "materialism," nor does he suppose that virtues should be their own reward or that they should be rewarded exclusively in the afterlife.

31. *QL,* Pr, 559: "Souhaitez donc médiocrité: elle vous adviendra": *le souhait* is a masculine noun from the verb *souhaiter; la médiocrité* is feminine; *elle* grammatically refers therefore to *médiocrité.*

things than you have wished for, in due time."[32] The phrase, taken at its face value, and connected with either the following words that complete it or the preceding words about mediocrity, simply says: if you work away, you'll get better "duly," that is, in accordance with either the way you work or your properly mediocre wishes. The preacher says nothing about showers of riches from heaven.

The preacher's empty words are rejected with accuracy by his scabby back-country auditors: "But, you say, God could just as well have given me seventy-eight millions as the thirteenth part of a half [-penny]." This is the moment when the sermonizer thunders, "Quiet there! God has predestined everyone's fortunes and who are you to dare talk about it?"—which makes wishes great or small quite irrelevant.

Why does this displacement flow along so easily? It is, as I suggested in chapter 1, a question of not only Rabelais's personal skills as a storyteller and rhetorician but also of his use of the tools offered him by his context. The inchoateness of printed book conventions made it easier to think about mixtures of the rather rigid and narrow conventions of manuscript books with the panoply of oral storytelling techniques. Imitation of oral storytelling traditions rendered more rhetorically acceptable the shifts from one subject, one register of rhetorical appeal, one universe of discourse to others. Orality is flow; swift change and even inconsequence in subject matter is a condition of retaining contact with an easily distracted audience, in contrast to the concentrated attention on which one can count in readers. Awareness of the ironic effects in the prologue just noted depends in fact on readers' ability to turn back the pages and note with care the points at which the argument is dislocated. The presence of a countertext may be sensed in the swift-flowing movement from proposition to example to objection and back to apparent reiteration, but it can hardly be ascertained without the close reading that reveals gradual destruction of the initial proposition due to small phrases, grammatical referents, and polysemic slippage.

This situation of simultaneous sensitivity to oral and written techniques of persuasion and argument was Rabelais's context, not ours,

---

32. See Rabelais, *Gargantua and Pantagruel,* trans. J. M. Cohen, 448: "So wish in moderation. What you ask will come to you, and better things, too, if you toil hard at your own work in the meantime." Rabelais, *The Portable Rabelais,* trans. Samuel Putnam (New York, 1946), 547: "Do your wishing, then, in moderation, and you will get all you wish for and more still, providing that you only work and labor in the meanwhile."

which may be one reason why twentieth-century scholars have one-sidedly lionized his writing skills—and those of the other great story-tellers surrounding him in France—Marguerite of Navarre, Bonaventure des Periers, Noël du Faïl—not to mention those in other countries. They are analyzed and lauded too often one by one, so that the dual cultural atmosphere they shared and exploited—oral and written, printed and proclaimed—is only dimly perceived.

Rabelais's ironic retelling of the Aesopian tale of Ballocker not only undermines the sententious wisdom of Stoic-Christian prescriptions.[33] It also belies Pantagruelism. How did Ballocker get the attention of the gods and move them to their reward? By making an infernal racket. Ballocker bewailed his fate, his unfair fortune, his awful predicament, "calling aloud indefatigably after each chapter of his prayers, 'My hatchet, Jupiter! my hatchet, my hatchet! only my hatchet or the money to buy another! Alas, my poor hatchet!'" The clamor was so loud and long that "it was heard with great astonishment . . . in the very consistory of the gods. 'What devil is it down there?' asked Jupiter, 'howling so horribly?'"[34]

This behavior, not the Pantagruelists' gaily spirited disdain of fortuitous things, was adopted by the real author, in contrast to his prologue representation of himself.[35] Rabelais howled so loudly and horribly—witness the prologues to the *Third Book* and the 1548 incomplete *Fourth Book*—that the great gods of censorship in France answered his prayers. He paraded the results as proudly as Ballocker did his hatchets. The order of the first edition of the *Fourth Book* in early 1552 was: title page; dedicatory letter "To the most illustrious prince and most reverend monseigneur Odet, Cardinal of Châtillon" dated January 28, 1552; privilege in the name of Henry II, King of France, dated August 6, 1550 and signed "By the King, Cardinal Châtillon present, countersigned Du Thier"; prologue; and text.

33. Undermines but does not undo it. The example of Zachaeus's modest wish to see Jesus, and Jesus' reward to him by visiting him and blessing his family, is told without irony: *QL,* Pr, 547. The points of unsatirized seriousness in the prologue—this is not the only one—function to set off the irony of the rest more strongly.

34. *QL,* Pr, 549.

35. See the discussion of Pantagruelism near the end of ch. 8, which includes quotation of the definition at the beginning of this prologue, *QL,* Pr, 545.

It is as if Rabelais intended his readers to see first his appeal for help
and then its results, even though this order inverts the dates of composition of the dedication and privilege. The publisher, Fézandat in
Paris, probably did not choose this order, since it was in the publisher's
interest to manifest royal authorization as clearly and hence as quickly
as possible in terms of the book's pagination. The wordy and circum-
stantial royal privilege, rather unusual for the times, seems almost to
have been dictated in some parts by Rabelais.

> On behalf of our dear and well beloved M. François Rabelais, doctor in
> medicine, it has been represented to us that, . . . having given to be
> printed several books . . . including certain volumes concerning the he-
> roic deeds and sayings of Pantagruel, no less useful than delectable, the
> printers had corrupted, depraved, and perverted the said books in a num-
> ber of places. They had further printed some other scandalous books
> under the name of the suppliant to his great displeasure, prejudice and
> ignominy, books totally disavowed by him as false and counterfeit.[36]

Or, as the dedicatory letter put it, and as the reader had already been
informed if reading through the edition of 1552,

> King Francis . . . was informed about these slanders [concerning Rabe-
> lais's alleged heresies] and, having heard and comprehended these my
> several distinct books (I say it [i.e., he specifies that the Pantagrueline
> novels were issued in several separate volumes] because certain other
> false and infamous counterfeit ones have been attributed to me) . . . had
> found no passage suspect, [although one fellow] based mortal heresy on
> an N placed where an M should have been through the fault and negli-
> gence of the printers.

Francis's son, "our so good, so virtuous, heavenly blessed King
Henry (may God preserve him long among us) also had [heard the
public reading?], so that he granted to you for me a privilege and particular protection against the slanderers."[37] Thus the privilege assures
that:

> We, agreeing fully to the supplication and request of the said M. François
> Rabelais . . . give the right . . . to him to have printed and again placed
> on sale all and each of the said books and the sequel to Pantagruel . . .
> and at the same time to suppress those which have been falsely attributed
> to him. . . . Ceasing and causing to cease all troubles and impediments
> to the contrary, for such is our desire.[38]

36. Privilège du Roy, 339.
37. *QL,* DL, 543.
38. Privilège du Roy, 339–40.

Little wonder that the final paragraphs of the dedicatory letter approach the limits of encomiastic hero-worship. Cardinal Odet's favor leads the author to hope that "you will be to me, against my slanderers, like a second Gallic Hercules in knowledge, wisdom, and eloquence, a [Hercules] Alexicacos in virtue, power, and authority, one of whom I may truthfully say what was said of Moses . . . by the wise King Solomon." A long quotation from the book of Ecclesiasticus ensues, which calls Moses and hence Odet a man chosen of God, made "like to the glorious saints . . . so that his enemies stood in fear of him."[39] The praise is indeed grandiose. Are they Ballocker's naive tactics or Lucian's mocking ones, treading a tightrope "between protocol and parody"?[40]

This near syncophancy is neither greater nor more serious than that exhibited in the fresco covering a half-dome space in the family chateau of Tanlay near Châtillon-sur-Loing, where the three brothers Châtillon, with Diane de Poitiers, King Henry II, and some other courtly figures, are depicted as Olympian gods and goddesses looking down in a row, frontally posed, on whoever happens in, with many of the women and some of the men voluptuously, virilely nude. Rabelais is playing the courtier's game, using a different but complementary rhetoric to that employed in the prologue, a rhetoric that allows him, as in the rest of his writing, to remain so well masked as to be nearly invisible.[41]

To little avail. The *Fourth Book*, published at the end of January, was condemned on March 1 by Parlement at the request of the Sorbonne. Rabelais did not abandon his tactics; he redoubled them. As Michael Screech and Stephen Rawles have demonstrated, a new edition was hastily assembled in which an amended version of the prologue appears.

In the opening paragraphs of the prologue where the subject is personal health and how to retain it, Rabelais includes another of his mocking plays upon legal principles, the one in question being "the dead seizes upon the living" (*le mort saisit le vif*). This principle had been explicated by a one-time friend of Rabelais, André Tiraqueau, with whom the author was apparently irritated for a number of reasons, among other things because of Tiraqueau's omission of Rabelais's

39. *QL*, DL, 543–44.
40. Schwartz, "Rhetorical Tensions," 27.
41. The rather risqué scene, whose chief subject is the Judgment of Paris, is reproduced in Louis Réau, *Richesses d'art de la France: la Bourgogne, la peinture* (Paris, 1929), plate 13.

name from a list of famous doctors cited in one of Tiraqueau's works.[42] Already in the first edition of the *Fourth Book* Rabelais paid back this slighting omission by according the legist manifestly excessive mention in this passage:

> Good God! Good fellows! Is it not prescribed and practiced by the ancient customs of this most noble, most flourishing, most rich and triumphant realm of France, that the dead seizes upon the living? Note the recent exposition of this principle by the good, the learned, the wise, the most humane, most gracious and just And. Tiraqueau, counsellor of King Henry, second of that name, in his most dreaded Parlement at Paris.[43]

Ah, yes. Tiraqueau was among those who as a royal lawyer in the Parlement of Paris influenced in one way or another, by omission or commission, the condemnations of Rabelais's books. That too played its part in the composition of this reference whose context in the fantasmatic prologue, as opposed to similar hyperbole about Odet de Châtillon in the dedicatory letter, makes countertextual mockery very probable. Not so the changes that Rabelais made in the second edition of this passage, probably between April and June 1552.[44] The references to Henry II and his kingdom are augmented and inflated, while the rest of the words remain the same:

> Is it not prescribed and practiced by the ancient customs of this most noble, *most venerable, most beautiful,* most flourishing, most rich realm of France. . . ? Note the recent exposition . . . by . . . Tiraqueau, counsellor of the *great, victorious,* and *triumphant* King Henry.[45]

Screech and Rawles suggest that this amended edition was presented to King Henry and his place in it displayed. That is the reason, it is conjectured, that further legal proceedings against the *Fourth Book* were quashed.

42. See Schwartz, "Rhetorical Tensions," 30, n. 14, on this question. There were other issues between the two longtime acquaintances, having to do with Tiraqueau's comments on marriage laws, which play a part in Rabelais's *Third Book*. See Screech, *Rabelais,* esp. 213, 273.

43. See the first edition (Jan. 1552; not reprinted in *QL,* Pr, 547) in *NRB,* 238, Fig. 46.2, a facsimile from the first edition.

44. See *NRB,* 244, and the preceding discussion, 242–44, in portions of which some contradictory statements about the probable date of the second edition are made.

45. *NRB,* 239, Fig. 46.4, a facsimile from the second edition; italics added.

Jerome Schwartz concludes from his perspicacious reading of the liminary texts to the *Fourth Book* that the dedicatory letter and prologue are written for "two audiences, two levels of the social hierarchy . . . two sets of standards and values." One uses "grand, rhetorical style" to influence the great; the other "invokes in comic style the humble *goutteux* [gouty ones] in their modest, simple, limited hope for life and health." But Schwartz's very perception of the mocking and self-critical details in *both* documents undermines any such clear division.[46] Three kinds of readers are envisioned, not two, and the eyes of all of them would peruse all, not one rather than another in the whole proud parade of documents opening the *Fourth Book*: one category of reader includes high, elite, official, or exalted persons socially and culturally; the second mixes persons high and low in social estate and is unpretentious and popular in taste; the third, also indeterminate socially but not so easy to describe culturally, is an audience of mockers, a group of readers not necessarily Pantagruelist although certainly not slanderers, identified less by ideological inclinations or particular cultural style than by the ability to interpret signs at several, often conflicting levels of meaning.

The three audiences have been amply indicated in preceding pages with respect to the prologue to the *Fourth Book*. They are equally present in the dedicatory letter. Rabelais begins by placing himself in the same milieu as that of the persons he addresses: you are aware, prince, of how many great persons have been urging me to continue my Pantagrueline fictions, he writes. As he inaugurates his first theme he maintains this cultural context. It is the theme of the doctor concerned for his patients' health, the theme of the writer who heals his readers' grieved spirits with amusing stories.[47] But humor is a rhetorical slide. It pulls discourse toward mixed effects and mixed audiences. Physicians should present a happy mien to ailing patients, Dr. Rabelais explains; they should never depress them through arrogance or indifference. A sick man once asked the physician Callianax—the narrator obviously still addresses primarily elite readers here, people who are humanist students of the classics—about his disease, "questioning him in the

46. Schwartz, "Rhetorical Tensions," 35–36. Schwartz deals with the question of mocking undertones by calling them "tensions," such that the two writings, functioning "dialectically," diverge as well as complement each other.

47. The theme is present from the first of the prologues onward.

fashion of noble Pathelin: 'Does not my urine tell you I shall die?'" You won't, answered the flippant doctor, provided that "'Latona, mother of Apollo and Diana, was the one who bore you.'"

You and I, my Cardinal, have seen or heard of the famous play about a shyster lawyer named Pathelin. With this reference to an anonymous farce written several generations before Rabelais's time, Rabelais beckons to a second audience.[48] "'You've had your lunch, doctor; your breath smells of wine,'" runs Rabelais's next anecdote. "'Yours smells of fever,' the doctor replied." Urination and fever, breathing and smelling: such bodily references mix all classes of readers. What are they doing here, if Rabelais is only interested in wheedling the cardinal for political ends? He isn't.

In the fashion of the "noble" Pathelin trickster, writes Rabelais. This false social designation is the first mocking move, the first signal to the reader to take his distance from these representations. The second comes in the following paragraph, as Rabelais moves to his chief theme, the slanders upon him and the support of kings and courtiers. Although the surface context shifts back to an elite conversation between the author and an exalted person about others high and low, the subcontext remains satiric and also broadly popular. The slanderers who regard the author as a heretic treat Rabelais's nourishing books as if they were stones, snakes, and scorpions. Rabelais sarcastically employs Jesus' words to his disciples (Luke 11:11–12) against his sanctimonious adversaries; the reference would have been recognized not only by prelates like Odet but by the many whose daily, weekly, yearly bread, fish, and eggs were the preacher's homilies.[49] Rabelais's dramatic offer to heap up wood and offer himself like a phoenix to the flames, should any "spark" of heresy be found in him to ignite such a pile, is another piece of self-consuming bravado: The phoenix burns only to be reborn. We have already discussed the ambivalence of the final paragraphs, threading their way between hyperbole and parody.

In the dedicatory letter as in the prologue Rabelais asks readers to perceive the representation of two audiences of mixed social origin but contrasting social status and power and a third audience of mockers and skeptics. There are two kinds of reader-listeners with their faces crowded around the book, well-clothed or shabby, sedate or silly, and there is a third kind further away, reflective and smiling. My guess,

48. *Maistre Pierre Pathelin*, ed. Richard Holbrook (Paris, 1967); this play is one of the most well-known examples of late medieval French popular theater.
49. See the quotation on p. 212.

pending further probes, is that Rabelais's orientation to these three different audiences emerges with stylistic distinctness after the mid-1540s. Nurtured during the eleven years of compositional silence (except for revisions) between 1535 and 1546 as Rabelais apparently pondered the metatexts gathering around his works and name, incipient in the prologue and through the text of the *Third Book* as well as in the prologue of 1548, the triple appeal became inseparable from composition of the full *Fourth Book* and inseparable too from its full understanding then and now.

There are no limits to Rabelais's irony in the *Fourth Book*. His countertextual proclivity for disingenuous hyperbole is transferred without compunction from the prologue of 1548 to the dedicatory letter of 1552, that is, from a paratextually designated "secondary" world of factitious ambassadorial politeness to a paratextually designated "primary" world of pragmatic officialdom.

Complacency:

> 1548:   "You say what? That you have not been irritated by anything in all my books?" "It is a wonderful thing to be praised by the praiseworthy," as Horace used to say, as Cicero reports about Hector, etc.[50]

> 1552:   King Francis "found no passage suspect. . . . King Henry . . . granted to you for me a privilege and particular protection," which you, Cardinal Odet, mentioned to me at Cardinal du Bellay's St. Maur chateau, that "paradise of salubrity, amenity, serenity, commodity," etc.[51]

Innocence:

> 1548:   "You say the wine of the *Third Book* was to your taste and that it is good. . . . And you copiously invite me to continue the Pantagrueline history, alleging the utilities and fruits received from its reading by all men of worth" writes the doctor-monk-official; he adds that he graciously pardons the ambassador-reader for laughing at his books, explaining that he is "not so savage [farouche, as in Ferocious Island, as on the Hyères Islands] or implacable as you think."[52]

50. *QL*, Pr 1548, 754–55.
51. *QL*, DL, 543.
52. *QL*, Pr 1548, 754–55.

> 1552: "Gay fooling there is in plenty, offensive neither to God nor the King. . . . Heresies there are none, unless one were . . . to interpret them in such a way that I would a thousand times rather have died."[53]

Accusation:

> 1548: "You pronounce judgment. What? To whom? All the old quarters of the moon to the caphards, cagots, matagots. . . . If by these terms you mean the slanderers of my writings, you could more properly call them devils. For in Greek calumny is called diabole. You see how detestable the sin of calumny is before God and the angels (that is, when one impugns good deeds or speaks evil of good things) since . . . they are named and called devils of hell," although they are "properly speaking" only the "ministers" of hell's devils.[54]

> 1552: "The slander of certain cannibals, misanthropes, and age-lastes was so outrageous and beyond all reason that I lost all patience." Such people have fallen into the clutches of a "slandering demon, a *diabolos* [in contrast to the 1548 prologue, the word is printed here with Greek letters] who uses them to accuse me of such a crime" as heresy.[55]

But of course every courtier knows that the world of official politeness is as artificial as any world of the imagination. This was even more true in the sixteenth century than at later periods because both kinds of world were less defined than they later became vis-à-vis their ambience of intersecting social groups. The world of literature gradually attained a certain autonomy; so did the state.[56]

The author is always masked. The question to ask about the real author's relation to text is not what or who represents him or her but where do the author's personae place themselves with respect not only

---

53. *QL*, DL, 542.
54. *QL*, Pr 1548, 755.
55. *QL*, DL, 542.
56. Like the doctrine of *raison d'état,* which gradually raised state power and the officials embodying it above and beyond the play of social interests characteristic of feudal political institutions, the success of doctrines suggesting the

to represented but to real contexts. The reason for developing answers to this question of "where" by emphasizing the paratexts is that Rabelais more than most authors seems to have sought to place his authorial personae as precisely as possible halfway between his fictional contexts and the contexts beyond them. Not distinctions of intertextuality but the unraveling of Rabelais's inter*con*textuality has been a major purpose of this study. Pursuit of such distinctions is most valuable in explaining how Rabelais was led to stud his text with contemporary references broad and narrow, particular and generalizing, a technique that has made his writing opaque to later generations, obscuring not only its verbal beauties but much of its comedy.

The paratexts do not function in these novels as an exit from everyday life into a new world but as a gate between two kinds of reality, a gate that swings both ways. Instead of using paratext to pull readers in one direction only, into a book world separate from readers' lives, Rabelais uses it to peek out on the world beyond. "Ha, ha! . . . I see you!"

People say my gay fooling causes mischief, that I should be silenced—but consider Ballocker. Did he cease to squabble? No, of course not. And in the end he went proudly to Chinon with his badges of triumph round his neck, to Chinon, that "famous town, noble town, ancient town, the finest town in the world, as learned Hebrew scholars maintain."[57] Chinon is Rabelais's home town. The author peeks out and pulls what he sees back in, and not only in the prologues, of course. Readers, like authors, are folded into the tale. "You are making fun of me here, boozers. . . . Go see for yourselves. . . . It was on Ferocious Island, I give you its name." The communities of the tale, the writing of the author, spill over into the sphere of readership. The mode of communication presupposes shared interests and shared activities. Dispersing the narrator transforms the sender of this communication into a member of groups that include the readers rather than establish him beyond the reach of the narrative and therefore also beyond the ken of readers. By the same device space is created for conflict among narrative voices without the disruption of all meaning. Narrative discontinuities

---

independence of literature was a result of new social and cultural circumstances in the seventeenth and the eighteenth century. Schwartz's idea that Rabelais wrote for two quite distinct audiences in the dedicatory letter and prologue applies better to paratextual protocol in Racine's time and afterward.

57. *QL*, Pr, 556.

function as comic play rather than as the bottomless pit of split personality.[58]

But these tactics are only gestures, not realities, for the gates of signification are moveable by authors of books only toward other words, not deeds. Only under one set of conditions, perhaps, does the word spinner of fictions reach beyond language in enduring and efficacious ways: the conditions of ritual. When speaker and audience share the same opinion of the way in which signifying systems apply to reality—the kind of trust given in tribal societies to myth-telling masters of ritual—collective fictions may seem truth; dancing may lead to rain. Such shared understanding of fictions' performative power diminishes in proportion to the impersonality of the sender-receiver tie. As it disappears, the fiction writer's words are more and more liable to be misinterpreted. Dog-faced sourpusses rend the cultural consensus.[59] The fiction writer is tempted to stop writing altogether.

This is Rabelais's context. Greeting his readers, flattering his patron, he insists at the entrance to the *Fourth Book* that readers and patron develop a second strategy in addition to Silenus-box reading of surface and subtext, for in this way they, the scattered heterogeneous crowd of his well-wishers, may still be able to laugh at the dissonant irreconcilables around them.

Do not read simply above and below the lines, but obliquely, athwart the text's seeming thrust. Do not attend alone to the enfolding embrace of my words, to the mixture of cultural milieus, to the kaleidoscopic variety of my changing social alliances. Develop precisely by means of my evocation of an ideal social compatibility founded in communal closeness, in resonance with my invocation of an impossible Pantagruelist social calm founded on the sense of human identity, a detachment from the text, these words, and any others.[60]

The paratextual parade of 1552—dedicatory letter, royal privilege, prologue amenities, and some months later a prologue amended to offer further gratification to His Majesty Henry II—was not simply de-

---

58. See the beginning of ch. 8 and ch. 8, n. 4, on the modern literary episteme. The readerly groups in the *Fourth Book,* unlike earlier books, have been restricted at the outset to "well-wishing readers." The reduced and more defensive communalism affirmed in the *Fourth Book* allows this folding-in of readers to continue.

59. That is, "cannibals." See Appendix 3.

60. See n. 11 above concerning communalism as social ideal, not social description.

veloped on political grounds or, still more simply, out of elitist disgust with and despair about the attitudes of common readers. One-dimensional interpretations like these cannot account for such seemingly minute revisions in 1552 as adding the morally selective "Good people" to the salutation of the prologue to the *Third Book* and the socially selective "worthy people" to the narrator's apostrophic turn toward readers near the end of it, while *not* deleting the popularizing references to riff-raff boozers and sufferers from gout which the emendations accompany.[61] Rabelais's new system augments references at the surface of the text to those whom I call his third audience, the audience of ironic readers. It renders the text more shifty even as it accommodates the text to more officious uses. Rabelais disconnects his imaginary world from that of the hard-to-discern and even harder-to-calculate world of miscellaneous cultural milieus; he seeks to protect it from the cross-sawing exigencies of diverse ideological interests by playing the courtier's game. But he retains representation in his imaginary world of the rough-and-tumble world of miscellaneous social milieus. This was essential. This is where his stories get their salt. It is why his text is studded with contemporary references. Seen from the referential angle of meaning, the text is woven of attacks on law, medicine, theology, monasticism, and—more circumspectly, but no less unmistakeably—on royal politics. That his stories are offensive to neither God nor King are the most duplicitous words Rabelais ever wrote.

Rabelais's later career was passed not with recalcitrant monks, vagabond students, youthfully ambitious humanists and idealist evangelicals, but with grave men of power, usually generous-minded as far as we can ascertain but nonetheless ponderous with responsibilities and dangerous because of that. There is certainly in the *Fourth Book* a shift in Rabelais's sense of what is socially possible; that is implicit in the developing importance of ironic reading. But no determinate social or political philosophy can be found there. Nor should the shift in social sentiment be taken to imply any change in the author's subversive cultural sensibility. Rabelais remains inclined to bring the high low, to identify with the broadly popular, to expose to phallic and scatological ridicule every high and mighty pose, whatever the impulse to grant greater fictional sanction to his society's most deeply rooted communities: family, peasantry, royalty, the Christian church.

The advice offered readers in the prologue to *Gargantua* was Panta-

61. *TL,* Pr, 341, 350.

gruelist in tone and assumptions. Given time and the appetizing presentation of agreeable words, a text will be savored like wine and
sucked like a bone for its marrow. Surface and subtext will come to
coordinated comprehension. The advice offered readers in the prologue
to the *Fourth Book* is neither so direct nor so optimistic: restrain yourselves; things are not what they seem. Although surface and subtext
may show harmony, it is not necessarily so. Pantagruelist attitudes to
the text are neither discouraged nor denied, but they are put in question
by their ironic supplement.[62] Dr. Rabelais and his worthy initial interlocutors in the prologue fade away *pari passu* with the disappearance
first of the moral theme and then of the moral meaning. At the end we
are back with the usual crowd listening to the usual speaker: that town-
square and village-tavern bookseller, amateur of Galen, storytelling
minstrel, and good-time-Charley whose function, it finally appears, is
not so much to amuse, instruct, or impress, to preach, orate, or bore—
let alone to mystify *à plus hault sens*[63]—as simply to render the reader
immune to the blandishments of any and all of these, treacherous or
well meaning as they may be.

What cues does Rabelais offer readers to develop such immunity?
Most obviously he accents the falsehood of his representations of himself, his readers, and their mode of contact. Less obviously he constructs contrasts between the patterns of oral and written discursive-
ness. The prologues initiate these books in conversational or oratorical
style; the texts begin just as regularly in the mode of written chronicle.
The plot unfolds with the largesse and meandering ease of an oral storyteller's audience-attentive art. It is interrupted ever and again by law-
book, medical-book, shipfaring, warmaking, grammaticalizing, poetiz-
ing passages that play upon written forms of communication. The
reader is ever being urged to move on, turn the page, and follow the

62. Thus the Pantagruelist last phrase of the prologue of 1552 (*QL*, Pr, 559:
"Or, en bonne santé toussez un bon coup, beuvez en trois, secouez dehait vos
aureilles, et vous oyrez dire merveilles du noble et bon Pantagruel") seems to
shake off the immediately preceding repetition of the morality of moderation.
Conversely, however, this same preceding moralism (a reference to the avari-
cious Genoese) casts doubt on the meaning of the brief, subsequent reappear-
ance of the Pantagruelist trait: the latter may be simply a convenient way of
turning to the text. Each of the last two turns of the prologue lends irony to
the other.

63. That is, to find a higher, recondite meaning within the text. See the
discussion of the prologue to *Gargantua* in ch. 8.

flow; but the accumulation of contrastive styles whispers that it would be well to reverse the action, flip back the pages, review the running discourse and note the implications of its illogic. The pages of a printed, bound, handy-sized book of moderate cost allowed the latter to be done with a frequency and facility unknown in the age of manuscripts.

Demonstration of the communalist assumptions found in the Rabelaisian text centered on the way authorial and readerly personae, given multiple form, overlap without replicating each other. Faced with an impersonal medium, using the inchoateness of its new printed form, Rabelais created a peculiar type of paratext in which the scattered and distant partners in printed communication appear pressed together, jostling each other and the author in remarkably sensuous ways. Giving them an artificial and embodied closeness, Rabelais moved the more easily among heterodox discourses, varying praise and abuse, high titles and low, friendliness and scorn.

For Rabelais the social fact of communal closeness led on naturally to the social ideal of conviviality. Conviviality was not represented simply as an atmosphere generated among the Pantagruelian actors in his books; allegiance to it, acceptance of its importance to good living was considered, at least in the early books, as indispensable to the real reader's understanding of the real author's intentions. Such were the implications to be drawn from the prologue to *Gargantua*. Correct understanding of my books, Rabelais implies, arises in the atmosphere of conviviality, just as it has been part and parcel of my composition of them. Pantagruelism, which in this early book is nearly identical with conviviality, is not a Platonic Christian essence, acquired through moral exercise and divine help. It is a materially and communally engendered aspect of the body social and arises, like the flow of animal spirits from heart to brain in the body natural, from good fellowship and good imbibing.

This connection of "wine"-inspired reading with "wine"-inspired writing signified the embracing cultural action enacted and hence indirectly advocated by Rabelais in his earlier novels. Of course literature, distilling experience, offers readers as well as creators an intoxicating realm of special, ideal meanings. But the creation as well as the understanding of such a secondary world always takes place in reciprocity with daily life, with a first world in connection with—not in reflection of—the intercontexts through which and by means of which writers and readers think, feel, and conclude. At their fullest, words thus act upon those who distill them and imbibe them like double-action drugs, cheering up lives with light-hearted stories while injecting at the same time a dozen kinds of other thoughts and referents and verbal felicities.

This construction foundered. The obsessively reiterated denunciations of those attacking him make Rabelais's statements in the dedicatory letter about losing all desire to write relatively credible. Although the books never ceased to sell and patrons never abandoned him, Rabelais seems to have needed some more express response from the generality of his readers or perhaps less express response from the minority of his enemies. We have indicated a number of culturally and historically conditioned reasons for such attitudes in these enemies, in contemporary readers, and in Rabelais himself; one might add to these reasons, as far as Rabelais goes, the factors of the author's age and acquired experience. Whatever the reasons, Rabelaisian idealism declined. The character of Pantagruelism changed. In 1534 Pantagruelists "live in peace, joy, and good health, always making good cheer"; communalism is consonant with humanism, anyone may potentially join with anyone else in such conviviality. By 1552 it has become a personal faith, an individual's mode of resistance to life's troubles. The communalism that continues to exist in the *Fourth Book* is no longer necessarily part of Pantagruelism.[64]

In the midst of the *Fourth Book* even this chastened redefinition of Pantagruelism seems to break down. Rabelais shows Pantagruel erupting in anger at the behavior of the dog-faced men, incapable of laughter, who are Anti-Nature's children. Pantagruel betrays Pantagruelism, at least at the surface of the text. From a countertextual point of view, however, the situation is less clear.

By making explicit, as he habitually does, the differences between the position and points of view of author, narrator, and narrative actors, Rabelais requires his readers to regard any utterance by any of his characters as having several aspects. "Pantagruel" erupts, or rather Alcofri-

---

64. One might consider, however, the selective communalism of the *Fourth Book* to be in consonance with the new definition of Pantagruelism in the prologue to the *Third Book:* "those who possess it [Pantagruelism] never take in bad part . . . whatever they recognize as springing from a good, frank, loyal heart." Here persons are joined to one another through individualizing judgments of their "heart," just as Dr. Rabelais proposes to do in addressing only "well-wishing readers" in the *Fourth Book*'s prologue.

bas by means of Pantagruel, or rather Rabelais-the-person via Rabelais-author, Alcofribas-narrator, and Pantagruel-putative hero. Then, by adding names designating real persons—Calvin, Postel, DuPuyher-bault—Rabelais the author asks readers to step away from these fictional frames toward a world where denunciations could have fatal consequences. The author asks readers, moreover, as his well-wishers to agree with him in denouncing these real persons. But at the same time the author obliges them—the fictive audience of well-wishers for his fiction—to take that step in the company of Pantagruel, a person who exists only by means of a threefold fabrication. The pretense of stepping beyond fiction is thus itself mocked.

One must conclude that it is a fictive being who has exclaimed about an issue existing primarily in the fiction and only secondarily and obliquely beyond it, the abstract and general question of the proliferation of Anti-Nature's children. Such a question has little to do with Pantagruelism, that scorn of particular, real vicissitudes such as Rabelais the person faced. The author's transfer of the angry attack on calumny to Pantagruel's mouth from Dr. Rabelais's (the accusatory epithets in the prologue of 1548 are the very ones repeated here)[65] filters the anger at the same time as its verbal expression is magnified.[66]

Far from documenting a complete desertion of earlier faiths, the dark, vindictive representations that may be seen in parts of the *Third Book* and the incomplete *Fourth Book* turn out to be forerunners of the more complex and efficacious way of expressing them in the full *Fourth Book*. Mockery, serving heretofore as a defensive shield, becomes a weapon. Just as there had perhaps always been three voices in the author's head—Pantagruelist-humanist, misanthropic-divisive, and ironic—so also, the author now suggests, must the reader allow all three to operate upon his understanding. Pantagruel and Pantagruelism no longer even pretend to integrate the text with sovereign confidence; yes, society's parts and roles overlap, but they neither balance nicely

65. See the quotation referred to in ch. 9, n. 17, and the associated discussion.

66. For those reading Rabelais's text with Plato's *Symposium* in mind (see ch. 3, n. 39), the anger is also filtered by its contrast to Aristophanes' gaily naturalistic encomium of these spherical beings, the original form of humanity. That is why Rabelais's signal to his readers to consider the ancient sources of Pantagruel's discourse is pertinent. While readerly awareness of Calcagnini's moralistic fable augments the disruptive character of Pantagruel's tale, the presence of the Platonic subtext draws Pantagruel's eruption back toward the wider comic tenor of the episode.

nor laughingly agree. You and I, author and reader, find ourselves ridiculously, ironically near and far from each other and from the life we would like to dominate but cannot. The best we can do is to try and trick it into compliance with our immoderate desires and moderate estate.


In the seventeenth and the eighteenth century critics, far from worrying about the difference between forms of authorial and readerly representation, let alone about the relation of ironic to other kinds of understanding demanded by the text, became obsessed with clearing away narratological illusions in order to get at the actual allusions Rabelais was thought to have concealed for reasons of political safety. The Elzevier editors added a four-page key identifying Gargantua and Gargamelle and Pantagruel and the other characters as kings and queens and other contemporary personages, Ferocious Island as the Touraine country, and so on. Jean Bernard, who in 1741 reedited in augmented form Le Duchat's edition of 1711, reproached his predecessor for not having treated in sufficient detail the contemporary references hidden in Rabelais's text, allusions that made of his work an "image-devinette."[67]

One reason for this obsession was, as we suggested, the disappearance of Rabelais's contexts. But why did people seek to remedy this disappearance in such a pointillist fashion and why, for such a long time, did all metatextual criticism of Rabelais pursue meaning in this shallowly realistic way? Such uniformity suggests the pervasive, structural influence of that Foucauldian "classical episteme," with its logic of separate partitions, its Cartesian clear distinctions, and its politico-rationalist insistence that everything be recognizable and organized. In this "classical" ambience to read Rabelais's text was no longer a matter of imbibing a bit of Pantagruelism and a bit more of Menippean skepticism, and of lending one's understanding by turns to an ideal of communal relations that joined humanism, roguery, Christianity, and festival in leisurely conversational terms and to descriptions of social relations that set the same factors at sword's points. As scholarship and society, literature and manners, sought with greater and greater efficacy

67. That is, a set of riddlelike images. Bernard's prefatory remarks are cited in Fraser, *Le Duchat, First Editor of Rabelais,* 178.

to individuate, organize, and control belief and behavior, it became impossible to read Rabelais's works in crosscutting, complementary ways.

Polished society in the later seventeenth century came to reject Rabelais not simply because his bonhomie came to look like maudlin prattle. Rabelais was full of "filthy corruption."[68] His phallic vulgarity and scatology, the gaiety with which he depicted violence became unacceptable. Rabelais had to be expurgated, his satire saved but his ill manners put aside. Reactions like these ran parallel to the development of a courtly civil society in which nobles no longer shared the mores of the country folk among whom they had earlier lived and in which bourgeois elites gradually withdrew from the behavior patterns of the workmen who still occupied the ground story of their home-located businesses. As the new society emerged, built on individual enterprise, juridico-moral equality, and the privatized nuclear family, membership in groups became more voluntary, based on interest and belief rather than on birth, occupation, and residence.[69]

These changes ruined understanding of the communalist assumptions characterizing Rabelais's text. His books idolize a carefree youthful male camaraderie in education, sport, adventure, and love that had its correlatives, although certainly not its realizations, in contemporary society. In later centuries these correlatives largely disappeared, as the orderly supervision of a minutely graded, morally stringent schooling and confessional took hold. Perhaps the difference should be put even more strongly. Family life is kept in the background in these novels, as is work. A polymorphously "perverse" freedom characterizes the life of the male protagonists nearly without interruption from the time Gargantua's nursemaids tie ribbons about his pretty little thing to the end of the *Fifth Book*,[70] when it seems likely that Pantagruel and his double Panurge will soon be married. Insofar as Mikhail Bakhtin is correct about the carnivalesque essence of the Rabelaisian text, such carnivalism arises from not only the permanent atmosphere of leisure utopianly assured the Pantagruelians but also their one-sided sexuality and youth-

68. See La Bruyère's comments, cited near the end of ch. 6.

69. The best general depiction of this process in France remains Philippe Ariès's *Centuries of Childhood* (New York, 1962).

70. The reference is to *G*, ii, 60–61, which concludes with a castration threat: "'Ha couper! . . . coupez vous la chose aux enfants? Il seroyt Monsieur sans queue.'"

fulness. After the sixteenth century, as childhood, adolescence, and young male confraternities were increasingly regulated, the behavior associated earlier with this zone of freedom came to seem bizarre, reprehensible, and irrelevant.

The change from communalist to individualistic assumptions about social behavior was not sudden. Individuation and some ethics of individualism—salvation of the individual soul, for example—are already present in the tenth century and in the first, for that matter. But the balance of power between communal and individual modes of living, as publicly recognized norms, shifted decisively toward individualism in the eighteenth century. This had not happened in Europe since the advent of Christianity. The changed balance was ideal as well as practical, for the ideal of individualism was seen more clearly the more that practical means were forged for people to live separate, autonomous existences, and the reverse was equally true. From the eighteenth century onward idea and practice reinforced each other.

Even if communal membership more than individual peculiarity defines character in Rabelais's works, much also speaks for individuality. Panurge is not just the type of the rogue. Unlike the narrator in Nashe's *Unfortunate Traveller,* he is more than a boisterous voice who articulates an expansive social scene with his restless energy. Unlike the author of *Lazarillo de Tormes,* Rabelais shows not only what is done to the rogue and how he reacts to it but also how Panurge's character shapes action and propels plot, most notably in the *Third Book.* The growth and changes in character of Pantagruel have particularly engaged critics, to the point of denying nearly all connection between the giant sketched on the model of oral popular tales and the wise Stoic Christian of the *Third Book* and the *Fourth Book.*[71]

Because the Rabelaisian text takes for granted the notion that people's character is a consequence more of the way they behave with others than of their inward wits, it is rather misleading to trace the development and even the growth in character of Rabelais's heroes one by one through the different books of his text. The communal ambience, the framing action of each part of the text, is primary. But within the parameters of this generalization one must note the voice of empathy in Rabelais's work. It is a "characterological" voice, used most con-

71. This is the thesis of Richard Berrong's *Rabelais and Bakhtin.* Pantagruel's emergent Stoic Christianity is especially emphasized by Screech in *Rabelais.*

spicuously to animate Pantagruel, Panurge, and Friar John, making them vivid individuals. This empathetic talent is also what gives horrifying individuality to the portrait of Quaresmeprenant: the devastation he has wreaked (on his own anatomy as well as on Ferocious Island) is shown as the consequence of psychophysical peculiarities developed in correspondence with the demands of socially prescribed customs. However monstrously strange he is, Quaresmeprenant is depicted not only as a personification but also as a person, confronting the conflicting demands of two normative notions of daily life.

Both empathetic, characterological voices and sympathetic, sociable voices play over the text. The individualizing kind of voice supplements the voice that merges, the tavern voice that enfolds itself alcoholically into the group, the shipboard voice and the adventurer's voice that recognize situations not as yours and mine but ours.

What has led commentators toward historicizing or psychologizing realism has probably been less the edges in the text of an individualistic understanding of personality than Rabelais's gift for sharply defined yet many-faceted characterization, a quality as well shown in the portrayal of events as in the description of protagonists. The "Council of Chesil": the yawning procrastination and at the same time the numb-witted arrogance of the Church's attempt to hold back the tides of reform is struck off in a single phrase. Anti-Nature's children, somersaulting through life as if their heads and feet had turned into ball-bearing roller skates; Sausages scampering up trees like squirrels or martens; cook soldiers with names like Hotpot and Sourbacon swarming out of the belly of an iron sow: the images are indelible.

# 10

# Bakhtin's Discovery

In the twentieth century, as recognition of the breakdown of individual identity has become a commonplace of literary practice, Rabelais's use of communally shaped symbols has begun to influence criticism. Analysis of the folkloric, "medieval," oral-popular side of the writer's work has intensified.[1] The most powerful evocation of the communal side of Rabelais's writing has come from a man who lived in Lenin's and Stalin's Russia during the construction and destruction of the Marxian ideal of community. Bakhtin's carnivalesque interpretation of Rabelais's communalism was a supremely political act of communication in the sense in which we have used this phrase. It has more than any other single work dislodged Rabelaisian metatexts from their wonted individualist-humanist assumptions; with respect to Bakhtin's more immediate intellectual context, it has had wide-ranging influence as an effectively disguised voice of protest against Stalinist "community."[2]

The interpretation is nonetheless a distortion. If carnivalism means the limitless inversion of official norms during a privileged time of festive freedom, then that kind of inversion can scarcely be found in either Rabelais's text or the behavior of people during Carnival and similar festive moments in the later Middle Ages and Renaissance. Masked defiance there was, in fistfuls. But it was limited and directed by the nature of communalism, which is local, unlike the nature of socialism, which is general.

1. Aside from Bakhtin (and such older studies as those of Nemours Clement, Marcel Françon, and Etienne Gilson), one may mention the works of Carol Clark, Guy Demerson, Claude Gaignebet, Jean Larmat, John Parkin, and John Lewis. Of course, the great modern editors and commentators on Rabelais, like Abel Lefranc and Jean Plattard, never entirely neglected this side of the author.

2. See Michael Holquist, "Bakhtin and Rabelais: Theory as Praxis," *Boundary 2*, vol. ii, nos. 1 and 2 (Fall–Winter 1982): 12–17, for the Russian intellectual debates influencing Bakhtin in the 1930s when he began work on the Rabelais book. See more generally the intellectual biography by Holquist and Katerina Clark, *Mikhail Bakhtin* (Austin, Tex., 1984).

Rabelais's procedures are less carnivalesque than communal and less festively inversive than mockingly masked. The procedures are as various as his ways of participating in popular tastes and amusements and also in the interests of all kinds of corporate elites, medicinal, educational, ecclesiastical, and noble. Rabelais's communal memberships were nearly all partial and nonexclusive. There was no concrete totality to which he could belong, vis-à-vis which fractions of the whole or rival totalities must appear unjust or evil—unless one counts the emergent totalisms of Catholic and Protestant Christendom, which indeed gave Rabelais trouble. There was no broad undifferentiated populace into which he was pulled regardless of intent, so that the totality of the people seemed more like the Sausages, inconstant and silly, than like the monstrous Physeter, so alien and aggressive.

To say that Rabelais's communalism has little to do with the binarily reductive mass/elite and popular/official divisions of later European history or with a carnivalism that laughingly places the interests of the whole people above those of its fractions, does not mean that the Rabelaisian text offers no vision of totality or any space to the carnivalesque spirit. The varied oral, literary, and performative practices to which Bakhtin draws attention did not cohere to form a unified tradition of folk-created carnivalism, and Rabelais did not bend his text to serve the ideological purposes of such a carnivalism. But these "ritual spectacles," "comic verbal compositions," and "various genres of billingsgate,"[3] however disparate their source and purpose, are nevertheless important sources of what Bakhtin calls Rabelais's "nonofficial" view of the world—along with such elite-inspired comic elements as the myth of Anti-Nature's children and the image of the Sausages' flying pig deity. Rabelais's worldview, elite and popular by turns, is always nonofficial and hence frequently subversive, inversive, and carnivalesque. The links between the parts of Rabelais's text that are inversive and subversive and those parts that, even when supporting king and church, do so nonofficially (humorously, humanistically, fabulously), might be more accurately characterized as organicist and spiritualist than as popular and carnivalesque.

Organicism: against the mechanical, against the dogmatic, against rules and those dedicated to rules and regularity like the children of Anti-Nature; for matter, for fertility, for life-that-grows, for energy-that-unleashes. Spiritualism: for matter that grows when it "dies," for

3. Bakhtin, *Rabelais*, 5.

the mysteries of birth and creation, for the ever-unfinished body; against inert matter and inert acceptance of the world that is. Spiritualized organicism links Rabelais's naturalism and humanism, his "medieval" feudal corporatism and "Renaissance" civic Platonism, his commonplace anticlericalism and reforming evangelism. Organicist, not carnivalesque, spirit supplies the energy that empowers Rabelaisian comedy.[4] Rabelais's spring of "animal spirits" would have remained dry, the author assures Cardinal Odet; Pantagruelism is gaily pickled "spirit"; Alcofribas Nasier's abstraction of "quintessence" harmonizes the effects of his storytelling with the nature of the world, just as the alchemist attempts to imitate nature's production of precious metals by studying the relations among the world's organic essences.[5]

For Bakhtin the most attractive aspect of these venerable Western notions of spirit-impregnated mineral and animal life is embodiment. Embodied spirit, unlike inert, inanimate matter, bubbles forth in animal good humor, in gaiety and laughter. "He [Rabelais] was consistently materialistic, and moreover approached matter only in its bodily aspect." Bakhtin's idea of "materialism" is dialectically Marxist. He refers frequently to the regenerative nature of the body in Rabelais's work, whereby that which dies is already a stage in that which is reborn. "The material components of the universe disclose in the human body their true nature and highest potentialities; they become creative, constructive, are called to conquer the cosmos, organize all cosmic matter."

To document this view of Rabelais's materialism Bakhtin quotes the

---

4. Rabelais's burlesque of spiritualism in the episode about Ruach Island ( *QL*, 43–44, 677–81) does not indicate that he saw any manner of escaping its toils. Michel Jeanneret formulates Rabelais's commitment to spiritualism in the *Fourth Book* vis-à-vis his commitment to the dialogic polyvalence of signs, implicit in his communalism, with exactness and elegance in his "Quand la fable se met à table," 178: "L'interrogation des signes [par Pantagruel] comme symboles d'un sens caché, l'intériorisation de l'événement, la prééminence du spirituel, fonctionnent alors comme normes et confèrent aux valeurs inverses— celles des amis [de Pantagruel]—le statut du burlesque: le sensuel, le littéral, le farcesque ne sont alors que l'envers, ou le dévoilement qui fait rire, des choses sérieuses." A fuller account of Rabelais's organicist spiritualism would require distinguishing his Renaissance version from that of Romantics. The Renaissance form was founded upon Christian creation: God made the world in this organic-spiritual way, by means of a single fiat. The Romantic form was founded upon process, not act: history (divinely inspired in its turn or not) demiurgically produces a world made in this way.

5. See *QL*, DL, 544, for animal spirits; *QL*, Pr, 545, for "gaily pickled spirit"; *G*, 23, for *Gargantua*, a "book full of Pantagruelism" by Alcofribas, "abstractor."

passage at the end of the *Third Book* about the wondrous plant called Pantagruelion. The "divination and apotheosis of man," Bakhtin writes, is expressed in the comic eulogy of Pantagruelion,[6] when the gods, terrified at the power the herb has given to men, hold a council to discuss the dire consequences of its discovery, concluding, as Rabelais writes, that

> [Pantagruel] will soon marry and his wife will have children. . . . Perhaps his children will invent some herb with the same productive capacity [semblable énergie], by means of which humans would be able to visit the source of hail, the springs of rain, and the workshop of lightning; they could invade the regions of the moon, intrude into the territory of celestial signs and take up residence there, some at the [constellation of the] Golden Eagle, others at the Ram, others at the Crown.[7]

Bakhtin comments: "After the invention of aviation (which Rabelais foresees), man will direct the weather, will reach the stars and conquer them. This entire image of the triumph of mankind is built along the horizontal line of time and space, typical of the Renaissance. . . . Not the biological body, which merely repeats itself in the new generations, but precisely the historic, progressing body of mankind stands at the center of this system of images."[8]

All of this modernizes Rabelais's words exorbitantly. Bakhtin, commenting on the Pantagruelion chapters, abandons demonstration of his interpretive keynote, Rabelais's inveterate carnivalesque spirit. Submitting to the exigencies of an ideological code to which he apparently adhered, whether wittingly or grudgingly, consciously or unconsciously, Bakhtin passes over the episode's burlesque qualities, its caricature of the terrified Olympians, and considers it only from the serious side, as a progressive vision of man's technical future. Thus he concludes his meditation on this episode, stressing the epochal significance of Rabelais's "concept of the body": such a concept represents "not abstract thought about the future but the living sense that each man belongs to the immortal people who create history."[9] From the biological body to the historically creative body, the ever-becoming of Humanity: this is a Hegelian-Marxist interpretation, it is true, but Marx's own thought was, especially in its early development, indebted not only

6. Bakhtin, *Rabelais,* 366.
7. *TL,* 51, 531.
8. Bakhtin, *Rabelais,* 367.
9. Ibid.

to Hegel but also to the broad Western tradition of Platonic humanism.[10] Bakhtin's metatext reveals new aspects of Rabelais's text because
it is an ideological descendant of many of that very text's thought patterns.[11] It obscures other aspects because it is written in the light of the
post-Rabelaisian development of those thought-patterns.[12]

What, then, is Bakhtin's metatextual discovery, if it is neither this
materialism which overmodernizes Rabelais nor the idea of an immemorial life of the people expressed in its carnivalesque spirit, an idea
that postulates an ahistorical pan-Carnivalism so that the text can ap-

10. See, e.g., Louis Althusser, "Marxism and Humanism," in his *For Marx*
(New York, 1970), 221–47.

11. In a book-length essay first written in the 1930s when he was working on
his Rabelais book, but revised before publication in the 1970s, Bakhtin gives an
even more Hegelian formulation to his organicist view of Rabelais. The general
consistency of this earlier essay with the passage just quoted excludes the possibility that the hyperbole is ironic. Ch. 8 of this essay describes a Rabelaisian
"chronotope," that is, literally, time-place; the word is a neologism designed to
show how assumptions about time generate a notion of space and "to a significant degree the image of man in literature as well" (Bakhtin, *The Dialogic
Imagination*, 85). "A new chronotope was needed that would permit one to link
real life (history) to the real earth. It was necessary to oppose to eschatology a
creative and generative time, a time measured by creative acts, by growth and
not by destruction" (ibid., 206). Bakhtin explains: "The passage of time marks
. . . a movement toward flowering and ripening. Insofar as individuality is not
isolated, such things as old age, decay, and death can be nothing more than
aspects subordinated to growth and increase, the necessary ingredients of generative growth" (ibid., 207). This type of temporal-historical vision was created
long before Rabelais by "folklore," he adds; Rabelais merely adapted the vision
to his uses. "Folkloric time" was "positive" except for its "cyclicity," a feature
that "limits the force and ideological productivity of this time. . . . Time's forward impulse is limited by the cycle. For this reason even growth does not
achieve an authentic 'becoming'" (ibid., 209–10). It was Rabelais's task to
move beyond this limitation with his realistic vision, while at the same time
retaining links with the "folkloric base" through his exploration of "laughter"
(ibid., 236–42).

12. One of these aspects is Rabelais's acceptance, within limits not clearly
defined in his writings, of a "vertically" defined, Neoplatonically inspired
theory of the relation between body and spirit, as in his poem "to the spirit of
the queen of Navarre" (see Appendix 3). This sense of spirit, existing in a realm
beyond Nature, was certainly involved in Rabelais's Christian beliefs and must
have had a connection to the social and biological engendering of spirit Rabelais elsewhere affirms. Bakhtin ignores this kind of ideological polyvalence
when he declares in the same passage from which we have been quoting that
"nothing remains of the medieval hierarchic vertical" notion of humanity, due
to Rabelais's triumphal construction of man's "horizontal" development in
time and space.

pear as its reflection? To isolate this discovery requires a distinction between Rabelais's authorial individuality and his participation in a broad current of European thinking and writing stretching from Boccaccio's time to Ben Jonson's. This current may be defined as the effort to synthesize three heterogeneous bodies of culture: the stories, myths, medicine, ritual, and festive performances of nonliterate folk and popular culture; the literate non-Christian science and literature of antiquity; and the literate Christian worldview of medieval times. If one characterizes this effort as carnivalesque, then one implies with Bakhtin that the first of these heterogeneous elements provides the basis of integration for the others. A closer look at the text suggests that any of the three elements may, in a given passage, serve as an organizing principle for incorporating particular elements—proverbs, myths, science, stories, etc.—from any of the three bodies of culture. Other writers and thinkers did the same kind of thing: Thomas Dekker in *The Shoemaker's Holiday,* Agrippa von Nettesheim in *On the Vanity of Sciences,* Jean Bodin in the *Demonology,* not to mention the works of Erasmus, Shakespeare, and Cervantes to which Bakhtin also draws attention. There is nothing unique about Rabelais with respect to the synthesizing effort and its variable accent, sometimes elite, sometimes specifically carnivalesque, and sometimes broadly popular.

But Bakhtin also analyzes Rabelais's work at a different level, less concerned with Carnival images and their aggregate importance in Rabelais or the Renaissance. This analytic level deals with the philosophic implications of images of banqueting, of praise and abuse in the marketplace, of birth, death, copulation, defecation, dismemberment, and so on. Bakhtin shows that the aggressiveness and "cruelty" of folk-cultural and popular-cultural humor, its "grotesque realism," its temporal principle of cyclic birth and rebirth, its spatial principle of reversal and inversion, its organic principle of incompleteness and "unfinished" bodiliness, have greater philosophic breadth and more mutual coherence than anyone suspected. Bakhtin asserts that these principles lying behind Rabelais's images were folkloric from time immemorial, but the evidence he cites in support of this view is nearly all literate and highly discontinuous. What derives from what, and where and how it did so, is not pursued.

If one leaves aside the historicization of these principles and their one-sided attribution to the "people," however, one finds a very new way of understanding Rabelais in particular, a way closer to Foucault's perception of the logic *implied* by a text's ideas and expressions than to the nineteenth-century Romantic-Hegelian historicism that overlays Bakhtin's writing like a patina.[13] Rabelais's authorial individuality, on Bakhtin's reading, consists in his philosophic deepening of folkloric principles left inchoate and implicit by other writers, as of course they were also left inchoate and implicit by those who acted upon them in the town square, at the market, on saints' days, in battle camps, and indeed wherever men and women mixed and shared their everyday sense of life in public or private.[14]

The salient characteristic of this everyday folkloric sense of life is the absence of any commanding criterion of truth. Truth is irrelevant. This is so for Rabelais as well. Rabelais begins his books by upsetting the sovereign throne of truth in books, the prefatory meeting place between author and reader, and situating instead false authors and false readers in false marketplaces, manor houses, churches, and taverns.

Rabelais's images are often but not always folkloric. Rabelais's "systems of images" are similarly varied in their logical implications, sometimes folkloric and sometimes not.[15] Whether future interpreters of Rabelais agree with Bakhtin's idea of the predominantly folkloric character of both the images and their system, they will in any case have to deal with both levels that the Russian critic has discerned. Bakhtin has shown that the logic of folklore is as richly productive of verbal virtuosity as the art of the *rhétoriqueurs,* Platonic philosophy, Lucianic storytelling, or Erasmian wise foolishness. It is no longer possible after Bakhtin's metatextual discovery to treat Rabelais's "low," popular aspects as incidental decor to an essentially elite masterpiece.[16]

13. The differences between Foucault's mode of intellectual history and the German tradition of *Geistesgeschichte* have not yet been clarified. Foucault defines his method's deviation from the customary French *histoire des idées* in *The Archeology of Knowledge* (New York, 1976), 135–40.

14. This is Michel de Certeau's theme in *The Practice of Everyday Life.*

15. The phrase, "systems of images," is used repeatedly by Bakhtin without becoming the object of any methodological discourse (see Bakhtin, *Rabelais,* 254, 258, 386, 408, etc.). As is shown by Bakhtin's commentary on Pantagruelion, quoted above, the phrase was sometimes used to support Bakhtin's amalgamation of folkloric with Hegelian ideology.

16. The same cannot be said for Claude Gaignebet's endeavor in *A Plus Hault Sens.* Although Gaignebet's enterprise is similar to Bakhtin's because it takes Rabelais's folkloric elements to be part of a serious philosophic discourse rather than to be mere decor, Gaignebet endeavors to show that Rabelais's folkloric procedures esoterically express spiritualist-mystic truths. Its "low"

Not carnivalism but communalism, conviviality, and subterfuge: Rabelais depicts the varied and sometimes hostile, sometimes masked encounter of heterogencous communities and heterogeneous ideologies, not their amalgamation in a universally valid synthesis, low or high, popular or elite. He does not construct an "image of the triumph of mankind." He uses the "horizontal line of time and space" to show the problematic qualities of any and every pretense to triumphal hegemony. By means of the rarely carnivalesque and not always folkloric principles to which Bakhtin draws attention, Rabelais draws into connection and clash within the humanized arena of a fiction many realms that are usually kept ontologically separate. Allegorical figures like Quaresmeprenant and the Sausages or Nature and Anti-Nature are placed on the same level as the Pantagruelians, and the Pantagruelians, by means of Alcofribas, are placed on the same level as you and us, readers and narrators-authors. Quaresmeprenant and the Sausages belong to the popular-cultural world of orally and gesturally transmitted proverbial and festive practices that took form in the Middle Ages; Nature and Anti-Nature belong to the humanistically transmitted lore of literate antiquity; the verbal and bodily behavior of the Pantagruelians identifies them as enlightened representatives of the sixteenth-century Christian-feudal world. Beyond these levels Rabelais's fiction also makes room within the same humanized arena for the pre-Christian gods who hold comic counsel about their fate due to the discovery of Pantagruelion, for the place where the dead are lodged after their disappearance from this world, and for the arcane space within a giant's mouth, no less than for Asclepius falling off a staircase, misanthropic Diogenes, the butchers of Cande, King Henry II, Cardinal Odet, and the sly narrator-author himself.[17]

Rabelais's communalism is broad-gauged, but not all-embracing. His construction integrates much of what was seen as hell in the Christian Middle Ages and as heaven in Greco-Roman antiquity; but Chris-

parts, properly interpreted, can then be revealed, for all their scatology and obscenity, as having a single "high" essence. Bakhtin does not reduce Rabelais's "system of images" to an essence or philosophic doctrine.

17. Asclepius's fall is discussed in ch. 8, n. 71; the butchers of Cande are mentioned in the Carnival-Lent episode (*QL*, 29, 642), as is Henry II, "the great king of Paris." One of the most remarkable effects of enfolding real with fictive personages is the passing mention of "Rabelays" among the followers of Guillaume du Bellay who were present at his deathbed (*QL*, 27, 637–38).

tian heaven remains securely in place beyond the fixed sphere of the stars with its revolving constellations, so that it acts as a kind of limit to what can be given narrative form. The Creator and the Savior can be referred to metaphorically, in the guise of an ancient god, like Pan. But they cannot be incorporated into the action. In spite of this limit, the extraordinarily widened world of the Rabelaisian text disrupts, as Bakhtin insists, any vertically integrated understanding of reality, in which the human world could be lodged securely below heaven and above hell. Fiction, allegory, and history, French place names and Utopian geography,[18] nautical accuracy and nautical fantasy, authentic and imaginary written sources of ancient and medieval lore, like the impossibly intimate communication between author and readers, disrupt by their varying levels of concreteness and abstraction every pretension to stable meaning.

Nature and humanity have no fixed forms. The world has no fixable frontiers except for that at the end of the stars. Rabelais's organicist and spiritualist premises conjugate polemically with elements, which from official and elite points of view—Christian or feudal, ancient pagan or modern bourgeois—are "below." In Rabelais the natural world, the material world, the world of work and of craftsmanlike prowess, the "lower bodily stratum" of sex and death and excrement and fecundity, are in fertile, cyclic contact with *nearly* all that is "above," so that the interplay (I emphasize *play*) throws meaning and morals ever and again into disarray, prohibiting the consolidation of different interpretive levels.[19]

Bakhtin's exaltation of Rabelais as the leader of the Renaissance chorus of subversively laughing people is misleading in its overtones: Rabelais's effort at totalism was ultimately cultural more than social, and it was limited by a supernaturalism implicit in the instruments upon which he relied for synthesis, organicism and spiritualism. But in terms of Bakhtin's strategy toward both his immediate public, the audience of state censors without whose imprimatur his book would be in danger, and toward his remoter, larger public of twentieth-century students of cultural history, emphasis on the carnivalesque side of Rabelais's

18. Gargantua is king of Utopia, and Pantagruel the heir apparent; they reign in the Loire country.

19. The concluding words of this sentence follow Elizabeth Chesney's astute generalization in her *Countervoyage of Rabelais and Ariosto*, 82.

energies was astute. It explains the text in a manner that perfectly suits our divisive, mass-cultural context—our context, not Rabelais's.[20] In Rabelais's context there were only partitive communities and emergent individuals, only mixed Carnivals, jointly invented by elite and popular groups, and only Carnival-Lent traditions in flux: no totality, no triumphal humanity, no triumphal Church, either, or at least none in visible, living, organic form; not even a Nature sovereign enough to hold Anti-Nature in check.

Knowingly or unknowingly, Bakhtin adopted something of what I have called Rabelais's late-developed encouragement of oblique readings of text. Seemingly devoted to examining Rabelais's adherence to an ideological program of commitment to the people, his text in fact inculcates a sense of Rabelais's semiotic mode of developing textuality: the systemization of images, not the representation of Rabelais's populist orthodoxy, is Bakhtin's secret theme. Linearly read, Bakhtin's book idealizes and so falsifies its ostensible object, the Rabelaisian text/context. Obliquely read, Bakhtin's book shows that his subtext, the theory that Rabelais wrote easily in the popular vein because he used systems, not single folkloric images and themes, has in its turn a subversive corollary. Bakhtin's ideas are formalist and structuralist no less than socialist in their premises. But he could neither proclaim that publicly nor perhaps think out the meaning of that privately in the land of socialist realism any more than Rabelais could explain or think through his naturalist supernaturalism in a century of state and church inquisitions. Criticism, like literature, may in such conditions have recourse to special strategies for dealing with the danger of cultural submission to

20. Holquist and Clark, *Mikhail Bakhtin*, 388, admiringly cite the view of Sidney Monas concerning Bakhtin's "relation" to Rabelais and to James Joyce, a view that well expresses the appeal for twentieth-century Westerners of this dislocation of Rabelais, Carnival, and "folklore" from their late-medieval and Renaissance contexts: "Sidney Monas has defined the relation between Rabelais, Joyce, and Bakhtin best by insisting that the link between them all is 'folklore—a deep involvement in the most ancient, most basic and folkloric traditions. Not, certainly, sentimental *folklorico* in the manner of the Celtic twilight. Really the most fundamental stuff: fertility rituals, assisted by ritual clowns, who, like the Zuni clowns, drink their own urine, the celebration of life-out-of-death, degradation and renewal, debasement and resurrection . . . reaching back beyond Christian times to the Roman Saturnalia and beyond that to the prehistoric.' Monas, 'Verbal Carnival: Bakhtin, Rabelais, *Finnegans Wake,* and the Growthesk,' paper read at International Bakhtin Conference, Queen's University, Kingston, Ontario, Oct. 8, 1983."

social ends. From Rabelais's time to Bakhtin's, one strategy has been
fiction's capacity—and hence also criticism's capacity, in dealing with
such fiction—for bewilderingly recursive communication (who is the
author? where is the reader?) and bitingly ambivalent polysemy (how
does a text refer, coordinate, mean?).

Bakhtin's methodological insistence that fictions be read not only
page by page and symbol by symbol but also as coherent wholes, and
his discovery that the Rabelaisian text can be perceived, when so read,
as a series of image systems, is not demonstrated point for point in his
book. The argument is loosely woven, its documentation sporadic. For
that reason perhaps it is all the more suggestive. I have used Bakhtin's
idea of image systems in various ways here, without referring to it as
such. One way is to use it as an informal means of testing Rabelais's
texts for the presence of countertext. A series of images, it seems to me,
requires at least three components to constitute a system. Can I find a
recurrence of at least three linked meaning-clusters or "images," ironically propounded, first in the 1548 prologue and later in the supposedly
straightforward text of the dedicatory letter? I think I have.[21]

Another way to use it is more constructively heuristic. Suppose that
the commonplace symbolic series, sausage is like penis is like woman,
can be established as occurring in Rabelais's text. So what? If this is
truly an image system, then it should have the three aspects that words
regularly display. What corresponds on the levels of thought pattern
and referent pattern to the series of symbols or linguistic vehicles? Sausages gratify male bodily desire as the penis gratifies male bodily pride
and women gratify men's bodily pleasure. This psychophysical thought
pattern is found in a number of different Rabelaisian passages, and in
turn it corresponds to a related series of socially oriented propositions,
a recurrent pattern referring to the way society is perceived to function:
the pride of possessing the penis is socially displayed in the assumptions
of patriarchy (hierarchical power over sexual relations is equivalent to
hierarchical power over social relations); women's subordination to
male pleasure is socially displayed by their subordination in marriage;
and sausages' desirability is socially displayed as male-female familial
fecundity, as pretty, fatty, wriggly, babylike bodiliness. The referent pattern seems to be displayed in the social arrangements (and absences) on
Ferocious Island; phallocentrism and patriarchy emerge as consistent
subtexts.

21. See ch. 9.

Bakhtin's emphasis on the word "image" is well chosen. What makes the systems something more than dismayingly repetitive common-places, however interesting their connections, is the aesthetic power of the linguistic vehicles. What matters most is Rabelais's ability to give his meanings imaginative embodiment.

The Rabelaisian metatext has changed twice: first in consonance with individualistic society and culture and its emphasis on exploring personality, and second in harmony with mass society and culture and its emphasis on exploring the ironic countereffects and inversions of individual aspiration. This book lives in and by means of the second context. Pluralism, psychologism, nostalgia for a communal age inspire in no small measure the metatext which you well-wishing readers hold in your hands.

I have defended Bakhtin's subtext and countertext as a way of explaining the excesses of his book's surface. Bakhtin's explanation of the way "folkloric" principles function systematically to relate images previously understood as trivial and unconnected is fundamental. He has changed our sense of how to investigate the text/context connection. We must widen our investigations of sixteenth-century popular life, as previous generations widened our awareness of Rabelais's learned sources.

The investigation of Rabelais's Carnival, which began in Parts One and Two from a Bakhtin-inspired concept of the text's context, led from reconstruction of sixteenth-century Carnival-Lent customs to quite another kind of research in the second half of this book. It is one thing to suggest that Quaresmeprenant, the physeter, the Sausages, the flying pig, and the Pantagruelian warriors may be seen as a puppetlike parade of Carnival excesses, on the model of traditional Carnival-Lent combats on mardi gras. It is another matter to prove that such a model of the episode in the *Fourth Book* is more adequate textually and contextually than these chapters' usual interpretation as three separate episodes in which the first supposedly deals rather clearly with Lenten excess.

Text/context thus led not merely to the history of metatext but to a theory of how metatexts evolve. It led to reconstruction of both the seventeenth- and eighteenth-century misconception of the passage and also the reasons for twentieth-century conservation of the misconception, long after Rabelais's satiric, anticlerical, and supposedly "Protestant" proclivities had been reconsidered. As long as the sixteenth-century nonliterary context of Rabelais's writing is considered irrelevant, "intertextual" reading of these chapters will be inclined to interpret Quaresmeprenant as an ambiguous idea of Lent rather than ambivalent figure of Carnival. Reading Quaresmeprenant as Quaresme is more generally consonant with the twentieth-century's remoteness and impatience with issues of Christian ritual; it is simpler to read "directly" from the text.

To escape this impasse—after all, does not each epoch have a right, perhaps even an obligation, to generate its own version of a classic text?—required a third circle of investigations. In this circle I used semiotic and structural distinctions. By their means the current critical fashion of treating Rabelais's text as linguistically rather than folklorically carnivalesque—that is, as an extreme "carnivalism," or as a kind of infinitely playful intertextuality—was related to the ideological sources of Bakhtin's metatext. Implicit in the analysis of Bakhtin's spiritous, organic "materialism" is the trace of a similar but unperformed analysis of intertextuality as an antispiritual, mechanistically articulated science of interpretation. For different but equally cogent reasons, historicizing organicism and mechanistic science *both* suit our age.

A text acts upon readers because it comes to them attached to their apprehension of the contexts interacting with it. Readers' apprehension of the text/context connection grows as awareness of the author's "sources" grows, that is, as readers immerse themselves in the scholarship displayed in metatext. But this aid is a snare. At any given time metatext, the tradition of interpreting a text, is for readers who are coming to the text for the first time a part of the text's context. The difference of metatextual acumen from that of the original author and that of the new readers becomes apparent only insofar as new readers, having pursued enough metatextual history to allow them to disentangle that history from the author's context, map for themselves the horizon and then the intervening space that have led them here and now to read.

# *Afterword*

How, then, can the creation of normalized texts and idolized authors be restrained, since it cannot be prevented?[1] This is our problem with Rabelais's text: there may be many other places in it as misshapen by normalized commentary as the Carnival-Lent episode. It was also Rabelais's problem: his text was so misinterpreted in his own lifetime that it threatened, if not his bodily, then certainly his mental well-being.

Rabelais solved his problem first in one way and then in another, first with the interpretive system explained in the prologue to *Gargantua* and later with the countertextual techniques developed especially in the last books he published. The interpretive system supposed that even if particular readers, including the author as reader of his or her own text, may not grasp its meaning entirely, proper and full understanding of literary texts does potentially exist. In time our gnawing at its recalcitrant surfaces sucks out its marrow. Does it not follow that in time, too, misinterpretations contrary to the author's and his contemporaries' "usage of reason and common language" will fall away?[2]

Rabelais does not say this. I read this idea into his text. It may be anachronistic, for, although Rabelais had a Renaissance humanist's sense of temporal change, of progress and decline, he also had a Platonic and Christian sense of timeless measures of truth. Dr. Rabelais-Alcofribas-Pantagruel nastily—and ironically—barks at Rabelais's detractors in the name of Truth. The Pantagruelians more amiably—and comically—agree that truth depends on group witnessing. I suspect that Rabelais did not know how time would deal with mistaken metatexts and thus he played ironically and comically with theories of interpretation. Certainly he did not develop what a later age would call a historicist sense of the way text is related to metatext.[3]

1. See Foreword.
2. *QL*, DL, 542. See the discussion of the passage at the end of ch. 8.
3. An immense amount of Rabelaisian criticism is concerned with Rabelais's alleged hermeneutics. See, e.g., David Quint, *Origin and Originality in Renais-*

If he had done so, he would have been as mistaken about the future of his books as he actually was with what seems to have been a Christian humanist idea of temporal change. Historicist theory, as developed by its chief exponents in the nineteenth century, postulates continuity among time's epochs and describes change as the gradual individuation of earlier generalized meanings.[4] But understanding Rabelais's text has not been a matter of ever closer reading of ever more individuated and coordinated passages, such that we attain gradually fuller understanding of the whole. Metatextual history proceeds in jolts. When an author's context has been sufficiently obscured, recognition begins of meanings the author and contemporaries never knew were there. The normalized text no longer appears normal. Contextual catastrophe—not reason, common linguistic understanding, or the smooth unfolding of time—is the precondition for new critical insight. Understanding a text's larger meanings requires first losing its smaller ones.

Critics, reading the text with new eyes because of their context, appropriate it and misinterpret some of its parts due to insight into other parts. The new insight waits patiently for the contextual catastrophe that will expose it in turn. Each genuinely new metatext provides the impetus for its own destruction because it too is a distortion.

So the smashing of idols is inevitable? Of course, but this is little comfort to an author fried in fire because his message shakes the foundations of his age too profoundly. What can an author do to favor time's insights? What can critics do to guard against the narrowness of their metatextual *partis pris*? I have suggested four kinds of defensive action, four kinds of critical self-awareness, each of them forecast by Rabelais's own strategies.

*sance Literature: Versions of the Source* (New Haven, Conn., 1983), 172–86. One passage repeatedly explored in this connection is that concerning "frozen words" (*QL*, 55–56, 711–16). See, e.g., Gérard Defaux, "Vers une définition de l'herméneutique rabelaisienne: Pantagruel, l'esprit, la lettre, et les paroles gelées," *Etudes rabelaisiennes* 21 (1988): 327–37.

4. Among the many accounts of the development of historicism as a theory of temporal change two of the most solid and critical analyses are Otto Hintze, "Ernst Troeltsch und die Probleme des Historismus," *Historische Zeitschrift* 135 (1927): 188–239, and Friedrich Meinecke, *Historicism: the Rise of a New Historical Outlook* (London, 1972). The Renaissance roots of the theory, neglected by them both, are explored in Kelley, *Foundations of Historical Thought* (see esp. for the general thesis, 4–8, 12–15). Twentieth-century scholars have expanded the meaning of the word in different and sometimes quite unrelated directions; witness the name of the series in which this book appears. See ch. 5, n. 23.

First, because text and context are interwoven, let authors and critics alike embrace their inconclusive and ultimately indefinable relation instead of pretending to capture context in the text's mirror or to escape from it through definition of a textual construction of timeless artistry. (The gate of textual significance swings to and fro. Rabelais gives it a push instead of trying to lock it shut.)[5]

Second, because idols are created not by the relation of context to text but by the relation of a metatext's context to metatextual propositions, authors should forestall and critics thwart unidimensional interpretations with irony. (The Rabelaisian countertext mockingly obliges the reader to reread.) The point needs elucidation. As long as the author's contextual assumptions match in large part those of readers, little metatext is produced except for expressions of admiration or disgust— that is, reactions so extreme that, however irritating or assuaging they may be, they simply confirm the author's conscious or unconscious provocations.[6] But later on and elsewhere, when authorial and readerly assumptions no longer match, the alien context produces significant metatext. Only significant metatexts, congruent with an alien context's ideological apparatuses, eventuate in idols. Ideological apparatuses— for example, public education, the media, the churches, and governmental propaganda agencies to further the preservation and dissemination of a society's heritage—are not concerned directly with text but with the metatextual comments on it. Formed to regulate the social mind, ideological apparatuses are worried only by a text's referential power, its ability to provoke change in the mental climate. The apparatuses measure that ability by the amounts and kinds of metatextual commentary on a text. Hence, while metatexts work to adapt the text to their context, ideological apparatuses work away to trap and control, and if possible supervise, the metatextual shifts.

This three-way tugging about of the text by shifting contexts, ideo-

---

5. I refer to the metaphor developed in ch. 10. Signification, an author's or critic's sign-making activity, is like a gate which opens in only one direction, toward further sign-making. But significance, the meaningfulness of an author's or critic's words in readers' lives, the active results which such words inspire, is reflexive and diversive; it may change lives as well as thoughts and should jar and shift one's apprehension of the relation between words, lives, and thoughts.

6. This is the case with works that become "classics." Those that turn out to be nonclassical encounter no such problems, often enough because they are not really very provocative. Moderately praised and moderately damned, they move sedately to oblivion.

logical apparatuses, and metatexts was beyond the ability of Rabelais or others in his time to perceive. His canny strategies posed no effective defense against the tugging; irony is of no use when the texts of a "classic" prescribed for schoolroom use, for example, simply delete the irony.

Third, let authors develop and critics seek the polymorphic perversity of the text, by varying emphasis among the three angles of insight, the three opportunities for creation around which human language turns, literary, ideational, and pragmatic, allowing each to supplement and each to challenge the others. (Rabelais sought to affect his times with his pseudo-physical gestures toward readers and to probe his epoch's measures of truth, no less than to indulge his verbal virtuosity.)

Fourth and finally and especially, let critical authors and authorlike critics lace their language with sex and drink and dung and festive talk.

It sometimes seems as if Rabelais has only survived in snickers. He is still an author of mass appeal today, at least in bits and pieces, at least to the readers of *Playboy*.[7] This is in part because seventeenth-century metatext, turning phallic and fecal exuberance into naughty scandal, still rhymes with certain politico-economic repressions of great profit to certain institutions. Even so, this moral barnacle clinging to Rabelais's ribald text carries the classic ever and again to those readers for whom it was made—not humanists, not academics, not elite well-wishers and not populists, either; not any social class or abstract totality, but that corner of everybody's mind which responds to hilariously freewheeling talk about natural functions, desires, and pleasures. (Rabelais's writing is not just well wrought and not just profound. It's funny enough to get you drunk.)

7. Rabelais's sexy parts have tended to be reprinted more often than either the scatological or the inebriate allusions.

# *Appendix 1: Context*

Context is the bane of criticism. Everyone uses it; no one knows how to encompass it. Context cannot be connoted or defined because its boundaries themselves depend on context, as I shall try to show with henceforth noncircular arguments.

Context can be *de*noted insofar as the variable textual boundaries to which it pertains can be indicated. Is one discussing a word, a chapter, an entire book, a corpus of writings by one or several people? Con-text denotes that which is relevant to a specifically defined text because it participates in that text. It is *with* the text and integral to it; it is not simply a more or less interesting aid to its understanding. How it participates involves at least six aspects explored at various points in this book.

The first three may be summarized in these terms: (1) general versus specific aspects of context; (2) intratextual, intertextual, and inter-semiotic aspects; and (3) authors' versus critics' and editors' representations of context. The fourth and fifth aspects derive from the third way of categorizing context: (4) Students of contextual forms need to distinguish in authors' representations of contexts between their stated and their implied forms; (5) in critics' representations of context they need to distinguish (a) the contexts that critics, including textual editors, represent as influencing author's sources for and preparation of a text, from (b) the contexts of reading the text that such critics represent. These distinctions among critics' contexts involve, consciously or unconsciously, critics' appraisal of the history of criticism of the work in question. (6) The sixth aspect, more general in character, concerns the physical and institutional modes by means of which a text comes into existence and continues to exist. Brief elaborations of these aspects follow.

1. Context participates in the text generally and specifically. Generally: certain aspects of an author's time and place affect textual composition in large, diffuse ways. One critical metaphor for this kind of gen-

eral participation is climate of opinion: diffuse factors of ideology, such as supernatural notions of that which could not be materially defined and explicated were as integral to Rabelais's mentality as breathing air. The advantage of the metaphor is its emphasis on the vastness and impersonality of certain kinds of assumptions at play in the text; its disadvantage is the tendency to forget that what is breathed in is also breathed out, affecting and changing subsequent environments. Climate of opinion as a metaphor also leads one to think of everyone as subjected on the same scale to the same pervasive fog. But microclimates are everywhere, and some people, like Rabelais, like Erasmus, like Luther, have larger lungs than others.

Specifically: other aspects of an author's time and place affect composition at particular points of a text rather than generally. They include events (the death of King Francis I, the condemnation of Rabelais's *Third Book* by Parlement, the extraordinary sales of *Pantagruel*), what an author reads (DuPuyherbault's *Theotimus*), and what an author does (Rabelais's travels to the pope's court at Rome, to the king's court at Paris, to the bookstalls at Lyon in 1532[?]).[1] These contextual factors arise from the regular operation of the institutions in which an author participates no less than from exceptional or unique occurrences.

2. Context participates in the text verbally and nonverbally. Verbally: All the other words of a text affect any particular part of it in variably near and far ways, linguistically, ideationally, and referentially (intratext). The particular words whose verbal context is being investigated are also affected by the same and similar words in other authors of the same epoch or of other epochs whose influence on the author can be shown (intertext). The meaning of a particular passage nearly always also involves various nonverbal images, gestures, sounds, and other kinds of semiotic performance characteristic of the author's time and place, so that the meaning of particular words is clarified by examining related performances, customs, events, and institutions in their own setting, just as one verifies words of a text by comparing and contrasting their contextual use elsewhere (intersemiosis).[2]

1. The reference is to the circumstances in which Rabelais developed and published his first novel, *Pantagruel,* at Lyon in 1532. In the prologue to *Pantagruel* Alcofribas takes the voice of a bookseller speaking in some public place and refers to the high sales of the anonymous *Great . . . Chronicles of . . . Gargantua* as his model. See the introduction above.

2. This aspect of text/context interpenetration is described at the end of ch.

3. Context participates in a text through not only authors' representations but also critics' and editors' representations. An author's representation of the contexts in which he or she supposes the text will be received and conceived is typically found in paratextual elements, not only in the overt form of introductions, acknowledgments, footnotes, and the choice of categories in indexes, but also in the more hidden manner of the disposition of materials in sections and chapters and in the cooperation of author with editors and publishers to design the book or other writing, including its nonverbal emblems and illustrations. Critics' representation of the text's contexts affect the text in their paratextual additions to it, when they provide introductions, footnotes, and critical apparatuses. Editors' representation of the text's contexts affect the text by translating its words, changing paragraphs, changing the spelling, and even deleting materials, maliciously, negligently, or conscientiously, in accordance with ideological or economic pressures and precepts.

4. Analyzing authors' representations of context, as I have done particularly in chapters 1, 8, and 9, shows that one should distinguish between stated and implied forms of these representations. Implied forms are in authors like Rabelais singularly complex. By the time he wrote the *Fourth Book,* he obliged readers not only to consider various subtextual themes, implied directly by the surface text, but also to develop a way of reading against or across the subjects and opinions communicated and implied. Rabelais's countertextual strategies do not introduce other contexts, but they do require the reader to do more than simply look at surface and subtextual items one by one, in an ironic manner. The presence of a countertext implies that one can document an alternative perspective consistently developed over some pages or even several chapters. However simple or complex the fictional author's strategies, there will necessarily be some difference between represented and implied contexts because such an author is compelled by the nature of printed fictions—as opposed, say, to handwritten personal letters or printed government proclamations—to offer some representation of context.

---

7 as a set of rarely perfect compositional compromises between the linguistic vehicles, ideas, and referents with which an author is in contact, knowingly or unknowingly, and his textual inventions.

5. Pursuing the critics' and editors' representations of context, as we have done particularly in chapters 6 and 7, shows that one should distinguish between such critics' and editors' representations of the contexts influencing the author's sources for the text or the author's preparation of text on one hand and their representations of readers' contexts, influencing their responses to the text on the other. In treating readers' contexts, it is important for critics and editors to separate those readers' responses that are contemporary to the author's work from those of subsequent readers. The context of contemporary response involves reconstructing a critical ambience that will be similar to that in which the author participated; when several editions or several extensions of a work are made by an author, as in Rabelais's case, the ambience created by the reciprocities between author and readers (including those readers who act as mediators of the text, such as editors and publishers) needs to be considered. The context of noncontemporary response, on the other hand, consists of three-cornered reciprocities between the work in the form in which it has arrived in the noncontemporary present (a form deformed by the inevitable interventions of textual mediators), its new readers, and its critics. A critical tradition evolves that clings to the work at certain points more than others and that therefore forms not only new critics' but new editors' and publishers', and also new readers', consciousness of the work. A critical tradition influences the context of noncontemporary response no less than do the new climates of opinion and events amid which and by means of which new readers meet Rabelais.

6. The media used to pass the text from authors to readers are not only semiotic (editorial and critical work) but physical: the context of a text also includes paper size and paper quality, typefaces and their spacing on the page, margins, chapter breaks, subheadings, and, at a more general level, the sensuous abstractness of words printed on a page, compared to manuscript writing or face-to-face discourse. Beyond or rather enfolded into the semiotic and physical ingredients in this system of "contact," as information theorists call this sixth aspect of context, lie politico-economic elements and social customs: the patronage available to an author; the readerly market, with its economic and social rewards; the ways of licensing, censoring, and criticizing books, with their effects on distribution to different reading publics; and most crucial of all, perhaps, the means by which books are conserved over time in public and private, official and unofficial deposito-

ries. Analysis of a book's production should thus be supplemented by considering the customs and laws affecting its exchange, distribution, consumption, and conservation. These customs and laws dictate—peripherally in some cases, centrally in others—what authors write, to whom they direct their writing, and who receives it. In these ways the politics, economics, and sociology of contact systems also affect the variable boundaries of text/context.

# Appendix 2: The Carnival-Lent Tradition and Quaresmeprenant

Few poems and narratives that drew upon the Carnival-Lent tradition of calendrical opposition depicted Rabelais's personage Quaresmeprenant. None did so with such light poetic skill and allegorico-calendrical precision as Charles d'Orléans (1391–1465). In his "Rondel 244" an anonymous reveler is awakened by Saint Valentine, presumably to share in the wine, meat, and good cheer for which everyone is clamoring "at present," on "this day of Quaresmeprenant":

> Qu'est-ce là qui vient si matin?
> —Se [*sic:* ce?] suis-je—Vous Saint-Valentin,
> Qui vous amaine maintenant?
> Ce jour de Karesme prenant
> Venez-vous départir butin?
>
> A présent nully ne demande
> Fors bon vin et bonne viande
> Banquetz et faire bonne chière

This "present" must be the very morning of mardi gras, the day on which Lent arrives to challenge Fleshliness, telling him to leave "for a time":

> Car Karesme vient et commande
> A charnaige, tant qu'on le mande
> Que pour ung temps se tire arrière.

Thus for Charles d'Orléans's fifteenth-century reveler the *prospect* of Fleshliness's exile during Lent becomes a troublesome mental reality on the day of Quaresmeprenant, the last day of Carnival:

> Ce nous est ung mauvais tatin,
> Je n'y entens nul bon latin;
> Il nous fauldra dorénavant
> Confesser penance faisant:

But because it is still Carnival on Quaresmeprenant day, the reveler has a recourse:

> Fermons lui l'uys à tel hutin,
> Qu'est-ce là qui vient si matin?

Saint Valentine and the reveler will now, it seems, join forces against the importunate arrival of Lent.[1]

The poem shows that, as long as the Carnival-Lent opposition was thought about primarily within a calendrical frame, Quaresmeprenant, whether represented as a day or a personage, was on the side of Carnival. The poem also shows that people's psychological ambivalence about Carnival and Lent was exploited long before Rabelais. To liberate this psychological way of depicting the Carnival-Lent contrast simply required diminishing the sense of calendrical boundaries. Quaresmeprenant in Rabelais is scarcely a time period at all. The monster is indirectly rather than directly related to the calendar, representing a permanent state of mind and body brought about by obsession with the customs peculiar to this moment in the year.

1. The invocation of the gay saint of lovers may mean that Charles d'Orléans wrote this poem in 1412 or 1458, the only dates in his lifetime on which Valentine's Day coincided with mardi gras. I have used the text given in Charles d'Orléans, *Poésies,* ed. Champollion (Paris, 1842), 377.

# Appendix 3: Cannibals, Pantagruel, and the Spirit of the Queen of Navarre

"La calumnie de certains Canibales, misantropes, agelastes avoit tant contre moy esté atroce et desraisonnée qu'elle avoit vaincu ma patience," Rabelais explains in his dedicatory letter to Cardinal Châtillon.[1] The three words he chose to denounce his opponents seemed unusual enough to the anonymous writer of the *Briefve Declaration* to warrant definition in that key to difficult words in the *Fourth Book*.[2] Misanthropists (from Greek *misanthropos*, man-hating) are described as those "haissans les hommes, fuyans la compaignie des hommes." Agelastes (from Greek *agelastos*, nonlaughing) are people "poinct ne rians, tristes, fascheux." These definitions are unexceptional, making "agelastes" and "misanthropists" nearly synonyms. But surprisingly "canibales" receives a punning definition in the *Briefve Declaration*, which explains its odd presence in the same phrase with the other two words.

Instead of referring to man-eating barbarians in the Caribbean—a meaning of which Rabelais was aware[3]—the author of the *Declaration* suggests that the word designates "peuple monstrueux en ayant la face comme chiens [cf. Latin canis] et abbayant en lieu de rire." Dog-men (*cynocephali*) and cannibals (*anthropophages*) were among the monstrous races associated with India, Ethiopia, Africa, and the "East" since classical times. They were discussed by church fathers like Jerome and Augustine and illustrated in medieval and Renaissance books of marvels.[4]

1. *QL*, L, 542.
2. On the date and usefulness of this "Brief Clarification" see ch. 4, n. 37, and ch. 6, n. 5.
3. See R. Arveiller, "La *Briefve Declaration* est-elle de Rabelais?" *Etudes rabelaisiennes* 5 (1964): 9–10, who cites the following passages referring either to the Caribbean home of cannibals or to their man-eating habits: *G*, 56, 181; *P*, 12, 244; *P*, 34, 333; *QL*, 66, 746.
4. Timothy Husband, *The Wild Man in Medieval Myth and Symbolism* (New York, 1980), 39–47, discusses the sources of the medieval tradition and includes illustrations of an eleventh-century cannibalistic giant (Fig. 16) and of fifteenth- and sixteenth-century dog-men (Figs. 20, 21).

Did Rabelais intend to displace the meaning of cannibal from man-eater to dog-man by associating it with a Latin word instead of Spanish *canibal,* from the Caribbean Indian word *caniba?* The move would certainly have been recognized by most educated readers, like the author of the *Briefve Declaration,* for whom Latin was nearly as familiar a tongue as French. For most sixteenth-century readers the kinship to Latin was probably more obvious than the reference to a Caribbean people's customs.

If Rabelais did intend to play upon *canis,* then the word game is one more mockery among many. Surely he did not mean for readers to discard the reference to man-eaters. He certainly thought of his remorseless critics as such, but were they not doggy creatures as well? The association of "canibales" with two Greek words referring to antisocial behavior enriches the list with a double meaning, invoking two kinds of monstrous being from the popular anthropological lore of Western tradition. It seems probable that this special meaning of cannibal is also intended later in the *Fourth Book* when Rabelais includes the word among the vituperative epithets denouncing the children of Anti-Nature.[5] The reason is obvious enough: not to laugh is to go against nature, "Pour ce que rire est le propre de l'homme," as the dixain which prefaces *Gargantua* explains.[6]

The definition of "canibale" in the *Briefve Declaration* not only helps specify the meaning of a denunciatory word in the Anti-Nature myth. It may also throw light on a possible inconsistency between what I have said in chapter 10 about Rabelais's organic spiritualism and his poem at the beginning of the *Third Book,* "François Rabelais to the spirit of the Queen of Navarre." This poem, addressed to King Francis I's sister Margaret (1492–1549), affirms in the most traditional terms the superiority and high celestial origin of spirit. Margaret's *disembodied* spirit is addressed, a spirit that has left organic, earthly life behind: "Esprit abstraict. . . . / Qui frequentant les cieulx, ton origine, / As délaissé ton hoste et domestic, / Ton corps concords."

Organic spirit, those animal spirits whose renewed flow issued in the

5. *QL,* 32, 651.

6. *G,* verso of title page, 24: see the text and translation in the latter part of ch. 1. André Tournon, "La *Briefve Declaration* n'est pas de Rabelais," *Etudes rabelaisiennes* 13 (1976): 133–38, convincingly demonstrates that this exegetical list of 178 terms in the *Fourth Book* is not by Rabelais. He concludes like Arveiller that the unknown exegete was mistaken about Rabelais's meaning in these two passages. The exegete was not, I think, mistaken; merely incomplete.

*Fourth Book* after the mood of lassitude and ill humor brought by the cannibals had been overcome, seems to have no place here.[7] Margaret's spirit, when it descends from the skies, renders the body not only harmonious with but also obedient to it: "Ton corps concords, qui tant se morigine / A tes edictz, en vie pérégrine."

There are, however, consequences to such an orderly arrangement of heaven and earth, spirit and body, and toward these consequences Rabelais has aimed his adroit compliments. A spirit drawn out from the body (*abstraict*) is "Sans sentement et comme en apathie": It lacks the vivacity of embodied spirit because it is no longer connected to senses and muscles. "Vouldrois-tu poinct faire quelque sortie / De ton manoir divin, perpétuel, / Et ça bas veoir une tierce partie [i.e., the *Third Book*] / De faictz joyeux du bon Pantagruel?" Heaven's perpetuity holds many treasures, but neither those of joyous deeds nor, perhaps, those of infectious laughter are among them.

One might arrange the three terms, cannibals, Pantagruel, and Margaret's spirit, in a standard Neoplatonic manner: Cannibals are less than human persons, Pantagruel is fully human, and Margaret's spirit is more than human. But such a series leaves out laughter and the company of others joining in and provoking laughter. Organic spirit functions organically when it is connected not just to muscles and sense but to society, to an ambience of social well-being. The company of others mixes up, disrupts and subverts the orderly obedience of body to spirit. It shakes the organism and in so doing enlivens the spirit, maintains the body in good health, and engenders man's generic quality, laughter. Rabelais does not say this in so many words, but is it not implicit in that preeminently sociable ending to the *Fourth Book*'s prologue: "Or en bonne santé toussez un bon coup, beuvez en trois, secouez dehait vos aureilles, et vous oyrez dire merveilles du noble et bon Pantagruel"?[8] Pantagruelist "gaiety of spirit"[9] is a virtue that can only be realized on earth among natural organic beings—not, however, among unnatural ones like cannibals, "countrefaicts en despit de Nature."[10]

7. *QL*, DL, 544.
8. *QL*, Pr, 559.
9. *QL*, Pr, 545.
10. *QL*, 32, 651.

# Appendix 4: Friar John's Breviary, and Others

One reason that critics have tended to identify Quaresmeprenant with Lent is Friar John's protest that he has found him following the moveable feasts. But this statement, as indicated in chapter 6, is fraught with ambiguity, not least of all because of the contents and arrangement of breviaries, which were standardized in 1568 by an ordinance of Pope Pius V and have not essentially varied since then. In what follows I shall compare modern breviaries with one made in Paris about 1450 for Duke Philip the Good of Burgundy.

The modern breviary begins with a table of moveable feasts that lists the varying dates at which church celebrations occur during a thirty- or forty-year period. Tables in two breviaries I consulted, published one hundred years apart,[1] include the same list of seven moveable feasts, printed in columns from left to right across the page: Septuagesima (the Sunday ten weeks before Easter; the beginning of Lent for many orders of the clergy today and the beginning of the liturgical drama culminating in Easter since the Middle Ages),[2] Ash Wednesday, Easter, Ascension, Pentecost, Corpus Christi, and the first Sunday of Advent. To the left of the column concerning Septuagesima are columns providing means to calculate the dates of moveable feasts by extrapolation for

1. See, e.g., *Breviarium romanum ex decreto sacrosancti concilii tridentini*, 4 volumes (Regensburg, 1863), and *The Hours of the Divine Office in English and Latin*, 3 volumes (Collegeville, Minn., 1963).
2. For Jacobus de Varagine (also sometimes spelled Voragine), *The Golden Legend* (written ca. 1280), ed. Granger Ryan and Helmut Ripperger (New York, 1941), 133, the drama beginning with Septuagesima extends from this Sunday to the week following Easter. "Septuagesima designates the time of the Fall, Sextagesima the time of the abandonment, Quinquagesima the time of forgiveness, and Quadragesima the time of spiritual penance. Septuagesima begins with the Sunday on which during the mass we sing '*Circumdederunt me*'—'the sorrows of death surround me'—and lasts until the first Saturday after Easter."

years other than those in the table (golden number, dominical letters, epact number). To the right is a column giving the number of Sundays between the last moveable feast in late spring (Trinity Sunday following Pentecost) and the first moveable feast in late fall (Advent, beginning the new church year). Quadragesima, from which the French word for Lent is derived ( *Quaresme* or *Carême*) is not a word included in the tables of moveable feasts; it is found further on, when the liturgy is given for Quadragesima. A table of moveable feasts like these is thus not where Friar John would have found Quaresmeprenant-as-Lent, at least not after the breviary was standardized by Pope Pius.

When we examine the breviary made for Philip the Good, we realize that Friar John could not have found Quaresmeprenant indicated in a calendrical way here either. In this manuscript breviary, published with a valuable commentary in 1929, there is no table of moveable feasts. Instead, the manuscript volume for the "winter season," extending from Advent to the end of May, begins with an *ordo officii* for Advent.[3] This "order of [divine] service" explains the liturgical alterations to be made in daily services, depending on the annually shifting relation between the date of Advent and the date of Christmas. After this section, which occupies the first thirteen folios, comes the liturgy to be used from day to day from the eve of Advent to that of Trinity Sunday, which occupies more than two hundred folios. The third section is a calendar of saints' days and other celebrations, occupying six folios; each month is given a separate page. The calendar for the entire year is given, and it follows a lay sequence, perhaps reflecting its destiny for a secular patron: the calendar begins with January 1, not Advent. After the calendar come three other sections dealing with liturgical use of the psalms and with saints' days.

Placing the calendar at the middle rather than at the beginning of the breviary was unusual but by no means unique, according to the editor of this manuscript. Other breviaries from Rome, Coutances,

---

3. See *Le breviaire de Philippe le Bon, un breviaire parisien du quinzième siècle,* ed. Victor Leroquais (Brussels, 1929), 1: 18–42, where the main divisions of the breviary are described. As indicated in the subtitle, this breviary seems to have been written and illuminated at or near Paris sometime around 1450. The breviary was made in two volumes: one for the winter and the other for the summer of the liturgical year. The calendar for the entire year is given in each of the two halves, and in each case follows a lay sequence; the calendar begins with January 1, not with Advent.

Limoges, Le Mans, Paris, and Tours (a town not far from where Rabelais served in a monastery) also place it in the middle.[4] Where Friar John thinks that he found Quaresmeprenant in his breviary, therefore, would depend on his monastery's customary way of ordering this book. In the 1550s there was no authoritative rule to follow; each ecclesiastical body followed regional tradition, which is why information about those monastic customs with which Rabelais might have been familiar—as at Tours—is pertinent.

A French word like Quaresmeprenant would not in any case be literally found in a Latin breviary either in the fifteenth century or in one of the ancestors of Pius V's model, which possibly used a table of moveable feasts rather than the clumsier calendrical form. Hence the first of the possibilities suggested above, Quaresmeprenant's written presence, could only have been true in an unusual and otherwise undocumented sense. *Carnisprivium,* that is, "cessation of meat," which seems to be the chief Latin word for Carnival in French medieval sources, might conceivably be found in some local breviary, but, if so, it has not been noted by scholars any more than the Latin equivalent of Fat Tuesday.

In fact the only word resembling Quaresmeprenant anywhere in either the fifteenth-century example or in modern breviaries is Quadragesima. In Duke Philip's breviary calendar, as in the modern breviaries' tables of moveable feasts, not Quadragesima but Septuagesima appears;[5] Quadragesima appears in both kinds of breviary only in the section devoted to liturgy. It is the ordinal form of the Latin word for forty, and it names the Sunday following Ash Wednesday. *Dominica Quadragesima,* the "Fortieth Sunday," denoted the day on which in very early medieval times the six weeks and forty days of fasting before Easter were initiated; fasting was to begin after Quadragesima Sunday and to end on Holy Saturday, the eve of Easter, thus making forty days.

4. Ibid., 1: 20–21.
5. See ibid., 2: Plate 74: The last date on which Septuagesima might fall, depending on the moveable date of Easter, is indicated for February 21 ("IX Kal. Mar. Ultima Septuagesima"). The inferiority of the calendrical system used here, compared to the modern table of moveable feasts, which offers a clear way of calculating how dates change as well as providing a thirty- or forty-year list of the changing dates, is shown in this calendar, which does not list the first possible dates of Septuagesima, Easter, Ascension, etc. However, dominical letters are provided before each day listed in the calendar, and presumably its users knew how to apply the other mathematical instruments necessary to calculate location of moveable feasts in other years.

Since the ninth century it was customary to exempt from fasting the other five Sundays in Lent and to add fasting on Holy Saturday. The beginning of Lent was thus moved to Ash Wednesday before Quadragesima Sunday in order to conserve the forty days. Thus the Latin word Quadragesima by Rabelais's time did not usually refer specifically to the beginning of Lent. "Dominica Quadragesima," "Fortieth Sunday," as it appears in the liturgical section of Philip the Good's breviary, designates the first Sunday *in* Lent. (I should mention, however, that some locales, not accepting the church's revision that began Lent on Ash Wednesday, continued to begin Lent on Quadragesima Sunday.)

Duke Philip's breviary indicates the *beginning* of Lent not as Ash Wednesday (*dies cinerum*) but simply as "the Wednesday on which fasting begins" (*Feria IIII in capite ieiunii*). However, Quadragesima also occurs in other phrases which indicate that it means Lent in general (e.g., "Nota quod singulis diebus per totam quadragesimam XXV psalmi dicuntur ad Primam").[6] Hence in Duke Philip's breviary the word Quadragesima is used to refer to both Lent in general and to the first Sunday in Lent.

If Friar John's words, "follows after," are interpreted loosely to mean an occasion that follows in the sense of being something observed in accordance with the general pattern of moveable feasts, and if Friar John makes the mistake most commentators have made by identifying Quaresmeprenant with Quadragesima as Lent in general, then, as mentioned in chapter 6, his words make sense, but they are redundant. Quadragesima follows the pattern of moveable feasts because it *is* a moveable feast. If Friar John instead takes Quaresmeprenant to mean, as Rabelais does, a personification of the inclination to move toward Lent, then when does this movement begin, and in what sense could such a movement "follow" the moveable feasts? Here we must introduce the fact that, while the fasting aspect of Lent was supposed to begin on Ash Wednesday for the laity, it was for many clerics supposed to begin on Quinquagesima Sunday preceding Ash Wednesday.[7] In the

6. *Le breviaire,* 1: 20, 187, from folio 113.

7. De Varagine, *The Golden Legend,* 135: "Firstly we were to fast for 40 days . . . but in fact we fast for only 36 days, since the Sundays are not fast-days. . . . In compensation for these four days taken from the time of fasting the Church established the last four days of [the week preceding Quadragesima Sunday, called] Quinquagesima. Then the clergy, wishing to give the people an example of sanctity, resolved to fast during the two preceding days, and so was formed a whole week of fasting."

liturgical sense to which breviaries were devoted, Lent's themes began not on Quadragesima, Ash Wednesday, or Quinquagesima, but on Septuagesima.[8] As I pointed out in chapter 6 in connection with this problem, the moveable feasts of the church year then and now begin in November, but those of the lay year normally began on either Septuagesima or Quinquagesima for clerics, and on either Ash Wednesday or Quadragesima for laity. To say that the occasion of Lent-taking-hold "followed after" any of the latter four occasions would be false because they indicate the beginning of Lent; to say that the occasion followed after Advent is true but would hardly locate it. One is hence inclined to choose the reading "flees"—but only inclined—because it makes the text a bit more interesting.

8. Cf. the quotation in n. 2.

# Bibliography

Abundance, Jehan d'. *Le Testament de Carmentrant*. See Aubailly, Jean-Claude.

Albarel, Dr. "La psychologie et la tempérament de Quaresmeprenant." *Revue des études rabelaisiennes* 4 (1906): 49–58.

Althusser, Louis. *For Marx*. New York, 1970.

———. *Lenin and Philosophy*. Boston, 1972.

Antonioli, Roland. *Rabelais et la médecine*. Geneva, 1976.

Ariès, Philippe. *Centuries of Childhood*. New York, 1962.

Arveiller, R. "La *Briefve Declaration* est-elle de Rabelais?" *Etudes rabelaisiennes* 5 (1964): 9–10.

Aubailly, Jean-Claude, ed. *Deux jeux de Carnaval de la fin du Moyen Age: La Bataille de Sainct Pensard à l'encontre de Caresme et le Testament de Carmentrant*. Paris, 1978.

Auden, W. H. *Secondary Worlds*. New York, 1969.

Babcock, Barbara. "The Novel and the Carnival World." *Modern Language Notes* 89 (1974): 911–37.

Bakhtin, Mikhail. *The Dialogic Imagination*. Austin, Tex., 1981.

———. *Rabelais and His World*. Cambridge, Mass., 1968.

Barthes, Roland. *S/Z: An Essay*. New York, 1974.

*Bataille de Caresme et de Charnage*. Ed. G. Lozinski. Paris, 1933.

*Bataille de Sainct Pensard à l'encontre de Caresme*. See Aubailly, Jean-Claude.

Beaujour, Michel. *Le jeu de Rabelais*. Paris, 1968.

Beduschi, Lidia. "La vecchia di mezza quaresima." *La ricerca folklorica* 6 (1982): 37–46.

Bernier, Jean. *Jugement et nouvelles observations sur les oeuvres . . . de Maitre François Rabelais, D.M., ou Le Véritable Rabelais Réformé*. Paris, 1697.

Berrong, Richard. *Rabelais and Bakhtin*. Lincoln, Nebr., 1986.

Berry, Alice. "'Les Mithologies Pantagruelicques': Introduction to a Study of Rabelais' *Quart Livre*." *PMLA* 92 (1979): 471–80.

Bloch, R. Howard. *The Scandal of the Fabliaux*. Berkeley, 1986.

Boulenger, Jacques. *Rabelais à travers les âges*. Paris, 1925.

Bowen, Barbara. "Lenten Eels and Carnival Sausages." *L'esprit createur* 21 (1981): 12–25.

———. "L'épisode des Andouilles: esquisse d'une méthode de lecture." In *Le comique verbal en France au seizième siècle*, ed. Halina Lewicka, 111–26. Warsaw, 1981.

*Le breviaire de Philippe le Bon, un breviaire parisien du quinzième siècle.* Ed. Victor Leroquais. 2 volumes. Brussels, 1929.

*Breviarium romanum ex decreto sacrosancti concilii tridentini.* 4 volumes. Regensburg, 1863.

Breviary (English translation). *The Hours of the Divine Office in English and Latin.* 3 volumes. Collegeville, Minn., 1963.

Brown, Huntington, ed. *The Tale of Gargantua and King Arthur.* Cambridge, Mass., 1932.

Buonarroti, Michelangelo. *Cicalate.* In M. Buonarroti, *Opere varie.* Florence, 1894.

Burke, Peter. *Popular Culture in Early Modern Europe.* New York, 1978.

Camporesi, Paolo. *La maschera di Bertoldo.* Turin, 1976.

Cave, Terence. *The Cornucopian Text: Problems of Writing in the French Renaissance.* Oxford, 1979.

Certeau, Michel de. *The Practice of Everyday Life.* Berkeley, 1984.

Charpentier, Françoise. "La Guerre des Andouilles, Pantagruel, IV, 35–42." In *Etudes seizièmistes offerts à V. L. Saulnier,* 119–35. Geneva, 1980.

Chartier, Roger, and Henri-Jean Martin. *Histoire de l'imprimerie française.* Volume 1. Paris, 1983.

Chaytor, Henry. *From Script to Print.* London, 1945.

Chesney, Elizabeth. *The Countervoyage of Rabelais and Ariosto.* Durham, N.C., 1982.

Chiappelli, Fredi, ed. *First Images of America: The Impact of the New World on the Old.* Berkeley, 1976.

Cholakian, Rouben. *The Moi in the Middle Distance: A Study of the Narrative Voice in Rabelais.* Madrid, 1982.

Clark, Carol. *The Vulgar Rabelais.* Oxford, 1985.

Clouzot, Henri. "Les commentaires de Perreau et l'alphabet de l'auteur français." *Revue des études rabelaisiennes* 4 (1906): 59–73.

Coleman, Dorothy. "Language in the *Tiers Livre.*" In *Rabelais in Glasgow,* ed. J. Coleman and C. Scollen-Jimack, 37–53. Glasgow, 1984.

——. *Rabelais, a Critical Study in Prose Fiction.* Cambridge, 1971.

Coleman, James, and Christine Scollen-Jimack, ed. *Rabelais in Glasgow.* Glasgow, 1984.

Cooper, Richard. "Les 'contes' de Rabelais et l'Italie: une mise au point." In *La nouvelle française à la Renaissance,* ed. Lionello Sozzi, 183–207. Geneva, 1981.

Cotgrave, Randle. *Dictionarie of the French and English Tongues.* London, 1611.

Croce, Giulio Cesare. *Invito generale . . . per veder segare la vecchia.* Bologna, 1608.

——. *Processo overo esamine di Carnevale.* Bologna, 1588.

Davis, Natalie Zemon. *Society and Culture in Early Modern France.* Stanford, Calif., 1975.

Defaux, Gérard. "D'un problème l'autre: herméneutique de l' 'altior sensus' et 'capatatio lectoris' dans le Prologue de 'Gargantua.'" *Revue d'histoire littéraire de la France* 85 (1985): 195–216.

————. "Rabelais et son masque comique: *Sophista loquitur.*" *Etudes rabelaisiennes* 11 (1974): 89–135.

————. "Vers une définition de l'herméneutique rabelaisienne: Pantagruel, l'esprit, la lettre, et les paroles geleés." *Etudes rabelaisiennes* 21 (1988): 327–37.

Delen, Adrien. *Histoire de la gravure dans les Pays-Bas.* 2 volumes. Paris, 1935.

Demerson, Guy. "Les calembours de Rabelais." In *Le comique verbal en France au seizième siècle,* ed. Halina Lewicka. Warsaw, 1981.

Demerson, Guy, and Christian Lauvergnat-Gagnière, eds. *Le disciple de Pantagruel.* Paris, 1982.

Derrida, Jacques. *Of Grammatology.* Baltimore, 1974.

Dontenville, Henri. *Histoire et géographie mythiques de la France.* Paris, 1973.

Droz, Eugénie. "Frère Gabriel DuPuyherbault, l'agresseur de François Rabelais." *Studi francesi* 10 (1966): 401–27.

Duchet, Claude. "L'illusion historique: l'enseignement des préfaces (1815–32)." *Revue d'histoire littéraire de la France* 75 (1975): 245–67.

Duval, Edwin. "Interpretation and the 'Doctrine absconce' of Rabelais' Prologue to *Gargantua.*" *Etudes rabelaisiennes* 18 (1985): 1–17.

————. "La Messe, la Cène, et le Voyage sans fin du *Quart Livre.*" *Etudes rabelaisiennes* 21 (1988): 130–40.

Eco, Umberto. *The Role of the Reader.* Bloomington, Ind., 1979.

Eisenstein, Elizabeth. *The Printing Press as an Agent of Change: Communications and Cultural Transformations in Early Modern Europe.* 2 volumes. Cambridge, 1980.

Elias, Norbert. *The Court Society.* New York, 1983.

————. *The History of Manners.* New York, 1978.

Eluard, Paul, ed. *La poésie du passé.* Volume 1. Paris, 1960.

Erasmus, Desiderius. *Adagiorum Chilias quatuor.* In Erasmus, *Opera omnia,* Volume 2. Leyden, 1703.

————. *Ausgewählte Werke.* Ed. Hajo Holborn and Annemarie Holborn. Munich, 1933.

Erlich, Victor. *Russian Formalism: History-Doctrine.* Paris, 1965.

Eskin, Stanley. "Physis and Anti-Physie: The Idea of Nature in Rabelais and Calcagnini." *Comparative Literature* 14 (1962): 167–73.

Fabre-Vassas, Claudine. "Le soleil des limaçons." *Etudes rurales* nos. 87–88 (July–December 1983): 63–93.

Febvre, Lucien. *The Problem of Unbelief in the Sixteenth Century: The Religion of Rabelais.* 1942; trans. Cambridge, Mass., 1982.

Febvre, Lucien, and Henri-Jean Martin. *L'apparition du livre.* Paris, 1958.

Fish, Stanley. *Is There a Text in This Classroom?* Berkeley, 1980.

Fontaine, Marie-Madeleine. "Quaresmeprenant: l'image littéraire et la contestation de l'analogie médicale." In *Rabelais in Glasgow,* ed. J. Coleman and C. Scollen-Jimack, 87–112. Glasgow, 1984.

Foucault, Michel. *The Archeology of Knowledge.* New York, 1976.

————. *The Order of Things.* New York, 1971.

————. *This is Not a Pipe.* Berkeley, 1983.

Françon, Marcel, ed. *Le Vroy Gargantua.* Paris, 1949.

Fraser, Theodore. *Le Duchat, First Editor of Rabelais.* Geneva, 1971.

Gaignebet, Claude. *A plus haut sens: l'ésotérisme spirituel et charnel de Rabelais.* 2 volumes. Paris, 1986.

———. *Le folklore obscène des enfants.* Paris, 1979.

———. *Le Carnaval.* Paris, 1974.

———. "Le combat de Carnaval et de Carême de P. Brueghel." *Annales: économies, sociétés, civilisations* 27 (1972): 313–45.

Garasse, François. *La doctrine curieuse des beaux esprits de ce temps.* Paris, 1623.

———. *Le Rabelais réformé.* Brussels, 1619.

———. *La recherche des recherches d'Etienne Pasquier.* Paris, 1622.

Genette, Gérard. *Introduction à l'architexte.* Paris, 1979.

———. *Palimpsestes.* Paris, 1981.

———. *Seuils.* Paris, 1987.

Glauser, Alfred. *Les fonctions du nombre chez Rabelais.* Paris, 1982.

———. *Rabelais Créateur.* Paris, 1964.

Glück, Gustav. "Die Darstellungen des Karnevals und der Fasten von Bosch und Brueghel." In *Gedenckbock Vermeylan,* 263–68. Antwerp, 1932.

Gray, Floyd. *Rabelais et l'écriture.* Paris, 1974.

Grève, Marcel de. "François Rabelais et les libertins du XVIIᵉ siècle." *Etudes rabelaisiennes* 1 (1956): 120–50.

———. "Les érudits du XVIIᵉ siècle en quête de la clef de Rabelais." *Etudes rabelaisiennes* 5 (1964): 41–63.

———. *L'interprétation de Rabelais au XVIᵉ siècle.* Geneva, 1961.

Grinberg, Martine. "Des géants au Carnaval de Metz en 1498: innovation folklorique et politique urbaine." In *Etudes et documents du Cercle royal d'histoire et d'archéologie d'Ath et de la région.* Volume 5, 319–26. Ath, 1983.

Grinberg, Martine, and Samuel Kinser. "Les combats de Carnaval et de Carême: trajets d'une métaphore." *Annales: économies, sociétés, civilisations* 38 (1983): 65–98.

Groos, Robert. "The Enigmas of Quaresmeprenant: Rabelais and Defamiliarization." *Romanic Review* 69 (1978): 22–33.

Hauser, Henri, and Augustin Renaudet. *Les débuts de l'âge moderne.* Paris, 1956.

Heidegger, Martin. *On the Way to Language.* New York, 1971.

Higman, Francis M. *Censorship and the Sorbonne: A Bibliographical Study of Books in French Censured by the Faculty of Theology of the University of Paris 1520–1551.* Geneva, 1979.

Hintze, Otto. "Ernst Troeltsch und die Probleme des Historismus." *Historische Zeitschrift* 135 (1927): 188–239.

Hobbes, Thomas. *Leviathan.* New York, 1962.

Holquist, Michael. "Bakhtin and Rabelais: Theory as Praxis." *Boundary 2,* 11, nos. 1–2 (Fall–Winter 1982): 1–17.

Holquist, Michael, and Katerina Clark. *Mikhail Bakhtin.* Austin, Tex., 1984.

Huchon, Mireille. *Rabelais grammairien.* Geneva, 1981.

Hudson, William, and John Tingey, ed. *Selected Records of the City of Norwich.* Volume 1. London, 1906.

Huguet, Edmund. *Dictionnaire de la langue française du seizième siècle.* Paris, 1932.

Husband, Timothy. *The Wild Man in Medieval Myth and Symbolism.* New York, 1980.

Ingarden, Roman. *The Literary Work of Art.* 1930; trans., Evanston, Ill., 1973.

Iser, Wolfgang. *The Implied Reader.* Baltimore, 1974.

Jauss, Hans R. *Untersuchungen zur mittelalterlichen Tierdichtung.* Konstanz, 1959.

Jeanneret, Michel. "Alimentation, digestion, réflexion dans Rabelais." *Studi francesi* 27 (1983): 405–16.

———. "Quand la fable se met à table." *Poétique* 54 (1983): 163–80.

Kämmel, Heinrich. *Geschichte des deutschen Schulwesens in Übergang vom Mittelalter zur Neuzeit.* Leipzig, 1882.

Keller, Abraham C. "The Idea of Progress in Rabelais." *PMLA* 66 (1951): 235–43.

Kelley, Donald R. *Foundations of Modern Historical Scholarship: Language, Law, and History in the French Renaissance.* New York, 1970.

Kinser, Samuel. "*Annaliste* Paradigm? The Geohistorical Structuralism of Fernand Braudel." *American Historical Review* 86 (1981): 63–105.

———. "Combats." See Grinberg, Martine, and Samuel Kinser.

———. "Ideas of Temporal Change and Cultural Process in France, 1470–1535." In *Renaissance Studies in Honor of Hans Baron,* ed. Anthony Molho and John Tedeschi, 703–55. Florence, 1971.

———. "Presentation and Representation: Carnival at Nuremberg, 1450–1550." *Representations* 13 (Winter 1986): 1–41.

———. "Saussure's Anagrams; Ideological Work." *Modern Language Notes* 94 (1974): 1105–38.

———. *The Works of Jacques-Auguste de Thou.* The Hague, 1967.

Kline, Michael. *Rabelais and the Age of Printing.* Geneva, 1963.

Koopmans, Jellie, ed. *Quatre Sermons Joyeux.* Geneva, 1984.

Koselleck, Reinhard. *Futures Past.* Cambridge, Mass., 1985.

Krailsheimer, Alban. "The Andouilles of the *Quart Livre.*" In *François Rabelais: ouvrage publié pour le 4e centenaire de sa mort, 1553–1953.* 226–32. Geneva, 1953.

Kristeva, Julia. *Le texte du roman.* Paris, 1970.

———. *Semiotiké.* Paris, 1968.

La Bruyère, Jean de. *Les caractères et moeurs de ce siècle.* Paris, 1941.

Lebègue, Raymond. "Rabelaisiana." *Bibliothèque d'humanisme et Renaissance* 10 (1941): 159–68.

Le Double, Anatole. *Rabelais anatomiste et physiologiste.* Paris, 1899.

Lefranc, Abel. "Garasse et Rabelais." *Revue des études rabelaisiennes* 7 (1909): 492–500.

———. *Les navigations de Pantagruel.* Paris, 1905.

Lentz, Tony. *Orality and Literacy in Hellenic Greece.* Carbondale, Ill., 1988.

Lestringant, Frank. "L'insulaire de Rabelais, ou la fiction en Archipel. Pour une lecture topographique du 'Quart Livre.'" *Etudes rabelaisiennes* 21 (1988): 249–74.

Lewicka, Halina, ed. *Le comique verbal en France au seizième siècle.* Warsaw, 1981.

Lindahl, Carl. *Earnest Games: Folkloric Patterns in the Canterbury Tales.* Bloomington, Ind., 1987.

Lowry, Martin. *The World of Aldus Manutius*. Ithaca, N.Y., 1979.

Magnus, Olaus. *Carta Marina*. Ed. Erik Gamby. Uppsala, 1964.

*Maistre Pierre Pathelin*, ed. Richard Holbrook. Paris, 1967.

Man, Paul de. *Blindness and Insight*. Oxford, 1971.

Mannheim, Karl. *Man and Society*. London, 1940.

Manzoni, Luigi, ed. *Libro di Carnevale dei secoli XV e XVI*. Bologna, 1881.

Marcel-Dubois, C. "Fêtes villageoises et vacarmes cérémoniels, ou une musique et son contraire." In *Les Fêtes de la Renaissance*, Volume 2, 602–16. Paris, 1975.

Marichal, Robert. "*Quart Livre:* Commentaires." *Etudes rabelaisiennes* 5 (1964): 65–162.

———. "Rabelais et les Censures de la Sorbonne." *Etudes rabelaisiennes* 9 (1971): 134–51.

Marshack, Alexander. *The Roots of Civilization*. New York, 1971.

Meinecke, Friedrich. *Historicism: The Rise of a New Historical Outlook*. London, 1972.

Mérimée, Henri. *Spectacles et comédiens à Valencia*. Toulouse, 1913.

Meyer, Christian, ed. *Quellen zur Geschichte der Stadt Hof*. Hof, 1894.

Montaiglon, Anatole de, and James de Rothschild, eds. *Recueil de poésies françaises des XVe et XVIe siècles*. Paris, 1875.

Moreau, François. *Un aspect de l'imagination créatrice chez Rabelais*. Paris, 1982.

Moser, Hans. "Städtische Fasnacht [*sic*] des Mittelalters." In *Masken zwischen Spiel und Ernst*, 135–202. Tübingen, 1967.

Nashe, Thomas. *The Unfortunate Traveller*. Harmondsworth, Eng., 1972.

*A New Rabelais Bibliography* (*NRB*): see Screech and Rawles.

Nicot, Jean, and Aimar de Raconnet. *Thresor de la langue francoyse, tant ancienne que modern*. 1621; reprint, Paris, 1960.

Ogden, C. K., and I. A. Richards. *The Meaning of Meaning*. London, 1923.

Ong, Walter. *Presence of the Word*. New York, 1967.

Orléans, Charles d'. *Poésies*. Ed. Champollion. Paris, 1842.

Oudin, Antoine. *Curiositez françoises*. Paris, 1656.

Paris, Jean. *Hamlet et Panurge*. Paris, 1971.

———. *Rabelais au futur*. Paris, 1970.

Pineau, Leon. "Notes et enquêtes." *Revue des traditions populaires* 4 (1889): 368.

Plan, Pierre-Paul. *Les éditions de Rabelais de 1532 à 1711*. Paris, 1904.

Plattard, Jean. *L'oeuvre de Rabelais*. Paris, 1910.

Psichari, Michael. "Les jeux de Gargantua." *Revue des études rabelaisiennes* 6 (1908): 1–37, 124–81, 317–61.

Quint, David. *Origin and Originality in Renaissance Literature: Versions of the Source*. New Haven, Conn. 1983.

Rabelais, François. *Gargantua and Pantagruel*. Trans. J. M. Cohen. Harmondsworth, Eng., 1955 (Penguin ed.).

———. *Gargantua und Pantagruel*. Ed. and trans., Johan Gottlob Regis. 2 volumes. Leipzig, 1832–1841; reprint, Munich, 1911.

———. *Oeuvres*. 2 volumes. Amsterdam, 1663 (Elzevier ed.).

———. *Oeuvres*. Ed. Jacob Le Duchat. 6 volumes. Amsterdam, 1711.

————. *Oeuvres*. Ed. Jean Bernard. Amsterdam, 1741.

————. *Oeuvres*. Ed. Esmangart and Eloi Johanneau. 9 volumes. Paris, 1823–1826.

————. *Oeuvres*. Ed. Abel Lefranc, et al. 6 volumes. Paris, 1913–1955.

————. *Oeuvres*. Ed. Jacques Boulenger. Paris: Bibliothèque de la Pleiade, 1955.

————. *Oeuvres complètes*. Ed. Pierre Jourda. 2 volumes. Paris, 1962.

————. *Oeuvres complètes*. Ed. Guy Demerson. Paris, 1973.

————. *The Portable Rabelais*. Trans. Samuel Putnam. New York, 1946.

————. *Le Quart Livre, édition critique*. Ed. Robert Marichal. Geneva, 1947.

————. *The Works of François Rabelais*. Trans. T. Urquhart and P. [Le] Motteux. 2 volumes. London, 1708.

————. *The Works of François Rabelais*. Ed. John Ozell. 2 volumes. London, 1737.

Réau, Louis. *Richesses d'art de la France: la Bourgogne, la peinture*. Paris, 1929.

Regalado, Nancy. "Speaking in Script: The Re-creation of Orality in Villon's *Testament*." Paper presented at the conference on Oral Tradition in the Middle Ages, Center for Medieval and Early Renaissance Studies, State University of New York at Binghamton, October 22, 1988.

Riffaterre, Michael. *Text Production*. New York, 1983.

Rigolot, François. "Cratylisme et pantagruelisme: Rabelais et le statut du signe." *Etudes rabelaisiennes* 13 (1976): 115–32.

————. *Les langages de Rabelais*. Geneva, 1972.

————. *Le texte de la Renaissance*. Geneva, 1982.

————. "Prolégomènes à une étude du statut de l'appareil liminaire des textes littéraires." *L'Esprit Créateur* 27, no. 3 (Fall 1987): 7–18.

Roller, Hans. *Der Nürnberger Schembartlauf*. Tübingen, 1965.

Sabry, Randa. "Quand le texte parle de son paratexte." *Poétique,* no. 69 (February 1987): 83–99.

Sachs, Hans. *Werke*. Ed. Adelbert von Keller and E. Goetze. 26 volumes. Hildesheim, 1964.

Sainéan, Lazare. *L'influence et la réputation de Rabelais*. 2 volumes. Paris, 1930.

————. *La langue de Rabelais*. 2 volumes. Paris, 1922–1923.

Saulnier, Vernon L. *Rabelais dans son enquête: étude sur le Quart et le Cinquième Livre*. Paris, 1982.

Saussure, Ferdinand de. *Course in General Linguistics*. 1916; trans., New York, 1959.

Schwartz, Jerome. "Rhetorical Tensions in the Liminary Texts of Rabelais's *Quart Livre*." *Etudes rabelaisiennes* 17 (1983): 21–36.

Screech, Michael. *Rabelais*. Ithaca, N.Y., 1979.

Screech, Michael, and Stephen Rawles, ed. *A New Rabelais Bibliography: Editions of Rabelais before 1626*. Geneva, 1987.

Segre, Cesare. *Avviamento all'analisi del testo letterario*. Turin, 1985.

Skorup, Povl. "Le Physétère et l'Ile Farouche de Rabelais." *Etudes rabelaisiennes* 6 (1965): 57–59.

Smith, Paul J. *Voyage et écriture: etude sur le Quart Livre de Rabelais*. Geneva, 1987.

Spitzer, Leo. "Rabelais et les rabelaisants." In *Etudes de style,* 134—65. Paris, 1970. (First published in *Studi francesi* 4 [1960]).

———. "Zu *carnaval* im Französischen." *Wörter und Sachen,* 5 (1914): 193—96.

Stridbeck, C. G. "'Combat between Carnival and Lent' by Pieter Brueghel the Elder." *Journal of the Warburg and Courtauld Institutes* 19 (1956): 96—109.

Suleiman, S. R., and I. Crosman, ed. *Reader in the Text: Essays on Audience and Interpretation.* Princeton, 1980.

Swarzenski, Hanns. "The Battle Between Carnival and Lent." *Bulletin of the Museum of Fine Arts* (Boston) 49 (1951): 2—11.

*The Tale of Gargantua and King Arthur:* see Brown, Huntington.

Taylor, John. *Works.* Ed. Charles Hindley. London, 1872.

Tetel, Marcel. *Rabelais.* New York, 1967.

Thou, Jacques-Auguste de. *Historiarum sui temporis libri CXXXVIII.* London, 1733.

Thuasne, Louis. *Etudes sur Rabelais.* 1905; reprint, Paris, 1969.

Tournon, André. "Le Paradoxe ménippéen dans l'oeuvre de Rabelais." *Etudes rabelaisiennes* 21 (1988): 309—17.

———. "La Briefve Declaration n'est pas de Rabelais." *Etudes rabelaisiennes* 13 (1976): 133—38.

Varagine, Jacobus da. *The Golden Legend.* Ed. Granger Ryan and Helmut Ripperger. New York, 1941.

Vaultier, Roger. *Le folklore pendant la guerre de Cent Ans d'après les lettres de remission du Trésor des Chartes.* Paris, 1965.

Visconti, Gaspare. *Il transito di Carnevale.* In his *Rithmi.* Milan, 1493.

*Le Vroy Gargantua:* see Françon, Marcel.

Widman, Enoch. *Hofer Chronik.* In *Quellen zur Geschichte der Stadt Hof,* ed. Christian Meyer. Hof, 1894.

Wilden, Anthony. *The Language of the Self.* Baltimore, 1968.

Zapperi, Robert. *L'homme enceint, l'homme, la femme, et le pouvoir.* Paris, 1983.

Zingerle, Oswald, ed. *Sterzinger Spiele nach Aufzeichnungen des Vigil Rabers.* Volume 1. Vienna, 1886.

Zumthor, Paul. *Introduction à la poésie orale.* Paris, 1983.

———. *La lettre et la voix de la "littérature" médiévale.* Paris, 1987.

# Index

Agrippa von Nettesheim, Cornelius,
  123n.24, 253
Alcofribas, 5n.7, 20, 23, 24, 31, 33, 39, 41,
  46, 67n.6, 78, 79, 98, 101, 102, 108n.41,
  109, 111, 124, 190n.3, 191, 192, 194, 198,
  200–208, 210, 211n.53, 212, 242–43, 250,
  255, 261, 266n.1
Allegory, 47–58, 59, 63, 84, 94–95, 123,
  148–49, 158–59
Alphabet author, 134–42, 156–57
Ambiguity, 13–14, 84, 116, 135–42, 260
Ambivalence, 13–14, 72, 84, 107n.40, 117,
  143, 212, 260
Anti-Nature, 13, 80n.22, 87–92, 100n.19,
  113, 114n.10, 116, 119–20, 129, 146n.27,
  190, 210, 242–43, 247, 249, 255, 257, 273
Aristophanes, 39, 88n.39, 243
Asclepius, 224n.23
Aubigny, Agrippa d', 10, 97n.9
Auden, W. H., 164
Audiences, Rabelais's, 17–33, 37–40, 44–
  45, 59–60, 127–34, 152–60, 184, 205–6,
  210, 214, 233–36, 239, 243
Augustine, Saint, 272

Badebec, 112
Bakhtin, Mikhail, x-xi, 12–13, 33, 42–43,
  73, 154, 166, 185, 245, 248–60
Ballocker, 112n.4, 223–29, 231, 237
Balzac, Honoré de, 160
Barnacles, metatextual, 154–55, 162, 170,
  264
Barthes, Roland, 14n.10
*Bataille de Caresme et de Charnage,* 51–52,
  66n.3
*Bataille . . . de Sainct Pensard à l'encontre
  de Caresme,* 2n.1, 85–86, 105n.29
Beaujour, Michel, 43n.56, 80n.23, 91–92,
  93n.1, 166, 173, 219n.10
Bernard, Jean, 145n.25, 244
Bernier, Jean, 133–134, 142–46, 155, 156
Berquin, Louis de, 22
Berrong, Richard, 217n.7, 246n.71
Berry, Alice, 109n.43
Beza, Theodore, 39

Boccaccio, Giovanni, 253
Bodin, Jean, 253
Bosch, Hieronymus, 47, 48, 50
Bowen, Barbara, xii n.2, 58, 98–99,
  106n.34
Braccelli, Giovanbatista, 88n.40
Breviaries, Roman Catholic, 72, 74n.11, 75,
  78, 134–41, 221, 275–79
*Briffaulx,* 89
Brueghel, Pieter, the Elder, 47, 48, 50, 51
Bruni, Leonardo, 101
Budé, Guillaume, 189, 202n.27
Burckhardt, Jacob, 187
Burke, Peter, 41n.54, 217n.7
Bussy-Rabutin, Roger, 158

*Cagotz, cagots,* 34, 89, 90, 193, 210, 211, 222,
  236
Calcagnini, Coelio, 88n.39, 100n.19,
  243n.66
Calvin, John, 34, 89, 90, 95, 129, 131, 146,
  150, 226, 243
*Caphars,* 34, 89, 90, 193, 210, 211, 222, 236
Carnap, Rudolf, 149–50
Carnival: personification of, 10–14, 47–57,
  76, 85, 89, 105n.32, 109, 142, 270–71;
  practice of, 39, 41, 46–58, 66, 69, 97–98,
  132; psychology of, 127; theory of, x-xi,
  117–22
Carnivalesque and Carnivalism, x-xi, 30–
  33, 42, 43n.56, 69, 78, 85, 97–98, 100–05,
  107–8, 245–46, 248–57, 260
Carnivalization, 42–43, 260
Carnival-Lent, literary genre of, 17–57, 63,
  66, 89, 103, 123
Carte, Thomas, 152n.41
Cartier, Jacques, 64, 112
Cave, Terence, 124n.26, 172–73
Censures, Censorship, 21–22, 32–37, 44,
  128, 131n.2, 146, 158–59, 215–16, 222, 229–
  32
Châtillon, Cardinal Odet de, 35, 41, 191,
  203, 208, 215, 229, 231, 232, 272
Charles V, Holy Roman Emperor, 4, 35,
  59, 79, 94–95, 211n.53

Charles VI, king of France, 102
Charpentier, Françoise, 114n.10
Chauliac, Guy de, 74
Chesney, Elizabeth, 107n.40
Cholakian, Rouben, 198, 206–7
Cicero, Marcus Tullius, 174–75, 235
Climate of opinion, 29n.26, 35–41, 128–33, 159n.52, 160–61, 266
Coleman, Dorothy, 165, 166, 206–8
Columbus, Christopher, ix
Communalism, 187–213, 219–20, 237–50, 255–57, 259
Communication, politics of, 44, 183–85, 189–90, 219; theory of, 167, 237–38, 258
Context, xi, 14–15, 17–18, 32, 43–45, 98–99, 136–37, 149–50, 155, 174–79, 237, 244–45, 257, 259, 262–64, 265–69
Countertext, 216–20, 235, 258, 259, 267
Criticism, literary. *See* Metatexts and literary criticism
Cuspidius, Ioannes, supposititious will of, 2

Dante Alighieri, 155
Davis, Natalie Zemon, 29n.25, 132n.4
Defaux, Gérard, 166, 205–6n.37, 207n.39, 262n.3
Dekker, Thomas, 253
Demerson, Guy, 89, 123, 248
Derrida, Jacques, 29n.26
Des Periers, Bonaventure, 229
Diogenes, 20, 193, 211, 255
*Disciple of Pantagruel (Le disciple de Pantagruel)*. *See Voyage et navigation de Panurge*
Dolet, Etienne, 5, 22, 26, 28, 35
Du Bellay, Guillaume, 4, 255
Du Bellay, Jean, 4–5, 35, 39, 79, 95
Du Bellay, Joachim, 39
Du Faïl, Noël, 21, 106, 229
Duperron, Cardinal Jacques Davy, 156
DuPuyherbault, 34, 39, 89, 90, 95, 129, 150, 154, 156, 243, 266
Duval, Edwin, 107–8, 201–5

Eco, Umberto, 26, 150n.36
Eluard, Paul, 80n.21
Elzevier edition of Rabelais, 128, 133–34, 155–58, 244
Embodiment, Renaissance, 55–57, 96, 250, 259
Epistemon, 166, 189
Erasmus, Desiderius, 3, 23n.15, 58, 87n.38, 100n.20, 103, 106n.36, 108n.42, 205, 253, 266
Esmangart, Charles, 160n.57

Estienne, Henri, 10, 131
Evangelism, 22, 171, 250

Faba, Guido, 52n.8
Fabre-Vassas, Claudine, 11n.6
Febvre, Lucien, 23, 38, 39, 166, 170
Fiction. *See* Novels
*Fifth Book* (Rabelais[?], 1564), 34, 129n.4, 143, 245
Folengo, Teofilo, 66n.4, 209
Fontaine, Marie Madeleine, 73–74, 76–78, 80n.22 and 23, 88n.40, 92n.46, 171
Foucault, Michel, 82n.26, 200n.22, 253–54
Francis I, king of France, ix, 4, 35, 158, 266, 273
Friar John, 3, 46, 67, 72, 93, 96–97, 102, 107, 112, 119n.18, 134–42, 198n.21, 247, 275–79
*Fricassée crotystylonée*, 71

Gaignebet, Claude, 43n.56, 48n.4, 71, 85, 166, 170, 248n.1, 254n.16
Galen, 2, 4, 24, 25, 74, 77, 156, 203, 224n.23, 240
Gallandus, Peter, 224
Gargamelle, 1, 244
*Gargantua* (Rabelais, 1534 or 1535), 3–5, 12n.8, 18–19, 22n.14, 26–28, 33n.33, 39, 67n.6, 109n.43, 112, 152, 153, 191, 192, 194, 198, 200–205, 206, 207n.39, 208–9, 211n.53, 213, 214, 216n.6, 217, 239–41, 245, 250, 261, 273
Gaster, Gastrolators, 118–19
Genette, Gérard, 17n.1, 38n.44, 150nn. 37 and 38
Giants, Carnival, 57–58, 66, 74
Giovio, Paolo, 101
Gladman, John, 50
Glauser, Alfred, 80n.23, 105n.29, 166
*Grandes et Inestimables Cronicques . . . de Gargantua*, 1, 23–24
Grandgosier, 1
Gray, Floyd, 74, 172, 206n.38
*Great Chronicles. See Grandes et Inestimalbes Cronicques . . . de Gargantua*
Grève, Marcel de, 38n.45, 159n.52
Gymnaste, 105, 107, 185

Heidegger, Martin, 29n.26
Henry II, king of France, ix, 33, 35, 128, 158, 229–32, 238, 255
Henry IV, king of France, 128, 157
Henry VIII, king of England, 148, 188–89
Hermeneutics, 26n.3
Hippocrates, 2, 4, 20

Historicism, New, 122n.23, 262n.4
Hjelmslev, Louis, 149–50
Hobbes, Thomas, 6n.8
Hoghenberg, Frans, 48–52, 121
Homer, 155, 200–203, 217
Homosexuality in Rabelais's *Fourth Book*, 113
Horace, 36n.41, 190n.3, 201, 203n.28, 235
Huchon, Mireille, 4
Hugo, Victor, ix, 160
Humanism, 3, 9, 22, 38, 41, 88, 101, 202–3, 210, 219, 242, 250

Ideology, 121–22, 252, 266
Idols or icons, plaster, ix-x, 40, 175, 261–64
Images, system of, 254, 257–59
Individualism, 187, 193, 246–47, 259
Intertext, 14, 17, 43n.56, 115–17, 168, 260, 266
Irony, 21n.12, 35n.37, 103, 106, 217–44, 263–64, 273–74

Jeanneret, Michel, 109n.43, 250n.4
Jerome, Saint, 272
Johanneau, Eloi, 160n.57
Jonson, Ben, 253
Jourda, Pierre, 12n.9, 135n.12
Joyce, James, 190–91, 257n.20
*Joyous Sermon of Saint Ham and Saint Tripe-Sausage. See Sermon Joyeux de Saint Jambon et de Sainte Andouille*
Julius II, Pope, 71

Kelley, Donald R., 202n.27, 262n.4
Kline, Michael, 38n.45
Koselleck, Reinhard, 177n.22
Krailsheimer, Alban, 58n.24, 59, 79n.20, 95n.6
Kristeva, Julia, 14, 43n.56

La Bruyère, Jean de, 159, 245n.68
Lacan, Jacques, 178n.23
La Fontaine, Jean de, 21n.12
La Noue, François de, 39
La Ville, Claude, 26–28, 59n.25
Le Double, Anatole, 83n.29, 89n.41, 113n.7, 160n.57
Le Duchat, Jacob, 69, 70, 75, 84, 128, 146–48, 151–52, 155–56, 160, 162n.1, 170, 244
Lefèvre d'Etaples, Jacques, 205
Lefranc, Abel, 64n.2, 131n.1, 170, 248n.1
Le Motteux, Pierre, 59n.26, 98n.12, 133–34, 142–48, 154, 155, 162n.1, 170
Leo X, pope, 71
Leonardo da Vinci, 187

Lévi-Strauss, Claude, 150n.36
Linguistic vehicles or "symbols," 111, 117, 163–73, 177–79, 258–59, 266n.2; defined, 163
Literacy and literature. *See* Oral and written literature; *see also* Paratext
Literariness, 165–66, 171, 177
Literary criticism. *See* Metatexts and literary criticism
Lope de Vega, 54
Louis XIV, king of France, 132
Lucian, 39n.49, 58, 64, 101, 115, 231, 254
Luther, Martin, 23, 145, 149, 187, 266

Magnus, Olaus, 64–66, 93, 99, 103, 104
Mannheim, Karl, 178n.22
Manutius, Aldus, 22n.14
Mardi Gras, 9n.3, 106–7, 120–21; Rabelais's personification of, 72, 101, 105, 121, 146, 148, 166, 185
Marguerite d'Angoulême, queen of Navarre, 10, 229, 252, 272–73
Marichal, Robert, 12n.9, 34n.35, 95n.6, 110n.45, 135n.12, 151, 154
Marot, Clément, 10, 38
Marshack, Alexander, 29n.26
Marsy, Abbé de, 128, 148–49, 156, 159n.52
*Marvellous Conflict Between Lent and Fleshliness*, 66, 103
Mary, queen of England, 148
*Matagotz*, 34, 89, 90, 222, 236
Medicine, 3–6, 69, 73–83, 113
Médicis, Catherine de, 128
Médicis, Marie de, 128
Melusine, 11, 111
Metatexts and literary criticism, ix, 36, 40, 133, 149–55, 162–65, 172–79, 183, 216, 244, 248, 252, 259–64, 268; defined, ix, 149–55; history of, 36–37, 174–76, 183; history of Rabelaisian, 127–61, 216, 244–48, 252–54, 259
Michelet, Jules, 160, 187
Midlent, 75–76, 85
Minerva, 106–9
Montaigne, Michel de, 10, 173, 195
Montmorency, Anne de, constable of France, 35
Moralism, 123, 223–26, 240n.62

Nashe, Thomas, 188–89, 246
Naturalism, 90–92, 119–20, 219, 250, 252n.12, 256–57, 272–74
Nature (Rabelais's Physis), 87–89, 91, 114n.10, 119, 252n.12, 257
Navarre, Marguerite de. *See* Marguerite d'Angoulême, queen of Navarre

*Navigatio sancti Brendani,* 66n.5
New Historicism, 122n.23, 262n.4
Niphleseth, 107, 111–16, 119
Novels: nature of, 164; history of, 190–91, 219

Oblique reading. *See* Perspectival and oblique reading
Ogden, C. K., 163–65, 168
Oracle of the Holy Bottle, 46, 70
Oral and written literature, interaction of, 28–32, 101–2, 228–29
Organicism, 249–50, 252n.11, 256, 260
Orléans, Charles d', 84n.2, 95, 270–71
Oudin, Antoine, 19, 157n.49
Ovid, 200
Ozell, John, 160, 162n.1

Pansard, Saint: in Rabelais, 140n.18. See also *Bataille . . . de Sainct Pensard*
*Pantagruel,* (Rabelais, 1532), 1–3, 5, 20, 22n.14, 23–24, 25n.18, 30, 33n.33, 38, 58, 59n.25, 152, 191, 194, 198, 208, 210, 211n.53, 214, 217, 266
*Pantagrueline Prognostication* (1533), 56, 70, 78, 85
Pantagruelism, 120, 190, 208–11, 217, 223, 229, 241–44
Panurge, 3, 10n.5, 20n.10, 46, 71, 78, 79n.20, 93, 112, 114, 115, 189, 190, 198, 203–4, 208, 245–47
*Papelars,* 89
Paratext, 17, 20–21, 23n.15, 25, 30, 31, 37, 44, 46, 90, 132, 150–54, 162, 184, 194–98, 214–16, 220, 229–39, 241, 267
Paré, Ambroise, 187
Paris, Jean, 43n.56
Parlement of Paris, 5, 21, 32, 33, 222, 232
Pasquier, Etienne, 10, 39, 131n.1
Pathelin, Maître, 234
Patriarchy, 114, 258. *See also* Phallocentrism
Patrons, patronage, 4, 35
Peirce, C. S., 163
Pérau, Abbé, 128
Perreau, author of "Explanation," 75, 134n.8, 156–58
Personifications of Carnival and Lent (non-Rabelaisian), 47–58, 85–86
Perspectival and oblique reading, 123–24, 127, 218–19, 257–58
Petrarch, Francesco, ix, 174
Phallocentrism, 111–15. *See also* Priapism
Philip the Good, duke of Burgundy, 139, 275–78
Philology, 159n.52, 202–3
Physeter, "spouter," 63–66, 93, 116, 123n.25, 147, 249, 259

Physis. *See* Nature
Pius V, pope, 136, 275
Plato and Platonism, 58, 88n.39, 106, 122, 123, 171, 200, 202, 241, 243n.66, 250, 252, 254, 261, 274
Pliny, 63, 64, 67n.5
Plutarch, 200, 201
Poitiers, Diane de, 231
Postel, Guillaume, 89–90, 95, 243
Priapism, 98–99, 102, 195, 224–25
Printing, 22–32, 36–37, 44–45, 136–37, 152, 163, 183–84, 195, 241
Privilege, royal, for printing, 5, 21–23, 33–36, 215–16, 229–30
Protestant use of Rabelais's text, 128–30, 143–48
Protestants, German, aided by France, 4, 59, 94–95
Psychology, psychologism, 55–56, 81–87, 113, 114, 141–42, 176, 259
Puppets, Carnival, 57, 66, 83, 119, 169

Raber, Vigil, 56n.18
Ramus, Peter, 77, 224
Readers. *See* Audiences, Rabelais's
Referents and referent patterns, 163–71, 266n.2
Regis, Johan Gottlob, 10n.5
Representation, 25–26, 55–60, 117, 122n.23, 267–68
Residues, metatextual, 154–55, 162
Richards, I. A., 163–65, 168
Richelieu, Armand Jean du Plessis, cardinal de, 128, 132n.2
Riffaterre, Michael, 14, 80n.23, 171–72, 174n.21
Rigolot, François, 15n.10, 17n.1, 37n.44, 123n.25, 124n.26, 166, 195n.17, 197n.18, 206–7
Ronsard, Pierre de, 39, 173

Sachs, Hans, 55, 86n.35
Saenger, Paul, 25n.18, 31n.30
Sainéan, Lazare, 105n.31, 145n.25, 160n.56
Sainte-Beuve, Charles Augustin, 15n.10, 166
Sainte-Marthe, Scévole de, 39
Satirist, Rabelais as, 77, 80n.23, 91–92, 108, 109n.44, 121, 219, 221
Saulnier, Vernon, 123n.25, 166
Scheler, Lucien, 9n.1, 127n.1
Schwartz, Jerome, 214n.1, 215n.5, 224, 227n.30, 231, 233, 237n.56
Screech, Michael, 3n.5, 12n.9, 35n.38, 58n.24, 87n.38, 89n.42, 90, 107n.39, 123n.25, 129, 166, 193n.14, 231–32, 246n.71

Semiotics, x, 14, 83n.29, 163–68, 173, 178–79, 194, 257, 260, 268; and semiology, 173n.20

*Sermon Joyeux de Saint Jambon et de Sainte Andouille*, 111–12

Sévigné, Marie de Rabutin-Chantal, marquise de, 158

Sexuality, 71–72, 75–76, 111–16, 223–25, 245–46, 264

Shakespeare, William, ix, 253

Skorup, Povl, 64

Smith, Paul J., 64n.2, 66n.5, 93n.1

Socrates, 200, 202

Solomon, king of Israel, 231

Sorbonne (Faculty of Theology of University of Paris), 4, 5, 21–22, 32–35, 38n.48, 152, 212, 222, 231

Spiritualism, 249–52, 256, 273–74

Spitzer, Leo, 84, 166

Structuralism, x, 14n.10, 122n.23, 150n.36, 257

Structural theory of semantics, 163–79, 260

Structures of Rabelaisian metatexts, 244–45

Subtext, 216–18, 221, 240, 257–59, 267

Suleiman, Susan, 26n.20, 174n.21, 206n.38

Surrealism, 80n.21, 87

Symbols. *See* Linguistic vehicles or "symbols"

Taylor, John, 70n.2

*Third Book* (Rabelais, 1546), 3, 5–6, 20, 22, 46, 192–94, 198, 201, 203, 209, 211, 213, 214–15, 217, 221, 229, 242–43, 251, 266, 273–74

Thou, Jacques-Auguste de, 152n.41, 197n.20

Thought patterns, 168–72

Thuasne, Louis, 66n.4, 89n.42, 209n.47

Tiraqueau, André, 231–32

Tournon, André 224–25, 273n.6

Trent, Council of, 35, 70–71, 95n.6, 115, 128, 136, 148

Valentine, Saint, 270–71

Valla, Lorenzo, 202n.27

Varagine, Jacobus de, 275n.2, 278n.7

Vega, Lope de, 54

Vesalius, Andreas, 77, 89n.40

Vigneulles, Philippe de, 58n.23

Villon, François, 19n.5

Voltaire, 159n.53

*Voyage et navigation de Panurge, disciple de Pantagruel, Le* (1538), 5, 58–59, 64, 94, 98n.15, 115

Wildman, 57, 97

Xenomanes, 9–11, 46, 63, 69–70, 72–73, 78, 80, 82, 94, 111, 149, 198

Compositor: Graphic Composition, Inc.
Text: 10/13 Galliard
Display: Galliard
Printer: Edwards Brothers, Inc.
Binder: Edwards Brothers, Inc.